Readings on Color

Volume 1: The Philosophy of Color

D1285095

Readings on Color

Volume 1: The Philosophy of Color

edited by Alex Byrne and David R. Hilbert

A Bradford Book
The MIT Press
Cambridge, Massachusetts
London, England

This book was set in Times Roman on the Monotype "Prism Plus" PostScript Imagesetter by Asco Trade Typesetting Ltd., Hong Kong and was printed and bound in the United States of America.

Library of Congress Cataloging-in-Publication Data

Readings on color / edited by Alex Byrne and David R. Hilbert.
   p. cm.
  Includes bibliographical references and index.
  Contents: v. 1. The philosophy of color — v. 2. The science of color.
  ISBN 0-262-02424-1 (v. 1 : hardcover : alk. paper). — ISBN 0-262-52230-6 (v. 1 : pbk. : alk. paper). — ISBN 0-262-02425-X (v. 2 : hardcover : alk. paper) — ISBN 0-262-52231-4 (v. 2 : pbk. : alk. paper)
  1. Color. 2. Color—Philosophy. I. Byrne, Alexander. II. Hilbert, David R., 1959–   .
  QC495.R32 1997
  152.14′5—dc21
                                96-44539
                                  CIP

Contents

Acknowledgments   vii

Sources   ix

Introduction   xi

1   On Some Criticisms of a Physicalist Theory of Colors   1
J. J. C. Smart

2   Color and the Anthropocentric Problem   11
Edward Wilson Averill

3   Smart and the Secondary Qualities   33
D. M. Armstrong

4   Reply to Armstrong   47
J. J. C. Smart

5   Colour Concepts and Colour Experience   51
Christopher Peacocke

6   An Objectivist's Guide to Subjectivism about Colour   67
Frank Jackson and Robert Pargetter

7   Colour as a Secondary Quality   81
Paul A. Boghossian and J. David Velleman

8   Physicalist Theories of Color   105
Paul A. Boghossian and J. David Velleman

9   How to Speak of the Colors   137
Postscript: Visual Experience
Mark Johnston

10   A Simple View of Colour   177
John Campbell

11   The Autonomy of Colour   191
Justin Broackes

12   Phenomenal Character   227
Sydney Shoemaker

13   Explaining Objective Color in Terms of Subjective Reactions   247
Gilbert Harman

14   Colors and Reflectances   263
       Alex Byrne and David R. Hilbert

15   Reinverting the Spectrum   289
       C. L. Hardin

       Bibliography   303
       Contributors   313
       Index   315

Acknowledgments

Larry Hardin gave us good advice on selecting papers for this volume. We are also grateful to Larry and to Ned Block, Andrew Botterell, Fiona Cowie, Ned Hall, Katie Hilbert, Steven Palmer, Jim Pryor, Daniel Stoljar, and Judith Thomson for comments on the Introduction, although we are quite sure the final result will not satisfy all of them. Austen Clark and Joe Levine helped with the early stages of the project. Peter Ross made some last-minute corrections to the Bibliography. Betty Stanton, Jerry Weinstein, and Katherine Arnoldi at The MIT Press were, as usual, indispensable. Finally, Ned Block needs to be thanked again, this time for his enthusiastic support for this project.

Sources

1   J. J. C. Smart, On Some Criticisms of a Physicalist Theory of Colors. Reprinted with permission from *Philosophical Aspects of the Mind–Body Problem*, ed. C. Cheng, Honolulu: University Press of Hawaii. © 1975 University Press of Hawaii.

2   Edward Wilson Averill, Color and the Anthropocentric Problem. Reprinted from *Journal of Philosophy* 82 (1985), pp. 281–304, by permission of the author and *The Journal of Philosophy*.

3   D. M. Armstrong, Smart and the Secondary Qualities. Reprinted from *Metaphysics and Morality: Essays in Honour of J. J. C. Smart*, ed. P. Pettit, R. Sylvan, and J. Norman (1987), by permission of Blackwell Publishers.

4   J. J. C. Smart, Reply to Armstrong. Reprinted from *Metaphysics and Morality: Essays in Honour of J. J. C. Smart*, ed. P. Pettit, R. Sylvan, and J. Norman (1987), by permission of Blackwell Publishers.

5   Christopher Peacocke, Colour Concepts and Colour Experience. Reprinted from *Synthese* 58 (1984), pp. 365–82, with kind permission from Kluwer Academic Publishers.

6   Frank Jackson and Robert Pargetter, An Objectivist's Guide to Subjectivism about Colour. Reprinted with permission from *Revue Internationale de Philosophie* 41 (1987), pp. 127–41.

7   Paul A. Boghossian and J. David Velleman, Colour as a Secondary Quality. Reprinted from *Mind* 98 (1989), pp. 81–103, by permission of Oxford University Press.

8   Paul A. Boghossian and J. David Velleman, Physicalist Theories of Color. From *Philosophical Review* 100 (1991), pp. 67–106. © 1991 Cornell University. Reprinted by permission of the publisher and the authors.

9   Mark Johnston, How to Speak of the Colors. Reprinted from *Philosophical Studies* 68 (1992), pp. 221–63, with kind permission from Kluwer Academic Publishers. Postscript: Visual Experience. Written specially for this volume.

10   John Campbell, A Simple View of Colour. Reprinted from *Reality, Representation, and Projection*, ed. J. Haldane and C. Wright (1993), by permission of Oxford University Press.

11   Justin Broackes, The Autonomy of Colour. © Justin Broackes 1992. Reprinted from *Reduction, Explanation, and Realism*, ed. D. Charles and K. Lennon (1992), by permission of the author and Oxford University Press.

12   Sydney Shoemaker, Phenomenal Character. Reprinted from *Noûs* 28 (1994), pp. 21–38, by permission of Blackwell Publishers.

13   Gilbert Harman, Explaining Objective Color in Terms of Subjective Reactions. Reprinted with permission from *Philosophical Issues* 7 (1996), ed. E. Villanueva (Atascadero, CA: Ridgeview Publishing Co.).

14   Alex Byrne and David Hilbert, Colors and Reflectances. Written specially for this volume.

15   C. L. Hardin, Reinverting the Spectrum. Written specially for this volume.

Introduction

Color is a peculiarly striking aspect of the world as it appears to us. It is therefore a natural starting point for any investigation into appearance and reality. No surprise, then, that philosophy has always taken an interest in color. And even when colors have not been the topic, they have often been used to stain a specimen under the philosophical microscope: Hume's missing shade of blue; G. E. Moore's comparison of good with yellow; Nelson Goodman's "grue" and "bleen"; Frank Jackson's super-scientist Mary who doesn't know what it's like to see red.[1]

As C. L. Hardin remarks in the expanded edition of *Color for Philosophers*, a "small chromatic zeitgeist has been loose in the philosophical world" (1993, p. xix), its presence being significantly due to the influence of Hardin's book. But *Color for Philosophers* has done more than stimulate philosophers to work on color: it has also made them (or, anyway, some of them) familiar with the main findings of color science. And greater sensitivity to the empirical facts has certainly raised the level of debate.

This volume contains a selection of recent philosophical papers on color and a comprehensive bibliography. Its companion volume, *Readings on Color, vol. 2: The Science of Color*, is a broad collection of current scientific work on color and color vision.

Philosophers have become increasingly aware of the relevance of science to philosophy. This is a welcome trend, and we hope these two volumes will do something to reinforce it. But how relevant is philosophy to science? Here we can only point to the papers in this book.

1 Summary of This Volume

There is a central concern shared by nearly all the papers collected here (and most contemporary philosophical discussions of color), namely, to answer the following questions: Are physical objects colored?[2] And if so, what is the nature of the color properties? These questions form the problem of *color realism*.

Eliminativists answer no to the first question. They think that although physical objects seem to be colored, this is no more than a peculiarly stable illusion. Thus C. L. Hardin: "We are to be eliminativists with respect to color as a property of objects, but reductivists with respect to color experiences" (1993, p. 112). Eliminativism is of course controversial, but so is the second of Hardin's claims, namely that there is a physicalist reduction of color experiences. In his contribution to this volume (chapter 15) Hardin attempts to overturn objections to the latter. An extended case for eliminativism is given by Paul Boghossian and David Velleman (chapters 7, 8). For arguments against it, see Mark Johnston's chapter 9.

If, *contra* the eliminativists, the answer to the first question is yes, then what is the answer to the second? *Dispositionalists* say that the property green (for example) is a disposition to produce certain perceptual states: roughly, the disposition to *look green*. Johnston (chapter 9 and its postscript), E. W. Averill (chapter 2), and Christopher Peacocke (chapter 5) argue for versions of dispositionalism.[3] It receives a wide variety of criticism from Boghossian and Velleman (chapter 7), Justin Broackes (chapter 11), and Gilbert Harman (chapter 13).

Physicalists claim that colors are physical properties (for instance, that green is a certain property of selectively reflecting incident light). J. J. C. Smart (chapter 1, 4) is the father of this view[4]; Smart's position is criticized by Averill (chapter 2) and defended by D. M. Armstrong (chapter 3). Physicalism (in various versions) is also held by Frank Jackson and Robert Pargetter (chapter 6), Sydney Shoemaker (chapter 12), Harman (chapter 13), and Byrne and Hilbert (chapter 14). Johnston argues against physicalism by taking Jackson and Pargetter's version as representative, and Boghossian and Velleman (chapter 8) attack a wide range of physicalist theories.

Primitivists agree with the physicalists that objects have colors, and that these properties are not dispositions to produce perceptual states. But they also hold that colors are sui generis, and so they deny, in particular, that colors are identical to physical properties. John Campbell (chapter 10) defends this position, and Broackes (chapter 11) is officially agnostic as between primitivism and physicalism. An argument against primitivism can be found in Johnston's chapter 9.

For those wanting a more leisurely tour of the territory, the following section explains various views in the philosophy of perception. In subsequent sections this material is drawn on to elaborate the main philosophical accounts of color.

2   Visual Experience: Some Distinctions

2.1   *Red-Representing Experiences and Red-Feeling Experiences*

If you have normal vision, then when you see a ripe tomato in good light, it looks red and round. If the world is as it appears to be—that is, if your visual experience is *veridical*—then the tomato is red and round. Now certainly sometimes objects do not have the colors or shapes they appear to have. Let us suppose this is so in the case of the tomato; in particular, suppose that although the tomato *looks* red, it *isn't* red. Then the world is not, or not exactly, as it appears to be—your visual experience is at least partly illusory.

Because a visual experience may be veridical or illusory, we may speak of visual experiences *representing* the world to be a certain way. For example, when you look at a tomato, your visual experience represents the world as containing, inter alia, a round red object in front of you. That is, the *representational content* (content, for short) of your experience includes the proposition that there is something red and round before you.

It will be useful to classify visual experiences by their contents.[5] Let us say that a visual experience is *red-representing* just in case it represents that something is red.[6] (Henceforth, "experience" will mean *visual* experience.)

Provided you take conditions to be normal, and are uncontaminated by philosophy, you will also believe that the tomato is red. This belief, like the experience, represents the world as being a certain way, and so has representational content (the proposition that the tomato is red). The belief and the experience, then, have content in common. Might the connection between experience and belief be even more intimate? Could we *identify* the experience with a cluster of (occurrent[7]) beliefs? (The cluster would presumably be something like: the belief that the tomato is red, that it is a certain shape, that it is a certain distance from the perceiver, etc.) The answer is no. One reason why is that the experience may occur unaccompanied by the cluster of beliefs: you may not take conditions to be normal, and hence not believe the testimony of your senses. It is possible, for example, to have an experience that represents that something is red without believing that something is red. Another reason for not identifying experiences with clusters of beliefs is that, intuitively, one's perceptual beliefs are *based on* the deliverances of experience: experience provides us with reasons for perceptual beliefs. That suggests that experience and belief are quite distinct.[8]

There is a third reason why, prima facie, experience is a different animal from belief. There need be nothing "it is like" to believe—or even consciously to believe—that something is red. (At any rate, if there is something it's like to have such a belief, the accompanying phenomenology does not necessarily distinguish this belief from the belief that something is green, or square.) And—admittedly a further step—no distinctive phenomenology need accompany a large cluster of conscious beliefs. But, notoriously, there is something quite distinctive it's like to look at a ripe tomato.

So, in addition to classifying experiences by their contents, we may classify them by their phenomenology. Experiences as of red objects resemble one another in a salient phenomenological respect. In that respect, they resemble experiences as of orange objects more than they resemble experiences as of green objects. Let us say that a *red-feeling experience* is an experience of the phenomenological kind picked out by the following examples: the typical visual experiences of ripe tomatoes, rubies, blood, and so forth.[9,10]

Are any important questions being begged by our claim that experiences may be classified by their phenomenology? No. Admittedly, some philosophers will profess only to understand "red-feeling experience" as another name for an experience that represents that something is red.[11] For these philosophers, this apparently new distinction between red- and green-feeling experiences is just the previous distinction between red- and green-representing experiences, relabeled. But their position is accommodated, because we are not insisting that these are *different* distinctions (although, as we shall see, many hold that they are).

We can all agree that, at least typically, a red-feeling experience is red-representing, and conversely.[12] (And similarly for the other colors.) Could these two ways of classifying visual experiences come apart? That is, could someone either have a red-feeling experience that was not red-representing, or else have a red-representing experience that was not a red-feeling experience? Different answers to this question mark important divisions among philosophical views of perception.

If the two ways of classifying experiences are inseparable, then, of necessity, any red-feeling experience represents that something is red, and conversely. First, let us take the left-to-right direction: the thesis that, necessarily, all red-feeling experiences are red-representing:

COLOR-FEEL → COLOR-REP
For all possible subjects S, and possible worlds w, if S is having a red-feeling experience in w, S is having a red-representing experience in w. (Similarly for the other colors.)

Now for the right-to-left direction: the thesis that, necessarily, all red-representing experiences are red-feeling experiences:

COLOR-REP → COLOR-FEEL
For all possible subjects S, and possible worlds w, if S is having a red-representing experience in w, S is having a red-feeling experience in w. (Similarly for the other colors.)[13]

Let CONTINGENCY be the thesis that both COLOR-FEEL → COLOR-REP and COLOR-REP → COLOR-FEEL are *false*. CONTINGENCY says that there is only a contingent connection between red-feeling experiences and red-representing experiences: red-feeling experiences can occur without being red-representing, and red-representing experiences can occur without being red-feeling experiences.

Famously, a case that forms the basis for an argument for CONTINGENCY was described by Locke, in his *Essay Concerning Human Understanding*. Suppose, Locke said, that "by the different Structure of our Organs, it were so ordered, That *the same Object should produce in several Men's Minds different* Ideas at the same time; *v.g.* if the *Idea*, that a *Violet* produced in one Man's Mind by his Eyes, were the same that a *Marigold* produced in another Man's, and *vice versa*" (Locke 1689/1975, II, xxxii, 15).[14] In our terminology, Locke is supposing that a person might have yellow-feeling experiences when he looks at violets, and blue-feeling experiences when he looks at marigolds. (On Locke's view, this case is merely possible, not actual, because he thinks that, as things have turned out, "sensible *Ideas*, produced by any Object in different Men's Minds, are most commonly very near and undiscernably alike" (ibid).)

Let us suppose that Invert is "spectrally inverted" in the way that Locke describes, and has been since birth.[15] Let Nonvert be a normal human: he has blue-feeling experiences when he looks at violets, and yellow-feeling experiences when he looks at marigolds. Nonvert and Invert both speak English: at any rate, they both call marigolds "yellow" and violets "blue." Now if we also stipulate that Nonvert and Invert are exactly alike physically, or exactly alike in internal functional organization, or even exactly alike behaviourally, then we shall run into controversy, for some will deny that the resulting case is possible (see Hardin, chapter 15). But for present purposes we do not need to make any of these stipulations.[16]

In normal humans blue-feeling experiences and blue-representing experiences go together. So Nonvert's experience, when he looks at a violet, is a blue-representing experience. What about Invert's experience, when he looks at a violet? It is a yellow-feeling experience, but is it also yellow-representing? Many philosophers have thought not, often on the basis of the two following arguments.

First argument. It seems plausible that Invert means by "blue" just what Nonvert and the rest of us mean. When Invert describes how violets look to him, then, he will say and believe that they do look blue and don't look yellow. But if his experience when he looks at a violet is yellow-representing, Invert is mistaken about how things look (how things are visually represented) to him. Violets in fact look yellow to him, although he believes that they look blue. This is a counterintuitive result. Hence Invert's experience when he looks at a violet, although yellow-feeling, is blue-representing.

Second argument. Consider Nonvert and Invert, each looking at a violet. Since nothing can be yellow and blue all over, if Invert's experience is yellow-representing, then at most one of Nonvert and Invert's experiences is veridical. Now since we may fairly suppose that violets *are* blue, it follows that if Invert's experience is yellow-representing, it is not veridical. But, again, this is a counterintuitive result. After all, presumably Invert can use his color vision to navigate the world successfully. Given this fact, there is at least a presumption against the view that he systematically misperceives the color of things. So Invert's experience is blue-representing as well as Nonvert's.

Of course, if either of the above arguments is persuasive, we can also show by similar reasoning that Invert's experience when he looks at a marigold is yellow-representing.

Suppose we accept these conclusions about the content of Invert's experiences. We can now argue for CONTINGENCY as follows. Take blue as an example, and consider Invert, looking at a marigold. Invert is having a blue-feeling experience. But his experience is representing the marigold to be yellow and so, given that yellow and blue are contraries, is not representing it to be blue. So Invert is having a blue-feeling experience, but is not having a blue-representing experience.[17] That falsifies COLOR-FEEL → COLOR-REP.

Now take Invert again, this time looking at a violet. His experience is representing the violet to be blue, and so is blue-representing. But his experience is a yellow-feeling experience. So Invert is having a blue-representing experience, but is not having a blue-feeling experience. That falsifies COLOR-REP → COLOR-FEEL. Hence, since COLOR-FEEL → COLOR-REP is also false, CONTINGENCY is true.

So runs the argument. For those who endorse it, an obvious candidate for the property blue is Locke's "the Texture of a *Violet*" (op. cit.): the physical property that typically causes blue-feeling experiences (in Nonvert) and yellow-feeling experiences (in Invert). (For this line of thought, see especially Jackson and Pargetter [chapter 6], and Shoemaker [chapter 12].)[18]

If CONTINGENCY is true, the texture of a marigold, which typically causes yellow-feeling experiences in human beings, typically causes, in some possible world, normal perceivers of some species (Martians, say) to have blue-feeling experiences. Hence, if CONTINGENCY is true, there is some motivation to say—and Jackson and Pargetter do say—that there is no *single* property blue, but rather a family of properties: blue-for-humans, blue-for-Martians, etc.[19]

2.2 *Phenomenal Properties*

We can unpack COLOR-FEEL → COLOR-REP thus:

COLOR-FEEL → COLOR-REP
There is a property P such that, for all possible subjects S, and all possible worlds w, if S is having a red-feeling experience in w, then:

(i) S's experience represents an object as having P

and:

(ii) P is the property red.

(Similarly for the other colors.)

Let us call the thesis obtained by deleting (ii) from COLOR-FEEL → COLOR-REP, COLOR-FEEL → PROPERTY-REP. Now return to the argument against COLOR-FEEL → COLOR-REP. That only attempted to show that there is no one *color C*, such that, necessarily, all yellow-feeling experiences represent something as having *C*. So if this argument is correct, it only provides a reason for rejecting COLOR-FEEL → COLOR-REP, and not COLOR-FEEL → PROPERTY-REP. For all that has been argued is that if there *is* a property that is represented by all (actual and possible) yellow-feeling experiences, this property is *not* yellow. And that is consistent with there being such a property. So, even granting the argument against COLOR-FEEL → COLOR-REP, COLOR-FEEL → PROPERTY-REP might yet be true.

And, one might think, COLOR-FEEL → PROPERTY-REP *is* true. Surely, what all yellow-feeling experiences have in common, in whatever possible world in which they occur, is that something *looks to be a certain way*, which we can gloss as: looks to have a certain property. What else can the common element be, if not part of the content of all yellow-feeling experiences? As Shoemaker puts it, "If one is asked to focus on [an] experience without focusing on its intentional aspect, or its representational content, one simply has no idea of what to do" (chapter 12, p. 237). So, Shoemaker thinks, yellow-feeling experiences, although not all yellow-representing, nonetheless represent *some* common property.

Call the property that, by COLOR-FEEL → PROPERTY-REP, is represented by all yellow-feeling experiences, *phenomenal-yellow* (similarly for the other colors). The phenomenal-colors are examples of—in Shoemaker's terminology—*phenomenal properties*. Now suppose that Nonvert and Invert are looking at a violet. Since they are enjoying, respectively, yellow- and blue-feeling experiences, their experiences are, respectively, phenomenal-yellow- and phenomenal-blue-representing. Hence, unless the violet has *both* properties, at least one of their experiences is not veridical. But, it might be thought, it is not plausible to suppose that either Nonvert or Invert is the victim of an illusion. (Compare the second inverted spectrum argument for CONTINGENCY in the previous section.) If this is right, we can conclude that the violet, at least when Nonvert and Invert are looking at it, is both phenomenal-yellow and phenomenal-blue.

After considering a number of candidates for being phenomenal-yellow, Shoemaker argues that this property is, in our terminology, the relational property of "producing in a viewer" yellow-feeling experiences (chapter 12, p. 241). The violet is producing in a viewer (Nonvert) yellow-feeling experiences, and is also producing in a viewer (Invert) blue-feeling experiences. It is therefore both phenomenal-yellow and phenomenal-blue, as desired. (For an objection to Shoemaker, see Harman, chapter 13; see also Shoemaker 1996 and Harman 1996.)

2.3 *Sensational Properties*

According to the arguments of section 2.1, when Invert looks at the leaves and flowers of a marigold, he is having a red-feeling experience (and a blue-feeling experience) that represents the leaves to be green (and the flowers to be yellow). So he is having a red-feeling experience that is not red-representing. But there are alleged to be other kinds of examples, where a red-feeling experience is not red-representing because the experience does not represent an object to have a property at all. Boghossian and Velleman (chapter 7, pp. 91–2) describe a case of this kind, that of having a red afterimage. According to them, having a red afterimage, although a red-feeling experience, is not red-representing. When you have a red afterimage, and so a red-feeling experience, they say your experience does not—or at any rate need not[20]—represent anything as having any property: a fortiori, it does not represent anything as being red.[21]

This second kind of case presents an obvious difficulty for COLOR-FEEL → PROPERTY-REP. There cannot be a property things are represented as having by all (possible) red-feeling experiences if some red-feeling experiences are not representational at all. Some philosophers have argued that these sorts of examples show that the content of an experience does not determine the phenomenology of the experience. Take the experience of having a red afterimage and the experience of having a green afterimage. The experiences are phenomenologically different. But if Boghossian and Velleman are correct, there need be no difference in content between the two experiences, and so the content of an experience does not determine its phenomenology.

Nonetheless, even if we grant that in the case of a red afterimage, the experience does not represent that something is red, or phenomenal-red, it seems that, when one is having a red afterimage, one can be "aware," in some sense, of the presence of a distinctive property, a property of which one is not aware when one is having a green afterimage. Following Christopher Peacocke (1983), let us call these properties *sensational properties*, and label the sensational property one may be aware of when having a red afterimage, "red'" ("red-prime"). Sensational properties are not supposed to be properties that experiences may *represent* objects as having. According to Peacocke, they are properties of "regions of the visual field" (chapter 5, p. 60). (Such regions bear a close resemblance to the *sense-data* of twentieth-century empiricism.) With Peacocke's conception of sensational properties thus explained, it is not suprising that he takes red' to be a property of a region of one's visual field not just in the case of afterimages, but whenever "a normal human sees a red object in daylight" (chapter 5, p. 58).[22]

2.4   Three Kinds of Experiential Property

The distinctions made so far can be further clarified by employing this threefold classification: properties *of* experiences; properties *represented by* experiences; and properties *presented in* experiences. Suppose you have normal vision and are looking at a ripe tomato in good light. Let *e* be the visual experience you are currently enjoying. *e* is an event, and it has certain properties, for example the property of occurring at a certain time. More relevantly, *e* also has the property of *being a red-representing experience*, and of *being a red-feeling experience*. So we may say that these are properties *of* your experience. On one usage of the term, *qualia* are certain properties of experiences; e.g., one *quale* your experience currently instantiates is the property of being a red-feeling experience. Qualia, on this conception, are properties in which almost everyone can believe. For, as noted above in section 2.1, someone may take red-feeling experiences to be, simply, those experiences of something's looking (i.e., being visually represented as) red.

Now, because your experience *e* is a red-representing experience, red is a property *e* represents something to have. So we may say that red is a property *represented by* your experience. Of course, from the fact that a property is represented by an experience, one cannot conclude that anything *has* this property: the experience may not be veridical.

If, like Shoemaker, you believe in phenomenal properties, then you will say that there is *another* property that is represented by *e*, namely the property phenomenal-red. What is that property? There are a variety of possible views here, but as we saw, Shoemaker takes it to be the property of "producing in a viewer" red-feeling experiences. The phenomenal property that Shoemaker thinks is *represented by e*, then, is defined partly in terms of a *property of e*: such properties of experience being qualia in the sense explained above.

If, like Peacocke, you believe in sensational properties, then you will say that there is a property (red′), which is neither a property *of e*, nor a property *represented by e*, but instead a property of a region of your visual field, of which you can be aware when you are having *e*.[23] Such properties, we may say, are *presented in* experiences. (On another usage of "qualia," qualia are properties like red′; to avoid confusion, the term is really best avoided.) Like properties *of* an experience, but unlike properties *represented by* an experience, if a property is *presented in* an experience then, necessarily, something (namely, a region of one's visual field) really does have this property.

With these distinctions in hand, we can use them to elaborate and sharpen the four main responses to the problem of color realism.

3 Eliminativism

Eliminativism about color is the thesis that no physical objects are colored. Since physical objects certainly look to be colored, eliminativism charges experience with widespread misrepresentation. Eliminativism is, perhaps surprisingly, a perennial favorite, and goes back at least to the early Greek atomist Democritus. The connection between atomistic metaphysics and eliminativism has seemed to many fairly immediate: if the physical world ultimately consists of colorless atoms in the void, how can colors find a place in it? Although Democritean atomism has not survived, the apparent conflict between the world as described by physics and the world as we perceive it has remained. Galileo and, following him, an impressive parade of philosophers including Descartes and Locke seem to have thought that modern science straightforwardly shows that physical objects are not colored. Many contemporary color scientists are of the same opinion. This fact gives color science a dubious honour not shared by many other fields of scientific enquiry.

Eliminativists will convict experience of different sorts of error, depending on their other views about the nature of visual experience. For an eliminativist who takes the visual field to be populated by sensational properties like red′, the natural view to take is that we mistakenly take red′—a property of regions of the visual field—to be a property of material objects.[24] (Such an eliminativist may, like Frank Jackson [1977], take red′ to *be* red,[25] and so hold that *some* things are red, but not physical objects like tomatoes. But this is an optional extra.) Boghossian and Velleman (chapter 7, 8) hold this sort of "projective" eliminativism, which is, on some interpretations, a close cousin of the traditional Galilean view.

A more straightforward sort of eliminativism, which does not depend on a commitment to sensational properties, is simply that experience falsely represents objects as being colored. We do enjoy red-representing experiences, but they are never veridical. The most prominent recent defender of this view has been C. L. Hardin (1984, 1993), who reinforces it further in chapter 15. (See also Mackie 1976; Landesman 1989; Averill 1992; Maund 1995.)

4 Dispositionalism

According to Locke, "a Violet, by the impulse of such insensible particles of matter of peculiar figures, and bulks, and in different degrees and modifications of their Motions, causes the *Ideas* of the blue Colour ... to be produced in our minds" (op. cit., II, viii, 13). Moreover, he thinks, such an idea of blue does not "resemble" anything in the violet; and by this he arguably means that violets, although they are *represented* to be blue, are not in fact blue. That is the eliminativist strand in Locke. But he is somewhat equivocal on the point. One property a violet certainly has is "a Power to produce those Sensations in us" (ibid., II, viii, 15): an example of a *secondary quality*. And Locke often speaks as if the power or disposition to produce ideas of blue may, without undue violence to ordinary talk, be fairly called "blue."

Although Locke was not the first to formulate the thesis that colors are dispositions to cause certain kinds of visual experiences,[26] his discussion is the point of departure for contemporary versions of dispositionalism. Taking blue as an example, the basic claim of the dispositionalist is something of the following form:

(D)   The property blue = the disposition to cause in perceivers P in circumstances C, visual experiences of kind K.[27]

What is the status of (D), once the schematic letters are filled in appropriately? According to Johnston (chapter 9), it does not express our naive conception of blue (which, strictly speaking, does not apply to anything), but rather a conception that, for pragmatic reasons, we should adopt. According to other philosophers, no such revision is required: our naive conception of blue is correctly analyzed as such a disposition (see, for example, Evans 1980, McGinn 1983, McDowell 1985).

There remains the question of how to fill in the schematic letters. As far as the first two are concerned, dispositionalists have been usually content with "normal" perceivers in "standard" conditions, without properly explaining what these terms mean (for some of the problems, see chapter II of Hardin 1993; for a response see Johnston's chapter 9). What about the "visual experiences of kind K"? If these are specified in terms that explicitly or implicitly employ the concept of the color in question (blue, in our example) then let us say that the resulting dispositionalism is *nonreductive*, and *reductive* otherwise.

It is here that issues about visual experience intrude. Suppose the "visual experiences of kind K" are specified in terms of what *colors* they represent things as having; in the case of blue, this will amount to specifying the experiences as *blue-representing*. Then evidently this will be a version of *non*reductive dispositionalism: the property blue has not been analysed in terms that do not employ the concept of blue, because blue-representing experiences are introduced by saying that they represent that something is *blue*. Of course, the nonreductive dispositionalist's thesis is circular (that is just another way of saying that it is nonreductive). Circularity as such is no vice, but Boghossian and Velleman argue in chapter 7 that here it is fatal.

In any case, if *reductive* dispositionalism is to be an option, there must be some way of picking out the visual experiences in question without recourse to their color contents. In section 2.1 above, we said that experiences may be classified by their distinctive phenomenology, as well as by their contents. So could a reductive dispositionalist simply identify the desired visual experiences, not as *blue-representing*, but as *blue-feeling*?

That depends. Blue-feeling experiences are those that saliently resemble, in respect of what it is like to undergo them, standard visual experiences of clear sky, Levi 501s, and lapis lazuli. As we noted in section 2.1, the introduction of this terminology is innocuous: it is quite compatible with the tightest of conceptual connections between blue-feeling and blue-representing experiences. In particular, it is compatible with the claim that "blue-feeling experience" can only be understood by presupposing that such experiences are also blue-representing. And if this claim is right, then characterizing dispositionalism in terms of blue-feeling experiences leaves it firmly nonreductive.

Therefore, if nonreductive dispositionalism is to get off the ground, it must be argued that "blue-feeling experience" can be understood without presupposing that such experiences are blue-representing. The most straightforward way to do this is to argue that blue-feeling experiences can occur without being blue-representing. And the most straightforward way to do *that* is to argue for the CONTINGENCY thesis of section 2.1.

5 Physicalism

Physicalism about color is, to a first approximation, the view that colors are physical properties that we sometimes veridically perceive objects to possess. The "physical" is a notoriously slippery notion, but fortunately those problems are not relevant here. The leading idea behind physicalism is not so much that colors are *physical* properties, but rather that colors are to be identified with properties whose natures (a) are specifiable in ways that do not employ our color concepts, and (b) are not constituted by relations to the psychological states of perceivers. That being so, the obvious candidates for such properties are either certain kinds of dispositions to affect incident light, or the diverse kinds of microphysical properties that realise such light-affecting dispositions. (On the former, see Land, *Readings on Color, vol. 2*, chapter 5, Wandell, *vol. 2*, chapter 6; on the latter, see Nassau, *vol. 2*, chapter 1.) As it happens, such properties are paradigmatic examples of physical properties, at any rate as philosophers have come to use this term; but that is incidental.

Because of (a), physicalism is *reductive*. Sometimes, because of (b), it is classified as "objective," the intended contrast here being with dispositionalism, said to be "subjective." But this can be misleading. Consider, for example, the physicalism of

Jackson and Pargetter (chapter 6; see also Jackson 1996). According to them, something like the following is a priori: green is that property that would standardly cause an object which has the property to look green.[28] So, on their view, it's a priori that something is green just in case it has a disposition to look green. But they also think that "dispositions do not cause their manifestations" (p. 69) (the "manifestation" in this case being the visual experience of the object's looking green). Hence, as the property green plausibly does cause such experiences, they decline to *identify* green with the disposition to look green. Rather, they say, green is the categorical base of the disposition, which science tells us is a physical property of some kind. As Johnston points out, the difference between physicalism in the style of Jackson and Pargetter and the corresponding version of dispositionalism "must really be quite subtle" (chapter 9, p. 148). It is not obviously helpful to characterize this difference by locating Jackson and Pargetter's account at the objective end of the spectrum.

Rather than employing the subjective/objective distinction to distinguish physicalism from rival views, it is more useful to classify accounts of color as subjective to the extent that they claim a substantive a priori connection between being a certain color and causing certain visual experiences. On this latter usage, dispositionalism, and Jackson and Pargetter's physicalism, both count as subjective. Armstrong, on the other hand, advocates a physicalism that cuts "all logical links between colours and what happens in the perceivers of colours" (chapter 3, n. 13),[29] a view that he says is also held by Smart. Armstrong, then, holds an objective version of physicalism; and so do Harman, and Byrne and Hilbert.

While Jackson and Pargetter identify colors with (disjunctions of) microphysical properties, Byrne and Hilbert identify them with dispositions to affect light (see also Hilbert 1987, Matthen 1988). Harman, on the other hand, suggests that colors are dispositions "to produce a certain reaction in normal perceivers, where the relevant reaction is identified in part with reference to the mechanisms of color perception" (chapter 13, p. 259). As Harman makes clear, this is not strictly a version of dispositionalism, because the "relevant reactions" are supposed to be specified "in terms of *biological* mechanisms of color perception" (p. 255), not as (say) red-feeling experiences or red-representing experiences.[30] All these three views are in part driven by their proponents' conceptions of visual experience. As noted at the end of section 2.1, Jackson and Pargetter hold CONTINGENCY. They also agree with Peacocke that there are sensational properties.[31] Harman, and Byrne and Hilbert, disagree on both counts. Harman, unlike Byrne and Hilbert, finds some insight in reductive dispositionalism, but his denial of CONTINGENCY prevents him from fully endorsing it.

6 Primitivism

An obvious, although in practice quite uncommon, view of the colors is to align them closely with paradigmatic "primary qualities," shapes. The property of being square, for example, is not reducible (to properties specified in nonspatial terms, at any rate); is not identical to the disposition to look square; and often our visual perceptions as of square things are veridical. According to the primitivist, colors are just like shapes in these respects. And especially in view of the problems that are widely held to afflict other views of color, primitivism can seem an attractive option.

A primitivist may hold that colors do not even supervene on physical properties of objects, a view to which Hardin (1993, pp. 60–1) rightly objected.[32] If there could be two physically alike objects that differ in their colors, then since both objects will affect light in the same way, it seems that the color of an object is causally irrelevant to the way it affects light. And if so, then vision does not *detect* the colors; but without visual detection, we have no reason to think that objects have the colors they look to have.

The primitivist, then, would be well-advised to claim that colors, although not identical to any physical properties, at least supervene on them. This is precisely what John Campbell does (chapter 10).

One of the most compelling, yet elusive, ideas in philosophical thinking about color is that the nature of the colors is fully revealed, or is transparent, to us in visual experience (Johnston, in chapter 9, calls this *Revelation*). Since it is not evident in visual experience that colors are physical properties, physicalism is not consistent with Revelation, and arguably any form of dispositionalism has the same failing. Hence one obvious motivation—apparently Campbell's—for primitivism comes from taking the metaphors about transparency seriously.[33]

Whatever Revelation amounts to exactly, it is not compatible with CONTINGENCY, as Campbell implicitly recognises. Return to Invert and Nonvert (section 2.1). They are both looking at a marigold and are enjoying, respectively, yellow- and blue-feeling experiences. If their experiences are *both* representing the marigold to be yellow, then intuitively it does not seem that the nature of yellow is transparent to either of them: their experiences are merely a sign or indication of yellow, rather than exposing its underlying nature.[34]

It is too much to expect that the foreseeable future will produce a philosophical consensus on the question of color realism. For one thing, the content and phenomenology of perceptual experience are topics that have only recently been treated with anything like the sophistication they demand. But this itself is genuine progress, suggesting new positions, and exposing new flaws in old ones. For those of us who prefer solutions as opposed to problems, contemporary philosophical work on color provides some grounds for hope.

Notes

1. Hume 1740/1978, p. 6; Moore 1903/1993, §§7, 10; Goodman 1983, chapter 3; Jackson 1982. It is no accident that the colors used in these examples are all unique hues (the four unique hues are red, green, blue, and yellow). It is interesting to speculate whether Moore would have thought a binary hue such as orange also an example of a "simple and indefinable quality." On the perceptual and linguistic salience of the unique hues, see Kay and McDaniel 1978 (chapter 17 of *Readings on Color, vol. 2*). On their connections with psychophysics and physiology, see Hurvich 1981, and De Valois and De Valois 1975 (chapters 3 and 4, respectively, of *vol. 2*).

2. For simplicity, we shall concentrate on surface color, and ignore the fact that colors also appear to be properties of light sources, transparent volumes, and expanses such as the sky. On these modes of color appearance, see Katz 1935.

3. Averill also argues that, although "green" should be analyzed in terms of perceptual effects on ourselves, "color" should not. The color of an object, according to Averill, is (simplifying a bit) the (maximally determinate) way the object affects visible light. (See also Hilbert 1987, pp. 98–9.) On Averill's view then, green is *not* a color and so, by his own lights, he is not a dispositionalist about *color*.

4. As Smart says, the midwives were David Lewis and D. M. Armstrong.

5. Some caveats. First, it is not clear in general just what the content of a given experience is. Does visual experience represent objects as being *tomatoes*, as opposed to being red and bulgy? Second, it is not clear whether there is such a thing as *the* content of an experience. Without more said about the individuation of experiences, perhaps talk about their contents is somewhat ill-posed. However, "observational" properties like the colors provide relatively uncontroversial examples of properties that visual experiences—however they might be individuated—represent objects as having, and that will do for present purposes.

6. Here we just assume for simplicity that the content of experience is existentially quantified: when you look at a tomato, your experience represents, inter alia, that there is a red object. An opposing view is that the content takes the form: that *o* is red.

7. The occurrent/nonoccurrent distinction is hard to make precise. But the rough idea is that a belief is occurrent to the extent that it is playing an active role in one's mental economy. Some writers reserve "thought" for this kind of belief.

8. See Evans 1982, pp. 122–4, p. 227. Evans also holds that experiences, unlike beliefs, have "non-conceptual content." But this further view is certainly not required in order sharply to distinguish belief and experience (see, e.g., McDowell 1994).

9. A visual experience, then, may be both a red-feeling experience and a green-feeling experience: for example, the visual experience one typically has when looking at ripe tomatoes on the vine.

10. It should be pointed out that if the phenomenological character of the visual experience of ripe tomatoes and the rest varies widely from person to person, this attempt to fix the reference of "red-feeling experience" will not do the trick! (See Block 1990, p. 57.) But for ease of exposition we shall assume that this is not the case.

11. Philosophers who think that that there are two distinctions here may well say that "looks red" has a use on which it means is *visually represented to be red*, and another on which it picks out the "phenomenological quality" characteristic of actual experiences of ripe tomatoes and the like. (Cf. p. 106 of Boghossian and Velleman's chapter 8.) Connectedly, they may say that "red" is ambiguous as between a property of physical objects and a property of mental objects or experiences. See, for instance, Block 1983 and Rosenthal 1990.

12. Tolliver (1994) excepted: he argues that visual experiences do not represent objects as having colors.

13. Here the restriction to *visual* experience is important. Many philosophers would claim that there could be another (non-visual) sense modality that represents things as having the property red (under a different "mode of presentation"). If so, and if the restriction to visual experience were dropped, COLOR-REP → COLOR-FEEL would be false.

14. The classic contemporary discussion is Shoemaker 1982.

15. More exactly, let us suppose, whether or not this was what Locke had in mind, that the inversion is not only with respect to blue- and yellow-feeling experiences. Let's stipulate that Invert's color-feeling experiences in a given circumstance *C* may be obtained from what a normal person's color-feeling experiences would be in *C* by the mapping that takes a point on the color circle to the point opposite it. (We are not supposing that such an inversion would be undetectable—see the text below.)

16. For the kind of evidence that color scientists have taken to be relevant to the discovery of such cases, see Alpern et al. 1983 (chapter 9 of *Readings on Color, vol. 2*) and Boynton 1979, pp. 380–2.

17. Strictly speaking, we need the further assumption that Jones's experience is not blue-representing for other reasons (as it would be if there were a violet next to the marigold, for instance).

18. See also Shoemaker 1986. For a more elaborate thought experiment, designed to support, inter alia, the same conclusion while avoiding some objections to the spectrum inversion case described above, see Block 1990.

19. See also Averill 1992.

20. Having a red afterimage with one's eyes closed would presumably be a case, according to Boghossian and Velleman, of having a red-feeling experience that was not representational at all. An experience of having a red afterimage with one's eyes open will typically have *some* content, however.

21. Or so we interpret Boghossian and Velleman. Bigelow et al. (1990) claim that afterimage experiences are not representational, but deny that this is Boghossian and Velleman's view.

22. For critical discussion of chapter 5 see Smith 1986 and Peacocke's reply (1986).

23. In his book *Sense and Content* (1983) Peacocke often writes, although not exclusively, as if sensational properties were properties *of* experiences, rather than properties *presented in* experiences. However, in chapter 5 of this volume (an elaboration of part of chapter 2 of *Sense and Content*), he largely dispenses with this potentially confusing mode of expression.

24. Cf. Hume's famous metaphor: "The mind has a great propensity to spread itself on external objects" (1740/1978), p. 167.

25. Jackson later changed his mind: see this volume, chapter 6, n. 5.

26. See Boyle 1666/1979 and Descartes 1644/1970. A precursor is Galileo 1623/1957.

27. This is a slight oversimplification, for the dispositionalist may wish to distinguish between various kinds of disposition (on this point, see Johnston, chapter 9).

28. Although Jackson and Pargetter employ expressions such as "the experience of looking red," and "looking-red experience," they do not mean, in our terminology, *red-representing* experience. Rather, they mean *red-feeling* experience.

29. By the quoted remark Armstrong clearly means to be simply denying that any kind of dispositionalist claim is a priori. Of course, he would agree that there are *some* "logical links"; for example, it is a priori that an experience as of something's looking red is veridical only if the thing is red.

30. See also Smith 1987. Evan Thompson (1995) may perhaps be interpreted as holding a view similar to Harman's.

31. CONTINGENCY does not force acceptance of sensational properties. Shoemaker, for instance, holds CONTINGENCY but explains the similarity between red-feeling experiences in terms of properties *represented by* experiences—phenomenal properties. But Jackson and Pargetter agree with Peacocke rather than Shoemaker (see Bigelow et al. 1990, pp. 281–4, esp. n. 7).

32. Hardin attributes this position to James Cornman (1974, 1975). But although Cornman is certainly a primitivist, it is not clear to us that he also intends to deny supervenience.

33. Jonathan Westphal (1991) is a primitivist who appeals to the findings of color science to uncover the "real essence" of the colors. Hence his version of primitivism, unlike Campbell's, does not pretend to be consistent with Revelation. P. M. S. Hacker (1987) is a primitivist who would probably reject Revelation as conceptually confused.

34. Cf. Descartes: "Clearly, then, when we say we perceive colours in objects, it is really just the same as though we said that we perceive in objects something as to whose nature we are ignorant, but which produces in us a very manifest and obvious sensation, called the sensation of colour" (1644/1970, I, lxx).

References

Alpern, M., K. Kitahara, and D. H. Krantz. 1983. Perception of colour in unilateral tritanopia. *Journal of Physiology* 335, 683–97. Reprinted in *Readings on Color, vol. 2: The Science of Color.*

Averill, E. W. 1992. The relational nature of color. *Philosophical Review* 101, 551–88.

Bigelow, J., J. Collins, and R. Pargetter. 1990. Colouring in the world. *Mind* 99, 279–88.

Block, N. 1983. Mental pictures and cognitive science. *Philosophical Review* 92, 499–541.

Block N. 1990. Inverted Earth. In *Philosophical Perspectives 4*, ed. J. Tomberlin. Atascadero, CA: Ridgeview.

Boyle, R. 1666/1979. The origin of forms and qualities according to the corpuscular philosophy. In *Selected Philosophical Papers of Robert Boyle*, ed. M. A. Stewart. Manchester, England: Manchester University Press.

Boynton, R. M. 1979. *Human Color Vision.* New York: Holt, Rinehart & Winston.

Cornman, J. 1974. Can Eddington's 'two' tables be identical? *Australasian Journal of Philosophy* 52, 22–38.

Cornman, J. 1975. *Perception, Common Sense, and Science.* New Haven: Yale University Press.

Descartes, R. 1644/1970. *Principles of Philosophy.* Extracts in *Descartes: Philosophical Writings*, ed. and trans. E. Anscombe and P. T. Geach. Middlesex, England: Nelson.

De Valois, R. L., and K. K. De Valois. 1975. Neural coding of color. In *Handbook of Perception, vol. 5: Seeing*, ed. E. C. Carterette and M. P. Friedman. New York: Academic Press. Reprinted in *Readings on Color, vol. 2: The Science of Color.*

Evans, G. 1980. Things without the mind. In *Philosophical Subjects: Essays Presented to P. F. Strawson*, ed. Z. Van Straaten. Oxford: Oxford University Press.

Evans, G. 1982. *The Varieties of Reference.* Oxford: Clarendon Press.

Galileo, G. 1623/1957. *The Assayer.* In *Discoveries and Opinions of Galileo*, ed. and trans. S. Drake. Garden City, N.Y.: Doubleday.

Goodman, N. 1983. *Fact, Fiction, and Forecast* (fourth edition). Cambridge, MA: Harvard University Press.

Hacker, P. M. S. 1987. *Appearance and Reality.* Oxford: Basil Blackwell.

Hardin, C. L. 1984. Are 'scientific' objects coloured? *Mind* 93, 491–500.

Hardin, C. L. 1993. *Color for Philosophers* (expanded edition). Indianapolis: Hackett.

Harman, G. 1996. Qualia and color concepts. In *Philosophical Issues* 7, ed. E. Villanueva. Atascadero, CA: Ridgeview.

Hilbert, D. R. 1987. *Color and Color Perception.* Stanford: CSLI.

Hume, D. 1740/1978. *A Treatise of Human Nature.* Oxford: Clarendon Press.

Hurvich, L. M. 1981. Chromatic and achromatic response functions. Chapters 5, 6 of his *Color Vision.* Sunderland, MA: Sinauer Associates. Reprinted in *Readings on Color, vol. 2: The Science of Color.*

Jackson, F. 1977. *Perception: A Representative Theory*. Cambridge: Cambridge University Press.

Jackson, F. 1982. Epiphenomenal qualia. *Philosophical Quarterly* 32, 127–36.

Jackson, F. 1996. The primary quality view of color. In *Philosophical Perspectives* 10, ed. J. Tomberlin. Cambridge, MA: Blackwell.

Katz, D. 1935. *The World of Colour*. London: Kegan Paul, Trench, Trubner & Co. Ltd.

Kay, P., and C. K. McDaniel. 1978. The linguistic significance of the meanings of basic color terms. *Language* 54, 610–46.

Landesman, C. 1989. *Color and Consciousness*. Philadelphia: Temple University Press.

Locke, J. 1689/1975. *An Essay Concerning Human Understanding*. Oxford: Oxford University Press.

Mackie, J. 1976. *Problems from Locke*. Oxford: Clarendon Press.

Matthen, M. 1988. Biological functions and perceptual content. *Journal of Philosophy* 85, 5–27.

Maund, J. B. 1995. *Colours: Their Nature and Representation*. Cambridge: Cambridge University Press.

McDowell, J. 1985. Values and secondary qualities. In *Morality and Objectivity*, ed. T. Honderich. London: Routledge and Kegan Paul.

McDowell, J. 1994. *Mind and World*. Cambridge, MA: Harvard University Press.

McGinn, C. 1983. *The Subjective View: Secondary Qualities and Indexical Thoughts*. Oxford: Clarendon Press.

Moore, G. E. 1903/1993. *Principia Ethica* (revised edition). Cambridge: Cambridge University Press.

Peacocke, C. 1983. *Sense and Content: Experience, Thought, and their Relations*. Oxford: Clarendon Press.

Peacocke, C. 1986. Reply to Michael Smith. *Synthese* 68, 577–80.

Rosenthal, D. 1990. The colors and shapes of visual experiences. Report 28, Research Group on Mind and Brain, Perspectives in Theoretical Psychology and the Philosophy of Mind (ZiF), University of Bielefeld, Germany.

Shoemaker, S. 1982. The inverted spectrum. *Journal of Philosophy* 79, 357–81.

Shoemaker, S. 1986. Review of C. McGinn's *The Subjective View*. *Journal of Philosophy* 83, 407–13.

Shoemaker, S. 1996. Colors, subjective reactions, and qualia. In *Philosophical Issues* 7, ed. E. Villanueva. Atascadero, CA: Ridgeview.

Smith, M. A. 1986. Peacocke on red and red'. *Synthese* 68, 559–76.

Smith, P. 1987. Subjectivity and colour vision. *Proceedings of the Aristotelian Society Suppl.* 61, 245–64.

Thompson, E. 1995. *Colour Vision*. London: Routledge.

Tolliver, J. T. 1994. Interior colors. *Philosophical Topics* 22, 411–41.

Westphal, J. 1991. *Colour: A Philosophical Introduction*. Oxford: Basil Blackwell.

1 On Some Criticisms of a Physicalist Theory of Colors

J. J. C. Smart

I want to discuss some criticisms made by M. C. Bradley[1] of the account of colors in my book *Philosophy and Scientific Realism*. I shall put forward a modified account of colors, which was first suggested to me by David K. Lewis, though a rather similar view has been put forward by D. M. Armstrong.[2] In fact there turn out to be certain differences between Lewis' present view of colors and that which he first suggested to me, and also between Armstrong's and Lewis', as also between Armstrong's and mine (or Lewis' original one). However, these differences seem to me to be of no ontological significance, but are rather differences as to which account of colors best fits our ordinary ways of talking. I suspect that our ordinary color discourse contains enough obscurity to make the choice between various philosophical analyses to some extent an arbitrary one.

In *Philosophy and Scientific Realism* I elucidate colors as dispositions of physical objects to evoke characteristic patterns of discriminatory color behavior by normal human percipients in normal circumstances. (Color discrimination, it will be remembered, can be elucidated antecedently to the notion of color, and so there is no circularity here.) Bradley brings up two imaginary cases to show the inadequacy of this view. One was originally C. B. Martin's, and is as follows. All colors can be represented on a color circle, where the various radii represent the various hues, and hues which are nearly indistinguishable from one another correspond to radii which are near to one another. The various amounts of saturation of a color are represented by distances along the radii. Thus, points near the center of the circle represent a high degree of additive mixing of white. (For simplicity of exposition I am here neglecting differences of brightness, and hence that between white, gray and black, but the full story can easily be adapted to the full color cone, which takes these differences into account. For "color circle" read "any cross section of the color cone.") Now let us envisage a miraculous transformation of things in the world so that the colors of things change into the diametrically opposite colors on the color circle. Thus if O is the center of the color circle and P and P' are points on opposite radii such that O P = O P', a thing whose color is represented by P will change to the color which is represented by P', and vice versa. The only things that will not change will be those things (white ones) whose color is represented by the center O of the color circle.

In the envisaged case the physical constitutions of things will change and so will the wavelengths of the light radiated from them. That is, the change is a perfectly objective and scientifically detectable one. It might correctly be remarked that such a miraculous change would be physically inexplicable, and it would almost certainly lead to difficulties for even the existence of human life. Both food and human flesh would have to undergo changes in order for them to have the chemical constitutions required for the new colors. Moreover, we would have to make all sorts of assumptions about boundary conditions in order to keep our story compatible with the laws of physics. For example, we would have to suppose the nonexistence of rainbows. (For how could color interchange occur on a rainbow without there being a change in the laws of physics?) Such objections can probably be set aside as quibbles, because for the purposes of the objection we can even suppose the laws of physics to be different from what they are, so long as they remain the same throughout the story. After all, we are concerned with elucidating commonsense color concepts, which have mostly grown up before the rise of modern science.[3]

Now in the envisaged case, everybody will want to say (on the basis both of physics and of immediate experience) that there has been a systematic change of the colors of things in the world. Yet the patterns of discriminatory responses will *not* have changed. Normal human percipients will still find it hard to pick geranium petals from a pile of ripe tomatoes, but easy to pick them from a heap of unripe ones, and hard to pick out lettuce leaves from a distant part of the lawn, but easy to pick out delphinium petals which have fallen onto the lawn. Thus the systematic interchange in the constitutions of things will not lead to any change in discriminatory responses of normal human percipients. (This supposes, of course, that the nervous systems of normal human percipients will continue to function as before, even though the constitution of blood, nerve tissue, etc., may have changed. We have already agreed to neglect any objection of this sort as being something of a quibble.) On the basis of immediate experience, and also on the basis of physics, people will say that a systematic interchange of colors will have occurred. And yet there will be no change in the patterns of discriminatory responses which are evoked by things in the world. Consequently there must be something wrong with an account of colors in terms of powers to cause certain patterns of discriminatory behavior.

In my book I tried unavailingly to get out of this difficulty by bringing in color experiences; in the envisaged case we should notice that our color experiences had changed. I elucidated the experience of something looking red in terms of "something going on in me which is like what goes on in me when I am in normal health and in normal light and there is something in front of my eyes which *really is* red." That is, the experience of red is elucidated in terms of the redness of objects. (Not the other way round, as by John Locke, although my account is like the Lockean one, insofar as it elucidates colors as powers. But to elucidate redness as the power to cause red ideas or sense data, as in Locke, leads to obvious difficulties for a thoroughgoing physicalism.) Bradley shows convincingly that if I modify my account so that redness becomes not just the power to cause a certain pattern of discriminatory responses but the power to cause the experience of "seeing something red" as well, I am caught in a vicious circularity. Colors are elucidated in part in terms of color experiences, and these are elucidated in terms of colors, which are elucidated in part in terms of experiences, which are. . . .

I admit that this objection from color reversal is damaging to my original account of colors. I am therefore disposed to give up my original account in favor of a different one which is, however, equally compatible with physicalism. In correspondence, David Lewis asked me why I did not say that a color is a physical state of the surface of an object, that state which normally explains certain patterns of discriminatory reactions of normal human percipients. (Fairly obvious modifications would have to be made to deal with the colors of public yet illusory objects, such as the sky or a rainbow.) I replied at the time that I did not like this because the state would be a very disjunctive and idiosyncratic one. In effect, Lewis replied, "Very disjunctive and idiosyncratic—so what?" And I then thought to myself, "So what?" Let me explain this.

Consider the following absurd piece of fiction. A man (Smith, say) has a peculiar neurosis. If he sees a tomato, a rainbow, a bulldozer, or an archbishop, he goes red in the face and stands on his head. No other objects produce this odd behavior. Then doubtless the property corresponding to the open sentence "tomato x or rainbow x or bulldozer x or archbishop x" would be of some interest to this man and to his psychiatrist. It is a perfectly objective property, but because of its peculiar disjunctiveness (the oddity of the different components of the disjunction occurring within the same disjunction) it is both a disjunctive and an idiosyncratic property. Let us call this disjunctive and idiosyncratic property "snarkhood." Now, although snarkhood is a perfectly objective property, it is only Smith's neurosis which makes it of any interest to anyone. Were it not for Smith's neurosis, neither he nor his psychiatrist would have any reason to single it out from the infinity of other highly disjunctive and idiosyncratic properties. Similarly, the disjunction of physical properties which is the physical property of greenness seems to be a very disjunctive and idiosyncratic physical property. We single it out only because of certain highly complex facts about the human eye and nervous system. This is because infinitely many different mixtures of light of various wavelengths and intensities can produce the same discriminatory response. Just as the property of snarkhood is of no interest except to Smith or his psychiatrist, so we need not expect the physical property of greenness to be of any interest to extraterrestrial beings, who would have differently constituted eyes and nervous systems.

A simple formula F might be suggested which would describe all the mixtures of wavelengths which would give rise to the same color behavior (and color experience) in a normal percipient. For this reason Armstrong is tempted to say that if there is no such simple formula there are not really any colors, because it is an aspect of our color perception that all red things look to have some simple and nondisjunctive property in common. Compare the case in which a disease is described by some complex syndrome, and medical scientists come to divide it into two diseases characterized by different (although possibly overlapping) parts of the syndrome and ascertainably different etiologies. We would be inclined to say in such a case that the scientists had discovered the existence of two new diseases, and also the nonexistence of the original disease. There seems to be a choice here: we could redescribe the old disease as a disjunction of the two new diseases, or else say that the old disease is nonexistent. My own inclination in the case of colors would be to take the analogue of the former choice. That is, if no suitable F exists Armstrong would say that there are not really any colors. I do not think that any ontological issue depends on the difference, even if the simple formula F exists.

It may be worth recalling my reason for thinking that no simple formula exists. Consider an arrangement of three photoelectric cells in a circuit which approximately simulates the human visual system (as elucidated by the three-color theory of vision).[4] We should have to choose three cells with appropriately related characteristic curves (current plotted against wavelength of light) such that the shapes of the curves were such-and-such, and their maxima were such-and-such. These specifications would have a quite arbitrary look about them and would be dictated by the nature of the human visual system. In this way the properties of physical objects which explain human visual discriminations are idiosyncratic properties. Presumably they are disjunctive properties because quite different mixtures of light can lead to the same visual response. Moreover, a mixture of light for which the intensity-wavelength curve is single-peaked, say at wavelength λ, can produce the same reactions as light with a many-peaked intensity-wavelength curve, and this last curve may even have a trough around λ. Nevertheless, there *may* be a nondisjunctive specification of the physical properties which are colors of objects although it is at least not obvious what this might be. I shall, however, mention an ingenious suggestion which David Lewis has communicated to me in correspondence. Consider a hyperspace of infinitely many dimensions, indeed as many dimensions as there are points in the real number continuum. A particular spectrum could be represented by a point in this hyperspace. Suppose that we give the space a metric, perhaps by taking the interval between two points in the hyperspace to be the mean square difference of intensities (for the two spectra) averaged over all wavelengths. Then, according to Lewis, it is possible that a color might correspond to (be the power to reflect light corresponding to) a simple shaped volume in this hyperspace. But at any rate is seems clear that if there is a simple formula of the sort for which Armstrong hankers, it cannot be anything very obvious, such as the capacity to reflect light of such-and-such a single wavelength. And if color should be such a simple property, so much the better. My defense of physicalism, however, will allow that it can be as idiosyncratic and disjunctive as you wish; like snarkhood it will nevertheless be a perfectly *objective* property.

Let me now revert to the earlier "So what?" A highly complex, disjunctive or idiosyncratic property would be objectionable at one end of a correlation law (nomological dangler). The assertion, however, that the color *is* the property, however disjunctive and idiosyncratic it may be, does not lead to this trouble. (If it should turn out to be less disjunctive or idiosyncratic than I fear, so much the better.) If the color *is* the physical property, then we have no nomological dangler depending from the property.

The property of snarkhood is disjunctive in that it might be defined by means of the disjunction:

Snarks $x =_{df}$ tomato x or rainbow x or bulldozer x or archbishop x.

Nevertheless snarkhood could also be described nondisjunctively as the property which things have if and only if they cause the neurotic behavior in question. Snarkhood is the property which *causes* or which *explains* the peculiar behavior; it is the property such that it is a *lawlike* proposition that, if and only if Smith is presented with something possessing the property, then he stands on his head. Such a description of the property makes use of words like "causes," "explains," "is lawlike." (Another possibility, related to the last one, is that we teach "snarks x" ostensively; snarkhood would then in a sense be indefinable, but we would be teaching someone to come out with the word "snarks" on any of a disjunctively describable set of occasions, whether or not he was aware of the disjunctiveness of the property of snarkhood.)

Notice that the identification of snarkhood with the property which causes the behavior in question is a contingent one. There is no difficulty about the contingent identification of properties, although it has for some reason been hard for many philosophers (including myself) to come to see this.[5] To use an example which I got from Lewis in correspondence, consider the statement that the property of conductivity is identical with the property measured by the piece of apparatus with such-and-such serial number. This statement is quite clearly a contingent and factual one. We must resist the temptation to suppose that all true statements of identity of properties would have to be necessary. It is clear, then, that although colors may be disjunctive and idiosyncratic physical properties, it need not be the case that those who use color words need know that this is so. For them, colors are described in a purely topic-neutral way (neutral between physicalist and nonphysicalist metaphysical theories). They are the properties, whatever they are, which could explain the characteristic patterns of discriminatory responses of normal human percipients. It would be perfectly possible for an Aristotelian type of person to agree with the analysis, but to suppose that the property which explains the pattern of responses is a nonphysicalist, emergent, and perhaps nondisjunctive one. We, with our scientific knowledge, will suspect that it is an idiosyncratic and possibly very disjunctive, purely physical property of the surfaces of objects. Not at first knowing or suspecting that the property is an idiosyncratic and possibly very disjunctive one, people might wrongly claim that they know that it is not an idiosyncratic and disjunctive one.

Armstrong suggests that mistakes of this sort can arise from a tendency of mind which gives rise to the headless woman illusion.[6] To cause this illusion, a dark cloth is put between the woman's head and the audience, and the background is similarly dark. Armstrong points out that the illusion arises from the tendency to suppose that because we do not perceive the woman to have a head we think that we perceive that she does not have a head, and he holds plausibly that a similar error causes people to think that they have an intuition that experiences are not brain processes. Such an error could occur in thinking about the possible identity of colors and physical states.

(I do not mean to say that Armstrong approves of this particular application of his idea about the headless woman illusion. He has told me that because all red things look to have something in common he does not think that the apparent simplicity of colors can be explained by a failure to perceive a real disjunctiveness.)

Notice now that though greenness is the very property which (in normal circumstances) explains a certain pattern of discriminatory reactions, a different color could explain the same pattern in the case of the miraculous color reversal. Two different things can explain the same thing. There is no reason why we should not therefore say that the colors had changed over. No doubt our inner experiences and memories would incline us to take this course because there will be a systematic change in our color experiences. (I go along with Martin and Bradley in supposing this; it seems to be probable. But since there would also have to be a complete change in our semantic habits we might simply feel dizzy or go mad.) Percipients will notice the change and will say (for example) that tomatoes are blue and that delphiniums are red. They will want to rewrite the *Concise Oxford English Dictionary* and interchange the entries "shades ... seen in blood" (see the definition of "red") and "colored like the sky" (see the definition of "blue"), though they might allow "red" and "blue" to be defined as "the shade *formerly* seen in blood" and "the color *formerly* of the sky." In short, then, the revised account of colors, which defines colors as the physical states of objects which (in our normal world) explain a pattern of discriminatory reactions, allows us consistently to describe the color reversal case: A and B can be different and yet each can explain the same phenomenon C. The trouble which arose for the account of colors as simply powers to cause patterns of discriminatory reactions does not arise. The colors are the physical states which explain these powers, but other states could explain the very same powers after the miraculous interchange.

I think that the revised account of colors also saves the physicalist from Bradley's objection that it is conceivable that everyone might have the appropriate discriminatory responses so that they would satisfy the behavioral tests for color vision, and yet everything would look gray to them. I am not completely sure that Bradley's case really is conceivable, because if someone has not at least a tendency not to discriminate (with respect to color) red things from gray things, can he really see red things as gray? Just as in Martin's example, however, the inability to think through the example in a scientific manner probably does not suffice to discredit the *philosophical* potency of the example, and so I shall waive this point. Now I think that we can accommodate this case to the revised account of colors as follows: Colors are the (perhaps highly disjunctive and idiosyncratic) properties of the surfaces of objects that explain the discriminations with respect to color of normal human percipients, and also the experiences of these percipients, the looking red, or looking blue, etc., of objects. They would also, however, help to explain the abnormal experiences of the people in Bradley's proposed case.

We might consider that there would be some abnormality in the brains of people who always had inner experiences of seeing gray even though their behavior showed a complete range of color discriminations. Then colors (properties of surfaces of objects) would help to explain the normal discriminatory behavior of these people and would also help to explain the abnormal color experiences of the people with the abnormal brains. It is interesting to speculate whether and in what sense these people would have a color language. They might learn color words purely by reference to discriminatory behavior and would have no words for color experiences. They would doubtless be able to describe illusory color perceptions, in the sense that someone might in slightly abnormal circumstances want to match A with B even though a normal human percipient (behavioristically speaking) would not want to do so. They would need at least a behavioristic analogue of "B looks the color of A."

Let us revert to Bradley's case. He strengthens it (so as to avoid the considerations of the last paragraph) by supposing that both the discriminatory color behavior and the looking gray of everything were *ex hypothesi* inexplicable. Then could I say, as I have done, that the colors of things are those objective physical properties (perhaps highly disjunctive and idiosyncratic) which explain the patterns of discriminatory behavior of human beings? If the answer is negative, I do not see how Bradley can suppose that there could be a color vocabulary at all. Surely a certain degree of explicability is presupposed by any color vocabulary? How would we teach or learn a purely private language of color discrimination or of color experiences? Both colors (which I am arguing to be objective properties of the surfaces of objects) and color experiences (which in my view are physical processes in human brains) are identified by their typical causes and effects (in the case of the colors themselves, mainly by effects, and in the case of color experiences, mainly by causes). This does not mean that for the purpose of giving sense to our color language we need strict causal laws, which would give strict necessary or sufficient conditions for color behavior or color experiences. The difficulties into which philosophical behaviorism has run provide sufficient evidence of the fruitlessness of a search for such strict conditions. Typical causes and effects in typical conditions are all that we need.[7]

I think that the revised account of colors will even enable us to follow Bradley in saying that color discriminations must be on "the different observed appearances of things."[8] For (a) we hypothesize colors as the (perhaps highly disjunctive and idiosyncratic) physical states of the surfaces of objects which in fact explain (from the side of the objects) typical color discriminations, and also (b) we hypothesize color experiences as those processes which (from the side of the person—in fact, the brain) explain this same discriminatory behavior. That the causal chain goes not direct from the surface of the object to behavior but goes via the person (his brain and hence his inner experiences) is perfectly consistent with the physicalist thesis.

A color sensation, in this view, is what is hypothesized as a typical cause of the typical response of normal color percipients in typical circumstances. ("Normal" can be defined without circularity.) Such a sensation will also partially serve to explain the nontypical false reports of percipients who suffer from illusion or from intention to deceive. (Illusion leads to false reports about external things, while intention to deceive can also lead to false sensation reports.) I therefore see no difficulty for the amended view in Bradley's remarks about false sensation reports which arise from intention to deceive.[9] Nor shall I touch on Bradley's argument[10] from the alleged incorrigibility of sensation reports, since he no longer subscribes to this argument.[11]

I have no doubt that I have been unable to do justice to all of Bradley's criticisms or even to the full subtlety of any of them, but I hope that I have been able to explain why I think that, although my earlier account of colors must be given up, there is nevertheless another physicalist account of colors which avoids these objections.

Ideally, for Quinean reasons, I should like to supplant my talk of colors as properties by a more extensional set theoretic account.[12] Ideally, too, the notion of "explains" or "causes" which comes into the account should rest on an extensional account in terms of the syntax (or possibly semantics) of the language of science.[13] It should be noticed, in any case, that this property talk, as well as the use of the concept of explanation ("colors are the physical states of objects which explain certain discriminatory behavior") is needed only to identify the colors of our ordinary commonsense talk with physicalist properties, that is, as a defense against someone who thinks that a physicalist world view leaves something out. Once this is conceded, we can drop the words "property" and "explain" within our statement of world view. But it would be good to do the job set-theoretically, rather than in terms of properties.

Acknowledgments

I wish to thank Professor D. K. Lewis and Professor D. M. Armstrong for commenting on an earlier version of this paper.

Notes

1. In his "Critical Notice of *Philosophy and Scientific Realism*," *Australasian Journal of Philosophy* 42 (1964): 262–283, and also in his "Sensations, Brain Processes and Colours," ibid. 41 (1963): 385–393.

2. D. M. Armstrong, *A Materialist Theory of Mind* (London: Routledge & Kegan Paul, 1968), pp. 256–260, 272–290.

3. It may be questioned whether the concept of the sort of color change which we are envisaging can be made structurally consistent. See Paul E. Meehl, "The Compleat Autocerebroscopist: A Thought-Experiment on Professor Feigl's Mind-Body Identity Thesis," in Paul K. Feyerabend and Grover Maxwell, eds., *Mind, Matter and Method: Essays in Philosophy and Science in Honor of Herbert Feigl* (Minneapolis: University of Minnesota Press, 1966), pp. 103–180, especially pp. 147–148. Also Bernard Harrison, "On Describing Colours," *Inquiry* 10 (1967): 38–52. I welcome such considerations if they can be made out, but even so I do not want my defense of physicalism to have to depend on them.

4. P. J. Bouma, *Physical Aspects of Colour* (Eindhoven, Netherlands: Philips Industries, 1949), pp. 154–156.

5. I myself learned this point from Lewis. N. L. Wilson argued, however, for the possibility of contingently identifying properties in his interesting paper, "The Trouble with Meanings," *Dialogue* 3 (1964): 52–64.

6. D. M. Armstrong, "The Headless Woman Illusion and the Defence of Materialism," *Analysis* 29 (1968): 48–49.

7. David K. Lewis, "An Argument for the Identity Theory," *Journal of Philosophy* 63 (1966): 17–25, especially 22.

8. Bradley, "Sensations, Brain Processes and Colours," p. 393.

9. Bradley, Critical Notice, p. 269.

10. Bradley, Critical Notice, pp. 272–278.

11. Bradley, "Two Arguments against the Identity Theory," in R. Brown and C. D. Rollins, eds., *Contemporary Philosophy in Australia* (London: Allen & Unwin, 1969).

12. See my paper, "Further Thoughts on the Identity Theory," *The Monist* 56 (1972).

13. To elucidate "explanation" we need to elucidate "law." A law is a universally quantified sentence which occurs either as an axiom or a theorem of an important and well-tested theory (or, in an informal theory, somehow "follows from" it) or is such that we guess that it will one day be incorporated in such a theory. Thus to elucidate "explanation" we seem to need value words (e.g., "important"). Value expressions enable us to avow preferences; there is nothing contrary to physicalist metaphysics about them.

2 Color and the Anthropocentric Problem

Edward Wilson Averill

By the phrase 'anthropocentric account of color' I mean an account of color that makes an assumption of the following form: two objects are the same color if and only if they would appear to be exactly similar in color to normal human observers under such-and-such viewing conditions. Anthropocentric accounts are distinguished from one another by the way in which they fill in the viewing condition. The purpose of this paper is to compare anthropocentric and nonanthropocentric accounts of color and to argue for a certain nonanthropocentric account.

An anthropocentric account of color that fills in the viewing condition with 'normal viewing conditions' will be called an *a-nor account*. Every nonphysicalist account of color that I am aware of is an a-nor account. Since I want to compare anthropocentric and nonanthropocentric accounts of color without getting into too many other questions, I will consider only physicalist accounts of color in this paper. However, I believe that the criticisms that will be made of J. J. C. Smart's physicalist a-nor account of color can be extended to all nonphysicalist accounts of color.

In part I a trilemma is set up which displays the consequences of giving up an a-nor account of color. More specifically, the working out of this trilemma in parts II and III shows that any account of color must have at least one of the following consequences: many things that appear to be the same shade of yellow to normal human observers under normal viewing conditions are not the same shade of yellow; or yellow is not a color and the various shades of yellow are not colors; or some a-nor account of color is correct.

The purpose of part II is to show that accounts of color that grasp the third horn of the trilemma have more problems than a certain account of color that grasps the second horn. In part II J. J. C. Smart's a-nor account of color is compared with an anthropocentric account which assumes that the viewing conditions should be filled in with 'all lighting conditions (but otherwise normal viewing conditions, e.g., no viewing of objects through light filters)'. Call any anthropocentric account of color which fills in the viewing condition this way an *a-all account*. No simple argument is given to show that Smart's a-nor account of color is false. Instead it is shown that Smart's account of color is vastly more complex and cumbersome than his presentation of that account suggests and that this complexity stems from Smart's a-nor assumption. By contrast the a-all account to be developed in part II is much simpler, even though this a-all account holds that neither yellowness nor its shades are colors, i.e., even though this a-all account grasps the second horn of the trilemma. On this a-all account every shade of yellow is a set of colors.

Part III is concerned with accounts of color that grasp the first horn of the tri-lemma. Such accounts of color are not anthropocentric. In part III an account of color is considered which treats yellowness as a natural kind. This account of color has the consequence that many things that appear to be the same shade of yellow to normal observers under normal conditions are not yellow. Of course, all accounts that grasp the first horn of the trilemma have this consequence. It is argued that this consequence makes all such accounts unacceptable.

By the end of part III I hope to have established that the best accounts of color grasp the second horn of the trilemma, as the a-all account of part II does. In part IV the problems raised in connection with Smart's a-nor account are generalized, and it is shown that the a-all account of part II cannot solve all these problems. To deal with these further problems an account of color is developed in part V which generalizes from the a-all account of part II in much the same way that the a-all account generalizes from Smart's a-nor account. But with this generalization the importance of humans drops out; i.e., the new account is not anthropocentric. On this new account the concept of color depends on the concepts of light and visibility (like the anthropocentric accounts of color and unlike the natural-kind account of color), but the distinctions between colors are no longer restricted to distinctions that are visible to normal human beings (unlike anthropocentric accounts of color).

I   The Trilemma

Objects that reflect very different combinations of wavelengths of light can appear to be the same color to normal human beings looking at these objects in sunlight. For example, the different combinations of wavelengths of light reflected by objects that appear to be any specific shade of white or yellow (except for the brightest, most saturated shades of yellow) are almost endless. Furthermore these combinations can be made up of light from many different parts of the spectrum. Given these facts, suppose that the paints in two pots, A and B, appear to normal humans to be the same shade of yellow in sunlight; and suppose that the paint in pot A reflects only light from the red and green parts of the spectrum and the paint in pot B reflects only light from the yellow and blue parts of the spectrum (the large majority of which will be light from the yellow part of the spectrum). A figure is painted on a canvas with paint from pot A, and the background is filled in with paint from pot B. The canvas now appears to be a uniform shade of yellow to normal human beings looking at it in sunlight. What is the color of this canvas? Clearly the following three statements are inconsistent:

(a) The canvas is a uniform shade of yellow.

(b) This uniform shade of yellow is one distinct color.

(c) The figure on the canvas is different in color from its background.

Before getting into the problems involved in resolving this inconsistency, consider some of the ways in which the reasoning leading to the inconsistency can be generalized. To begin with, the inconsistency does not need to be developed in terms of sunlight. It can be developed in terms of candlelight, firelight, or the light from the large majority of incandescent lamps, since under each of these sources pots *A* and *B* will reflect different kinds of light, but the canvas will appear to normal humans to be a uniform shade of yellow. So the conditions under which the above inconsistency was derived can be generalized from sunlight to normal lighting conditions. Note for later use that these conditions cannot be generalized to all lighting conditions, because if the canvas were placed under a light source that emitted light from the yellow band of the spectrum only it would appear to normal observers to have a black figure on a yellow background. Secondly, the pots might contain paint that appeared to be another color under normal viewing conditions, e.g., another shade of yellow or a shade of green. Finally, there is no need to limit the above reasoning to canvases or to reflected light. Any object will do which appears to normal human beings to be a uniform color under normal viewing conditions and which reflects or radiates light from one part of its surface different in composition from the light reflected or radiated from another part of its surface.

Given these generalizations, there are a great many actual and possible objects about which sets of three inconsistent statements could be generated that are like the above example. Each of these sets involves a-like, b-like, and c-like statements. All a-like statements, including (a) itself, will be called *shade-identity statements*. Similarly, b-like statements and c-like statements will be called *color-identity statements* and *color-different statements*, respectively.

How should the trilemma be resolved? It is tempting to begin by assuming that we can be sure that (a) is true. This seems reasonable, because it seems that the canvas passes the most basic test imaginable for being a uniform shade of yellow; i.e., it appears to be a uniform shade of yellow to normal observers who can inspect it as much as they want under normal viewing conditions. However, Saul Kripke[1] has taught us that there is a deeper test for being gold than appearing to be gold to normal observers under normal conditions; and similarly for other natural kinds. Furthermore, Kripke claims that yellow objects form a natural kind (354). This suggests that there might be a deeper test for being yellow than appearing to be yellow to normal observers, and that such a test might show that (a) is false. This solution to the trilemma will be taken up in part III.

J. J. C. Smart holds an a-nor physicalist account of color. So he accepts shade- and color-identity statements and rejects color-different statements. As I will explain in part II, there are good reasons for rejecting this view.

I think (b) is false. I think there are good reasons for holding that the specific shades of red, yellow, blue, etc., should be anthropocentrically defined, but that colors should not be anthropocentrically defined. It is one thing to argue that accounts of color which accept color-identity statements have problems and another thing to present a full-fledged account of color which keeps shade-identity and color- different statements and rejects color-identity statements. So I will start this latter task in part II and finish it in part V.

II Smart's Account of Color

Smart, in his essay "On Some Criticisms of a Physicalist Theory of Color,"[2] sums up his account of color this way:

Colors are the (perhaps highly disjunctive and idiosyncratic) properties of the surfaces of objects that explain the discriminations with respect to color of normal human percipients, and also the experiences of these percipients, the looking red, or looking blue, etc. of objects (60).

For example:

... greenness is the very property which (in normal circumstances) explains a certain pattern of discriminatory reactions (59).

Here the concept of colored (physical) object is being explained in terms of the con- cepts of color discrimination (those color discriminations made by normal human beings under normal viewing conditions) and color experience (those color experi- ences that normal human beings have under normal viewing conditions). Smart sends us to a previous work of his, *Philosophy and Scientific Realism*,[3] which explains how the concepts of color experience and color discrimination can be understood independently of the concept of colored (physical) object (75–84, and "Some Criticisms...," 54). The thesis that the concept of color experience or color discrimination is logically independent of the concept of colored (physical) object is controversial. Some authors who hold this thesis define color experiences or color discriminations in terms of color sensations, whereas others appeal to "color be- havior." I will not consider this thesis here because I think it can be successfully defended, and I want to get on to other considerations.[4] (Every account of color considered in this paper holds some version of this controversial thesis.)

There is a problem about exactly what Smart means by "same color" in the above passages. If color is a matter of explaining the sorts of discriminations Smart has in mind, then it would seem that, strictly speaking, greenness is not a color, but shades of green are colors. In his earlier work on color Smart addressed this problem.

What about the differences between Oxford blue and Cambridge blue? (Dark blue and light blue.) We call things of both these colours 'blue', but they are nevertheless from the present point of view different colours. A normal percipient will easily distinguish otherwise similar objects, one of which is Oxford blue and the other of which is Cambridge blue (78).

Since Smart refers us to the passages in *Philosophy and Scientific Realism* to explain the notion of discrimination that he uses in "On Some Criticisms of a Physicalist Theory of Colors," I feel safe in assuming that Smart holds an account of color that assumes that color-identity statements are true.

In summary, Smart explicitly adopts the following three assumptions. (1) The A-Nor Assumption: two objects have the same color if and only if they would appear to have the same color to normal human percipients under normal lighting conditions. This assumption makes (c), and other color-different statements, false. Furthermore, this assumption divides objects up into equivalence classes, such that there is one specific color associated with each class, and all and only the members of that class are the specific color associated with the class. To explain how shades are related to colors Smart holds the following shade assumption: (2) colors and shades have the same identity conditions. So color-identity statements are true, and the equivalence classes defined above are shades. For example, any specific shade of blue would be such a class. Notice that, strictly speaking, blue is not a color. From these first two assumptions it follows that shade-identity statements are true. (3) The Physicalist Assumption: the color of an object is that physical property of the object which causally explains which equivalence class the object belongs to.

Smart's a-nor account of color is to be compared to the following a-all account of color, which makes the following three assumptions. (1) The A-All Assumption: two objects have the same color if and only if the two objects would appear to have the same color to normal human percipients under all lighting conditions (other viewing conditions being normal). (Both on this view and on Smart's view it is assumed that, when a color comparison is being made between two objects under a light source, they are oriented in the same way toward that light source.) Like Smart's a-nor assumption, this a-all assumption also sorts objects into equivalence classes. We have already noticed that under certain light sources the figure on the canvas appears to be black against a yellow background. Given the a-all assumption, (c) is contingently true. To make (a) true we need the following assumption about the identity conditions for shades: (2) the shade of yellow on the canvas is a set of colors such that all and only those objects which appear to be this shade of yellow to normal human observers under normal viewing conditions have a color that is a member of this set. So (a) and other shade-identity statements are true, whereas (b) and other color-identity statements are false. Strictly speaking, the yellow shade of the canvas is not a color but a set of colors. Similar remarks hold for other shades. (3) The Physicalist Assumption: the color of an object is that physical property of the object which causally explains which equivalence class the object belongs to.

Before getting into the differences between these two accounts, it is interesting to note the following similarities between them. Strictly speaking, yellow is not a color on either account. On both accounts a shade of yellow is an "a-nor concept," because on each account two objects are the same shade of yellow if and only if the two objects would appear to be the same shade of yellow to normal observers under normal viewing conditions.

Smart says in "Some Criticisms ..." that his account of color may make colors highly disjunctive and idiosyncratic properties of objects, and for this reason he was at one time reluctant to accept it (56). (Note Smart's parenthetical remarks in the first quote cited above.) Smart explains why colors may be highly disjunctive properties in the following passage:

Presumably they (i.e., colors) are disjunctive properties because quite different mixtures of light can lead to the same visual response. Moreover, a mixture of light for which the intensity-wavelength curve is single-peaked, say at wavelength λ, can produce the same reactions as light with a many-peaked intensity-wavelength curve, and this last curve may even have a trough around λ (57). (my "i.e.")

For example, the intensity-wavelength curve of the paint in pot B is very nearly single-peaked in the yellow part of the spectrum, but the paint in pot A is double-peaked and has a trough in the yellow part of the spectrum.

So the shade of yellow on the canvas mentioned above is a disjunctive physical structure of either the same physical type as the paint in pot A, or the same physical type as the paint in pot B, or the same physical type as ... —and so on through all the many types of physical structures that look to normal humans this shade of yellow in sunlight. In this way the figure and the background of the canvas turn out to have the same physical property. Given the above a-all account, this shade of yellow is also a disjunctive physical property.

Consider how this disjunctiveness works out in the description of specific perceptual situations. Normal observers could see the figure on the canvas under normal lighting conditions by holding a filter in front of their eyes that screens out all and only light from the red part of the spectrum. To such observers the canvas appears to have a green figure on a yellow background. Since the figure is really yellow (both accounts take shade-identity statements to be true), this situation involves a hue illusion; i.e., the figure looks green when it is really yellow. This sort of an illusion is quite common, since the hue of many objects will appear to be different when seen under abnormal lighting conditions or when seen through filters.

Given Smart's account of color, this situation also involves a color-distinction illusion. Since the figure and its background are the same color (because Smart accepts the truth of shade- and color-identity statements), the apparent distinction in color between them is an illusion. Furthermore, the color-distinction illusion is different from the hue illusion because there are hue illusions that are not color-distinction illusions. For example, suppose that a figure on a canvas is painted with paint that reflects only light from the red and green parts of the spectrum (similar to the above case) but the background is filled in with paint that reflects only light from the blue part of the spectrum. If normal observers look at this canvas under normal light through a filter that screens out all and only light from the red part of the spectrum, then the figure on the canvas will look green against a blue background. Here there is a hue illusion, because the figure looks green when it is really blue. However, there is no color-distinction illusion because the figure and its background appear to be different in color and really are different in color.

Given Smart's account of color, the observers do not see a color distinction in the above situation. But they do see a real distinction. How should Smart describe the distinction that normal observers see in the above situation as a color distinction? When one sees the shade of yellow on the canvas described in part I, the object of perception is a disjunctive physical property. Since this disjunctive physical property can be an object of perception, the nondisjunctive components of this disjunction must also be objects of perception; otherwise the perception of the disjunctive property would be unintelligible. Hence it is a consequence of Smart's account of color that when normal observers see the color-distinction illusion described above they are really seeing the distinction between two nondisjunctive components of a certain shade of yellow, which in this case appear to be different in color even though they are not different in color. In order to describe this perceptual situation Smart will have to introduce types of this shade of yellow; one type for each nondisjunctive component of this disjunctive property.

Is there a nonillusionary way for normal observers to see the distinction between the components of this shade of yellowness, on Smart's account of color? Perhaps they could see the differences between the microstructures if they looked at the canvas through an electron microscope. However, there is no simple nonillusionary way to see this distinction. This makes the color-distinction illusion unusual because most visual illusions are contrasted with nonillusionary ways of seeing that do not require a lot of special equipment.

By contrast, the a-all account described above handles this situation quite easily. There is, of course, a hue illusion; i.e., the figure does not appear to be the shade that it really is. But there is no color-distinction illusion, because the observers looking at the canvas through the filter see the color distinction between the color of the figure and the color of the canvas. Clearly the a-all account describes this situation more simply than Smart's a-nor account.

So far we have considered the perceptions of normal humans. Since normal human observers can see the figure on its background under normal lighting conditions, when they have the appropriate filters in front of their eyes, it is easy to imagine that some unusual human observers should have eyes that can distinguish the figure from its background; i.e., it is easy to imagine that some humans should have the appropriate filter "built in." Perhaps genetic engineers or microsurgeons could create such people. In any case, there are two reasons for thinking that normal observers are color-blind to a color distinction that the unusual human perceivers could perceive. In the first place normal observers pass the basic test for color blindness (i.e., failure to see the figure on the canvas under normal lighting conditions) relative to the unusual perceivers. Secondly, under normal lighting conditions these unusual human perceivers see the figure as a figure that is different in color from its background. Thus, if (c) is true, as it would be if the a-all account described above were true, there is an easy and natural way to characterize the difference between normal observers and the unusual observers; i.e., normal observers are, and the unusual observers are not, color-blind to the difference in color between the figure and its background. (The unusual observers are also color-blind to distinctions that normal observers can perceive, e.g., they are color-blind to the difference between the color of an object that reflects light from the green part of the spectrum only and one that reflects light from the red and green parts of the spectrum.)

But suppose, as Smart does, that (c) is false. In this case there are not two colors on the canvas for the unusual perceivers to see. So, of course, normal observers are not color-blind with respect to these two colors. How then should we understand the difference between the unusual human observers and normal human observers? The unusual human observers perceive the figure on the canvas by perceiving a color-distinction illusion. On the a-all account described above there are two colors on the canvas for the unusual observers to see. On Smart's a-nor account there are two types of yellowness on the canvas for them to see. So Smart has to introduce as many objects of perception as the a-all account does. He also has to introduce color-distinction illusions that the a-all account does not need. But there is more to this example.

Smart points out that, given his account of color, color is idiosyncratic in this sense: if a machine were to be constructed that detected color distinctions, the specifications of this system "would have a quite arbitrary look about them and would be dictated by the nature of the human visual system" ("Some Criticisms . . .," 57; also see the parenthetical remarks in the first quote from Smart at the beginning of this part). Since the unusual human observers have a perceptual mechanism that responds to light unlike the perceptual mechanism that normal human observers have, they do not see colors insofar as their mechanism is different from ours. For example, when the unusual observers see a blue figure on a green background, they do see a color distinction, although they do not see a color distinction when they look at the canvas described above. In this way Smart's account of color implies that there is a radical discontinuity in the sorts of things that the unusual observers see. In some cases they see color distinctions, and in other cases they see color-distinction illusions. But surely we think of the unusual observers as seeing much the same sort of thing in these two cases, because the perceptual situations are so similar. For this reason the a-all account spelled out above describes what the unusual observers see in a better way than Smart's account does.

Consider a generalization of this "unusual human observers" case. Scientists have established that color perception in humans has a lot to do with cone cells in the eye, different groups of which are sensitive to different combinations of wavelengths of light, and to the way in which these cells are hooked together by the nervous system. Once one starts thinking about how such mechanisms might be different, and comparing our neural setup with those of other animals (including animals that we are very close to, such as those we evolved from and may evolve into), it is natural to think that a virtually endless variety of color perceivers is physically possible, despite what Smart says about the idiosyncratic nature of color. Such speculations assume that any animal that has groups of cells in a light-sensitive organ, i.e., an eye, which are differentially sensitive to combinations of wavelengths of light, perceives colors, even if those cells are not differentially sensitive to the same combinations of wavelengths of light to which humans' eyes are sensitive. But this assumption makes sense only if there are color distinctions associated with the different combinations of wavelengths of light; i.e., if color-different statements are true. In other words speculations about the color distinctions that other beings may see are not speculations about a large variety of color-distinction illusions, as they would have to be if color-different statements were false. But if color-different statements are not false, Smart's a-nor assumption is false. (Notice that this generalization of the argument given in the paragraph preceding this one does not assume that animals, who are sensitive to combinations of wavelengths of light to which humans are not sensitive, see colors by having color sensations that are similar to the color sensations that humans have. This was assumed for the unusual human observers above, in order to emphasize the point that Smart must hold that observers that are very close to normal human observers see the figure on the canvas by means of a color-distinction illusion, i.e., there is a discontinuity between what normal humans see and what those who are much like them see.)

One final point before leaving Smart. Smart says that colors *may be* highly disjunctive and idiosyncratic properties of objects, given his account of color and modern scientific accounts of the way humans perceive color distinctions. He does not say that they *are* disjunctive and idiosyncratic. Smart says that it could turn out that color properties have a simple nondisjunctive characterization in terms of modern physical theory, besides their present disjunctive characterization, which we are not aware of at this time. I do not see how this could be true. Suppose that the figure and its background have some common nondisjunctive property. The figure and its background react differentially to normal light. It could not be that this common property causally explains how both the figure and its background react to normal light, since the same cause cannot have different effects. Thus, it could not be that this common property causally explains the differential reaction of our retinas to the light reflected from the figure and to the light reflected from its background.

III   A Natural-Kind Account of Color

So far I have argued that color-different statements are true. If this is correct, then either shade- or color-identity statements are false. Consider shade-identity statements. Are there any good reasons for thinking that such statements are false? Although I do not know of any philosopher who ever argued that such statements are false (D. M. Armstrong may have[5]), it is easy to see how someone holding Kripke's position on color might construct such an argument.

Kripke holds that a description, or paradigm examples, can be used to fix the reference of a natural-kind term in a nonanalytic way, where the natural-kind term refers to some, perhaps unknown, deep structural property that all and only things of this kind have in common. About yellowness he writes:

... the reference of 'yellowness' is fixed by the description 'that (manifest) property of objects which causes them, under normal circumstances, to be seen as yellow (i.e., to be sensed by certain visual impressions)' (354).

Given what has been said above, there is no known nondisjunctive physical property that all and only things have in common which appear to be yellow to normal observers looking at them under normal conditions, nor does it seem that scientists are looking for such a property. There are several ways that Kripke might deal with these facts. For example, these facts may only show that the deep structural property in question might be disjunctive. However, what is interesting in this context is that Kripke could conceivably deal with them in a way that makes (a) false.

Kripke might hold that the scientific study of yellowness shows that many things that appear to be yellow are not really yellow (just as things may appear to be gold but are not really gold). In fact, all and only things that appear to be the most saturated and brightest yellow emit light from the yellow part of the spectrum only.[6] This is why the paint in pot B had to reflect a little light from the blue part of the spectrum in order to match the color in pot A. This phenomenon is even more pronounced for other hues; e.g., no mixture of light, from other than the green part of the spectrum, comes close to matching the bright rich green appearance of the light emitted from the green part of the spectrum. Thus Kripke might hold that the only things that are really yellow are those which emit light from the yellow part of the spectrum. More generally, the color of an object is the color of the spectral light that it emits. On this view the background of the canvas is yellow, or almost pure yellow, and the figure on the canvas only appears to be yellow but is not really yellow. The figure is really red and green. So, (a) is false. Since (b) presupposes (a), (b) is either false or incorrect in some way. Similar remarks are to hold for all shade- and color-identity statements.

The consequences of this position are interesting. To begin with, purple is not a color because there is no such thing as purple spectral light. Purple things are really red and blue. Of course white and black are not spectral colors either. If a white surface is one that reflects all light and a black surface is one that absorbs all light, then a white surface is really a combination of all colors and a black surface is colorless. More importantly for us, if shade-identity statements are false, then normal observers cannot tell in the large majority of cases that an object is yellow by simply looking at the object under normal viewing conditions; e.g., one cannot tell that the figure is not yellow but its background is yellow. Only in the relatively few cases where an object appears to be an example of the brightest, most saturated form of yellow can normal observers be reasonably certain that the object is indeed yellow.

Could normal observers tell what the color of an object is if they could see the object under different conditions, such as through a microscope? It might turn out that through a really powerful microscope the figure on the canvas, or the paint in pot *A*, would appear to be made up of little particles that looked red and green. It is also possible that the paint in pot *A* might be a compound whose total electron structure reflects light from the red and green parts of the spectrum in such a way that there are no particle parts of the compound, such as atoms, some of which reflect red light and some of which reflect green light.[7] So it seems that there are red and green things whose surfaces are not made up of spatially distinct red and green parts; i.e., they are red and green all over at the same time! The point is that in many cases there is no way that the color of an object can be determined by looking at it under normal lighting conditions, even if one is using a microscope.

This account has not completely abandoned the human eye. If a normal observer placed an object under light from a narrow band of the spectrum it would either appear to be black, because it did not reflect light from this part of the spectrum, or it would appear to be the color of the light shining on it, because it did reflect light from this part of the spectrum. By working through the spectrum, one narrow band at a time, a normal observer could determine the color of an object.

This account of color seems to be consistent, and is one that I believe is really used in some scientific work. But it is not an account of yellowness that captures our ordinary concept of yellow, because we could not use this concept of yellow and still quickly and easily identify yellow objects as yellow. Surely there is a sense of the term 'yellow' such that we quickly and easily identify the canvas mentioned above as a yellow canvas. Indeed the canvas is to be distinguished from other canvases that are two or more shades of yellow. We know what canvases that are two or more shades of yellow look like, and this is not one of them. For this reason I think that (a), and other shade-identity statements, are true.

Hilary Putman, who has supported a view about natural-kind terms that is much like Kripke's, has explained that there is a linguistic division of labor, such that some members of our society are the experts upon whom we call when we need to be sure about whether or not a particular object belongs to a particular natural kind.[8] For example, chemists use special equipment to determine whether an object is made of gold. But the yellowness of the canvas should not be thought of in this way. Although we need experts sometimes, we also need simple and easy methods of identification that do not require experts or special equipment. The concept of yellowness that I am concerned with in this paper forms part of the everyday methods we use in the identification of objects.

We have reached the following conclusions. Given the assumption that many different sorts of animals are like humans, in that they see objects by seeing color distinctions, color-different statements must be true. Given the assumption that shades of red, yellow, white, etc. are commonly recognized by normal observers under normal conditions in the everyday identification of things, shade-identity statements are true. To avoid inconsistency it must be that color-identity statements are false. In the next section it will be argued that the a-all account of part II does not satisfy the condition that many different sorts of animals who have eyes unlike ours see colors, for a broad enough range of animals.

IV Problems with the A-All Account of Part II

Consider the following perceptual object. A figure and its background each reflect light of the same wavelength (from the yellow part of the spectrum, say) and of the same intensity under normal lighting conditions. The light reflected from the background is diffuse. For each incident ray of light some of the light reflected from the figure is polarized in a plane perpendicular to the plane containing the incident ray and a line perpendicular to the plane of the figure. (Reflected light from beams that strike the figure perpendicularly are unpolarized.) Are the figure and its background the same color?

Given the a-all account developed in part II, the figure and its background are the same color, because humans are insensitive to the difference between polarized and unpolarized light. (Here I ignore the effect of polarized light on the human eye known as Haidinger's brush, because it is so slight.) However, the same sort of considerations that were raised against Smart's position in part II can now be raised against the a-all account of part II. Imagine normal observers who hold a filter in front of their eyes which screens out light that vibrates in some plane perpendicular to their line of sight. If light strikes the figure and its background at an oblique angle, then there will be some position from which the figure appears darker in color to the observers than its background. If the figure and its background are not distinct colors, then these observers see a color-distinction illusion. To deal with this the a-all account will have to introduce color types, much as Smart has to have types of yellowness. As on Smart's account, the description of color becomes very cumbersome in many perceptual situations, because partial polarization is a very widespread phenomenon. And, as on Smart's account, the physical property common to all objects that are one distinct color is a disjunctive physical property.

Consider another example. Imagine a being who is much like us, but who has only two types of retinal cells. Both types of cells will react to light of any wavelength. Covering each of the many type-one cells is a tiny filter that transmits only light waves or components of light waves that are in the plane determined by the two eyes and the direction in which the eyes are looking. A tiny filter in front of each of the many type-two cells transmits only light waves or components of light waves that are perpendicular to those that reach type-one cells. Stimulation of type-one cells give this imaginary being a sensation that is like our sensation of red, and stimulation of type-two cells produces a sensation that is like our sensation of green. Stimulation of type-one and -two cells simultaneously produces a yellow-like sensation. Under some normal lighting conditions there are perspectives from which the figure described above looks red and its background looks yellow to the imaginary being. Again it seems that normal observers are color-blind with respect to such an observer. (It is interesting to note that bees, and several other insects, can detect the vibration direction of linearly polarized light, and that the human perception of polarized light, i.e., Haidinger's brush and light seen through special filters, is seen as a color distinction.[9]).

If the criticisms given in part II worked against Smart's a-nor account, then the above arguments work against the a-all account of part II. To deal with this situation, another anthropocentric account of color could be introduced that made the viewing conditions more general than the a-all account allows: two objects have the same color if and only if they would appear to be the same color to normal human beings under all viewing conditions. Here the viewing conditions can include the use of any kind of filter, as well as any kind of light source. Should they include viewing equipment more exotic than filters?

Suppose there are two large cans of white paint that are physically identical. A drop of red paint is stirred into one of these cans. These two cans will appear to be the same in color to normal human observers under any kind of light when viewed through any kind of filter. So, given this last notion of same color, they will be the same color. But this result seems unsatisfactory. Since it has been argued that many different sorts of reactions to light count as color differences, it seems that the two cans of paint should be considered to be slightly different in color because they react to light in appropriately different ways. If there was a being that could see the difference between these two cans of paint as a color difference, then that being would be seeing a color distinction, not a color-distinction illusion. Thus, if we are going to have an anthropocentric account of color, the viewing conditions will be so broad that they will include special viewing equipment sensitive to minute differences between light waves. But now there seems to be no point to making colors conceptually dependent on the distinctions that humans can draw, because color seems to have little to do with human sensitivity. In other words an anthropocentric account must make the viewing conditions very broad, but these very broad conditions make the concept of same color depend upon a general notion of visibility rather than upon a more specific notion of what is visible to humans. (On Smart's a-nor account of color the two cans of paint are the same color, and the problems he will have in dealing with this consequence of his theory are not unlike those developed in part II.)

At this point one is inclined to hold that two objects are the same color if and only if they react to light in the same way. But this will not do. A perfect vacuum transmits all the light that strikes it without doing anything to the light. A perfect mirror reflects all the light that hits it without doing anything to it, other than changing its direction. Since no animal could see a perfect vacuum or a perfect mirror, these two objects are colorless. Yet they do react differently to light; so, by the above conception of same color, they are different in color. Hence this conception of same color is false. The problem with this conception of same color is that it has no notion of visibility. But this problem can be remedied.

V Another Nonanthropocentric Account of Color

If there is some real or imaginary animal that could see object O under light source L, then the reaction that O would have to L will be called a *visible light reaction of O* or a *vlr* of O. Assume the following: two (nonradiant) objects have the same color if and only if the two objects have the same visible light reactions to every light source.[10] (Again it is assumed when using this definition that the objects are oriented the same way toward the light sources.)

The colors that objects have are the equivalence classes implied by this conception of same color. To bring this idea out, note again that an object may react in one way to light of one sort and another way to light of another sort. For example, the figure on the canvas discussed in part I reacts differently to normal light than it does to light from only the yellow part of the spectrum. Each such vlr of an object is specified by describing the reaction of the object (which makes it visible) to a specific type of light. An object has as many vlrs as there are types of light under which it is visible. The task of giving a description of what goes on when an object reacts to light is left to the scientists. The color of an object is identical with its set of vlrs. Or: the color of an object is the set of dispositional reactions that it has to light of all kinds that make it visible. [For an object to be visible under a light source it is necessary, but not sufficient, that it have a vlr to the light source. If an object is visible to some animal, the object must also be different in color from the background against which it is seen. For this to happen the vlr of the object must be different from the vlr(s) of its background. Here I assume that animals see objects by seeing color distinctions. (Smart does not assume this, since he must hold that animals can see objects by seeing color-distinction illusions.)]

Scientific investigations of the way things react to light make it possible to explain and deepen this conception of color. Scientists begin with the commonsense assumption that an object reacts to light by reflecting, or absorbing, or transmitting the light shining on it. They have discovered that the reflected or transmitted light can be diffused (or scattered) in varying degrees or polarized in different ways (plane polarization being by far the most common). The reactions of an object that make it visible are absorbing some of the light that strikes it, or diffusing the light it reflects or transmits, or polarizing the light it reflects or transmits. Thus an object that did not absorb any light and that reflected or transmitted all the light shining on it without diffusing or polarizing it would not have a color. Intuitively, such transmissions and reflections do not mark the light with which they come in contact. In other words, some objects do not change the light that strikes them so that the light carries the information that it has been in contact with these objects.

Consider some examples. Clean air does scatter some of the light that strikes it (making the sky blue and also polarizing some sunlight in the process), but small volumes of air are close to colorless. A clear transparent piece of glass nondiffusely reflects and transmits light, but if the light striking the glass is not perpendicular to its surface it polarizes some of the light it reflects and transmits. Mirrors that we use around the house reflect nondiffuse light, but they also polarize some of this light. Since our eyes are not sensitive to the difference between polarized and unpolarized light or between light polarized in different ways, panes of glass and ordinary mirrors seem colorless to us; i.e., we can see objects through a pane of glass or in a mirror, but we do not see either the surface of the glass or the surface of the mirror. Most opaque objects are visible to us and to other animals because they reflect some light diffusely and absorb the rest. Black objects absorb all the light falling on them, and some white objects diffusely reflect almost all the light that strikes them. A red piece of glass absorbs all the light that strikes it which is not from the red part of the spectrum and may either diffuse the light it transmits (making it translucent) or not diffuse it (making it transparent).[11]

The rest of this paper is concerned with the assumptions that will have to be added to the vlr assumption given above to deal with the relationship between color and human observation. I begin with the often-made point that 'look' and 'appear' have an implication in some contexts which they do not have in others. Sentences of the form '*O* appears *A* to *S*' imply in some contexts that it is *S*'s best judgment, based on all that *S* believes and on his present perceptual experiences, that *O* is *A*. Call this sense of appears *appears*(j). At other times sentences of the form '*O* appears *A* to *S*' do not carry this implication. Most objects appear, but do not appear(j), to change color when the illumination we see them under changes. For example, our clothes do not appear(j) to change color as we step from direct sunlight into shadows or into the illumination of fluorescent lamps. Undoubtedly our clothes sometimes appear to change color, when we are aware of or paying attention to the fact that the light reactions of our clothes change as lighting conditions change. But the color we attribute to our clothes, i.e., the color we normally *see* our clothes as having under changing lighting conditions, remains constant. Given the vlr assumption, it is the dispositional property of our clothes to react to light of all kinds that remains constant under different lighting conditions.

There is a fundamental thesis that follows from the vlr assumption and some commonsense points, which connects the vlr conception of same color to the perception of color: two objects have the same color if and only if, for every light source, the two objects would appear to have the same color to all beings who could see the objects under this light source (assuming that there is no disturbing factor that affects the way the color perceivers perceive one of the objects but not the other,[12] and assuming that the objects are oriented in the same way toward the light sources.[13]) To establish this thesis, suppose, to begin with, that two objects are different in color. In this case the two objects would react differently to some light source (given the vlr assumption), and so under it they would reflect or transmit light differently. Hence, a light-sensitive organ with the appropriate receptor cells could be sensitive to this difference. Thus, the two objects would appear to be different in color to a perceiver with the appropriate sort of eyes. To prove the other side of the equivalence, suppose that two objects appear to be different in color to some perceiver under a given light source. In this case the eyes of the color perceiver are reacting differently to the reflected or transmitted light of the two objects. This could happen only if in fact the reflected or transmitted light of the two objects was different, which would make the two objects different in color. (Notice that this equivalence is established from the vlr conception of color and the commonsense point that objects react to light by reflecting it or transmitting it or absorbing it. So no scientific discoveries are needed to link the vlr conception of color to the appearance of objects.)

One consequence of the above thesis is this: if two objects appear to be different in color to us or to any other color perceiver, instruments included, under some light source (provided that the objects are oriented toward the light source in the same way), then the objects are different in color. The converse of this conditional is not true, as the yellow canvas mentioned earlier illustrates. This point can be developed further into a definition of 'shade', but first I need to say something about hues.

I assume that yellow is an anthropocentric causal concept: an object is yellow if and only if under normal lighting conditions the object's visible light reactions cause it to appear yellow to normal human perceivers who have the best possible view of it. (Sometimes a color spot will appear to be one color when viewed from a distance but appear to be made up of multicolored particles when viewed up close. One view of a color spot will be said to be *better* than another view if and only if more color distinctions can be made out from the former than from the latter view. For most people the best views of a color spot are between one and two feet from the spot.) Yellow is not a color. It is the set of all those colors which contain in their vlr sets vlrs to normal lighting conditions that cause objects to appear yellow to normal human beings. What has been said here about yellow holds for red, dark blue, black, white, etc. These sets will be called *color-sets*; so, although yellow is not a color, it is a color-set. There will be more on yellowness when we finish with shades.

Two objects are the same shade of yellow if and only if they are yellow and they appear to be the same color to normal human beings under normal viewing conditions. Clearly, *A* and *B* can be the same shade of yellow, *B* and *C* can be the same shade of yellow, and yet *A* and *C* not be the same shade of yellow. (This complication was ignored in part II because Smart ignores it.) To obtain well-defined sets, let '*O*' be the name of any object and let *O-set* be the name of the set of colors that include the color of *O* and the color of any object that normal humans cannot distinguish from *O* under normal lighting conditions. Shades are *O*-sets. *O*-sets are defined in terms of some object *O* (or group of objects, *O*s, that are assumed to have the same color). For example, 'sky blue' and 'lemon yellow' are the names of *O*-sets. Given these definitions, dark blue is better thought of as a color-set than as a shade. [Note that '*x* is the same length as *y*', like '*x* is the same color as *y*', refers to a transitive relation. But '*x* appears to be the same length as *y*', like '*x* is the same shade as *y*', refers to an intransitive relation (i.e., *A* and *B*, like *B* and *C*, may appear to be the same length to normal observers under some set of conditions, although *A* and *C* do not appear to be the same length under these conditions). A phrase like '3.26 ± .02 meters' functions something like a shade term in that it is often used to refer to a set of lengths that appear to be the same under some set of conditions. In general '*x* appears to be the same as *y* to so-and-so with respect to _____ under such-and-such conditions' does not pick out a transitive relation; so no wonder that '*x* is the same shade as *y*' is intransitive.]

The above conception of yellow needs to be applied with care when the phenomena of color constancy and color contrast are involved. If an observer is looking at snow under a clear blue sky, it may appear to be a bluish white to him even though it appears(j) white to him. The problem is that the observer may think that the snow appears white to him because he believes that he is discounting a perceptual judgment that he is not in fact discounting. We can determine that the observer is not discounting his perceptual judgments by arranging for him to see the snow and describe its color-set, when he does not know that it is snow he is perceiving. There is another problem with brightness-contrast and color-contrast phenomena. A small green patch on a large yellow surface appears blue. This does not mean that the patch really is blue, because in this case it is not the vlr of the patch alone that is causing the patch to appear blue but the combined vlrs of the patch and its background. These problems do not arise frequently, but when they do arise they can be solved by having normal observers, who are ignorant of what they are looking at, observe the object through a reduction screen, i.e., a screen with a hole in it that lets the observer see only a small part of the object's surface (small enough so that the observer can neither identify the object nor see its background).

A great deal of scientific work has been done on how the apparent color-set of an object is affected by lighting conditions. This work can be combined with the causal concept of color-sets given above to obtain a deeper analysis of color-set terms. To see how this can be done, note that two dependent variables, called *dominant wavelength* and *purity*, can be defined in terms of the physical features of a beam of light (i.e., the intensity of each wavelength in the beam). A third variable, called *brightness*, is determined by the physical features of a beam of light, although it is not defined in terms of those features.[14] Two beams of light may have entirely different physical features, even though their dominant wavelength, purity, and brightness are the same. This is the case with the light reflected from the paint in pots *A* and *B* discussed in part I. The important point is that dominant wavelength, brightness, and purity characterize (or are one way of characterizing) the features of light which affect the color-set to which an object appears to belong. Applying these discoveries to the causal concept of yellow given above, one gets the following: an object is yellow if, and only if, if the object is under normal lighting conditions and the reflected or transmitted light from the object reaches any normal observer unchanged in its journey to the observer's eye, then the dominant wavelength, purity, and brightness of the smallest beams of light that the eye can resolve into distinct points (when the observer is in the best possible position to see the object's color) cause the object to appear yellow.

Let us apply this analysis of yellowness to specific examples that we can compare with our intuitions. Suppose a surface that appears to be yellow (to normal observers under normal lighting conditions) is made up of tiny dots that cannot be distinguished without a magnifying glass. Seen through a magnifying glass these dots appear to be red and green. Even so, it would be very natural to say that this surface really is yellow, as it should be if the above theory is right. [But see note 5.] Are the dots really red and green? Given the vlr account, objects that are too small to be perceived with the naked eye could belong to a color-set only in a derivative sense. Suppose that this example is changed so that the dots can be perceived with the unaided eye if one is close enough to the surface, but the surface still appears yellow from a distance. Examples like this include parts of Seurat paintings, and a football field that looks yellow from an airplane but is divided up into a checker board of large red and green blocks. Given this vlr account, both the painting and the football field are really red and green although they appear to be yellow under some conditions.

One half of a circular disk is red and the other half is green. When the disk spins slowly it appears to be red and green, but as it speeds up it appears to be yellow. In this case the dominant wavelength of the light reaching the eye is changing faster than the reaction time of the eye. More exactly, the light reaching the eye from any fixed point above the disk during the reaction time of the eye is from both the red and green parts of the disk. In this sense the light reflected from, say, a red part of the disk does not reach the eye unchanged, but is mixed with light from other parts of the disk. Since it is not the vlr of such a red part of the disk alone that causes that part to appear yellow, its apparent yellowness is an illusion.

If the preceding analysis is right, the distinctions we make between color-sets and between shades go only as deep as the unaided human eye can go. This is unlike the distinctions we draw between colors, which go as deep as many of the distinctions between lightwaves. Although the distinctions between color-sets are not so deep as the distinctions between colors, they are for that very reason easier to apply and more suitable in the everyday identification of objects.[15]

Acknowledgments

I would like to thank Robert Audi, John Heil, and Evan Jobe, all of whom made helpful criticisms of earlier drafts of this paper. Special thanks are also due to the National Endowment for the Humanities for a fellowship which helped make this essay possible.

Notes

1. "Naming and Necessity," in Donald Davidson and Gilbert Harman, eds., *Semantics of Natural Language* (Boston: D. Reidel, 1972).

2. Chung-ying Cheng, ed., *Philosophical Aspects of the Mind-Body Problem* (Honolulu: UP of Hawaii, 1975). [chapter 1, this volume]

3. New York: Humanities, 1963.

4. Frank Jackson has argued that Smart's account of red cannot account for red afterimages, because afterimages do not have the appropriate physical structure to reflect any light, let alone light that causes humans to have the sensation of red. [See his *Perception: A Representative Theory* (New York: Cambridge, 1977), pp. 127/8.] Jackson is missing the point just made in the text. Smart's account of red takes the concept of an experience of red to be essentially different from the concept of a red physical object. Clearly, red afterimages are certain sorts of experiences and so do not, on Smart's account of red, need to reflect light in order to be red.

5. D. M. Armstrong may hold that shade-identity statements are false. He points out that under a microscope blood appears to be mostly colorless. Only a small area of the blood seen through a microscope appears to be red. He says ["Colour-Realism and the Argument from Microscopes" in Richard Brown and C. D. Rollins, eds., *Contemporary Philosophy in Australia* (New York: Humanities, 1969), p. 127]:

> A drop of freshly drawn blood looks red all over to normal perceivers in standard conditions, and is a very suitable object to teach a child 'what red is'. We can admit these facts, and still say it makes sense to deny the drop is really red all over.

Armstrong denies that the blood drop is red all over because it does not appear to be red all over through a microscope. And this shows, he claims, that the light actually reflected from the blood is not characteristic of red surfaces (124/5). Suppose that a drop of blood and a surface that really was red were indistinguishable to the unaided eye. Armstrong might claim that these two surfaces were not the same shade of red, since one of them was not red. But maybe Armstrong would not say this, because if the drop of blood is a suitable object to teach a child what red is, it may be red in some sense.

6. Yves Le Grand, *Light, Colour and Vision*, R. W. G. Hunt, J. W. T. Walsh, and F. R. W. Hunt, trans., 2d English ed. (London: Chapman & Hall, 1968), pp. 147 and 155.

7. For more on the physics of the color of objects, see Kurt Nassau, "The Causes of Color," *Scientific American*, CCXLIII, 4 (October 1980): 124–154. [chapter 1, *Readings on Color, vol. 2*]

8. "The Meaning of 'Meaning' " in *Mind, Language and Reality* (New York: Cambridge, 1979), pp. 227–229.

9. William A. Shurcliff and Stanley S. Ballard, *Polarized Light* (Princeton, N. J.: Van Nostrand, 1964), pp. 95–98.

10. For radiant objects we have the following principle: two radiant objects are the same color if and only if, for every nonradiant object, the vlr that the nonradiant object would have to each of these radiant objects would be the same.

11. Scientific discoveries have simplified the description of the color of some objects. For example, there is a law that makes a substantial part of the description of the color of an object particularly easy. When the intensity of the light of a given wavelength striking a surface is varied, the intensity of the reflected light of that wavelength is always a constant fraction of the intensity of the incident light. Hence, the description of how an object reflects light of a particular wavelength but varying in intensity involves just one fraction, for with this fraction one can deduce how the object will react to each of the infinite variations in the intensity of that wavelength. A complete description of how an object reflects light of all wavelengths is given by its reflection curve: the reflection curve of a surface is a graph that plots for each wavelength of light the fraction of the intensity of the incident light that the surface will reflect. Similarly, an object will have a transmission curve. Of course the reflection and transmission curves of an object form a large part of the description of that object's color. (Smart calls the reflection curve the "intensity-wavelength curve" in one of the above quotes from his work.)

12. For the sort of disturbing factors involved and how to deal with them, see Le Grand, *op. cit.*, pp. 134/5.

13. The notion of being "oriented in the same way to a light source" can now be spelled out. The vlr conception of same color and scientific discoveries about the reaction of objects to light imply the following: two objects have the same color (or no color) if and only if, for every light source, if the objects were to be oriented in the same way toward the light source then the objects would reflect, absorb, or transmit the same wavelengths of light with the same intensity for each wavelength and they would diffuse and

polarize the same amount of the light they reflected or transmitted, wavelength by wavelength. In practice, identically shaped slabs of a handy size which are made from different substances are tested for their reaction to light, wavelength by wavelength. Although these slabs are easily oriented in the same way toward a light source, the geometric notion of same orientation does not mean just that the surfaces to be tested be at the same angle and distance from the light source. The surfaces may also have to be lined up in the same way relative to each other, in order to deal with polarization. (If two slabs polarize sunlight that strikes them in the same way when they are at the same oblique angle to the sun *and* when they are appropriately rotated about an axis perpendicular to their surface, then to be oriented in the same way toward any light source they must always have this same relative position to each other. Without this or something like this condition, two identically made filters could be turned so that they polarized the light shining on them into different planes and hence were different in color. Also a slab that polarized light would change its color when rotated.) By making the important assumption that objects made of the same substance react in the same way to light, the color of any object whose chemistry is known can be found by knowing the color and chemistry of the slabs. Thus, given this important assumption, the problem of explaining in a general way what 'oriented in the same way toward a light source' means can be avoided. All of which is just as well, because there may be no general way of defining this phrase so that, for any light source, a highly curved surface and a flat surface can be oriented in the same way toward this light source.

14. For details see Le Grand, *op. cit.*.

15. A related structural account of color goes like this: the color of an object is that part of its structure which causes it to react to light in a way that makes the object visible. Thus, two objects have the same color if and only if they have exactly similar vlr structures. Two objects that are different in color according to the vlr account in the text are different in color according to this structural account, because different effects must have different causes. Two objects that are different in color according to the structural account might be the same in color according to the vlr account, because different causes can have the same effect. But this seems implausible; i.e., it seems implausible that two objects could be different in color although no conceivable animal or instrument could tell they were different in color by looking at them under any lighting condition. The reader may want to compare this argument with the last argument in part IV.

3 Smart and the Secondary Qualities

D. M. Armstrong

Jack Smart is a world figure in contemporary philosophy, in particular for the part he has played in developing scientific realism. But in Australia it is natural to turn to what he has done for philosophy in this country. There was a sort of pre-established harmony between the man and what he found when he came here.

His completely open and direct way of doing philosophy, springing from his completely open and direct personality, made an instantaneous appeal to students and colleagues. The appeal was all the stronger because it joined hands with Australian values. His philistinism—early in our acquaintance he told me that there was little need to bother about Shakespeare especially if you could look out of your study window at Mt Lofty instead—and his indifference to the history of his subject— why bother about those chaps who are dead?—did him no harm! His writing was straightforward and colloquial, although it did have a great deal of style thus covertly contradicting his declared indifference to aesthetic matters.

To this he has joined disinterested generosity of intellectual spirit, a readiness to praise the good as he saw it as soon as he saw it, and a habit of answering philosophical and other correspondence by return of post. The philosophers of Australia owe him a lot.

One of the topics about which he and I have exchanged letters and papers over many years is that of the secondary qualities. It is to this topic that I now turn. In the first part of this chapter I discuss the development of Smart's views on the secondary qualities, relating this to larger themes in his thought: the development of his scientific realism, his physicalism and his view of the mind. The account of the secondary qualities which he now rests in he had arrived at by 1968, although the paper which contained this account was not published until 1975.[1]

I think that this view is the true one, or close to the truth. So in the second part of this chapter I defend it against objections, in particular against the nagging feeling that it must be rejected because it does not do phenomenological justice to our perception of the secondary qualities.

The Development of Smart's View

If one had to sum up Smart's philosophical development in a phrase, one could say that he went from science to scientific realism. He was early inclined to believe that it is pre-eminently scientific investigation that gives us knowledge and rational belief about the nature of the world. But given the Oxford of his graduate studies, and his admiration for the work of Gilbert Ryle, this did not immediately translate into a realistic view of the entities that science speaks of, or appears to speak of.

I begin with the development of Smart's view of the mind. We each believe that it is rational to postulate other minds besides our own. The scientific realist will naturally see this as an inference to unobserved processes and states which are causes of much of the observable behaviour of bodies besides our own. It is a case of inference to the best explanation. The inference is perhaps suggested, and in any case is further supported, by the fact that we are able to observe such processes and states in our own case (introspection), and are even able, apparently, to observe the causal efficacy of some of these processes and states in producing our own outward behaviour.

At Oxford, Smart held no such view. Instead, he leaned to a reductive account which, putting it roughly, identified the mind with behaviour. No doubt, at the time this seemed to him to be the right line for a scientifically minded philosopher to take. For the philosophical orthodoxy of the time took it as obvious that if there were minds which lay behind, and which caused, behaviour, then these minds were immaterial things. At the same time, it seemed that no respectable science of the immaterial could be developed. It might appear that in our own case we have direct awareness of the distinction between our behaviour and our mental states. But this introspective faculty was thought to be a suspicious affair. Orthodoxy, stretching back to Descartes, held that its deliverances were indubitable or incorrigible. It was not easy to see how these characteristics of introspection were to be reconciled with a scientific view of human beings.

But after Oxford Smart made a most important break. In Adelaide, under the influence of U. T. Place, for the case of sensations and the phenomenon of consciousness he reversed what Russell in phenomenalist mood had called the supreme maxim of scientific philosophizing. Unlike Russell, he moved *from* logical constructions *to* inferred entities. But Place and he sought to preserve scientific plausibility by identifying the having of sensations and other conscious experiences with physical processes in the brain.

The Place-Smart view was a half-way house, of course, even if one which Place has continued to find satisfactory. Smart was later to move on to a fully scientific realist, and physicalist, view of the mental, where all mental processes, events and states are identified with physical processes, events and states in, or of, the brain.

A similar development appears to have taken place in Smart's view of the theoretical entities of physics. In his Oxford days he did not take a fully realistic attitude to such entities as molecules. I suppose that the old historical link between empiricism, on the one hand, and positivism and instrumentalism, on the other, was an influence here. That link was certainly present in Ryle's realism about the physical world—a realism about the entities of common sense, but not a realism about the entities that physicists, for the most part, think of as constituting the entities of common sense.

Here is Smart, in an article published in 1951, apparently poised between denying and asserting the literal reality of molecules:

unless we recognize the difference of language level between the various uses of 'particle' it might be misleading to say that a gas consists of particles. On the other hand it would not do to retain the use of the word 'particle' for things like billiard balls and refuse to say that a gas consists of particles. How else can we bring out the analogy on which the explanatory power of the theory consists?[2]

This soon changed. Concluding his article 'The reality of theoretical entities', published in 1956, he wrote:

The modern tendency in philosophy is to be opposed to phenomenalism about tables and chairs but to be phenomenalist about electrons and protons.[3]

However, just before saying this, he had made it clear that he had now repudiated this half-phenomenalism:

The naive physicist thinks that his science forces us to see the world differently and more truly. I have tried to defend him in this view.[4]

To adopt the physicist's view leads to certain difficulties, of course. For instance, one will be led to say that ordinary physical objects, as opposed to the collapsed, and hugely dense, state of matter found in neutron stars, are mostly empty space. But is not a desk, say, a paradigm of something in which, to use Parmenides's phrase about his One, what is stands close to what is?

This argument from paradigm cases is not very difficult to surmount, as most philosophers would now judge. It is perhaps sufficient to note that something which consistently appears in perception to have a certain character will serve as a perfectly good paradigm of that character for ordinary thought and language (and for teaching a child), even if it in fact lacks that character.

But a much more serious problem is posed by the secondary qualities. In the manifest image of the world, to adopt Wilfrid Sellars's expression, colour, heat and cold, sound, taste and smell, play a conspicuous part. Yet as far back as Galileo (with intellectual precedents stretching back to the Greek atomists) physicists could find no place for these qualities as intrinsic properties of physical things. The trouble is that these properties do not *explain* anything physical. Does the high-pitched sound shatter the glass? To superficial observation it might appear to do so. But investigation reveals that it is vibrations in the air which really break the glass. The secondary qualities do not even help to explain how they themselves are perceived. Contrary to earlier speculations, it is not the sensible species of colours, but rather patterns of light waves, that cause us to see the colours of the surfaces of objects.

What is the scientific realist to do? A traditional solution is to use the mind as an ontological dustbin, or sink, for the secondary qualities. Locke gave us a classical formulation. For him, the surface of a ripe Jonathan apple can properly be said to be red. But what constitutes its redness is only this. The surface has nothing but the primary qualities. In virtue of certain of these properties, however, properties of the micro-structure of the surface, it has the power to produce in the minds of normal perceivers in standard conditions (this last fills out Locke a little) ideas, or sense-impressions or sense-data, mental objects which have a certain simple quality, a quality unfamiliar to persons blind from birth. (Some philosophers, although not Locke himself, might then go on to *identify*, at least token by token, the redness of the surface with the primary qualities of the surface responsible for it having that power.)

This solution does have a phenomenological disadvantage, neatly captured by Berkeley in a little remarked passage: 'Besides, if you will trust your senses, is it not plain all sensible qualities co-exist, or to them appear as being in the same place? Do they ever represent a motion, or a figure, as being divested of all other visible and tangible qualities?'[5] By the 'sensible qualities' Berkeley means, of course, the phenomenological qualities. He is surely right that, for example, the sensible quality of redness looks to be an intrinsic (non-relational) property of certain surfaces. Phenomenally, the secondary and the primary qualities cannot be separated. The difficulty can of course be met by embracing a Representative theory of perception of *all* the sensible qualities, primary as well as secondary. But a Representative theory has its own disadvantages.

Here, however, I want to focus upon a much more serious difficulty, much more serious at any rate for one who, like Smart, has accepted a physicalist account of the mind. If we have not merely accepted a scientific realism about the physical world, as Locke did, but have also made the mind part of that world, then there is no hiding place down in the mind for the sensible secondary qualities. The same reasons that made one want to exclude them from the physical world will make one want to exclude them from the mind. So what is the *physicalist* to do with the secondary qualities?

It will help us to appreciate the physicalist's problem if we consider further the phenomenology of these qualities, that is, their characteristics as revealed, or apparently revealed, to observation.[6] In the first place, as we have already noted, they appear to be intrinsic, that is, non-relational, properties of the physical things, surfaces, etc. to which they are attributed. This seems clear enough for the cases of colour and heat and cold. Perhaps it is not so clear for sound, taste and smell. After all, we do have the view of Hume and others that qualities of these three sorts are not spatial. It seems to me on the contrary, as a matter of phenomenology, that sounds have sources and can fill areas, that smells hang around places, and that tastes are intrinsic properties of tasty objects. However, if Hume's view is phenomenologically correct (I do not know how we decide the issue) that will make the existence of the secondary qualities even harder to reconcile with physicalism. (The physicalist will have to say that sounds, tastes and smells *are* spatial but that their spatiality is not revealed to perception.)

Second, the secondary qualities appear as lacking in 'grain', to use Wilfrid Sellars's excellent term. Perhaps Locke was wrong in claiming that they appear to be simple. But they do have a uniformity, a lack of extensive structure, even if they have an intensive structure.

Third, despite the point just made, the different secondary qualities are not merely blankly different from each other. Each determinate quality is set in a logical space, a quality-space it has been called, which psychologists and others are trying (with difficulty) to map for us. Consider, in the case of the colours, the dimensions of hue, saturation and intensity and the resemblance-orderings which these dimensions are associated with.

Fourth, however closely primary and secondary qualities may be correlated, the two sorts of quality appear to be wholly distinct from each other.

So much for the way it seems. Why, now, do these secondary qualities *so conceived* constitute an embarrassment for the scientifically minded philosopher? We have already encountered one reason. The qualities seem to play no part in physical explanations of phenomena. In G. F. Stout's fine phrase, they are not part of 'the executive order of the material world'.[7] And if one takes a physicalist view of the mental, then no relief will be gained by transferring the location of the qualities to the mind.

However, the difficulty that Smart himself emphasized, although not unconnected with the point just made, was a bit different. It was this. If one treats the secondary qualities as qualities *additional* to the primary qualities, and as having the general nature that they appear to have, then one will require *laws* to connect them with the primary qualities. But these laws will have to have a very strange structure.

The laws will be emergent laws. When exceedingly complex assemblages of physical conditions occur (outside or inside the brain will make no difference), then in association with these conditions, relatively simple qualities emerge. Smart says that, as a scientifically minded person, he cannot believe in such laws. He used Herbert

Feigl's phrase: the qualities so conceived are 'nomological danglers', excrescences on the organized and beautiful structure of physical law that is beginning to appear. He also said that such laws had a bad smell!

So what solution to the problem does Smart offer? It is very interesting to notice that once again his first reaction was to look for an operationalist/behaviourist answer. The answer is adumbrated in 'Sensations and brain processes' (1959), expanded in 'Colours' (1961) and repeated in his major work *Philosophy and Scientific Realism* (1963).[8]

Smart's solution has a Lockean element to it, as he points out. Secondary qualities are identified with powers in the objects to which the qualities are attributed, powers which one might then identify with categorial characteristics of the objects. But these powers are powers to cause normal perceivers ('normal' is given a special definition which need not concern us) to be endowed with further powers: *discriminatory* powers. Thus to say something is red is to say, very roughly, that it would not easily be discriminated from, picked out from, a background of ripe tomatoes, but would easily be discriminated from, picked out from, a background of lettuce leaves.

Smart was immediately hit with two objections, objections of a sort very familiar to us today from contemporary discussions of Functionalism. The first was raised by Michael Bradley, and would now be called the 'absent qualia' objection. Is it not possible, asks Bradley, that we should see the world in a uniform shade of grey, and yet be able to make all the discriminations that normally sighted persons make on the basis of the perceived colours of things.[9] The second objection was raised by C. B. Martin, that of the 'inverted spectrum'. Could not the colours of things be systematically inverted (an objectivist form of the inverted spectrum), and yet our ability to discriminate between tomatoes and lettuce leaves remain exactly as before?[10]

Smart originally tried to meet these difficulties by admitting colour-*experiences* into his analyses. To say that something is red *both* says that the thing has the power to furnish a normal perceiver with appropriate discriminatory powers *and* (less important) that it has the power to furnish such a perceiver with the right visual experiences.

But this did not last long at Bradley's hands. Once again, the trouble is caused by Smart's physicalism about the mind. What are these experiences? For Smart they can only be brain processes, as indeed he emphasizes. Furthermore, he maintains, the only introspective notion that we have of these experiences is a topic-neutral one, a notion definable only by reference to the nature of the stimulus that brings the experiences to be. (The idea of a topic-neutral analysis of our mental concepts was, of course, one of Smart's major contributions to developing a central-state physicalism about the mind.) As a result, for something to look red to me (the right sort of experience) is for me to have something characteristically brought about by red things. Red things, however, in Smart's theory, are constituted red by the discriminations they cause, so for him experiences of red must be defined in terms of these discriminations, and cannot vary independently of the right discriminations. As a result, Smart's appeal to experiences adds nothing that will allow him to make sense of Bradley's (and Martin's) case.[11]

In a paper given to a conference at Hawaii in 1968, but not published until 1975, Smart accepts Bradley's criticism.[12] (This paper has not become widely known. I have discovered that many philosophers think that Smart is still committed to the quasi-Lockean quasi-behaviourist view that he held at the time he wrote 'Sensations and brain processes'.) As a result, he finally comes to a realistic account of the secondary qualities. They are objective qualities of objective things. What of the demands of physics, then? He meets these by accepting a suggestion that had been put to him by David Lewis: he identifies a colour, and by implication the other secondary qualities, with a *physical* property of the coloured object. It is a fact that this property is causally responsible for certain discriminatory responses of normal human percipients. It is also a fact that certain colours are associated with certain sorts of physical objects, in particular with their surfaces. When all this is filled out, it will provide identifying descriptions for the colours. Using Kripke's terminology (not that that would please Smart very much) we can say that the descriptions can, if we wish, be used as rigid designators. But the descriptions do not pertain to the essence of the colours.[13]

The only difference in all this from a naive view of colour is that the colour-properties are identified with primary qualities of the micro-structure of the surfaces of the coloured objects. Though realist, the view is reductionist. Smart shows how this account can deal with Bradley's and Martin's cases.

He goes on to explain why he originally rejected Lewis's suggestion. The reason had to do with the particular case of colour, and not the secondary qualities generally. According to Smart, the scientific evidence about the physical correlates of colour is such that a particular shade of colour would have to be a highly *disjunctive* and very *idiosyncratic* property. This, he thought, was a reason to reject the identification. Lewis simply responded by asking him what was wrong with a disjunctive and idiosyncratic property. And by the time Smart came to give his Hawaii paper, he had accepted Lewis's 'So what?'.

Defence of an Objectivist Physicalism About the Secondary Qualities

I proceed to defend a physicalist realism about colour and the secondary qualities. The first point I want to make is that there is no difficulty at all in the fact, if it is a fact, that a particular secondary quality is very *idiosyncratic*. In this respect, a certain shade of colour might be like a certain complex, idiosyncratically complex, shape. Such a shape might well be a repeatable, and so a clear case of a property, even though its idiosyncratic nature made it an unimportant property in physical theory. (It might still be important in biological theory. Consider the way that the young of many species of birds automatically cower when a hawk-like shape appears in the sky above.) The physicalist could well admit that, unlike, say, sensible degrees of heat, the colour-properties are not very important physical properties. Perhaps the point of colour-recognition is just to break up the perceptual environment to make it more manageable, or, as Ruth Millikan has suggested, to render more easy the re-identification of individual objects.[14]

That colour-qualities might have to be adjudged ineluctably disjunctive is perhaps a bit more worrying.[15] Certainly, it worried me for a long time. Suppose it turns out that surfaces which we judge by objective tests to be of the very same shade of colour cannot be brought under a genuinely unifying *physical* formula. At one stage, this led me to flirt with the idea that, if the so-called colour-properties really are irreducibly disjunctive in this way, then the proper moral for a physicalist to draw is that, despite their phenomenological prominence, colours do not really *exist*. In Berkeley's splendid phrase, which he of course used pejoratively, they are 'a false, imaginary, glare'.[16]

My problem was compounded in the following way. In the past, I had asserted that all genuine properties are universals. Now there are excellent reasons in the theory of universals to deny that there are *disjunctive* universals. One problem about disjunctive universals is that there would be no identity, no sameness, in the different instances. Let a instantiate universal P but not universal Q. Let b instantiate Q but not P. Both instantiate P *or* Q. But this would appear to yield what Peter Geach calls a 'mere Cambridge' sameness. For this and other reasons I was led to reject disjunctive properties.

But I would now reject the first premiss of this argument. While continuing to reject disjunctive *universals*, I think that we should be prepared to accept disjunctive *properties*. I am influenced by two points here. First, it seems clear that what are *ordinarily* called properties can for the most part only be explicated in terms of more or less tightly knit *ranges* of universals, ranges which must be understood disjunctively. (Wittgenstein on games is relevant here.) Second, I am fortified by the reflection that such properties—which Peter Forrest suggests should be called multiversals—are logically supervenient upon the instantiation of genuine universals, that is, properties and relations which are genuinely identical in their different instances. Given all the non-disjunctive properties of things, then their disjunctive properties are determined. The reflection is fortifying because, I think, what is supervenient is ontologically nothing over and above what it supervenes upon. If that is correct, then we can take disjunctive properties on board without making any addition to our ontology. They are a free lunch.

But what then of the phenomenological point? Suppose that we have two instances of what, despite close examination, appear to be surfaces of exactly the same shade of colour. Could we, if the science of the matter demanded it, accept that the two surfaces instantiate two quite different micro-structural characteristics, where the latter characteristics *constitute* the colour of the surfaces?

I think that we can, as the following simplified neurophysiological thought-experiment is meant to show. Let there be an *or* neuron which is fed by two or more incoming channels. Each channel is activated by a different sort of retinal stimulation, and ultimately by a different sort of distal stimulation: a different sort of surface. Let the neuron be situated at an early stage in the neural processing leading up to the perception of coloured surfaces. Since the neuron is an *or* neuron it will fire, and so pass on its message, even where only *one* incoming channel is activated. Furthermore, that message will be identical whichever channel is activated. Different causes, same effect. So for the higher-ups in the brain it will not be possible to sort out which incoming channel has fired. Hence different sorts of stimuli must be *represented* as the same at the higher level, even though they are not in fact the same.

This result will be enhanced by what I call the 'Headless Woman' effect. Here the failure to perceive something (say the head of a woman, where the head has been obscured by a black cloth against a black background) is translated into the illusory perception of seeming to perceive the absence of that thing. It seems to be illustrated by the case of introspective awareness. When we introspect, we are certainly not aware that what we introspect are brain processes. This, by an operator shift, gives rise to the impression that what we introspect are not brain processes. This impression is inevitable *even if what we introspect are actually brain processes*, as we physicalists hold.

In the present case, a failure to perceive the presence of disjunctivity in a certain property would translate into an impression of the absence of disjunctivity, that is, an impression of identity. I regret to say that Smart suggested this application of the Headless Woman principle in the 1975 paper but, as he records there, in correspondence with him I rejected this particular application. I cannot now see any good reason for my rejection. I think it was just hostility to disjunctive properties.

There is one other problem about taking colours or other secondary qualities to be disjunctive properties. The problem has been put to me by David Lewis, now a little worried about his own suggestion for dealing with Smart's problem. When we perceive the sensible qualities of physical things the quality must presumably play a causal role in bringing the perception to be. But now consider a disjunctive property. It cannot be thought that the disjunctive property itself plays any causal role. Only the disjuncts do that. So if sensible qualities are disjunctive, how can they be perceived?

It seems to me that this problem can be met by a legitimate relaxation of the causal condition for perception. Provided that each disjunct, operating by itself, would have produced exactly the same sensory effect, is it not reasonable to say that the perceiver is perceiving the disjunctive property? Consider, after all, that although the actual qualities that things have are determinate, yet they are not perceived as having some determinate quality. Even if a non-disjunctive account of colour is correct, it remains true that surfaces are perceived as having a certain shade of red but are not perceived as having an absolutely precise shade of red. As a result there will be a disjunctivity in the nature of what is actually registered perceptually. At the same time, it is the precise shades which act causally. And whatever account is given of this situation can presumably be applied to disjunctions of a more 'jumpy' sort.

Returning to the Headless Woman, she seems valuable in explaining two further phenomenological facts: (1) that the secondary qualities appear, if not simple, at least as lacking in grain; (2) that the secondary qualities appear to be quite distinct from the primary qualities.

The particular primary qualities with which Smart, Lewis and myself propose to identify the secondary qualities will fairly clearly be *structural* properties at the microscopic level. But the secondary qualities appear to lack structure ('grain'). How can the structured appear structureless?

What perhaps we need is an *and* neuron. If a cell has a number of incoming channels, each susceptible to different sorts of stimuli, but *each* channel has to fire before the cell emits a *single* impulse, then one could see how a complex structure might register perceptually as something lacking in structure. (It will be a bit more complicated if an irreducible *disjunction* of structures has to register both as a non-structural and non-disjunctive property, but no difficulties of principle seem involved.) Then the Headless Woman effect will explain why the lack of perception of structure gives rise to an impression of lack of structure.

But what of the point that the secondary qualities appear to be other than the primary qualities? The vital point to grasp here, I think, is that, with an exception or two to be noticed, our *concepts* of the individual secondary qualities are quite empty. Consider the colour red. The concept of red does not yield any necessary connection between redness and the surface of ripe Jonathan apples or any other sort of object. It does not yield any necessary connection between redness and any sort of discriminatory behaviour, or capacity for discriminatory behaviour, in us or in other creatures. It does not yield any necessary connection between redness and the way that the presence of redness is detected (eyes, etc.) in us or in other creatures. Finally, and most importantly, it does not yield any necessary connection between red objects and any sort of perceptual experience, such as looking red to normal perceivers in normal viewing conditions.

There may be a conceptual connection between redness and extendedness. But a physicalist, in particular, will think that this gives us little line on its form. There is certainly a conceptual connection between redness and the other colours: the complex resemblances and differences that the colours have to each other. But these conceptual connections do not enable us to break out of the circle of the colours.

With these exceptions, all we have are various identifying descriptions of redness. They identify it all right, but the identification is not conceptually certified. In my opinion, this conceptual blankness is all to the good if we seek to make intelligible a physicalist identification. For it means that there is no conceptual *bar*, at least, to such an identification. There is topic-neutrality. *Neither* the identity of redness with some primary quality structure *nor* its non-identity with such a property is given us. So if we can find a physical property which qualifies red things (what a good theory will tell us are red things) and bestows the same powers as the powers of red things, including their powers to act on us, then it will be a good bet that this property *is* redness. And I hope it is not overworking the Headless Woman to say that failure to perceive identity with primary qualities gives rise to the impression that that identity definitely does not obtain.

But still one may not be satisfied. Many will think that when we perceive a red surface under normal conditions, perceiving that it is red, we are directly acquainted with a quality, apparently an intrinsic, that is, non-relational, property of the surface, which is visibly different from any physical micro-structure of the surface, or physical micro-goings on at the surface. (And, it may be added, visibly different from any physical goings on in the brain.) I confess that I myself am still not fully satisfied with the physicalist reduction. I accept the reduction; I advocate it. But the phenomenology of the affair continues to worry me.

Here is something that may help to explain further this profound impression of concretely given intrinsic quality. Consider again the relations of resemblance that we perceive to hold between the members of the particular ranges of the secondary qualities. We are not merely aware of the difference in colour of different colour-shades, but also of their resemblances and the degrees of their resemblance. The different hues of red, for instance, do fall naturally together. Any red is more like purple in hue than it is like any blue. As we have already said, the colours exist in a colour-space exhibiting degrees of resemblance along different dimensions. The same holds for the other secondary qualities.

These resemblance relations are, like any resemblance relations, *internal* relations. They hold in every possible world. But if some physicalist account of colour is correct, then despite the rather clear way in which we grasp the resemblances we lack any concrete grasp of the nature of the qualities on which the resemblances depend.

Now I do not think that this creates any epistemological difficulty. It is commonplace for this sort of thing to happen in perception and elsewhere. Smart pointed this out when discussing that famous having of a yellowish-orange after-image which is *like* what goes on in me when an actual orange acts upon my sense-organs. He spoke there of 'The possibility of being able to report that one thing is like another, without being able to state the respect in which it is like'. He went on to say:

> If we think cybernetically about the nervous system we can envisage it as being able to respond to certain likenesses of its internal processes without being able to do more. It would be easier to build a machine which would tell us, say on a punched tape, whether or not the objects were similar, than it would be to build a machine which would report wherein the similarities consisted.[17]

No epistemological problem, then. But I suggest that it is the fact that we grasp these resemblances among the secondary qualities so clearly and comprehensively that generates, or helps to generate, the illusion that we have grasped in a concrete way the natures of the resembling things. In an unselfconscious way, we are all perfectly aware that resemblances are completely determined by the natures of the resembling things. So given resemblances, we automatically infer natures. We know further that in perception what is automatically inferred is regularly felt as directly given, as contrasted with being inferred. (Consider for example the way we pass from hearing words to the semantic intentions of speakers.) So in perception of the secondary qualities, we have a vivid impression of intrinsic nature.

Smart, Lewis and myself share a reductive (physicalistic) and realistic view of the secondary qualities. In the first section of this chapter I traced the path by which Smart reached this conclusion. In the second section I have tried to strengthen the defence of this position.

Notes

1. J. J. C. Smart, 'On some criticisms of a physicalist theory of colors', in Chung-ying Cheng (ed.), *Philosophical Aspects of the Mind-Body Problem*, Honolulu, University Press of Hawaii, 1975, pp. 54–63. [chapter 1, this volume]

2. J. J. C. Smart, 'Theory construction', *Philosophy and Phenomenological Research* 11 (1951), reprinted in A. G. N. Flew (ed.), *Logic and Language*, Second Series, Oxford, Basil Blackwell, p. 235.

3. J. J. C. Smart, 'The reality of theoretical entities', *Australasian Journal of Philosophy* 34 (1951), p. 12.

4. Ibid., p. 12.

5. G. Berkeley, 'First dialogue', in D. M. Armstrong, ed., *Berkeley's Philosophical Writings*, New York, Collier-Macmillan, 1965, pp. 157–8.

6. When considering the phenomenology of colours in particular, it is useful to draw a distinction between *standing* and *transient* colours. This is intended as a distinction in the coloured object, and is not perceiver-relative. The distinction may be illustrated by considering two senses of 'spherical' as applied to squash balls. There is a sense is which squash balls, to be any use for squash, must be and remain spherical. They may be said to be spherical in the standing sense. In the transient sense, however, squash balls are frequently not spherical, for instance when in more or less violent contact with a racquet or wall. To be spherical in the standing sense can be analysed in terms of being transiently spherical. If a ball is transiently spherical when the forces acting upon the ball are those found in 'normal', that is, unstruck conditions, then it is standing spherical.

Now consider a coloured surface such as a piece of cloth with fast dye which is subjected to different sorts of illumination. We often say that it presents a different *appearance* under the different illuminations. This seems misleading. In a standing sense the colour does not change. But *in a transient sense* it really does change colour. The mix of light-waves that leaves the surface is different. A standing colour is thus a disposition to have that transient colour in normal lighting conditions. (See my paper 'Colour realism and the argument from microscopes' in R. B. Brown and C. D. Rollins, eds, *Contemporary Philosophy in Australia*, London, Allen and Unwin, 1969. The terminology of 'standing' and 'transient' was suggested by Keith Campbell.)

We may think of transient colour as the painter's sense of (objective) colour. And if we are considering the phenomenology of colour, it is transient colour upon which we should concentrate.

7. G. F. Stout, 'Primary and secondary qualities', *Proceedings of the Aristotelian Society* 4 (1904), p. 153.

8. J. J. C. Smart, 'Sensations and brain processes', *Philosophical Review* 68 (1959), pp. 141–56; 'Colours', *Philosophy* 36 (1961), pp. 128–42; *Philosophy and Scientific Realism*, London, Routledge and Kegan Paul, 1963.

9. M. Bradley, 'Sensations, brain-processes and colours', *Australasian Journal of Philosophy* 41 (1963), p. 392.

10. J. J. C. Smart, *Philosophy and Scientific Realism*, London, Routledge and Kegan Paul, 1963, p. 81 (acknowledging Martin).

11. M. Bradley, Critical notice of *Philosophy and Scientific Realism*, *Australasian Journal of Philosophy* 42 (1964).

12. J. J. C. Smart, 'On some criticisms of a physicalist theory of colors.'

13. Or so I interpret Smart. In a very interesting recent paper ('Color and the anthropocentric problem', *Journal of Philosophy* 82 (1985) [chapter 2, this volume], Edward Wilson Averill appears to interpret Smart differently. He quotes from Smart's 1975 paper ('On some criticisms of a physicalist theory of colors'): 'Colours are the (perhaps highly disjunctive and idiosyncratic) properties of the surfaces of objects that explain the discrimination with respect to colour of normal human percipients, and also the experiences of these percipients, the looking red, or looking blue, etc. of objects'. Averill then seems to take 'explains' here as involving a logical tie. If that is correct, there is still a Lockean or subjectivist element in Smart's account. I, however, take Smart to be cutting all logical links between colours and what happens in the perceivers of colours. (It may be that I do this because I think that a complete objectivity, a complete realism, about the secondary qualities is the true view!)

But there is much of interest in Averill's paper. He points out that Smart assumes that two objects are the (very) same colour if and only if they would appear to be exactly similar in colour to normal human observers under normal viewing conditions. (He fails to note Smart's special definition of a 'normal' observer.) There is no doubt that this is Smart's assumption, even although, I take it, he does not assume that this is conceptual or definitional. But Averill's arguments seem to show that if the assumption is not taken to be a conceptual or definitional truth, then there is no reason to take it to be true *at all*. The moral for the complete anti-Lockean, the complete realist, about colour is that the link between objective colours and the colour-appearances presented to normal perceivers has to be very indirect indeed.

Averill, however, thinks that this is bad news for the full-blooded realist about colours. He thinks that Smart's normality assumption—which is, of course, the assumption generally made—is true, cannot be contingent, and must therefore be conceptual. However, he does concede that the full-blooded realist position might be maintained if the assumption is dropped. (A proposal I had already tentatively made in my 'Colour realism and the argument from microscopes'.) He even points to one advantage that dropping the normality assumption would have. It would become possible to evade saying that the objective colours are disjunctive properties. That would be a considerable gain. It may be noted that Averill's holding to the normality assumption is not without costs. He finds himself forced to say that e.g. yellowness is not (strictly) a colour.

14. Ruth Garrett Millikan, *Language, Thought and Other Biological Categories*, Cambridge, Mass., Bradford Books, MIT Press, 1984, p. 316.

15. Averill's work, cited in note 13, may show that the qualities involved are not after all ineluctably disjunctive. That will be all to the good. But it seems well worth a physicalist contemplating, and trying to deal with, a 'worst case' from the physicalist point of view.

16. G. Berkeley, 'Second dialogue', in Armstrong, ed. *Berkeley's Philosophical Writings*, p. 74.

17. J. J. C. Smart, 'Sensations and brain processes', *Philosophical Review* 68 (1959).

4 Reply to Armstrong

J. J. C. Smart

I must thank David for his very kind remarks about me. I do not deny the philistinism, about which I have just now said something. David may have given the impression that philistinism goes down well in Australia, and perhaps it does, though my first impression of Australia was very different. Never in Britain had I seen so many boys and girls walking about carrying violin cases as I did in the vicinity of the Adelaide University conservatorium! The question of whether Shakespeare or Mt Lofty (which at the time to which David refers had not been disfigured by its three television masts) does or ought to give the greater aesthetic pleasure raises an interesting quasi-philosophical problem. Shakespeare had the wonderful ability always to choose the right word, with a rarely equalled insight into human character. Contemplating him we feel great awe. Consider, however, the extraordinary interlocking complexities of the structure and biochemical processes of even one cell of one leaf of one gum tree on Mt Lofty. Consider again an outstanding sculpture of a human head. When I contemplate such a sculpture I am naturally impressed, but the impression is mixed up with the reflection that the sculpture has nothing between its ears, whereas my wife's beautiful head (for example) contains 10^{10} neurons (each neuron being of amazing complexity), not to mention blood vessels, glands and other extraordinary organs. It seems to me, therefore, that nature always far outstrips art. I leave it to aestheticians to tell me where I am wrong.

In his paper Armstrong begins by tracing the development of my own thinking about the secondary qualities: criticisms on the part of M. C. Bradley and C. B. Martin and a suggestion by David Lewis have helped me to move from the behaviourist account in my paper 'Colours' (1961)[1] to a position very close to the one to which Armstrong had already moved.[2] According to this later view of mine, colours are physical properties of the surfaces of objects. (I leave out qualifications about rainbows and the like.) My worry was that these properties must be highly disjunctive and idiosyncratic ones. Lewis said 'Disjunctive and idiosyncratic, so what?' Though disjunctive and idiosyncratic (that is, of interest to humans but not, say, to Alpha Centaurians) they could still be perfectly physical properties. To adapt an analogy used by Robert Boyle,[3] the shape of a lock might be of interest only because of a certain shaped key, but the shape of the lock is something perfectly physical— indeed geometrical—which can be described without reference to the key.

By and large I agree with Armstrong's positive theory of the secondary qualities, though I am not sure how far I can accept his theory of universals, and so I shall not comment on this. I do, however, want to comment on Armstrong's long note

(note 13), in which he remarks on E. W. Averill's important paper 'Color and the anthropocentric problem'.[4]

In this note Armstrong quotes a passage, also quoted by Averill, in which I say: 'Colours are the (perhaps highly disjunctive and idiosyncratic) properties of the surfaces of objects that explain the discrimination with respect to colour of normal human percipients, and also the experiences of these percipients.'[5] There is an important syntactical ambiguity here which may have misled Averill in his interpretation of me. (Armstrong has it right.) The words 'and also' are not meant to be governed by 'colours are' but by 'that explain'. However, I do not think that Averill's main arguments are affected by this matter.

In my article 'Colours' I introduce the notion of a normal human percipient, which is that of someone who can make at least as many discriminations as any other. Thus if Jones makes the best discriminations at the red end of the spectrum and McTavish the best at the blue end, the notion of a normal human percipient might be realized by Jones and McTavish acting in concert, or perhaps 'normal human percipient' might express an idealized notion, as does 'the mean sun' in astronomical chronology. I also assume that the discriminations are made in sunlight. I think this accords well with the ordinary use of colour words. However, there are pressures in another direction, to which Averill responds by relaxing the condition that canonical discriminations be made in sunlight, and also by relaxing the notion of a normal percipient by allowing super-discriminating humans who might be produced by genetic engineering, or who might even possess the power of responding to polarized light as bees do. Well, if all sorts of bug-eyed monsters are allowed, we do get away from anthropocentricity. Which is the right analysis of our concept of colours? I began on the slippery slope by allowing that a normal human percipient might be an idealization, or perhaps a syndicate. I am inclined to think that we capture ordinary usage best by sticking to illumination in daylight and not allowing, as Averill does, various special conditions of illumination which might allow discriminations to be made that cannot accord with what I take as ordinary usage. But whether it is he or I that is right about the ordinary use of colour words, or which of two contrary pressures to respond to, he does of course end up with a perfectly acceptable physicalist account of colour. I like it because of its rejection of anthropocentricity. With my account of colours the anthropocentricity exists but is as harmless as the key-centeredness of the shape of a lock. (Harmless, that is, so long as it is recognized for what it is. We must not get confused and project this anthropocentricity on to the perceived world.) Thus ontologically I see no need to disagree with Averill. I might say that when he talks of how coloured surfaces appear to percipients, I would rather talk about how these percipients discriminate (with respect to colour) various shapes on surfaces. I think that Averill could consistently be interpreted in this way. I should also like to remind the reader that, for me, 'discriminate with respect to colour' is a simpler notion than that of 'colour', just as in set theory 'equinumerous' is a simpler (or more fundamental) notion than that of number.

Notes

1. J. J. C. Smart, 'Colours', *Philosophy*, 36 (1961), 128–42.

2. On p. 6 Armstrong follows my use (in 'Sensations and brain processes', *Philosophical Review* 68 (1959), 141–56) of Feigl's expression 'nomological danglers' to refer to dangling entities, not, as Feigl did, to the dangling laws themselves. Subsequently I followed Feigl's usage.

3. Robert Boyle, *Origin of Forms and Qualities*, 1666.

4. E. W. Averill, 'Color and the anthropocentric problem', *Journal of Philosophy* 72 (1985), 281–304. [chapter 2, this volume]

5. Ibid.

5 Colour Concepts and Colour Experience

Christopher Peacocke

What is the relation between the concept of an object's being red on the one hand and experiences as of red objects on the other? That is the recalcitrant question to which this paper is addressed.[1]

The question contains the term of art "concept". This term will be used here correlatively at the level of properties as the phrase "mode of presentation" is used at the level of objects by Frege. Thus if the thought that an object presented in a given way is ϕ has potentially a different cognitive significance from the thought that it is ψ, then ϕ and ψ are different concepts. Our recalcitrant question concerns the realm of thought, informativeness and cognitive significance, rather than the realm of reference.

Why has the question, and similarly its analogue for any other secondary quality, proved so recalcitrant? The reason is that there exists an apparently straightforward dilemma about the relation between being red and experiences as of red things, i.e., experiences in which something looks red. There are arguments for saying that each must be more fundamental than the other. Someone does not have the concept of being red unless he knows what it is like to have a visual experience as of a red object; and the occurrence of such an experience is just an experience in which something looks red. The connection here is specifically with visual experience. Consider these two biconditionals:

A perceptible object is red iff it looks red in standard circumstances

and

A perceptible object is square iff it looks square in standard circumstances.

Both seem to be true, but they are not of the same status. For

A perceptible object is square iff it feels square in standard circumstances

is as acceptable as the visual version in the case of squareness; whereas "feels red" makes no sense. Again, the congenitally blind can understand "is square". For these familiar reasons, visual experience seems to occupy a special position in an explanation of what it is for something to be red that no particular sense modality occupies in an explanation of what it is for something to be square. The point is not just that squareness is accessible to more than one sense: rather, what it is for something to have the property of being square cannot be explained in sensory terms at all. (Other differences are consequential on this.) These points are precisely what we should expect if looking red is conceptually more fundamental than being red. Yet on the other hand the expression "looks red" is not semantically unstructured. Its sense is determined by that of its constituents. If one does not understand those constituents, one does not fully understand the compound; and conversely, with a general understanding of the "looks" construction and of some predicate ϕ for which "looks ϕ" makes sense, one can understand the compound without the need for additional information. Equally on the side of thought rather than language, being red is precisely how an experience as of something red presents that thing as being: the remark is platitudinous. So from this angle it appears that looking red could not be more fundamental than being red. How is this dilemma to be resolved?[2]

If colour is a coherent notion at all, it seems there are three possible types of response to this problem. These types are defined by the relations that they take to hold between the concept of being red on the one hand and concepts of experience on the other:

(i) The concept of being red is philosophically prior to that of looking red and to other experiential concepts. This is true not just in the uncontroversial sense that the phrase "looks red" contains "red" as a semantic constituent.[3] On this first type of view it is true also in the more substantial sense that an account of what makes an experience an experience as of something red must ultimately make use of the concept applicable to physical objects of being red where this concept is not to be explained in terms of properties of experiences. This we will label "the anti-experientialist option".

(ii) Neither being red nor any relevant family of concepts true of experiences ("experiential concepts") is prior to the other: both have to be characterized simultaneously by means of their relations to one another and to other notions. This is the no-priority view.

(iii) The concept of being red has to be explained in terms of experiential concepts: this can be done in a way not undermined by the fact that "looks red" semantically contains "red" and without any circular use of the concept of being red. This might be called "the pure experientialist view"—"pure" because the no-priority view is a partially experiential view. But for brevity we will call a view of this third type simply "the experientialist view".

These three positions exhaust the possibilities only for a given notion of priority. I have written, very loosely, of the relation "more fundamental than", "conceptually prior to", and "philosophically prior to". To be more precise, my topic here is a priority of definability. We can say that concept A is definitionally prior to concept B iff B can be defined illuminatingly in a given respect in terms of A: the fixed relation of priority with which we are concerned is definitional priority, and the respect in which we want to be illuminated is what it is to have the concept of being red. There are other notions of priority in the offing: I will return to one of them later.

I take first the anti-experientialist view. One form such a view might take has been developed by Shoemaker: he holds, by implication, that the fact that an experience is as of something red consists in the fact that it would, in the absence of countervailing beliefs, give rise to the belief that the presented object *is* red.[4] Alternatively, such an anti-experientialist might try to characterize such experiences as those playing a certain role in an experientially-based ability to discriminate red from non-red things. In either case, the property of being red is employed in the account of what it is for an experience to be as of something red.

What, then, can the anti-experientialist say about the property of being red? His view collapses into the third option, that taken by the experientialist, if he attempts to explain redness in turn by appeal to the properties of experiences. One cannot assess the anti-experientialist's view, and neither can he establish the special connection with visual experience, until he gives some positive account of colour properties of objects.

One response that is not immediately circular is to say that the predicate "red" in fact picks out either a dispositional property of objects to reflect light of a certain sort, or picks out the categorical ground of this disposition. This is Armstrong's view, later adopted by Smart.[5] Such a view may have a relatively sophisticated structure. It may be said that after being introduced to certain sample objects as being within the extension of "red" one goes on to act in accordance with the definition that "red" picks out that state S of these objects which causes human observers to be in some experiential state which tends to give rise to the belief that some object has S, or tends to give rise to an ability to discriminate things with the property S. Such methods of introducing "red" are not formally illegitimate and avoid circularity, provided that the states quantified over can be characterized in terms other than "states which produce experiences of such-and-such kind". For instance, in verifying that some physical state T conforms to this more sophisticated definition, one has to check that T is possessed by the initial sample objects and that it produces in humans the belief that some object has T, or produces an ability to discriminate objects with the property T. The objections at this point are not those of circularity.

Told only that a word refers only to a certain object, we are not in a position to know what way of thinking of the object that word is used to express. Similarly, we can draw a distinction between physical properties themselves and ways of thinking of them; and the move we are envisaging the anti-experientialist as making gives an account of which physical property the word "red" picks out, but gives no account of a way of thinking of that property the word expresses. We just said cautiously on behalf of the anti-experientialist that "red" picks out that state S of some initial sample of objects which causes human beings to be in some experiential state which tends to give rise to the belief that some object has S, or tends to give rise to the ability to discriminate things with the property S. But someone would equally be "acting in accordance with" such a specification if he employed some instrument which is sensitive to the reflectance properties of surfaces, and which gives this information in auditory form through a small loudspeaker. He may come to use this device unreflectively, and have beliefs about the properties of surfaces, beliefs which are caused by the auditory experience produced by the instrument, and which are not based on inference. Yet this person, if blind, need not have the concept of being red; and he does not fully understand "red" if he knows only that the word picks out the property he knows to be instantiated when he uses the instrument. This way of developing the anti-experientialist view lacks any component which would explain why possession of the concept and full understanding of the word is so closely tied to visual experience.

Since the anti-experientialist has an account only of the property "red" picks out but does not have any account of the way an understander is required to think of that property, the only propositional attitude and more generally psychological contexts containing "red" that he can explain are those in which it occurs transparently: contexts that say that someone believes of the property that such-and-such object has it, or of the property that it falls under so-and-so higher order condition. This leads to a difficulty in carrying out the anti-experientialist's programme of explaining the property of looking red in terms of being red, even when we confine our attention to visual experience.

Suppose that initially surfaces with a given physical reflectance property R look red, and those with a given physical reflectance property G look green. Then at a certain time, perhaps because of some effect on people's brains, things with R look green, and things with G look red. This is a case of universal intrasubjective change; it is detectable, and, we suppose, actually detected. The most difficult problem for our anti-experientialist is not whether in these circumstances things with R are no longer red—a question on which intuitions vary—but what account of "looks red" he can give which squares with the possibility of the case: for as the case is described, it is not in dispute that objects which have R no longer *look* red after the change (whether or not they really are red). How can the anti-experientialist secure this consequence?

The anti-experientialist may reply that immediately after the change experiences of a kind that before the change were produced by objects with R still tend to produce after the change the belief of the property R that the presented object has it. Such a belief, after the change, is false: but the anti-experientialist can argue that the case is analogous to those considered in discussions of proper names. If someone just like Quine kidnaps Quine early on in Quine's life and starts to act Quine's role, we will falsely believe this man to be Quine; in acquiring beliefs about him we also acquire beliefs that Quine is thus-and-so. The problem is rather that if the impostor continues long enough, the beliefs expressed in utterances of "Quine is thus-and-so" come to concern the impostor, so similarly in the anti-experientialist's account of the colour example: after a time it is correct to say that experiences in which something looks red tend to produce the belief that the presented object has physical property G, the one which before the change produced experiences as of green objects. In whatever sense Armstrong, for instance, would say that before the change experiences as of something red tend to produce beliefs (in a transparent sense) about physical property R, a long time after that change in that same sense such experiences will tend to produce beliefs about the different physical property G. For exactly the same relations hold between experiences in which things look red and the physical property G at a much later time as held before the change between such experiences and physical property R. This remains true if the change in the effects of R and G went unnoticed. (The same general point can also be made if the account of looking red in terms of red speaks of abilities to discriminate objects with property R.) But then the anti-experientialist account delivers the wrong answer on the question of the qualitative similarity of two experiences, one e before the change and another e' a sufficiently long time afterwards. e and e' may both be as of something red, but e tends to produce the belief of the presented object that it has physical property R (by Armstrongian standards), while e' tends to produce the belief that it has physical property G. It does not help to try to appeal to what would be the case if experience of the kind of e and e' occurred simultaneously to someone: for the *kinds* here will have to include determinate specifications of the experienced colour, and that is what we were asking the anti-experientialist to explain, and not just take for granted.

At this point the anti-experientialist may be tempted to argue that he can admit the possibility of intrasubjective inversion of the colour experiences produced by a given type of physical surface in fixed lighting conditions. He may argue that this possibility is allowed for in the fact that different central brain states may be produced by looking at such a physical surface at different times. But of course brain states may alter while experience remains the same: a change of brain state produced by the surface is not sufficient for a change in colour experience. To make this account work, our anti-experientialist needs to distinguish just those changes in brain state which produce or are correlated with change in the colour the object looks: and he cannot legitimately do so in explaining "looks red". The problem here is one of meaning or significance. We have a conception of colour experience on which such a change of brain state is not constitutively sufficient for change in colour experience (which is not to say that it may not in some circumstances be good evidence for it). A general principle is applicable here. Suppose one can conceive of evidence which counts in favour of a hypothesis: that does not suffice to show the hypothesis to be significant if it is also true that our conception of what it is for that hypothesis to be true allows that either the evidence could obtain and the hypothesis be false, or *vice versa*. The rationale for this principle is obvious: if either the hypothesis or the evidence can obtain independently of the other obtaining, then to cite possible evidence does not exhaust the content of the hypothesis. We could call this general principle the Principle of Significance. It is not itself intrinsically a verificationist principle: rather, it functions as a constraint, a condition of adequacy, on any substantive general theories of meaning together with views about the content of particular sentences.[6] The Principle gets a grip here because the anti-experientialist was citing as possible evidence for intrasubjective inversion altered brain states, which are not, as we ordinarily conceive it, sufficient for such inversion.[7]

The anti-experientialist may complain that too much is being asked of him. "Why", he may ask, "cannot the concept of being red have the priority I claim for it whilst that concept is not further explicable? To someone who does not possess it, one can convey it only by suitable training (or brain surgery)." The problem with such a position is that it still does not account for the special features of the ability such training or brain surgery induces. No one has the concept of redness unless his exercises of that concept stand in quite special relations to his visual experience: it is hard to see how the anti-experientialist can explain why this is so without moving, by bringing in experience, from the first position to the second or third of the possibilities we described. The difficulty seems endemic to the anti-experientialist view.

The second option was a no-priority view. A no-priority view must offer more than the observation that 'Red things in standard circumstances look red' and 'Being red cannot be eliminated from an account of what it is for an experience to be as of something red' are both constitutively true. For corresponding claims are true of being square, and yet being square does not have the special relationship with visual experience that being red does. It is a virtue of the pure experientialist view, the third option, that it is not left as a mysterious, inexplicable necessary truth that one cannot experience objects as red in modalities other than the visual: the impossibility is rather a simple consequence of an account of what it is for an object to be red which mentions specifically a feature special to visual experience. A no-priority theorist must explain the special relationship with visual experience.

A different no-priority theorist, one aware of this requirement, might try to explain both "red" and "looks red" in terms of the type of experience that is present when a certain experientially-based ability is exercised: something looks red to someone when this ability would be exercised with a particular result, and it is really red when it would be exercised with that result in standard circumstances. Now what would the ability be? One cannot say it is the ability on the basis of visual experience to discriminate red from non-red things. The occurrence of "red" in his description of the ability would prevent the resulting claim from being described as a no-priority view. But we ought to consider a bold modification of this idea, one on which we try to characterize the ability extensionally. We say that someone has a *reactive recognitional ability* (RRA) for a class A of objects in a given period (with respect to given physical circumstances) if and only if when trained to act in a particular way when he has a visual experience caused by objects in some sample subset of A, he goes on to act in the same way on the basis of the visual experience caused in him in the given physical circumstances by the remaining members of A, all in that period. An RRA is something one has in relation to a class, and so long as there is a class of red objects, one can speak of the existence of an RRA for a given class, and in terms of it explain "looks red" and "red" without initially using "red" and "looks red". Presumably the idea would be that there is a class with respect to which we have an RRA, a class such that when an object causes us (after training) to give on the basis of the visual experience it causes in us a positive response to it, we say it looks red: and it is red if it meets a similar condition in some standard specified circumstances. So the idea of this particular no-priority theory would be that both "red" and "looks red" are explained by reference to an RRA, and in such a way that certain connections—as that a red object looks red in standard conditions, etc.—are preserved between them.

This is a tempting theory, but the problems seem insuperable. If the properties of being purple and being shiny were coextensive, the corresponding RRA's would be identical, since they are identified by classes. The account needs to be thickened to distinguish between looking purple and looking shiny. This could not be done by appealing to counterfactual circumstances in which the responses for "purple" and "shiny" would come apart. This is not because they would not come apart—they would—but because the antecedents of the counterfactuals specifying the circumstances in which they come apart would either contain colour predicates or mention of the physical grounds of looking a particular colour. If they contained colour predicates, the account would be circular, while the physical grounds of looking red may alter.[8]

There is also a second problem. The definition of a RRA requires the ability to learn to produce a new response to red objects when conditioned anew. But the ability to learn new responses seems distinct from the enjoyment of colour experience, and may be absent in a creature though it does enjoy such experiences. It would be too weak to require only that in some circumstances the creature gives the same experientially based response to precisely the things in a certain class; for in some circumstances the response may not be to the colour of the object.

This does not exhaust the plausible no-priority theories. In particular, there is a form of no-priority view which tries to take on board the considerations in favour of the third option, that of the experientialist, and then goes on to claim that these considerations can all be accommodated within the no-priority view. We will be able to formulate this properly only after developing that third option, taken by the experientialist.

The experientialist can say that when a normal human sees a red object in daylight, there is a certain property possessed by the region of his visual field in which that object is presented to him. This property we can label "red$'$": the canonical form is that region r of the visual field is red$'$ in token experience e. Being purely a property of the visual field, rather than a property the experience has in virtue of representing the world as being a certain way, red$'$ does not require the possession of any particular concepts by the subject in whose experiences it is instantiated. It is true, of course, that we have picked out the property red$'$ of experiences by using the ordinary notion of redness; but it does not follow that someone could not manifest a sensitivity to the red$'$-ness of his experiences without already possessing the concept of redness. The experientialist may now say this: in mastering the predicate "red" of objects, one comes to be disposed to apply it to an object when the region of one's visual field in which it is presented is red$'$ and circumstances are apparently normal (and when one has indirect evidence that it would meet this condition were it so presented). The experientialist will say that this explains the inclination we feel initially to explain "red" in terms of "looks red". He will say that what is correct is to explain red in terms of red$'$: since normally when something looks red, the region of the visual field in which it is presented is red$'$, he will say that the inclination is not surprising. Since for him the property red$'$ of experiences and a sensitivity of one's judgements to its presence are the fundamental notions, rather than that of looking red, this experientialist does not need to deny the obvious fact that "red" is a semantically significant constituent of "looks red".

The experientialist is not committed to the consequence that anyone who can exercise the concept of redness also has to have the sophisticated concept of experience. All this experientialist requires for the possession of the concept of redness is a certain pattern of sensitivity in the subject's judgements to the occurrence of red′ experiences: this sensitivity can exist in a subject who does not himself possess the concept of experience. This experientialist can then agree with the letter of Wittgenstein's claims in these passages:

315. Why doesn't one teach a child the language-game "It looks red to me" from the first? Because it is not yet able to understand the rather fine distinction between seeming and being?

316. The red visual impression is a new *concept*.

317. The language-game that we teach him then is "It looks to me ..., it looks to you ..." In the first language-game a person does not occur as perceiving subject.

318. You give the language-game a new joint. Which does not mean, however, that now it is always used.[9]

It is important to note that the experientialist is operating with three, and not two, notions: that of being red′, that of looking red, and that of being red. The second of these is not in any simple way definable in terms of the first. However plausible it may seem at first blush, it is not true that anything which looks ϕ must be presented in a region of the visual field which is ϕ'. If one looks through a sheet of red glass at an array which includes a sheet of white paper, the sheet will be represented in the experience itself as being really white: anyone who has such an experience will, taking his experience at face value, be disposed to judge that the sheet really *is* white, and "white" here refers to the property of physical objects. It should be emphasized that this is not a matter of conscious inference: the surface of the paper is *seen* as white.[10] In such a case, it would be wrong to insist that the region of the visual field in which the paper is presented is white′ and wrong to insist that it is red′. We have here a new kind of experience, and any extension of these primed properties from the cases where the conditions of viewing are more normal seems partly stipulative. Certainly to insist that in this case the region of the visual field is obviously white′ seems to rely tacitly on the representational content of the experience in determining the application of the primed predicates: and since this representational content contains the concept of being white, the experientialist cannot on pain of circularity use such applications of primed properties in explaining colour predicates. The experientialist should, rather, agree that something can look ϕ without being presented in a ϕ' region of the visual field, and explain how this can be so as follows. Insofar as he is prepared to offer a definition of "x is red", it would be along these lines: "x is disposed in normal circumstances to cause the region of the visual field in which it is presented to be red' in normal humans". Now this concept of being red may enter the representational content of a subject's experiences. That it may so enter is an instance of a general phenomenon of concepts entering the representational content of experience. In possessing for instance the concept of complacency, one has the concept of a person who is unconcerned about something when there are available to him good reasons for concern: this is a trait that manifests itself in the man's thoughts. But one can also *see* a face or a gesture as complacent, and one can hear an utterance as complacent. The experientialist should say that the property red' stands to being red as the components of an account of being complacent stand to being complacent; while the property of an experience of representing something as red stands to being red in certain respects as the property of representing a gesture as complacent stands to being complacent. One must, then, beware of pinning an overly simple account of the property of representing something as red on the experientialist. In normal circumstances (and—unlike complacency—constitutively so) a thing presented in a red' region of the visual field is indeed seen as being red; but this is not the only way something can be seen as red, and the experientialist can acknowledge the fact.

We noted earlier that not all views of the no-priority type had yet been discussed. What we considered earlier were no-priority views which claimed that being red and looking red have to be simultaneously explained. It now appears that a much stronger type of no-priority view would be one on which the concepts which have to be introduced simultaneously are not those of being red and looking red, but rather those of being red and of being red'. Red objects are ones that in normal viewing conditions are presented in red' regions of the visual field: and red' is that property of regions of the visual field instantiated in regions in which red objects are presented in normal circumstances. Such a no-priority view can take over much of what we have already attributed to the experientialist, including the threefold distinction between red, looking red and red'.

But can these relations between red and red' really sustain the claim that we have here a no-priority view? We said that the sense in which the definition of being red in terms of red' was relevant to possession of the concept of redness is not that anyone who possesses it must be able to supply that definition, but rather that it captures a sensitivity to red' experiences which must be present in judgements that a presented object is red. Is it equally true that if someone possesses the concept red', there must be some appropriate sensitivity of his judgements involving *it* to the presence of redness, as opposed to other properties? One way to see that this is implausible is to consider a community the members of which not only often see things in normal daylight, but also often see them under ultraviolet light (perhaps at night). They might use "red$_{UV}$" as a predicate true of objects which are presented in a red$'$ region of the visual field when seen under ultraviolet light. Now we can ask: is it true that anyone who possesses the concept red$'$ must have a special sensitivity of his judgements involving it to the presence of redness as opposed to red$_{UV}$-ness? This seems to have no plausibility: if someone learns that red$'$ is that property of the visual field instantiated by regions in which red$_{UV}$ objects are presented in ultraviolet light, he can fully understand "red$'$". Indeed anything that tells him what that experiential property is, whether or not it mentions redness, will suffice to give him understanding. This seems to undermine the status of the view under consideration as a no-priority view: though one can indeed give definitions of each of "red" and "red$'$" in terms of the other, a sensitivity to red$'$-ness is essential in grasping the concept of redness, whereas a sensitivity to redness is not essential to grasping the concept of red$'$-ness in the same way. The result seems to be a priority of red$'$-ness, an experientialist rather than a no-priority conclusion.[11]

An objector might agree that it is false that red rather than red$_{UV}$ has to be used to explain red$'$; but he may nevertheless say that what is definitionally prior to both red and red$_{UV}$ is a certain *character*, in a suitable generalization of Kaplan's notion.[12] Different utterances of "I" may refer to different persons, but there is a single uniform rule for determining which person is referred to at any given context of utterance. The objector's point may be that we should adapt Kaplan's notion by replacing "context of utterance" with "condition of perception taken as standard". We could then say this: words differing as "red" and "red$_{UV}$" differ may refer to different properties, but there is a single uniform rule for determining which property such a word refers to if any given condition of perception is taken as standard. Thus in a certain sense the characters of our "red" and their "red$_{UV}$" are one and the same, and it is this character which is prior to red$'$.

This view would indeed circumvent the objection. But the difficulty for it lies in stating what the common character of "red" and "red$_{UV}$" is. What is the common rule which, applied to different conditions of perception taken as standard, gives the different properties of being red and of being red$_{UV}$? The objector can hardly say that for given conditions of perception the rule picks out the property of looking *red* under those conditions: for that brings back all the old problems. But if the objector were to say that the rule should advert to the property of being presented in a red$'$ region of the visual field, he has not shown red to be definitionally prior to red$'$.

There are other types of priority than the definitional. We can say that a concept *A* is *cognitively prior* to *B* if no one could possess the concept *B* without possessing the concept *A*. In the simplest case, this will be because a property thought of by way of the concept B has to be thought of as the property bearing certain relations to concept A. One should not assume that definitional priority and cognitive priority must coincide. It may be that in some cases one concept is definitionally prior to a second, while that second concept is cognitively prior to the first. This may be the case where the first concept is red$'$ and the second is that of being red.

If concept A is definitionally prior to concept B because a thinker has to use that definition in thought when he employs the concept A, and if one concept can be cognitively prior to another only because the latter has to be defined in terms of the former, then it might be that definitional and cognitive priority have to coincide. But in the case of red$'$ and red, the first antecedent of this conditional is false. A definition of an object's being red as its disposition to present itself in a red$'$ region of the visual field under certain conditions is good not because it captures the way everyone must think of being red; rather, as we said, the judgements of one who has the concept of being red are responsive to experience and evidence in exactly the same ways as would be the judgements of one who explicitly used this definition. If one wishes to maintain that red$'$ is definitionally prior to red, but cognitively posterior to it, then the fact that one can have an experience in which a region of one's visual field is red$'$ without having the concept red$'$ is crucial in avoiding circularity in the account of mastery of the concept of being red.

The reasons which might be given for saying that red is cognitively prior to red$'$ are subjects for other work.[13] It might, for example, be held that a necessary condition of possessing a conception of other minds according to which others can have red$'$ experiences in exactly the same sense as one can oneself is that red$'$ experiences, one's own and others, are alike thought of as experiences which bear certain relations to the property of objects, perceivable by oneself and others, of *being* red. (Such a reason would, if correct, have an a priori status, as required by the characterization of cognitive priority.) What matters for the present is just the possibility of such a position. For if it is possible, one must be careful before drawing any anti-experientialist conclusions from considerations of priority, and correspondingly careful in ascribing the anti-experientialist view to others. For someone's insistence that red is prior to red$'$ may be an expression of cognitive priority. Such a theorist may not be rejecting definitional priority in the reverse direction. If he is not, then it would be wrong to ascribe to him anti-experientialist views. Indeed, it may well be that Wittgenstein should be regarded as holding just such a combination of views. In a passage already displayed, he insists that "red" has to be learned before certain concepts of experience; while elsewhere he seems to hold at least that seeming to be a certain colour cannot be left out of an account of what it is to have that colour:

97. Don't we just *call* brown the table which under certain circumstances appears brown to the normal-sighted? We could certainly conceive of someone to whom things seemed sometimes this colour and sometimes that, independently of the colour they are.

98. That it seems so to men is their criterion for its *being* so.

99. Being and seeming may, of course, be independent of one another in exceptional cases, but that doesn't make them logically independent; the language-game does not reside in the exception.[14]

If Wittgenstein did or would have believed in the cognitive priority of red over red', but was nevertheless not an anti-experientialist, then according to the arguments I have been endorsing, his position was consistent.

The experientialist view also has consequences for the explanation of experience. In the case of primary qualities, it is legitimate, and arguably mandatory in normal cases, to explain someone's experience of an object as square by the fact that it really is square (or by something entailed by its being square). But on the experientialist view one could not explain in a central case an object's looking red to someone by citing the fact that is really is red—at least, not if this explanation were intended to leave open the question of whether there is any primary quality ground of redness. Genuine explanations cannot have a *virtus dormitiva* character. On the particular experientialist theory I suggested, for something to be red is for it to produce experiences of a certain kind, red' experiences, in standard circumstances. In central cases—those by reference to which possession of the concept of redness was analysed—for a thing to look red to someone is for it to produce red' experiences. So on the experientialist option, the conditional "If circumstances are standard, in a central case if an object is red, then it looks red" is *a priori*: it reduces to a logical truth of the form $\forall x((Sx \& (Sx \supset Rx)) \supset Rx)$. An expression might of course be introduced as an abbreviating ("descriptive") name for whatever physical state (if any) is the ground of objects' producing red' experiences. It is not clear, and perhaps not determinate, whether "red" is used in this way in English, but if it were what would make it legitimate to say "It's red" in explanation of something's producing red experiences in standard conditions would be the existence of some other, physical, characterization of the object that produces red' experiences.[15]

Acknowledgements

I have been helped by the comments of Rogers Albritton, Philippa Foot, John McDowell, and Colin McGinn on an ancestor of this paper written in 1980, and by Crispin Wright on a more recent version. This paper was written before, and the proofs corrected after, the final version of my *Sense and Content*, Oxford University

Press, Oxford, 1983. Where it differs from, or is more elaborate than, the treatment of colour concepts in *Sense and Content*, the paper supercedes the book. The book does, however, contain more elaboration of the idea of a sensational property, of which red' is but one instance.

Notes

1. This question is intimately related to another, also touched on by Wittgenstein, viz., 'What is the nature of the relation of qualitative sameness of two experiences of different subjects, or of one subject at different times?' An answer to that question is partly constrained by the correct answer to the question of this paper.
  The present paper is the first half of another, too long for inclusion in this special issue. The second half of the longer paper is concerned with sameness of experience between subjects and over time: I aim to publish that second part as soon as other pressures permit.
  The reader whose primary interest is the interpretation of Wittgenstein should be warned that, wanting to take into account the views of more recent writers on our question, I have adopted a more eclectic framework for the discussion than Wittgensteinian exegesis alone would dictate.

2. There is a passage in *The Concept of Mind*, Penguin, London, 1963 in which Ryle brings out the dilemma, but curiously leaves it untreated: "... when I describe a common object as green or bitter ... I am saying that it would look or taste so-and-so to anyone who was in a condition and position to see or taste properly ... It must be noticed that the formula "it would look so-and-so to anyone" cannot be paraphrased by "it would look *green* to anyone", for to say that something looks green is to say that it looks as if it would if it were green and conditions were normal." Having denied that this paraphrase is correct, Ryle is left explaining "green" by a definition which takes the phrase "looks so-and-so" as an unexplained primitive: this unacceptable price is what he pays to avoid the threatened circularity.

3. For emphasis on the importance of this relatively uncontroversial point, see Anscombe, 'The Intensionality of Sensation' in R. Butler (ed.), *Analytical Philosophy* (Second Series), Blackwell, Oxford, 1968, p. 172 and W. Sellars, 'Empiricism and the Philosophy of Mind' in his *Science, Perception and Reality*, Routledge, London, 1963, p. 141ff. Sellar's later explanation (p. 147) of why, as he puts it, it is a necessary truth that something is red iff it looks red to standard observers in standard circumstances is that standard conditions are just conditions in which things look as they are. This may be true, but it applies to any predicate F for which "looks F" has some application: it does not explain why the concept of being red has a closer connection with visual experience than does the concept of being square.

4. Shoemaker, 'Functionalism and Qualia', *Philosophical Studies* **27**, 1975, 291–315.

5. D. M. Armstrong, *A Materialist Theory of the Mind*, Routledge, London, 1968; J. J. C. Smart, 'On Some Criticisms of a Physicalist Theory of Colors', in Chung-ying Cheng (ed.), *Philosophical Aspects of the Mind-Body Problem*, University of Hawaii, Honolulu, 1975. [chapter 1, this volume]

6. The principle should also be accepted by criterial theorists of meaning, in the sense in which "criterion" is understood by, for instance, P. M. S. Hacker in *Insight and Illusion*, Oxford University Press, Oxford, 1972. Such a theorist would (or should) not admit the possibility that someone be in pain yet none of the criteria, however far one investigates possible defeating conditions, indicate that he is.

7. These remarks apply to Shoemaker, 'Phenomenal Similarity', *Critica* **20**, 1975, p. 267. They could also be applied *mutatis mutandis* to his remark in 'Functionalism and Qualia' that if two persons could fuse into a single subject of consciousness, "the behaviour of the resulting person could presumably settle [the question of whether their colour spectra were inverted relative to each other]"—N. Block (ed.), *Readings in the Philosophy of Psychology* (Reprint), Vol. 1, Harvard University Press, Cambridge, 1980, p. 264.

8. Extensionality also produces other problems: it is difficult to give a satisfactory account of how an object that is in fact red might not have been.

9. Ludwig Wittgenstein, *Remarks on the Philosophy of Psychology*, Vol. 2 (ed. G. H. von Wright and H. Nyman), University of Chicago Press, Chicago, 1980, p. 60e.

10. The red of a pane of red glass is a transparent film colour (Flächenfarbe) rather than a surface colour in the sense of psychologists of colour perception. The *locus classicus* is D. Katz, *The World of Colour*, Kegan Paul, London, 1935, p. 17ff. In seeing a snowman through a pane of red glass, one sees the pane as having a transparent film colour red and the snowman as having the *surface* colour white behind it. A red snowman by contrast would have the surface colour red. If the pane of glass is thick, the colour red may appear as a volume colour—one that is presented as occupying a volume of space. (See Katz, or again J. Beck, *Surface Colour Perception*, Cornell University Press, Ithaca, 1972, p. 20.) Anyone who doubts these points should look at a white surface through a coloured transparent bottle, or consult Plate 1 of Beck's book.

11. This point does not depend upon taking "red" and "red'" as natural kind terms. The view for which I am arguing is that for an object to be red is for it to be presented in a red' region of the visual field in certain conditions (external and internal to a perceiver). In the case of red and red_{UV} these conditions are different, and so the properties of being red and of being red_{UV} are different in at least one sense. There is no commitment in saying that an object is red_{UV} to how it would look in normal daylight.

12. David Kaplan, 'On the Logic of Demonstratives', *Journal of Philosophical Logic* **8**, 1978, 81–98.

13. I have discussed some of them in 'Consciousness and Other Minds', *Proceedings of the Aristotelian Society*, Supp. Vol. 1984.

14. Ludwig Wittgenstein, *Remarks on Colour* (trans. L. McAlister and M. Schättle), Blackwell, London, 1977, p. 29e.

15. In *Form and Content*, Blackwell, Oxford, 1973, Bernard Harrison argues that colours are not "natural nameables". These last are objects which are "defined as distinct objects of reference ... independently of linguistic convention". The experientialist does treat colours as natural nameables under this definition: the fact that something is a natural nameable in Harrison's sense does not exclude the possibility that an account of the nature of the object may have to make reference to human experience.

Harrison's own model of colour-naming is as follows: we fix a set of shades as name-bases, and apply the colour word associated with that name-base to any shade which more closely resembles that name-base than any other. He takes this to justify his view that colours are not natural nameables: yet it seems clear that the experientially caused actions of a nonlinguistic creature could manifest sensitivity to exactly the colour distinctions which are determined by Harrison's model of colour-naming as applied to, say, English.

6 An Objectivist's Guide To Subjectivism About Colour

Frank Jackson and Robert Pargetter

Locke saw that science teaches us something important about colour, but he wavered between saying that it taught that colour was a property of experiences (ideas), not objects, and saying that it taught that colour was the disposition in objects to produce those experiences. We suspect that he wavered because he did not care about the difference between the two positions. What he most wanted to say was that colour was *not* a non-dispositional, objective property of objects. It differs, thus, from shape and the other primary qualities in general, which are objective properties of objects, and even if some are dispositions, none is merely a disposition to cause certain kinds of experiences.

This paper is a defence of exactly what Locke most wanted to deny. It is a defence of the view that colours are non-dispositional properties of objects as 'primary' in their nature as shape and motion. Indeed, in the case of opaque objects, they are probably complexes of such properties of the object's surface and immediate surroundings, though we will not be going into the contentious scientific details.

This view is far from new. We first heard it expounded many years ago by David Armstrong.[1] What is, we trust, new is partly the argument path to the view, but mainly the way the particular version of the view that we will defend explains the special features many have perceived are characteristic of colours by contrast with shapes. (i) Colours are much more closely tied to the experience of colour than are shapes to the experience of shape. (ii) Something like 'To be red is to look red in normal circumstances' is a truism for standing colours; and something like 'To be red in C is to look red in C' is a truism for transitory colours. (iii) The argument from microscopes and similar subjectivist arguments really do show something important about colours which they do not show about shapes. (iv) The ascription of a certain shape to an object is related to the object's causal interactions with other objects in a way that the ascription of a certain colour is not.

Points like these have been independently noted by many writers on the distinction between primary and secondary qualities. They individually and collectively suggest an important difference between colours and shapes which justifies labelling the first 'secondary' and the second 'primary', and which in any case rules out identifying colours with physical properties of objects. Indeed, these points are why we did not accept Armstrong's view for many years. But we will see that this suggestion is a *suggestio falsi*.

We will start in Section 1 by suggesting a simple and plausible account of the meaning of colour terms. We will see how it leads, along with the empirical facts disclosed by science, to the thesis that colours are physical properties of objects. In

Section 2, we will see how to preserve the dispositional truism. In Section 3, we will show how to develop our theory so as to accommodate the basic insight that has wrongly led to subjectivism about colour; and the remaining sections will be concerned with causal interaction patterns, and with colours in the dark and in possible worlds where objects look a quite different colour from their actual colour.

1   Colour Terms

It is surely good methodology to start with what seems most obvious. What is most obvious about the colour terms, 'red', 'yellow', 'blue', and so on is that we use them to denote properties that we take to be presented to us in visual experience. Redness is visually presented in a way that having inertial mass and being fragile, for instance, are not. Our access to colour is through our visual experience of colour. If you do not know what looking red is like, you do not have our concept of redness. But if you do, what else do you need, in what way can your *concept* of redness then be defective? By contrast, it is clearly not enough in order to possess the concept of squareness to know what it is like for something to look square. Grasping squareness requires tactual experience and geometrical understanding as well as visual experiences of things looking square.

Accordingly, it would be quite wrong to say, as an account of their meaning, that the terms for shapes—'round', 'square', and so on—are simply terms for properties that present themselves in certain visual experiences. A much more complicated story than this is called for in the case of shapes. But not in the case of colours. Both shapes and colours present themselves in visual experience—things look green and look round—but only in the case of terms for colours is this fact plausibly the only essential ingredient in giving an account of their meaning. But we do not use 'red' as the name of the experience itself, but of the property putatively experienced. We examine *objects* to determine their colour, we do not introspect. We thus get the following clause for 'red': 'red' denotes the property presented in the experience of looking red, or, in more natural English, redness is the property objects look to have when they look red. If the last sounds like a truism, that is all to the good; it is evidence that we are on the right track. There will, of course, be similar clauses for 'yellow', 'blue', and so on.

We now face a difficult question. What is it for an experience to be the presentation of a property? How must experience E be related to property P, or an instance of P, for E to be the presentation of P, or, equivalently, for E to represent that P? One thing, though, is immediately clear. A necessary condition is that there be a causal connection. Sensations of heat are the way heat, that is, molecular kinetic energy, presents itself to us. And this is, in part, a matter of kinetic energy *causing* sensations of heat. We say 'in part', because, for instance, the causation must be in the 'right way'.[2] If a hot iron causes a burn mark on my shirt and seeing this burn mark startles someone holding a hot potato so that they drop it on my arm, thus causing a sensation of heat, I am not perceiving the heat in the iron although it caused my sensation of heat. The sensation of heat in my arm is not a presentation of the heat of the iron (although it is a presentation of the heat of the potato), or, in more natural English, the sensation of heat, though caused by the iron's heat, is not an apprehension of the iron's heat.

For present purposes, however, the causal part of the story is enough. We can work with the rough schema: redness is the property of objects which causes objects to look red, without worrying here about the needed 'add ons', that is, without worrying about what needs to be added to causation to bring it up to presentation.

For instance, despite its roughness, our schema makes it clear why the familiar dispositional treatment of colour is mistaken. Redness is not the disposition, power or capacity of an object to look red. For if it were, an object's looking red would not be the apprehension of that object's redness, because dispositions do not cause their manifestations. Their categorical bases do that. Fragility is not what causes a glass to break on being dropped. It is the very fact that it would break when dropped; and the fact that it would break when dropped is not what breaks the glass when it is dropped. Its internal molecular nature or whatever does that.[3] Holding that redness is the disposition to look red would commit us to denying the evident fact that a thing's looking red in the right circumstances is the *apprehension* of that thing's redness.

We are now ready to make use of what science tells us about colour. Colours are what cause (in the right way etc.) objects to look coloured. That is a piece of philosophy. What causes (in the right way etc.) objects to look coloured are physical properties—notably, certain highly complex primary properties involving shape, extension, motion and electromagnetic energy, though much is still unclear. That is a piece of science. Therefore, colours are physical properties.

The basic theory is now before you. We turn to the task of explaining the widely shared philosophical insights about colours in terms of it, or in terms of refinements of it that we will introduce as the need arises.

2   The Dispositional Truism

The popularity of the dispositional account of colours derives, of course, from the fact that something along the lines of: '*x* is red iff *x* looks, or would look, red in normal circumstances' sounds like a truism (as an account of standing colour). What more natural, then, than to identify redness with the disposition? But we can admit the truism while resisting the identification.

Consider the range of height which disposes towards victory in basketball, and tag it 'alcindor'. Alcindor is *not* a dispositional property; it is, say, being over seven feet tall, which is not a dispositional property (or, at least, not one towards victory in basketball). But 'x has alcindor iff x is disposed to win at basketball' is a truism, being in fact analytically true. The property is not itself a disposition, but earns the label 'alcindor' by virtue of conferring a disposition on what possesses it. We should say the same about redness. Redness is the categorical basis of the disposition, not the disposition itself, and it earns the name 'redness' by virtue of being the categorical basis of the disposition. (We consider shortly what to say if there are many bases of the disposition.) Thus, we can explain the dispositional truism without making colours dispositions to look coloured.

We could, of course, say something similar for fragility. (As David Lewis convinced us.) We *could* use 'fragility' to denote whatever (non-dispositional) property is responsible for an object being such that if it were dropped, it would break (the latter property would then need a new name). This would preserve the special status of something like 'x is fragile iff x would break on being dropped' without making fragility a disposition to breaking. There is, however, no reason to do this in the case of fragility. The trouble for identifying colours with dispositions to look coloured is that this is inconsistent with the prime intuition that colours are properties presented in the visual experience of having something look coloured. But it is not a prime intuition that fragility is a property presented in experience, and so we do not need to give it itself a causal role with respect to experience. We perceive colour, but infer fragility.

3 Subjectivism About Colour

If colours are physical properties of objects, then they are as objective and primary as shapes. The redness of a tomato is just as much an objective property of it as is its roundness. Thus we are flying in the face of the host of persuasive arguments for a broadly subjectivist account of colour. We think that the significance of these arguments has been completely misunderstood. They show something important about colour, but that important truth is not subjectivism.

The arguments turn on three truths about colours. (i) The fundamental ground for ascribing a certain colour to something is the colour it looks to have. (ii) The colour something looks to have may be highly variable, depending both on viewing conditions and on who is doing the viewing. (iii) There are clear cases—actual and also possible-but-not-fantastical ones—where the apparent colour of a given object is quite different in one set of circumstances from the apparent colour in another set of circumstances, and yet it is impossible in any non-arbitrary way to settle on which apparent colour, in which set of circumstances, should be the guide in ascribing a colour to the object.

As everyone knows, Berkeley said that the same goes for shape. But neither (i) nor (iii) applies to shape. The shape something looks to have is not *the* fundamental ground, but one among a number of grounds, for ascribing shape to an object. And, relatedly, as we will see, *non-arbitrary* choice between conflicting apparent shapes can always be made, at least in principle. How, then, do we avoid subjectivism, while granting so much to the arguments for it. We will introduce the leading idea by reference to taste instead of colour, because, as Jonathan Bennett observes, phenol affords a particularly striking example of the kind we are interested in.[4]

Phenol tastes bitter to about seventy percent of the population, and is tasteless to about thirty percent of the population. Is phenol bitter, or is it tasteless? There seems to be absolutely no reason to prefer one group's answer to the other's. The statistics could easily be changed in either direction by selective breeding; those to whom phenol tastes bitter are not generally better at perceptual discriminations than those to whom phenol is tasteless; the conditions under which the tastings are done are equally good in both cases; and so on and so forth. How then can we avoid giving a broadly subjectivist, or at least dispositional, account of being bitter? We avoid subjectivism by saying that bitterness for those to whom phenol tastes bitter is a *different* property from bitterness for those to whom phenol is tasteless. Bitterness for phenol tasters is not the same property as bitterness for phenol non-tasters. We are not saying that tasting bitter, the experience, is a different kind of experience for the two groups, but we are saying that the property presented to the first group when something tastes bitter is different from that presented to the second group when something tastes bitter. The idea is far less revolutionary than it may at first sound. We are familiar with the idea that pain for humans may be different from pain for dolphins, that what fills the pain-role may differ from one group of organisms to another (which is compatible with the experience being the same in both).[5]

We noted a moment ago that a *non-arbitrary* choice between conflicting apparent shapes can, in principle, always be made. Suppose an object looks spherical to Jim but looks slightly flattened at the ends to Fred. We settle the dispute by investigating the causal origins of Jim's and Fred's experiences and shape judgements. If the property of the object which causally explains the experiences and judgements is its

being spherical, Jim is right; while if it is its being oblate, Fred is right. The difference with taste is that this kind of investigation can easily fail to settle disagreements.
The majority declare phenol bitter, the minority declare phenol tasteless. We investigate which properties of the object causally explain the declarations, and find that
it is property, P, in each case—the difference in the declarations being due to the
different effects of P on the two groups. This result in itself gives us no reason to
favour one declaration over the other. It shows merely that P is bitterness for the first
group but not for the second. The crucial point with shape is that there is no question of one and the same property being one shape for one group and a distinct
shape for another group. Oblateness, for instance, is the same property for everyone
in all circumstances and at all times. Not so with taste.

And not so for colour. We said, in our rough schema, that redness is the property
of objects that causes them to look red. But which property it is that causes an
object, 0, to look red to a person, S, may depend both on the nature of S's internal
physiology at the time, t, and on the circumstances, C. Accordingly, a refinement of
our schema is:

Redness for S in C at t is the property which causes (or would cause) objects to
look red to S in C at t.

The point is that redness—though not the experience of having something look
red—may very from person to person, and, for a given person, from circumstance
to circumstance or from time to time. We say 'may', not 'will'. It is a question for
science if and when redness for one person is different from redness for another, and
redness in one lighting condition is different from redness in another lighting condition. For, in terms of our rough schema, it is the empirical question as to whether
the property which causes things to look red to S_1 in C_1 at t_1 is the same as the
property which causes them to look red to S_2 in C_2 at t_2; or, in terms of the presentation of properties in experiences, the question is whether the property presented
in the looking-red experience of S_1 in C_1 at t_1 is the same property as that presented
in the looking-red experience of S_2 in C_2 at t_2.

Subjectivists and dispositional theorists about colour taunt objectivists with the
notorious variability of apparent colour. They point out that an object 0 may look
one colour to typical percipient Fred in good viewing circumstances C_1, and another
colour to Fred in different, but still good, viewing circumstances C_2, and that there
may be no principled reason for discriminating between C_1 and C_2 in respect to
which are the best conditions for apprehending the properties of the world around
us. Accordingly, they ask how Fred could possibly make a *non-arbitrary* decision as
to the real colour of 0.

Our reply is to grant that it is wrong to insist that either Fred's robust declaration in C_1 that 0 is, say, red or Fred's equally robust declaration in C_2 that 0 is, say, yellow must be false. The subjectivist is right that it would be unacceptably arbitrary to do so. What we say instead is that *both* declarations may be true. The correct position is that 0 may be red in C_1 and yellow in C_2. How can we reconcile this with taking colours to be physical properties?

We need to distinguish two cases. One is where the change from C_1 to C_2 actually changes which physical properties cause the relevant experiences. This case is patently no problem for us. The difference in colours is matched by a relevant difference in physical properties. A white wall looking blue under blue light may be an example of this kind. The blue light may actually change the relevant physical properties of the wall's surface, in which case the right thing to say is that the wall under blue light *is* blue. The light actually *turns* the wall from white to blue. Acknowledging this does not, of course, prevent us from saying, as speakers of English typically do, that the wall is really white. The 'really' though has no metaphysical significance. It merely marks the existence of the convention in English that the colour an object has in white light is given, for reasons of convenience, a special label.

The hard case for us is where it is plausible that no change in the relevant physical properties occurs. Mountains seen from afar need be no different from mountains seen close up; putting blood under a microscope need not change its physical nature, yet its apparent colour changes from red to yellow. Our treatment of these cases turns on the point that despite initial appearances, the following triad is consistent: (i) 0 is red in C_1, and yellow in C_2, (ii) the relevant physical properties of 0 are the same in C_1 and C_2, and (iii) redness and yellowness are both physical properties.

The triad is consistent because the physical property which is redness in C_1 may be the physical property which is yellowness in C_2. The physical property which is redness for blood in normal viewing conditions is yellowness for blood under a microscope. The right thing to say in these cases is that which physical property is which colour changes, just as which property is bitterness is different for the two groups in the phenol case.

Three objections are likely to spring to mind at this point. The first is that if, as we grant is possible, redness in C_1 for me now is the same property as greenness in C_2 for me now, then when I say, in C_1, that 0 is red, and, in C_2, that 0 is green, I must be saying the same thing about 0. But clearly I am not. But if I say that Fred has the same height as the tallest man in France, and also that he has the same height as the tallest man in Britain, I am not saying the same thing about Fred even if the height of the tallest man in France is exactly the same as the height of the tallest man in Britain. Conversely, even if redness in C_3 for me now is a different property from redness in C_4 for me now, when I say that an object in C_3 is red and another in C_4 is red also, I am saying that they (and not just the experiences they may cause in me) have something in common. Both have what is redness for me now in their circumstances.

The second objection is that we go around saying that objects are red or green or blue or ..., we do not go around saying that they are red to S in C or green to T in D or .... But equally we go around saying that squash balls are round, yet much of the time—during rallies anyway—they are anything but round. Metaphysically speaking, the round shape a squash ball has at rest is no more its real shape than the flattened shape it has on impact against the back wall. Nevertheless, in normal circumstances it is 'Squash balls are round' that counts as true. It is clear, even without inquiring into how to analyse 'normal', that we interpret 'Squash balls are round' said without further ado, as 'Squash balls are round in normal circumstances'. Similarly, 'Tomatoes are red', said without further ado, is interpreted as 'Tomatoes are red to normal people in normal circumstances', and so is true iff 'Tomatoes have redness for normal people in normal circumstances' is true. But this in no way shows that redness for normal people in normal circumstances is, or is not, redness for you now, or whatever. Our position here is a natural extension of a common attitude towards the distinction between standing and transitory colour. Everyone grants this distinction, and many hold that it is the transitory colours which are basic, standing colours simply being transitory colours in normal circumstances.[6] Our view is that it is the 'transitory' colour to S in C at t, which is basic.

The third objection claims that we are taking unfair advantage of the earlier slide from presentation to causation. We claimed that the points we wished to make in what was to come were independent of what needed to be added to causation to get presentation, and so, that we could work with the rough schema. The fourth objection is that this claim is false. The difference between presentation and causation blocks the possibility of redness for S_1 in C_1 (at t_1) being different from redness for S_2 in C_2 (at t_2). But how could the 'add ons' make trouble for this possibility?

It might be argued that in order for an experience to be a presentation of a property of the objects around us, the experience and the objects need to share the relevant property. We must have resemblance, to put it in the Lockean terminology. Thus, as looking red is the same experience for different people in different circumstances, redness is the same presented property throughout. It is now widely believed that Berkeley won at least this part of the argument with Locke and that resemblance in any literal sense between ideas and mind-independent objects is a mystery. Moreover, however you stand on this question, you cannot hold that resemblance is a necessary condition for presentation. We do perceive the heat in objects, yet in no sense, literal or metaphorical, does molecular kinetic energy resemble sensations of heat. And, of course, very different experiences can be presentations of the same property. Seeing and feeling the roundness of something are very different experiences. We are merely insisting on the converse possibility that the same experiences may be presentations of different properties. Indeed, to insist that the same experiences must be the presentation of the same property may be plausible if we are talking about properties of experiences but not if we are talking about properties of objects presented in experience.

Therefore, the difference between causation and presentation does not block our view that redness for S_1 in C_1 at t_1 may be distinct from redness for S_2 in C_2 at t_2. But the difference does enable us to avoid an unwelcome consequence. Illusions concerning colour are surely possible. It is not always the case that an object that looks red is in fact red, even if it is a physical property of the object and its surroundings (and not of a brain probe) that is responsible for its looking red. Now if causation and presentation were the same, that physical property would automatically have to be redness in the circumstances for the person at the time; and so the object would *be red* in the circumstances for the person at the time, as well as looking red in the circumstances to the person.

4   An Empirical Complication

We now need to note a possible complication. The physics and physiology of colour vision is far from settled, and it may well turn out that the diversity of physical properties which cause (in the right way) objects to look red outruns the diversity of viewers, times, and circumstances. It may well be that even if we restrict ourselves to a given viewer, S, in a given circumstance, C, at a given time, t, there are a number of different physical properties, $P_1, \ldots, P_n$, that would cause an object, 0, to look red to S in C at t; that is, each P_i is such that were 0 to possess it, 0 would, in virtue of possessing it, look red to S in C at t.

There are two ways we might respond to this point. We might identify redness for S in C at t with the disjunctive property of being P_1 or ... or P_n. If we respond this way, we may not be able any longer to say that redness for S in C at t is the property which does or would cause an object to look red to S in C at t. For it is at least arguable that disjunctive properties of the kind in question do not cause anything. Being P_1 or ... or P_n may not be potentially causally efficacious, though *each* of P_1, ..., P_n may be. Accordingly, we would need to modify our account of redness to count a property as redness for S in C at t if it is a disjunctive property each disjunct of which is such that it does or would cause an object to look red to S in C at t. Of course, some have worried that being P_1 or ... or P_n is not enough for all red (or, on our approach, all red-for-S-in-C-at-t) objects to have in common in the possible case where the disjuncts are themselves unrelated. But they *are* related in the way that matters here. They have in common that they each cause things to look red in the right way for presentation.

The second response is to rest content with an account of the redness *of 0* for S in C at t, the redness of 0 for S in C at t being the property of 0 which does or would cause 0 to look red to S in C at t. In this case, the redness of 0 for S in C at t must actually be a property of 0; a property which may or may not actually be causing 0 to look red to S in C at t, for S may not actually be looking at 0. We cannot see any decisive reason to favour one response over the other.[7] Each enables us to say of any object in any possible world, whether or not it is red. In any case, we will suppress this complication in what follows.

5   Colours, Shapes, and Causal Interaction Patterns

"Square objects have characteristic interaction patterns. They do not, for instance, roll smoothly down flat planes. Red objects do not have characteristic interaction patterns. The red and white billiard balls behave in exactly the same way on the billiard table". Something like this is sometimes urged to be an essential difference between shape and colour. This is obviously incompatible with our view that colour is a physical property not different in kind from shape, so it is important for us to see that it is false.

Red and white billiard balls do not behave the same way on billiard tables. The red balls go down the pockets much more often. It may be objected that it is not their redness *per se* which is responsible. Rather certain physical properties of the red balls cause them to look red to the players, and that, along with the players' beliefs and desires causes the red balls to go into the pockets more often than the white balls. But this is a blatant *Petitio* as part of an argument against us. It is being *assumed* that redness is not a physical property in order to show that redness is causally inactive.

Perhaps the thought is rather that, by contrast with colour, the characteristic interaction patterns for, say, squareness are *partially definitive* of squareness; but the usual examples are unconvincing. It seems entirely contingent that square objects do not roll smoothly down flat planes. There are possible worlds without gravity, and ones where objects move through each other effortlessly. Rather, what does seem to be true is this. An object's interactions with other *non-sentient* objects constitutes evidence concerning its shape, and evidence which has roughly equal weight with those of its interactions with *sentient* creatures that are responsible for it looking or feeling to be a certain shape. By contrast, those of an object's interactions with sentient creatures responsible for it looking a certain colour have a very special status where colour is concerned. This, though, is very obviously no threat to our version of the view that colours are physical properties. For, on it, which physical properties are which colours (for which sentient creatures in which circumstances at which times) depends precisely on the kind of experiences they cause, that is, on their effects on sentient creatures.

6   Colours in the Dark and in Other Worlds

Locke asked whether porphyry was red in the dark. We will ask whether ripe tomatoes are red in the dark and in other possible worlds where they do not look red.

Are tomatoes literally red in the dark? We wish to enter a plea for tolerance on this question. Some writers answer it with 'Obviously, yes', others with 'Obviously, no'. But the very fact that opposite answers are found obvious shows that *neither* answer is *obvious*. How might we explain the disagreement? There is no disagreement about the underlying metaphysical facts of the matter. It is agreed that tomatoes do not look red in the dark, while having in the dark whatever physical basis it is that is responsible for it being the case that they would look red were they being viewed in daylight. Consequently, the obvious place to locate the disagreement is in an ambiguity in the question. Our treatment suggests a simple way of doing this.

We have lately spoken, not of redness, but of redness for S in C. Now, how should we relate redness for S in C, the *property*, to the truth or falsity of *sentences* about objects being red? Two things are immediately clear. First, we should count 'X is red in C for S' as true iff X has redness for S in C. Secondly, this observation is completely silent about what to say about 'X is red'. But the literature, particularly the parts concerned with the distinction between transitory and standing colours, suggest an obvious strategy. Count 'X is red' as true iff X has redness for normal perceivers in normal circumstances (however 'normal' is to be elucidated).

The ambiguity in the question, Are tomatoes red in the dark?, is now clear. On one disambiguation, it is the question, Do tomatoes have redness-in-the-dark? To which the answer is no, only fluorescent objects have that property, for only they red-present or look red in the dark. On the other disambiguation, it is the question, Do tomatoes have redness-in-normal-circumstances in the dark? To which the answer is, we take it, yes. The (physical) property which red-presents in daylight is a property that tomatoes have in the dark as well as in daylight. Turning the lights out does not remove the property, although it does stop it making tomatoes look red to us. We said 'we take it' because there is much about colour vision that is still a puzzle to scientists, and it just might turn out that the relevant property is only present in the daylight. In this case, the answer to the question, Are tomatoes red in the dark?, is no, on either interpretation. (And is not this just what we would say in this eventuality?)

A similar ambiguity infects corresponding questions about tomatoes in other possible worlds. Consider a world in which tomatoes look orange in daylight, not because they are different but because daylight is different. Are tomatoes red or are they orange in this world? Equivalently, had daylight been like sodium light, would tomatoes have been orange; or would they still have been red, despite looking orange to normal observers in normal circumstances.

One approach is to view the question as being as to whether certain descriptions should be read rigidly or non-rigidly. If 'redness' (or, as we would put it, 'redness in normal circumstances to normal perceivers') is short for the non-rigid, definite description 'the property responsible (in the right way) for things looking red', and likewise for 'orangeness', then *the* clear answer is that tomatoes are not red, and are orange, in our imagined world; while if 'redness' is short for the rigid, descriptive name 'the property *actually* responsible for things looking red', then *the* clear answer is that tomatoes are red in our imagined world. For, while not looking red in it, they do have in it the property responsible in the actual world for their looking red.

The trouble with this approach to the question is that, in either case, the answer is clear; though which answer it is that is clear is different. But the answer is manifestly not clear. People's *pre-theoretic* responses to, 'Had daylight been much more like sodium light so that tomatoes looked orange in it, would tomatoes have been red or orange (in normal circumstances)?' are notoriously all over the place. But not because of an underlying disagreement over the basic facts of the matter. The best explanation, therefore, is ambiguity of question and it is the non-rigid reading which allows an ambiguity. If we read 'redness' non-rigidly, our question, Are tomatoes red in our imagined world? is ambiguous as between, Do tomatoes have redness-in-our-world in our imagined world?' to which yes is the answer, and, Do tomatoes have redness-in-our-imagined world? to which no is the answer.

7 Conclusion

Science does not show that colours are properties of experiences or that they are mere dispositions to produce certain kinds of experiences. Rather, it shows that colours are physical properties of objects—highly complex and possibly largely extrinsic, though we have said almost nothing about the scientific details—which may vary according to person, circumstance, and time. Our case for this kind of view has been how it can explain what it ought to explain. In particular, we have seen how treating colours as physical properties, but possibly different ones for different persons, circumstances, or times can explain the features which have led philosophers to propound subjectivist or dispositional accounts of colour. Indeed, on our view, subjectivists have *mis-located* the subjective element in the story about colour. Colours are objective properties of the world around us, but it *is* a subjective matter *which* objective properties are which colours to which persons in which circumstances at which times.

Acknowledgments

Special thanks are due to Michael Smith and I. L. Humberstone for many fruitful discussions arising from earlier versions of this material, and to Keith Campbell for saving us from a blunder in Section 5.

Notes

1. In a paper which became chapter 12, of D. M. Armstrong, *A Materialist Theory of the Mind* (Routledge Kegan Paul, London, 1968). Similar views have been put to us in discussion by J. J. C. Smart and, particularly, David Lewis (to whom we also owe the idea for the title).

2. The corresponding point for intentional actions' connection with beliefs and desires, is discussed in Donald Davidson, 'Freedom to Act', reprinted in his *Actions and Events* (Clarendon Press, Oxford, 1980), pp. 63–81. For discussions of the point as it arises in the perceptual context, see, e.g. David Lewis, 'Veridical Hallucination and Prosthetic Vision', *Australasian Journal of Philosophy*, 58 (1980), pp. 239–249, and references therein.

3. For a detailed argument to this conclusion see Elizabeth W. Prior, Robert Pargetter, and Frank Jackson, 'Three Theses about Dispositions', *American Philosophical Quarterly*, 19 (1982), pp. 251–257.

4. Jonathan Bennett, 'Substance, Reality, and Primary Qualities', *American Philosophical Quarterly*, 2 (1965), pp. 1–17.

5. See, e.g., David Lewis, 'Review of Putnam', in *Readings in Philosophy of Psychology*, vol. I, ed. N. Block (Harvard University Press, Mass., 1980), and Frank Jackson, Robert Pargetter, and Elizabeth W. Prior, 'Functionalism and Type-Type Identity Theories', *Philosophical Studies*, 42 (1982), pp. 209–225. Note though that here and throughout we say nothing one way or the other about whether colour experiences can be understood physicalistically. For all we say, you can be a qualia freak and believe in sense-data—though you cannot think that sense-data are the real bearers of the colour properties. One author thus retracts this latter claim made in Frank Jackson, *Perception* (Cambridge University Press, Cambridge, 1977), chapter 5.

6. We are indebted here to Keith Campbell, 'Colours', and D. M. Armstrong, 'Colour-Realism and the Argument from Microscopes', both in *Contemporary Philosophy in Australia*, ed. R. Brown and C. Rollins (Allen and Unwin, London, 1969).

7. But note that the second style of response is not available for the corresponding problem for functionalist theories of mind, see the final section of Jackson, Pargetter, and Prior, *op. cit.*

7 Colour as a Secondary Quality

Paul A. Boghossian and J. David Velleman

The Galilean Intuition

Does modern science imply, contrary to the testimony of our eyes, that grass is not green? Galileo thought it did:

Hence I think that these tastes, odors, colors, etc., on the side of the object in which they seem to exist, are nothing else than mere names, but hold their residence solely in the sensitive body; so that if the animal were removed, every such quality would be abolished and annihilated. Nevertheless, as soon as we have imposed names on them, particular and different from those of the other primary and real accidents, we induce ourselves to believe that they also exist just as truly and really as the latter.[1]

The question whether Galileo was right on this score is not really a question about the content of modern scientific theory: aside from some difficulties concerning the interpretation of quantum mechanics, we know what properties are attributed to objects by physics. The question is rather about the correct understanding of colour concepts as they figure in visual experience: how do objects appear to be, when they appear to be green? Galileo seems to have found it very natural to say that the property an object appears to have, when it appears to have a certain colour, is an intrinsic qualitative property which, as science teaches us, it does not in fact possess.

Subsequent philosophical theorizing about colour has tended to recoil from Galileo's semantic intuition and from its attendant ascription of massive error to ordinary experience and thought. Thus, in a recent paper Sydney Shoemaker has written:

[S]ince in fact we apply color predicates to physical objects and never to sensations, ideas, experiences, etc., the account of their semantics recommended by the Principle of Charity is one that makes them truly applicable to tomatoes and lemons rather than to sense experiences thereof.[2]

Should a principle of charity be applied in this way to the interpretation of the colour concepts exercised in visual experience? We think not. We shall argue, for one thing, that the grounds for applying a principle of charity are lacking in the case of colour concepts. More importantly, we shall argue that attempts at giving the experience of colour a charitable interpretation either fail to respect obvious features of that experience or fail to interpret it charitably, after all. Charity to visual experience is therefore no motive for resisting the natural, Galilean response to a scientific understanding of light and vision. The best interpretation of colour experience ends up convicting it of widespread and systematic error.[3]

Charitable Accounts of Colour Experience

According to the principle of charity, the properties that objects are seen as having, when they are seen as coloured, must be properties that they generally have when so perceived. Two familiar interpretations of visual experience satisfy this principle.

The Physicalist Account

The first of these interpretations begins with the assumption that what objects appear to have, when they look red, is the physical property that is normally detected or tracked by that experience. Since the physical property that normally causes an object to be seen as red is the property of having one out of a class of spectral-reflectance profiles—or one out of a class of molecular bases for such profiles—the upshot of the present interpretation is that seeing something as red is seeing it as reflecting incident light in one of such-and-such ways, or as having surface molecules with one of such-and-such electron configurations.[4]

Now, we have no doubt that experiences of an object as having a particular colour are normally correlated with that object's possessing one of a class of spectral-reflectance profiles. But to concede the existence of such a correlation is not yet to concede that membership in a spectral-reflectance class is the property that objects are seen as having when they are seen as having a particular colour. Indeed, the claim that visual experience has this content yields unacceptable consequences.

In particular, this claim implies that one cannot tell just by looking at two objects whether they appear to have the same or different colours. For according to the physicalist interpretation, which colour one sees an object as having depends on which spectral-reflectance class one's visual experience represents the object as belonging to; and which spectral-reflectance class one's experience represents an object as belonging to depends on which spectral-reflectance profiles normally cause experiences of that sort. Hence in order to know whether two objects appear to have the same colour, under the physicalist interpretation, one must know whether one's experiences of them are such as result from similar spectral-reflectance profiles. And the latter question cannot be settled on the basis of the visual experiences alone: it calls for considerable empirical enquiry. The physicalist interpretation therefore implies that knowing whether two objects appear to have the same colour requires knowing the results of empirical enquiry into the physical causes of visual experiences.

But surely, one can tell whether two objects appear similarly coloured on the basis of visual experience alone. To be sure, one's experience of the objects will not necessarily provide knowledge of the relation between their actual colours. But the physicalist account implies that visual experience of objects fails to provide epistemic access, not just to their actual colour similarities, but to their apparent colour similarities as well. And here the account must be mistaken. The apparent colours of objects can be compared without empirical enquiry into the physical causes of the objects' visual appearances; and so the properties that objects appear to have, when they appear coloured, cannot be identified with the physical properties that are detected or tracked by those appearances.

Dispositionalist Accounts

We turn, then, to another class of theories that respect the principle of charity in application to colour experience. These theories are united under the name of dispositionalism. All of them are based, in one way or another, on the claim that the concept of colour is such as to yield a priori truths of the following form:

(i) x is red if and only if x appears red under standard conditions.[5]

Different versions of dispositionalism interpret such biconditionals differently and apply them to the vindication of colour experience in different ways.

Applying the Biconditionals: The Direct Approach   Perhaps the most direct way to argue from the dispositionalist biconditionals to the veridicality of colour experience is to point out that the biconditionals assert, as a priori truths, that there are conditions under which things appear to have a colour if and only if they actually have it, and hence that there are conditions under which colour experience is veridical. The possibility of global error in colour experience is thus claimed to be excluded a priori by the very concept of colour.

   We think that this version of dispositionalism misappropriates whatever a priori truth there may be in the relevant biconditionals. We are prepared to admit that the concept of colour guarantees the existence of privileged conditions for viewing colours, conditions under which an observer's colour experiences or colour judgements are in some sense authoritative. But colour experiences and colour judgements may enjoy many different kinds of authority, some of which would not entail that objects have the properties that colour experience represents them as having.

   Even philosophers who regard colour experience as globally false, for example, will nevertheless want to say that some colour experiences are correct in the sense that they yield the colour attributions that are generally accepted for the purposes of describing objects in public discourse. Of course, such a claim will yield slightly different biconditionals, of the following form:

(ii) x is to be described as red if and only if x appears red under standard conditions.

Our point, however, is that (ii) may be the only biconditional that is strictly true, and that (i) may seem true only because it is mistaken for (ii). If biconditional (ii) expresses the only genuine a priori truth in the vicinity, then the authority of experiences produced under standard conditions may consist in no more than there being a convention of describing objects in terms of the colours attributed to them in such experiences. As we shall argue at the end of this paper, such a convention may be perfectly justifiable even if all colour experience is, strictly speaking, false. Hence the intuitive support for biconditionals like (i) may not be such as to ground a vindication of colour experience.

In order for the dispositionalist biconditionals to vindicate colour experience, they must mean, not just that convention dictates describing objects in terms of the colours that they appear to have under standard conditions, but also that objects actually have the properties that they thereby appear to have. And we see no reason for regarding this stronger claim as an a priori truth.

Applying the Biconditionals as Content-Specifications   Another way of arguing from dispositionalist biconditionals to the veridicality of colour experience is to interpret the biconditionals as specifying the content of that experience. This argument proceeds as follows.

The first premiss of the argument says that the property that objects are represented as having when they look red is just this: a disposition to look red under standard conditions. The second premiss says that many objects are in fact disposed to look red under standard conditions, and that these are the objects that are generally seen as red. These premisses yield the conclusion that the experience of red is generally veridical, since it represents an object as having a disposition that it probably has—namely, a disposition to look red under standard conditions.

The first premiss of this argument corresponds to a biconditional of the following form:

(iii)   *Red* [i.e., the property that   a disposition to appear
        objects are seen as having   = def   red under standard
        when they look red]   conditions

The right side of biconditional (iii) can be interpreted in two different ways, however; and so there are two different versions of the associated argument.

Two Versions of Content-Dispositionalism   The first version of the argument interprets the phrase 'a disposition to look red' on the assumption that the embedded phrase 'to look red' has its usual semantic structure. The entire phrase is therefore taken to mean 'a disposition to give the visual appearance of being red'.[6] The second version interprets the phrase on the assumption that 'to look red' has a somewhat unusual structure. The predicate following 'look' is interpreted as expressing, not a property that a thing is disposed to give the appearance of having, but rather an intrinsic property of the visual appearance that it is disposed to give. The phrase 'a disposition to look red' is therefore taken to mean something like 'a disposition to cause reddish visual appearances'.[7]

Under these two interpretations, (iii) assigns two different contents to colour experience. Under one interpretation, the property that things are seen as having when they look red is defined as a disposition to give the visual appearance of being red; under the other, the property that things are seen as having is defined as a disposition to cause reddish visual appearances. In either case, the content of colour experience is claimed to be true, on the grounds that objects seen as red do have the appropriate disposition.

We regard both versions of the argument as faulty. In the next section, we shall raise an objection that militates against both versions equally. In subsequent sections, we shall consider each version in its own right.

A General Problem in Content-Dispositionalism   Both versions of the present argument are to be faulted, in our opinion, for misdescribing the experience of colour. In assigning colour experience a dispositionalist content, they get the content of that experience wrong.

When one enters a dark room and switches on a light, the colours of surrounding objects look as if they have been revealed, not as if they have been activated. That is, the dispelling of darkness looks like the drawing of a curtain from the colours of objects no less than from the objects themselves. If colours looked like dispositions, however, then they would seem to *come on* when illuminated, just as a lamp comes on when its switch is flipped. Turning on the light would seem, simultaneously, like turning on the colours; or perhaps it would seem like waking up the colours, just as it is seen to startle the cat. Conversely, when the light was extinguished, the colours would not look as if they were being concealed or shrouded in the ensuing darkness: rather, they would look as if they were becoming dormant, like the cat returning to sleep. But colours do not look like that; or not, at least, to us.

More seriously, both versions of (iii) also have trouble describing the way in which colours figure in particular experiences, such as after-images. The colours that one sees when experiencing an after-image are precisely the qualities that one sees as belonging to external objects. When red spots float before one's eyes, one sees the same colour quality that fire-hydrants and maraschino cherries normally appear to have.[8] The problem is that dispositionalist accounts of colour experience must analyse the appearance of colour in after-images as the appearance of a disposition to look red under standard conditions; and after-images simply cannot appear to have such a dispositional property.

This problem would not arise if after-images were full-blown illusions. That is, if seeing an after-image consisted in seeming to see a material object suspended in physical space, then that object, though in fact illusory, could still appear to have the same colour quality as any other material object. But after-images are not seen as material objects, any more than, say, a ringing in one's ears is heard as a real noise. The items involved in these experiences are not perceived as existing independently of being perceived. On the one hand, the after-image is seen as located before one's eyes, rather than in one's mind, where visual memories are seen; and the ringing is likewise heard as located in one's outer ear, rather than in the inner auditorium of verbal thought and musical memory. But on the other hand, one does not perceive these items as actually existing in the locations to which they are subjectively referred. The ringing is heard as overlaying a silence in one's ears, where there is audibly nothing to hear; and similarly, the after-image is seen as overlaying the thin air before one's eyes, where there is visibly nothing to see. The ringing is thus perceived as a figment or projection of one's ears, the image as a figment or projection of one's eyes: both, in short, are perceived as existing only in so far as one is perceiving them.

Thus, the possibility of a red after-image requires that one see something as simultaneously a figment of one's eyes and red. But how could something that looked like a figment of one's eyes also appear disposed to look a particular way under standard conditions? Because an after-image is seen as the sort of thing that exists only in so far as one is seeing it, it cannot be seen as the sort of thing that others could see nor, indeed, as the sort of thing that one could see again oneself, in the requisite sense. In seeing an after-image as a figment of one's eyes, one sees it as the sort of thing that will cease to exist when no longer seen and that will not be numerically identical to any future after-images, however similar they may be. One does not see it, in other words, as a persisting item that could be reintroduced into anyone's visual experience; and so one cannot see it as having a disposition to present this or any appearance either to others or to oneself on other occasions.

The foregoing, phenomenological problems are common to both versions of the dispositionalist argument currently under consideration. Each version of the argument also has peculiar problems of its own, which we shall now consider in turn. We begin with the first version, which understands a disposition to look red as a disposition to give the visual appearance of having the property red.

Problems in the First Version of Content-Dispositionalism The problem with this version has to do with the property expressed by the word 'red' in the phrase 'a disposition to appear red under standard conditions'—the phrase constituting the right side of biconditional (iii). Keep in mind that the entire phrase has itself been offered as expressing the property that objects are seen as having when they look red. When things are seen as red, according to the present argument, what they are seen as having is a disposition to appear red under standard conditions. But does the word 'red' here express the same property that the entire phrase purports to express?

Suppose that the answer to our question is no. In that case, what biconditional (iii) says is that the property that things are seen as having when they look red is a disposition to give the appearance of having some *other* property called red. This other property must naturally be a colour, since the property red could hardly be seen as a disposition to appear as having some property that was not a colour. For the sake of clarity, let us call this other property red*.

Now, in order for objects to have the property red that they appear to have, under the present assumption, they must actually be disposed to give the appearance, under standard conditions, of having the property red*; and in order to have that disposition, they must actually give the appearance of having the property red* under standard conditions. Thus, if the property that things are seen as having when they look red is a disposition to appear red*, then the experience of seeing them as red is veridical, as the dispositionalist wishes to prove, only if they also appear red*. And the question then arises whether red* is a property that things ever do or can actually have. The dispositionalist's argument does not show that the appearance of having red* is ever veridical, since that property is admitted to be different from the disposition whose existence the dispositionalist cites in vindicating the appearance of red. The consequence is that there must be colour experiences that the dispositionalist has failed to vindicate.

Suppose, then, that the dispositionalist answers yes to our question. That is, suppose he says that 'red' expresses the same property on the right side of (iii) as it does on the left. In that case, the dispositionalist's account of colour experience is circular, since in attempting to say what property things appear to have when they look red, he invokes the very property that is at issue.

The dispositionalist may refuse to be troubled by this circularity, however.[9] He may point out that a circular account of a property can still be true, and indeed informative, despite its circularity. For instance, to define courage as a disposition to act courageously is to give a circular definition, a definition that cannot convey the concept of courage to anyone who does not already have it. Even so, courage *is* a disposition to act courageously, and this definition may reveal something important about the property—namely that it is a behavioural disposition. The dispositionalist about colour claims that the circularity in his explication of red is similar.

We grant that circularity alone does not necessarily undermine a definitional equivalence. Yet the circularity in biconditional (iii) is significantly different from that in our circular definition of courage. Our definition of courage invokes courage in an ordinary extensional context, whereas the right side of (iii) invokes red in an intentional context expressing the content of a visual experience, an experience that happens to be the very one whose content (iii) purports to explicate. The result is that the visual experience of seeing something as red can satisfy (iii) only if it, too, is circular, and hence only if it is just as uninformative as (iii). Not only does (iii) fail to tell us which colour red is, then; it also precludes visual experience from telling us which colour an object has. The former failure may be harmless, but the latter is not.

Let us illustrate the difference between an unproblematic circular definition and a problematic one by means of an analogy. Suppose that you ask someone who Sam is and are told, 'Sam is the father of Sam's children'. This answer does not tell you who Sam is if you do not already know. But it does tell you something about Sam— namely, that he has children—and, more importantly, it places Sam in a relation to himself that a person can indeed occupy. In order for Sam to satisfy this assertion, he need only be the father of his own children. Now suppose, alternatively, that your question receives the answer 'Sam is the father of Sam's father'. This response also identifies Sam by reference to Sam; but it has a more serious defect. Its defect is that it asserts of Sam that he stands to himself in a relation that it is impossible for a person to occupy.

These two circular identifications of Sam are analogous to the two circular definitions that we are considering. The definition of courage as a disposition to act courageously is uninformative, but it places courage in a relation to itself that a disposition can occupy. In order to satisfy this definition, courage must simply be the disposition to perform actions that tend to be performed by someone with that very disposition. By contrast, the dispositionalist about colour not only invokes the content of colour experience in explicating that content; he places that content in a relation to itself that is impossible for it to occupy. For his explication says that the content of the visual experience of red must contain, as a proper part, the content of the visual experience of red. To see something as red, according to (iii), is to have an experience whose content is that the thing is disposed to produce visual experiences *with the content that it is red*. The experiential content that something is red is thus embedded within itself, and this is a reflexive relation that no determinate content can occupy. Consequently, (iii) requires that the visual experience of red have an indeterminate content that fails to represent its object as having any particular colour.

Under the terms of (iii), an experience can represent its object as red only by representing it as disposed to produce visual experiences that represent it as red. The problem here is that the experiences that the object is thus represented as disposed to produce must themselves be represented as experiences that represent the object as red, rather than some other colour—lest the object be represented as disposed to appear something other than red. Yet these experiences can be represented as representing the object as red only if they are represented as representing it as disposed to produce experiences that represent it as red. And here the circle gets vicious. In order for an object to appear red rather than blue, it must appear disposed to appear red, rather than disposed to appear blue; and in order to appear disposed to appear red, rather than disposed to appear blue, it must appear disposed to appear disposed to appear red, rather than disposed to appear disposed to appear blue; and so on. Until this regress reaches an end, the object's appearance will not amount to the appearance of one colour rather than another. Unfortunately, the regress never reaches an end.

One might attempt to staunch the regress simply by invoking the relevant colour by name. 'To appear red', one might say, 'is to appear disposed to appear red—and that's the end of the matter.' 'Of course,' one might continue, 'if you don't already know what red is, then you haven't understood what I've said. But that doesn't impugn the truth of my assertion, nor its informativeness, since you have learned at least that the property things appear to have in appearing red is a disposition to produce appearances.'

This reply cannot succeed. Staunching the regress with the word 'red' can work, but only if the word is not understood in the sense defined in biconditional (iii). We readily agree that red things do appear disposed to look red, and that they appear so without requiring the viewer to run an endless gamut of visual appearances. But what they appear disposed to do is to give the appearance of being red in a non-dispositional sense—the appearance of having a non-dispositional redness. And the way they appear disposed to give that appearance is usually just by giving it—that is, by looking non-dispositionally red.[10] Similarly, objects can appear disposed to look square just by looking square, but only because they look square intrinsically and categorically.

As we have seen, however, the dispositionalist cannot admit an intrinsic and categorical sense of the word 'red' into his formulation. For then he would have to acknowledge that objects appear disposed to look red, and do look red, in a non-dispositional sense. And he would then have acknowledged that an object's being disposed to look red does not guarantee that it is as it looks, in respect to colour, since the redness that it is thereby disposed to give the appearance of having is a different property from the disposition that it admittedly has. The dispositionalist must therefore say that although an object looks disposed to look red just by looking red, this looking red does not involve looking anything except disposed to look red. *In short, the object must look disposed to look a particular way without there being any particular way that it looks, or looks disposed to look, other than so disposed.* And that is why the vicious regress gets started.

Note, once again, that the problem created by the regress is not that we are unable to learn what red is from the statement that red is a disposition to look red. The problem is that, under the terms of that statement, the subject of visual experience cannot see what colour an object has. For he cannot see that particular colour of an object except by seeing the particular way the object tends to appear; and he cannot see the way it tends to appear except by seeing the way it tends to appear as tending to appear; and so on, *ad infinitum*. To be sure, a person can see all of these things if he can just see the object as having a colour, to begin with; but under the terms of dispositionalism, he cannot begin to see the object as having a colour except by seeing these dispositions; and so he can never begin to see it as having a colour at all.[11]

The Second Version of Content-Dispositionalism   The only way to save dispositionalism from its fatal circularity is to ensure that the disposition with which a colour property is identified is not a disposition to give the appearance of having that very property. Christopher Peacocke has attempted to modify dispositionalism in just this way.

According to Peacocke, the property that an object is seen as having when it looks red should be identified as a disposition, not to appear red, but rather to appear in a portion of the visual field having an intrinsic property that Peacocke calls red'. Let us call these portions of the visual field *red' patches*. We can then say that looking red, according to Peacocke, is looking disposed to be represented in red' patches under standard conditions—an appearance that can be accomplished by being represented in a red' patch under recognizably standard conditions, of course, but also in other ways as well, such as by being represented in an orange' patch when illuminated by a yellow-looking light. The upshot, in any case, is that objects often are as they look when they look red, because they both look and are just this: disposed to be represented in red' patches under standard conditions.

Peacocke's qualified dispositionalism eliminates circular experiential contents because it says that appearing to have a colour property is appearing disposed to present appearances characterized, not in terms of that very property, but rather in terms of a different quality, a 'primed' colour. Peacocke can also account for the role of red in the experience of seeing a red after-image, because he can say that the experience consists in a red' patch represented, in the content of one's experience, as a figment of one's eyes.

Peacocke's qualified dispositionalism differs from pure dispositionalism in that it introduces a visual field modified by qualities that—to judge by their names, at least—constitute a species of colour. Peacocke thus abandons a significant feature of the theories that we have examined thus far. Those theories assume that visual experience involves colour only to the extent of representing it. They analyse an experience of red as an experience with the content that something is red—an experience that refers to redness. Because the role of colour in experience is restricted by these theories to that of an element in the intentional content of experience, we shall call the theories intentionalist.

Peacocke's theory is not intentionalist, because it says that visual experience involves colour (that is, primed colour) as a property inhering in the visual field, and not just as a property represented in the content of that experience. We have two points to make about Peacocke's anti-intentionalism. We shall first argue that Peacocke is right to abandon intentionalism and to introduce colours as intrinsic properties of the visual field. But we shall then argue that, having introduced such properties, Peacocke is wrong to remain a dispositionalist about the colours that visual experience attributes to external objects. Peacocke's modification of dispositionalism is unstable, we believe, in that it ultimately undermines dispositionalism altogether.

The Case Against Intentionalism   Peacocke has argued elsewhere, and on independent grounds, for the need to speak about a sensory field modified by intrinsic sensational qualities.[12] We should like to add some arguments our own.

Our first argument rests on the possibility, noted above, of seeing an after-image without illusion. Consider such an experience, in which an after-image appears to you *as* an after-image—say, as a red spot obscuring the face of a person who has just taken your photograph. Since you suffer no illusion about the nature of this spot, you do not see it as something actually existing in front of the photographer's face. In what sense, then, do you see it as occupying that location at all? The answer is that you see it as merely appearing in that location: you see it as a spot that appears in front of the photographer's face without actually being there. Now, in order for you to see the spot as appearing somewhere, it must certainly appear there. Yet it must appear there without appearing actually to be there, since you are not under the illusion that the spot actually occupies the space in question. The after-image must therefore be described as *appearing in* a location without *appearing to be in* that location; and this description is not within the capacity of any intentionalist theory. An intentionalist theory will analyse the visual appearance of location as the attribution of location to something, in the intentional content of your visual experience.

But the intentional content of your visual experience is that there is nothing at all between you and the photographer.

The only way to describe the after-image as appearing in front of the photographer without appearing to be in front of the photographer is to talk about the location that it occupies in your visual field. In your visual field, we say, the after-image overlays the image of the photographer's face, but nothing is thereby represented as actually being over the photographer's face. The after-image is thus like a coffee-stain on a picture, a feature that occupies a location on the picture without representing anything as occupying any location. Similarly, an adequate description of the after-image requires reference to two kinds of location—location as an intrinsic property of features in the visual field, and location as represented by the resulting visual experience.

One might think that this argument cannot be applied to the after-image's colour, since you may see the after-image not only as appearing red but also as actually *being* red. But then intentionalism will have trouble explaining what exactly your experience represents as being red, given that the experience is veridical. Your experience cannot represent some external object as being red, on pain of being illusory. And if it represents an image as being red, then its truth will entail that colour can enter into visual experience as an intrinsic property of images, which is precisely what intentionalism denies. Hence there would seem to be nothing that the experience can veridically represent as being red, according to intentionalism. And if the experience represented something as merely appearing red, then our foregoing argument would once again apply. For how could you have a veridical experience that something appeared red unless something so appeared? And if something did so appear, it would have to appear *to be* red, according to intentionalism, which would be an illusion in the present case, unless images can be red.[13]

There are other, more familiar cases that refute intentionalism in a similar way. These, too, are cases in which something is seen without being represented in the content of experience as intentionalism would require. If you press the side of one eyeball, you can see this line of type twice without seeing the page as bearing two identical lines of type. Indeed, you cannot even force the resulting experience into representing the existence of two lines, even if you try. Similarly, you can see nearby objects double by focusing on distant objects behind them, and yet you cannot get yourself to see the number of nearby objects as doubling. And by unfocusing your eyes, you can see objects blurrily without being able to see them as being blurry. None of these experiences can be adequately described solely in terms of their intentional content. Their description requires reference to areas of colour in a visual field, areas that split in two or become blurry without anything's being represented to you as doing so.

The Case Against Peacocke's Dispositionalism   We therefore endorse Peacocke's decision to posit a visual field with intrinsic sensational qualities. What we question, however, is his insistence that the colours of external objects are still seen as dispositions. We believe that once one posits a visual field bearing properties such as red', one is eventually forced to conclude that objects presented in red' areas of that field are seen as red' rather than as possessing some other, dispositional quality.

The reason is that visual experience does not ordinarily distinguish between qualities of a 'field' representing objects and qualities of the objects represented. Visual experience is ordinarily naïvely realistic, in the sense that the qualities presented in it are represented as qualities of the external world. According to Peacocke, however, the aspects of visual experience in which external objects are represented have qualities—and, indeed, colour qualities—that are never attributed by that experience to the objects themselves. Peacocke thus gets the phenomenology of visual experience wrong.

Try to imagine what visual experience would be like if it conformed to Peacocke's model. The visual field would have the sensational qualities red', blue', green', and so on, and would represent various external objects; but it would not represent those qualities as belonging to those objects. Where, then, would the qualities appear to reside? What would they appear to be qualities of? They would have to float free, as if detached from the objects being represented, so as not to appear as qualities of those objects. Or perhaps they would seem to lie on top of the objects, overlaying the objects' own colours—which would be seen, remember, as different dispositional qualities. The result, in any case, would be that visual experience was not naïvely realistic, but quite the reverse. A veil of colours—like Locke's veil of ideas—would seem to stand before or lie upon the scene being viewed. But one does not continually see this veil of colours; and so visual experience must not conform to Peacocke's model.

The failure of Peacocke's model to fit the experience of colour can be seen most clearly, perhaps, in the fact that the model is a perfect fit for the experience of pain. When one pricks one's finger on a pin, pain appears in one's tactual 'field', but it is not perceived as a quality of the pin. Rather, the pin is perceived as having a disposition—namely, the disposition to cause pain, and hence to be presented in areas of the tactual field bearing the quality currently being felt. The ordinary way of describing the experience would be to say that by having an experience of pain one perceives the pin as disposed to cause pain. But this description can easily be transposed into Peacocke's notation, in which it would say that one perceives the pin as painful by perceiving it in a painful' patch.

Peacocke's theory is thus ideally suited to describing the experience of pain. Yet the experience of pain is notoriously different from the experience of colour. Indeed, the difference between pain experience and colour experience has always been accepted as an uncontroversial datum for the discussion of secondary qualities. The difference is precisely that pain is never felt as a quality of its apparent cause, whereas colour usually is: the pain caused by the pin is felt as being in the finger, whereas the pin's silvery colour is seen as being in the pin. Hence Peacocke's model, which fits pain experience so well, cannot simultaneously fit colour experience. When applied to colour, that model would suggest that the experience of seeing a rose contains both the flower's redness and the visual field's red'ness, just as the experience of being pricked by a pin contains both the pin's painfulness and the finger's pain.

One might respond that our objection to Peacocke is undermined by an example that we previously deployed against intentionalism. For we have already argued that seeing something blurrily involves a blurriness that is not attributed to what is seen. Have we not already admitted, then, that visual experience contains qualities that it does not attribute to objects, and hence that it is not always naïve?

We have indeed admitted that visual experience is not always naïve, but that admission is consistent with the claim that visual experience is naïve most of the time, or in most respects. Seeing blurrily is, after all, unusual, in that it involves seeing, as it were, 'through' a blurry image to a visibly sharp-edged object. It is an experience in which the visual field becomes more salient than usual, precisely because its blurriness is not referred to the objects seen. Peacocke's theory does manage to improve on intentionalism by explaining how one can blurrily see an object as being sharp-edged. But Peacocke goes too far, by analysing all visual experience on the model of this unusual case. He says that every perception of colour has this dual structure, in which the colours that are attributed to objects are seen through colour qualities that are not attributed to them. According to Peacocke, then, the redness of external objects is always seen through a haze of red'ness, just as the sharp edges of an object are sometimes seen through a blur.

The Projectivist Account

We have argued, first, that visual experience cannot be adequately described without reference to intrinsic sensational qualities of a visual field; and second, that intrinsic colour properties of the visual field are the properties that objects are seen as having when they look coloured. We have thus arrived at the traditional projectivist account of colour experience. The projection posited by this account has the result that the intentional content of visual experience represents external objects as possessing colour qualities that belong, in fact, only to regions of the visual field. By 'gilding or staining all natural objects with the colours borrowed from internal sentiment', as Hume puts it, the mind 'raises in a manner a new creation'.[14]

Talk of a visual field and its intrinsic qualities may seem to involve a commitment to the existence of mental particulars. But we regard the projectivist view of colour experience as potentially neutral on the metaphysics of mind. The visual field may or may not supervene on neural structures; it may or may not be describable by means of adverbs modifying mental verbs rather than by substantives denoting mental items. All we claim is that, no matter how the metaphysical underpinnings of sense experience are ultimately arranged, they must support reference to colours as qualities of a visual field that are represented as inhering in external objects.

Pros and Cons

The projectivist account of colour experience is, in our opinion, the one that occurs naturally to anyone who learns the rudimentary facts about light and vision. It seemed obvious to Galileo, as it did to Newton and Locke as well.[15]

The Principle of Charity as Applied to Visual Experience   Given the intuitive appeal that the projectivist account holds for anyone who knows about the nature of light and vision, the question arises why some philosophers go to such lengths in defence of alternative accounts. The reason, as we have suggested, is that these philosophers are moved by a perceived requirement of charity in the interpretation of representational content. External objects do not actually have the colour qualities that projectivism interprets visual experience as attributing to them. The projectivist account thus interprets visual experience as having a content that would be systematically erroneous. And it therefore strikes some as violating a basic principle of interpretation.

In our opinion, however, applying a principle of charity in this way would be questionable, for two reasons. First, a principle of charity applies primarily to a language, or other representational system, *taken as a whole*; and so, when rightly understood, such a principle is perfectly consistent with the possibility that large regions of the language should rest on widespread and systematic error. Second, what a principle of charity recommends is, not that we should avoid attributing widespread error at all costs, but that we should avoid attributing inexplicable error. And the error that a Galilean view of colour entails is not inexplicable; it can be explained precisely as an error committed through projection—that is, through the misrepresentation of qualities that inhere in the visual field as inhering in the objects that are therein represented.

We therefore think that the usual motives for resisting projectivism are misguided, on quite general grounds. Nevertheless, some philosophers have criticized projectivism for being uncharitable to visual experience in rather specific ways; and we think that these more specific charges deserve to be answered. We devote the remainder of this section to three of these criticisms.

Colours as *Visibilia* One argument in this vein comes from the dispositionalists. They contend that failing to see colours as dispositions to look coloured would entail failing to see them as essentially connected with vision, as *visibilia*.[16] But nothing can be seen as a colour without being seen as essentially connected with vision, the dispositionalists continue, and so colours cannot possibly be misrepresented in visual experience.

This version of the argument from charity relies on the assumption that the only way to see colours as essentially connected with vision is to see them as dispositions to cause visual perceptions. We reply that colours can be seen as essentially connected with vision without being seen as dispositions at all. In particular, they can be seen as essentially connected with vision if they are seen as the qualities directly presented in visual experience, arrayed on the visual field. The experience of seeing red is unmistakably an experience of a quality that could not be experienced other than visually. Consequently, red is seen as essentially visual without being seen as a disposition to cause visual perceptions.

A Berkeleyan Objection Another version of the argument from charity begins with the premiss that qualities of the visual field cannot be imagined except as being seen, and hence that they cannot be imagined as intrinsic and categorical qualities of material objects—qualities belonging to the objects in themselves, whether they are seen or not. This premiss is taken to imply that visual experience cannot possibly commit the error of representing colour *qualia* to be intrinsic and categorical qualities of objects, as projectivism charges, simply because it cannot represent the unimaginable.[17]

Our reply to this argument is that its premiss is false. The colour qualities that modify the visual field can indeed be imagined as unseen. Of course, one cannot imagine a colour as unseen while instantiated in the visual field itself, since to imagine a quality as in the visual field is to imagine that it is seen. But one can imagine a colour as instantiated elsewhere without being seen—by imagining, for example, an ordinary red-rubber ball, whose surface is red not only on the visible, near side but also on the unseen, far side.

What exponents of the present objection are pointing out, of course, is that one cannot imagine the unseen side of the ball as red by means of a mental image whose features include a red area corresponding to that side of the ball. Here they may be correct.[18] To form an image containing a coloured area corresponding to the unseen side of the ball would be to imagine seeing it, and hence not to imagine it as unseen, after all. But one's imagination is not confined to representing things by means of corresponding features in one's mental image. If it were, then one would be unable to imagine any object as being both opaque and three-dimensional; one would be reduced to imagining the world as a maze of backless façades, all artfully turned in one's direction. In actuality, one imagines the world as comprising objects in the round, whose unseen sides are represented in one's image indirectly and, so to speak, by implication. One can therefore imagine unseen colours, despite limitations on how one's imagination can represent them.

Visual experience has the same representational capacity, despite similar limitations. That is, although one cannot visually catch colours in the act of being unseen, one nevertheless sees the world as containing unseen colours—on the far sides of objects, in areas obscured by shadow, and so on. Just as one sees one's fellow human beings as having hair at the back, skin up their sleeves, and eyeballs even when they blink, so one sees them as possessing these unseen features in their usual colours. Thus, one has no trouble seeing colours as intrinsic and categorical properties that exist even when unseen.

Can Experience Commit Category Errors? A third version of the argument from charity alleges that according to projectivism visual experience commits not just a mistake but a *category* mistake, by representing external, material objects as having properties that can occur only within the mental realm.[19] Such a mistake is thought too gross for visual experience to commit.

It is not clear whether it is a necessary or merely contingent fact that external objects do not possess the sorts of property we understand colours to be; hence, it is not clear whether the mistake projectivism attributes to visual experience is categorial or merely systematic. But even if it were a category mistake, why should this necessarily be considered a difficulty for projectivism?

The assumption underlying the objection is that it is somehow extremely difficult to see how experience could commit a category mistake. But as the following remark of Wittgenstein suggests, just the opposite seems true.

Let us imagine the following: The surfaces of the things around us (stones, plants, etc.) have patches and regions with produce pain in our skin when we touch them. (Perhaps through the chemical composition of these surfaces. But we need not know that.) In this case we should speak of pain-patches just as at present we speak of red patches.[20]

In the normal experience of pain, pain is not perceived as a quality of its cause. As Wittgenstein remarks, however, this seems to be thanks only to the fact that the normal causes of pain constitute such a heterogeneous class. Were pain to be caused solely, say, by certain specific patches on the surfaces of plants, we might well experience pain as being in the plant, much as we now experience its colour. Far from being unimaginable, then, it would seem that nothing but a purely contingent fact about our experience of pain stands between us and a category mistake just like the one that projectivism portrays us as committing about colour.

Interpreting Colour Discourse

Thus far we have discussed colour concepts as they are exercised in the representational content of colour experience. Let us turn, somewhat more briefly, to the content of ordinary discourse about colour.

We assume that ordinary discourse about colour reports the contents of visual experience. The most plausible hypothesis about what someone means when he calls something red, in an everyday context, is that he is reporting what his eyes tell him. And according to our account, what his eyes tell him is that the thing has a particular visual quality, a quality that does not actually inhere in external objects but is a quality of his visual field. We therefore conclude that when someone calls something red, in an everyday context, he is asserting a falsehood. Indeed, our account of colour experience, when joined with the plausible hypothesis that colour discourse reports the contents of colours experience, yields the consequence that all statements attributing colours to external objects are false.

One would be justified in wondering how we can accept this consequence, for two related reasons. First, we will clearly want to retain a distinction between 'correct' and 'incorrect' colour judgements, distinguishing between the judgement that a fire-hydrant is blue and the judgement that it is red. And it seems a serious question what point we error theorists could see in such a distinction. Second, it seems perfectly obvious that colour discourse will continue to play an indispensable role in our everyday cognitive transactions. Yet how are we error theorists to explain this indispensability, consistently with our claim that the discourse in question is systematically false? We shall begin with the second question.

The Point of Colour-Talk   Consider one of the many harmless falsehoods that we tolerate in everyday discourse: the statement that the sun rises. When someone says that the sun rises, his remark has the same content as the visual experience that one has when watching the horizon at an appropriately early hour. That is, the sun actually looks like it is moving, and that the sun moves in this manner is what most people mean when talking about sunrise. So interpreted, of course, talk about sunrise is systematically false. When someone says that the sun rises, he is wrong; and he usually knows that he is wrong, but he says it anyway. Why?

When one understands why talk about sunrise is false, one also understands that its falsity makes no difference in everyday life. We do not mean that nothing in everyday life would, in fact, be different if the sun revolved around the earth, as it seems to. No doubt, the tides and the phases of the moon and various other phenomena would be other than they actually are. But those differences are not missed by the ordinary person, who does not know and has no reason to consider precisely how the tides and phases of the moon are generated. Consequently, someone who has a normal background of beliefs will find no evidence in everyday life to controvert his belief that the sun revolves around the earth. That belief will not mislead him about any of the phenomena he normally encounters; and it will in fact give him correct guidance about many such phenomena. His judgements about the time of day, the weather, the best placement of crops, the location of glare and of shadows at noon, will all be correct despite being derived from premises about a stationary earth and a revolving sun. Indeed, he is likely to derive more true conclusions from his belief in a revolving sun than he would from a belief in a rotating earth, for the simple reason that the consequences for earthlings of the former state of affairs are easier to visualize than those of the latter, even though those consequences would be the same, for everyday purposes. Talking about horizon-fall rather than sunrise would thus be downright misleading, even though it would be more truthful. Only an undue fascination with the truth could lead someone to reform ordinary discourse about the sun.

Talk about colours is just like talk about sunrise in these respects. That is, life goes on as if objects are coloured in the way that they appear to be. Experience refutes few if any of the conclusions derived from beliefs about objects' colours; and many true conclusions are derived from such beliefs. Most of those true conclusions, of course, are about how objects will look to various people under various circumstances. And these conclusions are extremely useful in everyday life, since one's ability to communicate with others and with one's future selves about the external world depends on the ability to describe how various parts of that world appear. The point is that such conclusions are more easily and more reliably drawn from the familiar false picture of colours than they would be—by the ordinary person, at least—from the true picture of wavelengths and spectral-reflectance curves. Why, then, should one replace such a useful false picture with a true but misleading one?

Correct vs. Incorrect Colour-Talk The case of colour differs from that of sunrise in one important respect. The sun never seems to do anything but move in a regular arc across the heavens, whereas objects often seem to have different colours in different circumstances. The ordinary speaker therefore finds himself drawing a distinction between the colours that objects really have and the colours that they only seem to have on some occasions. How can we countenance this distinction between real and illusory colours, given that our theory brands all colours as illusory?[21]

The answer is that classifying an object by the colour that it appears to have under so-called standard conditions is the most reliable and most informative way of classifying it, for the purposes of drawing useful conclusions about how the object will appear under conditions of any kind. Obviously, classifying an object by how it appears in the dark is not at all informative, since all objects appear equally black in the dark, even though they appear to have different colours in the light. Hence one can extrapolate an objects' appearance in the dark from its appearance in the light, but not vice versa. The same is true—though to a lesser degree, of course—for other non-standard conditions. For instance, distance tends to lend a similar appearance to objects that look different at close range; coloured light tends to lend a similar appearance to objects that look different in daylight; and so on. The common-sense calculus of colour addition and subtraction therefore enables one to infer an objects' appearance under non-standard conditions from its appearance under standard conditions, but not its appearance under standard conditions from that under non-standard conditions. That is why one set of conditions, and the accompanying colour-illusion, are privileged in everyday life.

There are notable exceptions to our claim about the varying informativeness of various colour appearances. But these exceptions actually support our explanation of why particular colour-illusions are privileged in ordinary discourse, because consideration of them leads the ordinary speaker to reconsider the distinction between true and illusory colour.

Some pairs of objects that appear to have the same colour in daylight—say, green—can appear to have different colours under incandescent lighting, where one may appear green and the other brown.[22] In these cases, how an object appears in daylight is not an indication of how it will appear under other less standard conditions.

Yet in these cases, one begins to wonder whether the object has a 'true' or standard colour at all. If an object's apparent colour does not vary, from one set of conditions to the next, in the same way as the apparent colour of objects that share its apparent colour in daylight, then one is tempted to say that the object does not have any one colour at all. Consider the object that looks green in daylight but brown in incandescent light, where most other objects that look green in daylight still look green. Is the object really green? really brown? Does it have any single 'real' colour at all?[23] Here intuitions diverge and ultimately give out. The reason, we think, is precisely that the common-sense notion of an object's real colour presupposes that it is the one apparent colour from which all its other apparent colours can be extrapolated, by fairly familiar rules of colour mixing. When that assumption is threatened, so is the notion of real colour.

Acknowledgments

We have benefited from discussing the material in this paper with: Sydney Shoemaker, David Hills, Larry Sklar, Mark Johnston, and participants in a seminar that we taught at the University of Michigan in the fall of 1987. Our research has been supported by Rackham Faculty Fellowships from the University of Michigan.

Notes

1. *Opere Complete di G. G.*, 15 vols, Florence, 1842, IV, p. 333 (as translated by E. A. Burtt in *The Metaphysical Foundations of Modern Science*, Doubleday, Garden City, NY, 1954, p. 85).

2. Sydney Shoemaker, 'Qualities and Qualia: What's In The Mind?' *Philosophy and Phenomenological Research* 50, 109–31.

3. One might be tempted to dissolve the conflict between the Galilean view and the charitable view of colour experience by rejecting a presupposition that they share. Both sides of the conflict assume that the properties mentioned in our descriptions of visual experience are properties that such experience represents objects as having. The only disagreement is over the question whether the colour properties that are thus attributed to objects by visual experience are properties that the objects tend to have. One might claim, however, that visual experience does not attribute properties to objects at all; and one might bolster one's claim by appeal to a theory known as adverbialism. According to adverbialism, the experience of seeing a thing as red is an event modified by some adverbial property—say, a seeing event that proceeds red-thing-ly. Not all adherents of adverbialism are committed to denying that such an experience represents an object as having a property; but adverbialism would indeed by useful to one who wished to deny it. For adverbialism would enable one to say that the phrase 'seeing a thing as red' describes a seeing event as having some adverbial property rather than as having the content that something is red. One could therefore contend that the question whether things really have the colour properties that they are seen as having is simply ill-formed, since colour properties figure in a visual experience as adverbial modifications of the experience rather than as properties attributed by the experience to an object.

Our view is that this extreme version of adverbialism does unacceptable violence to the concept of visual experience. Seeing something as red is the sort of thing that can be illusory or veridical, hence the sort of thing that has truth-conditions, and hence the sort of thing that has content. The content of this experience is that the object in question is red; and so the experience represents an object as having a property, about which we can legitimately ask whether it is a property that objects so represented really tend to have.

4. D. M. Armstrong, *A Materialist Theory of Mind*, Routledge & Kegan Paul, London, 1968; J. J. C. Smart, 'On Some Criticisms of a Physicalist Theory of Colors', in *Philosophical Aspects of the Mind-Body Problem*, ed. Chung-ying Cheng, University of Hawaii, Honolulu, 1975 [chapter 1, this volume] (as cited by Christopher Peacocke, 'Colour Concepts and Colour Experience', *Synthèse*, 1984, pp. 365–81, n. 5) [chapter 5, this volume].

5. The final clause of this biconditional is often formulated so as to specify not only standard conditions but a standard observer as well. But the observer's being standard can itself be treated as a condition of observation; and so the distinction between observer and conditions is unnecessary.

6. See John McDowell, 'Values and Secondary Qualities', in *Morality and Objectivity; a Tribute to J. L. Mackie*, ed. Ted Honderich, Routledge & Kegan Paul, London, 1985, pp. 110–29; David Wiggins, 'A Sensible Subjectivism?', in *Needs, Values, Truth*, Basil Blackwell, Oxford, 1987, pp. 185–214, p. 189; Gareth Evans, 'Things Without the Mind—A Commentary Upon Chapter Two of Strawson's *Individuals*', in *Philosophical Subjects; Essays Presented to P. F. Strawson*, ed. Zak van Straaten, Clarendon Press, Oxford, 1980, pp. 76–116, see pp. 94–100, esp. n. 30.

Wiggins and McDowell favour a similar strategy for vindicating our perceptions of other qualities such as the comic and perhaps even the good. See McDowell's Lindley Lecture, 'Projection and Truth in Ethics'.

7. Peacocke, 'Colour Concepts and Colour Experience'.

8. Perhaps the best argument for this claim is that no one who can identify the colours of external objects needs to be taught how to identify the colours of after-images. Once a person can recognize fire hydrants and maraschino cherries as red, he can identify the colour of the spots that float before his eyes after the flash-bulb has fired. He does not need to be taught a second sense of 'red' for the purpose of describing the latter experience.

9. See McGinn, *The Subjective View*, Clarendon Press, Oxford, 1983, pp. 6–8; McDowell, 'Values and Secondary Qualities', n. 6; Wiggins, 'A Sensible Subjectivism?', p. 189; Michael Smith, 'Peacocke on Red and Red'', *Synthèse*, 1986, pp. 559–76.

10. See McDowell, 'Values and Secondary Qualities', p. 112: 'What would one expect it to be like to experience something's being such as to look red, if not to experience the thing in question (in the right circumstances) as looking, precisely, red?'

11. When McDowell discusses dispositionalism about the comic, in 'Projection and Truth in Ethics', he tries to make the circularity of the theory into a virtue, by arguing that it blocks a projectivist account of humour. He says, 'The suggestion is that there is no self-contained prior fact of our subjective lives that could enter into a projective account of the relevant way of thinking'—that is, no independently specifiable subjective response that we can be described as projecting onto the world (p. 6). We would argue that the same problem afflicts, not just a projectivist account of the comical, but our very perceptions of things as comical, as McDowell interprets those perceptions.

12. *Sense and Content; Experience, Thought, and Their Relations*, Clarendon Press, Oxford, 1983, ch. 1. Other arguments are provided by Sydney Shoemaker in 'Qualities and Qualia: What's in the Mind?'.

13. Intentionalism cannot characterize the experience in question as being similar to, or representing itself as being similar to, the experience you have when you see redness as attaching to a material object. Such an experience would have a different content from the one you are now having, and so it would not be like your present experience in any respect that the intentionalist can identify. Of course, once we abandon intentionalism, we can say that your present experience and the experience of seeing a red material object are alike in their intrinsic qualities. But such qualities are denied by intentionalism.

14. David Hume, *Enquiry Concerning the Principles of Morals*, ed. L. A. Selby-Bigge, Oxford University Press, Oxford, 1975, Appendix 1. Of course, this passage is literally about the projection of value, not colour. But surely, Hume chose colour as his metaphor for value, in this context, because he regarded projectivism about colour as an intuitively natural view.

15. Isaac Newton, *Opticks*, Dover Publications, New York, 1979, Book I, part i, definition; John Locke, *An Essay Concerning Human Understanding*, ed. Peter H. Nidditch, Clarendon Press, Oxford, 1975, Book II, ch. viii. Jonathan Bennett has interpreted Locke as a dispositionalist about colour (*Locke, Berkeley, Hume; Central Themes*, Clarendon Press, Oxford, 1971, ch. IV). But the textual evidence is overwhelming that Locke believed colour experience to be guilty of an error, and a projectivist error, at that. Locke was a dispositionalist, in our opinion, only about the properties of objects that actually cause colour experience, not about the properties that such experience represents objects as having.

16. See McDowell, 'Values and Secondary Qualities', pp. 113–15.

17. See Evans, 'Things Without the Mind', pp. 99–100. Berkeley carried this argument farther, by claiming that unperceived qualities, being unimaginable, were also inconceivable and hence impossible. Berkeley's willingness to equate imagination with conception was due to his theory of ideas, which equated concepts with mental pictures.

18. We grant this point for the sake of argument; but we think that it, too, underestimates the representational powers of the imagination. For surely one can form a mental image that contains a 'cut-away' view, showing how the far side of the ball looks while implying that it is, in reality, unseen.

19. See Shoemaker, 'Qualities and Qualia: What's In The Mind?', p. 114.

20. *Philosophical Investigations*, Blackwell, Oxford, 1974, section 312. We do not necessarily claim that the use to which we should like to put this passage coincides with Wittgenstein's.

21. We should point out that a similar question will confront those who adopt a dispositionalist interpretation of colour discourse. For according to dispositionalism, the colours of objects are their dispositions to present the appearance of colour; and objects are disposed to present the appearance of different colours under different circumstances. Corresponding to every colour that an object ever appears or would appear to have, there is a disposition of the object to give that appearance under the circumstances then prevailing. Now, dispositionalism denominates only one of these innumerable dispositions as the object's real colour, and it does so by defining the object's colour to be that disposition which is manifested under conditions specified as standard. But surely, dispositionalism should have to justify its selection of dispositions—or, what amounts to the same thing, its selection of standard conditions. For if colour is nothing but a disposition to produce colour appearances, one wants to know why a particular disposition to produce colour appearances should be privileged over other such dispositions. And this is, in effect, the same question as why one colour-illusion should be privileged over other colour-illusions, given the assumption that all colours are illusory.

22. This phenomenon is called metamerism. See C. L. Hardin, *Color for Philosophers; Unweaving the Rainbow*, Hackett, Indianapolis, 1988, pp. 28, 45 ff.

23. People who spend much time considering these cases have been known to give up the notion of true colour entirely. We once asked a scientist who performs research on colour vision why people think that most opaque objects have a real colour. His answer was, 'They do? How odd.'

8 Physicalist Theories of Color

Paul A. Boghossian and J. David Velleman

The Problem of Color Realism

The dispute between realists about color and anti-realists is actually a dispute about the nature of color properties. The disputants do not disagree over what material objects are like. Rather, they disagree over whether any of the uncontroversial facts about material objects—their powers to cause visual experiences, their dispositions to reflect incident light, their atomic makeup, and so on—amount to their having colors. The disagreement is thus about which properties colors are and, in particular, whether colors are any of the properties in a particular set that is acknowledged on both sides to exhaust the properties of material objects.

In a previous paper [chapter 7] we discussed at length one attempt to identify colors with particular properties of material objects—namely, with their dispositions to cause visual experiences. Here we shall discuss a different and perhaps more influential version of realism, which says that the colors of material objects are microphysical properties of their surfaces.[1] We shall call this theory physicalism about color (physicalism, for short). In order to evaluate this theory, however, we shall first have to clarify some methodological issues. Our hope is that we can bring some further clarity to the question of color realism, whether or not we succeed in our critique of the physicalists' answer.

Metaphysics and Semantics

To say that the question of color realism is really about the nature of color properties is not yet to define the question sufficiently. One is tempted to ask, Which are the properties whose nature is at issue?

Of course, the latter question may seem like an invitation to beg the former. For in order to say which properties are at issue in the debate about the nature of colors, one would have to say which properties colors are—which would seem to require settling the debate before defining it. How, indeed, can one ever debate the nature of a property? Until one knows which property is at issue, the debate cannot get started; but as soon as one knows which property is at issue, it would seem, the debate is over.

Well, not quite. One can pick out a property by means of a contingent fact about it. And one can thereby specify the property whose nature is to be debated without preempting the debate. Such indirect specifications are what motivate questions about the nature of properties. One knows or suspects that there is a property playing a particular role, say, or occupying a particular relation, and one wants to know which property it is, given that playing the role or occupying the relation isn't the property in question.

The role in which colors command attention, of course, is their role as the properties attributed to objects by a particular aspect of visual experience. They are the properties that objects appear to have when they look colored. What philosophers want to know is whether the properties that objects thus appear to have are among the ones that they are generally agreed to have in reality.

Yet if the question is whether some agreed-upon set of properties includes the ones that objects appear to have in looking colored, then it is partly a question about the content of visual appearances. When philosophers ask whether colors are real, they are asking whether any of the properties acknowledged to be real are the ones attributed to an object by the experience of its looking colored; and so they are asking, in part, which properties are represented in that experience—which is a question of its content.

What is Looking Colored?

The foregoing attempt to define which properties are at issue in the question of color realism may seem viciously circular. For we identified colors as the properties that things appear to have when they look colored; and how can this description help to pick out the relevant properties? It specifies the properties in terms of their being represented in a particular kind of experience, but then it seems to specify the relevant kind of experience in terms of its representing those properties. Which properties objects appear to have in looking colored depends on what counts as looking colored, which would seem to depend, in turn, on which properties colors are—which is precisely what was to be defined.

This problem is not insuperable, however. The phrase "looks colored" and its determinate cousins—"looks red," "looks blue," and so forth—have a referential as well as an attributive use. That is, one learns to associate these phrases directly with visual experiences that are introspectively recognizable as similar in kind to paradigm instances. Paradigm cases of looking red fix a reference for the phrase "looks red," which then refers to all introspectively similar experiences. We can therefore speak of something's looking red and rely on the reader to know which kind of visual experience we mean, without our having to specify which property red is.[2] There is no circularity, then, in identifying red as the property attributed to objects by their looking red and, more generally, in identifying colors as the properties attributed to objects by their looking colored.[3]

Color Experience vs. Color Discourse

One might think that the references we have stipulated here are simply the references that color terms have anyway, in ordinary discourse. Surely, words like "red" and "blue" are sensory terms, designed to report what is seen. One may therefore feel entitled to presuppose that the term "red," as used in ordinary discourse, already denotes the property that things appear to have when they look red.

Yet the validity of this presupposition may depend on the answer to the question of color realism. For whether the ordinary term "red" always expresses the property that things appear to have in looking red may depend on whether that appearance is veridical or illusory. Suppose that an error theory of color experience is correct, in that the property that things appear to have when they look red is a property that they do not (and perhaps could not) have. In that case, the meaning of "red" in ordinary discourse will be subject to conflicting pressures. The term may still be used to express the property that objects are seen as having when they look red. Yet statements calling objects red in that sense will be systematically false, even if such statements tend to be made, and to garner assent, in reference to objects that have some physical property in common. In the interest of saying what's true, rather than what merely appears true, speakers may then be inclined to shade the meaning of "red" toward denoting whatever property is distinctive of red-looking objects.[4] The pressure towards speaking the truth will thus conflict with the pressure towards reporting the testimony of vision. How the meaning of "red" will fare under these conflicting pressures is hard to predict; it may even break apart, yielding two senses of the term, one to express the content of color experience and another to denote the property tracked by color attributions.

We are not here proposing or defending such an account of color language. We are merely pointing it out as a possibility and suggesting that this possibility shouldn't be excluded at the outset of inquiry about color. To assume that color terms denote the properties represented in color experience is to assume that terms used to attribute those properties to objects wouldn't come under pressure from the systematic falsity of such attributions—something that may or may not turn out to be the case but shouldn't be assumed at the outset. One should begin as an agnostic about whether color terms ordinarily denote the properties that are represented in color experience. If they are to be used in a debate about those properties, their reference to them must be explicitly stipulated.

Versions of Physicalism

If physicalism is to settle the debate over color realism, it must be formulated as a thesis about the properties at issue in that debate. When the physicalist says that colors are microphysical properties, he must mean that microphysical properties are the ones attributed to objects by their looking colored. Otherwise, his claim will not succeed in attaching the uncontroversial reality of microphysical properties to the properties whose reality is in question—that is, the properties represented in color experience. Physicalism must therefore be, in part, a thesis about which properties color experience represents.

The Naive Objection

When the physicalist thesis is so interpreted, however, it tends to elicit the following, naive objection. The microphysical properties of an object are invisible and hence cannot be what is represented when the object looks colored. One can tell an object's color just by looking at it, but one cannot tell anything about its molecular structure—nor, indeed, that it has such a structure—without the aid of instruments or experimentation. How can colors, which are visible, be microphysical properties, which are not?

Physicalists regard this objection as obviously mistaken, although different physicalists regard it as committing different mistakes. A particular physicalist's response to the objection will be conditioned by his brand of physicalism, on the one hand, and his conception of visual representation, on the other. We therefore turn our attention, in the next two sections, to these potential differences among proponents of physicalism.

Colors vs. Ways of Being Colored

The claim that red is a microphysical property can express either of two very different theses. On the one hand, the claim may state a strict identity between properties. In that case, it means that having a particular microphysical configuration is one and the same property as being red. On the other hand, the claim may mean that having this microphysical configuration is a way of being red and, in particular, the way in which things are red in actuality. In that case, the relation drawn between these properties is not identity. Rather, red is envisioned as a higher-order property—the property of having some (lower-order) property satisfying particular conditions—and the microphysical configuration is envisioned as a lower-order property satisfying those conditions, and hence as a realization or embodiment of red.

The difference between these two views is analogous to that between type-physicalism and functionalist materialism in the philosophy of mind. Physicalism says that pain is one and the same state as a configuration of excited neurons. Functionalist materialism says that pain is the higher-order state of occupying some state that plays a particular role, that this role is played in humans by a configuration of excited neurons, and hence that having excited neurons is the way in which humans have pain. Both views can be expressed by the claim that pain is a neural state, but this claim asserts a strict identity only when expressing the former view.

We shall distinguish between the corresponding views of color by referring to them as the *physical identity* view and the *physical realization* view, or *identity-physicalism* and *realization-physicalism*.[5] To repeat, only identity-physicalism says that red is one and the same property as a microphysical configuration; realization-physicalism says that the microphysical configuration is merely a way of being red.

Adherents of both identity-physicalism and realization-physicalism will dismiss the naive objection mooted above, but they will dismiss it on different grounds. A realization-physicalist can say that the naive objection confuses color properties with the properties that embody them. The ability to see which color an object instantiates is perfectly compatible, in his view, with an inability to see the particular way in which it instantiates that color. For in his view, seeing that an object is red consists in seeing that it has some property satisfying particular conditions; and seeing that an object has *some* such property need not entail seeing *which* such property it has. The invisibility of microphysical properties therefore doesn't preclude them from realizing or embodying colors.

This refutation of the naive objection is not available to the identity-physicalist, of course, since he doesn't draw any distinction between colors and their realizations. The identity-physicalist can still fend off the objection, however, by claiming that it misconstrues the use to which he puts the phrase "microphysical properties." The objection construes this phrase, he says, as articulating a mode of presentation under which colors are represented in visual experience—as expressing what colors are *seen as*—whereas the phrase is actually intended only to identify the nature of color properties. The physicalist points out that although one never sees anything as a layer of molecules—never sees anything under the characterization "layer of molecules"—one nevertheless sees things that are, in fact, layers of molecules, since that's precisely what the visible surfaces of objects are. Similarly, the physicalist argues, seeing nothing under the mode of presentation "microphysical property" doesn't prevent one from seeing things that *are* microphysical properties. And that colors *are* such properties is all that any physicalist means to say.

The Propositional Content of Visual Experience

Thus, the suggestion that physicalism requires colors to be seen under microphysical modes of presentation will be rejected by physicalists of all stripes. Some physicalists will go further, however, by denying that colors are seen under any modes of presentation at all. Whether a physicalist makes this further denial depends on his views about the propositional content of color experience.

On the one hand, a physicalist may take a fregean view of the visual representation of color. According to that view, the experience of seeing something as red has that content by virtue of the subject's relation to a proposition containing a concept, characterization, or (as we have put it) mode of presentation that is uniquely satisfied by instances of red. The property itself is not an element of the propositional content, as the fregean conceives it; rather, it is represented by an element of the content, namely, a characterization.

On the other hand, a physicalist might take a completely different view of how color is visually represented, a view that we shall call russellian. According to that view, the experience of seeing something as red has that content by virtue of the subject's relation to a proposition containing the property red—the property itself, not a conception, characterization, or presentation of it. A russellian believes that the property is introduced into the content of experience by something that directly refers to it. This item may be an introspectible, qualitative feature of visual experience, for example, or a word of mentalese tokened in some visual-experience "box." Whatever it is, it must be capable of referring to the property red directly—say, by virtue of a correlation or causal relation with it[6]—rather than by specifying it descriptively, in the sense of having a meaning uniquely satisfied by red objects.[7]

A strict russellian may believe that the mental symbol for red has no descriptive meaning at all—just a reference. A more liberal russellian may believe that it has a meaning, but that its meaning is not sufficient to specify the property red or to determine a complete proposition about redness, and hence that the content of seeing something as red must still be completed by the property itself, introduced via direct reference. The difference between these two variants of russellianism is analogous to that between two variants of the familiar causal theory about natural-kind terms. On the one hand, the word "gold" can be viewed as a name that has no descriptive meaning over and above its reference to gold (although this reference may have been fixed, of course, with the help of a description). On the other hand, "gold" can be viewed as having a descriptive meaning such as "a kind of matter," which is not sufficient to specify a particular kind of matter and must therefore be supplemented by a causally mediated relation of reference to gold. According to the latter view, "gold" and "silver" share the meaning "a kind of matter" but refer to different kinds of matter; and their contributions to the content of sentences must include not only their shared meaning but also their distinct referents. According to the corresponding view about the visual representation of color, there are mental symbols for red and orange that may contribute a shared meaning to the content of visual experiences—say, "a surface property"—while introducing different properties as their referents.

A proponent of this liberal russellianism will acknowledge that visual experience contains some characterization of colors, but his stricter colleague will not, since the strict russellian believes that red is introduced into visual content by an item possessing no descriptive meaning at all. The strict russellian will therefore deny that colors are seen under any modes of presentation. And he will consequently think of the naive objection to physicalism as doubly mistaken—not only in suggesting that he uses the phrase "microphysical property" to articulate such modes of presentation but also in suggesting that he acknowledges their existence.

Further Distinctions

The foregoing responses to the naive objection are cogent, as far as they go; but in our opinion, they don't go far enough. The physicalists have described a way in which microphysically constituted colors *aren't* represented in visual experience— namely, under microphysical characterizations—but they haven't yet told us how else such colors *are* represented. Similarly, the realization-physicalist has described what color properties are not—namely, microphysical properties—but he hasn't yet told us what colors are instead. The realization-physicalist therefore owes us an account of the higher-order properties that are identical with colors, in his view; and all of the physicalists owe us an account of how the properties with which they identify colors can be the ones represented in visual experience.

Once again, different physicalists are likely to respond differently. The distinction between fregeanism and russellianism and the distinction between the physical identity view and the physical realization view define a four-fold partition of physicalist theories. And within each cell of the partition, further variation is possible. For example, some physicalists believe that the experience of seeing something red normally has a distinctive, introspectible quality in addition to its representational content—a visual "feel," if you will—and that what the experience represents cannot be understood independently of how it feels. Others believe that a visual experience doesn't have intrinsic qualities, or that such qualities are in any case incidental to its content. Different physicalists are also motivated by different intuitions about how physically constituted colors are best identified and hence about how they are likely to be picked out in visual experience. Some identify colors as those physical properties which are common to various classes of objects; they consequently treat the perception of colors as the recognition of physical similarities and differences.[8] Others identify colors as those physical properties which cause particular visual effects, and consequently treat color perception as the recognition, via those effects, of their physical causes.[9]

These disagreements might be thought to require further subdivision of physicalist territory, into eight or even sixteen regions instead of four. But we begin to wonder, at this point, whether all of the resulting regions would be occupied by theories that were even remotely plausible. We shall therefore proceed less abstractly, by developing the latter intuitions about how to identify physically constituted colors. Each of these intuitions could in principle lead to eight different theories, as it is combined with fregeanism or russellianism, with identity theory or realization theory, and with credence or skepticism about qualia. As we have suggested, however, not all of the resulting permutations are viable. What's more, the lines of thought departing from these intuitions ultimately tend to converge. We shall therefore attempt to formulate only those accounts of color experience which are both plausible and distinct.

The First Intuition: Similarity Classes

One way of picking out an object as red is by saying that its surface shares a property with the surfaces of ripe tomatoes, British phone booths, McIntosh apples, and so on. Perhaps, then, an object can be visually represented as colored by being represented as sharing a property with certain other objects.

But do references to phone booths and tomatoes crop up in the visual representation of objects as red? Surely, people can see things as red without even having the concept of a tomato or a phone booth. Of course, this particular problem could be circumvented if each person's visual experience were conceived as characterizing red objects in terms of paradigms familiar to that person. But the resulting conception of visual experience would still be wrong, for two reasons.

First, the experience of seeing one thing as red makes no explicit allusion to other instances of the color, familiar or not. No matter how conversant one is with tomatoes, and no matter how centrally tomatoes may have figured in one's acquisition of color concepts, seeing a red fire engine doesn't appear to be an experience about tomatoes. Second, visual experience never represents objects as having their colors necessarily or trivially, whereas it would represent tomatoes (or some other objects) as necessarily and trivially red if it represented things as red by characterizing them as sharing a property with tomatoes (or with those other objects).[10]

The moral of these observations is not that an object's color isn't visually represented as a property shared with other objects; the moral is simply that if it is so represented, the other objects aren't specified individually. The possibility remains that the experience of an object as red represents it as sharing a property with objects in a set that includes tomatoes but which is specified without reference to them or to any other individual members.

Yet how can the appropriate set of objects be specified in the content of visual experience, if not in terms of its members? To suggest that it be specified in terms of a property characteristic of those members would defeat the point of the current intuition. The point of the intuition is that a color can be represented in terms of a set of objects precisely because it's the only property common to all members of the set. Specifying the set in terms of the property characteristic of its members would therefore require an antecedent capacity to represent the color—which would render specification of the set superfluous.

A Humean Proposal

Nevertheless, the intuition that an object's color is seen as a property shared with other objects can be preserved, with the help of a proposal dating back to Hume's *Treatise*.[11] Imagine that the experience of seeing an object as red has the indexical character "It's one of *that* kind," wherein the reference of "that kind" is determined by the subject's disposition, at the prompting of the experience, to group the object together with other objects. If the latter objects do constitute a kind, by virtue of possessing some common property, then the experience will have as its content that the former object belongs to that kind and hence that it possesses the characteristic property—a property that could easily be microphysical or realized microphysically.

This account of color experience is of the liberal russellian variety, since it suggests that visual content characterizes its object as belonging to a kind, but that the kind in question must be specified by direct reference rather than by a more specific characterization. Direct reference is mediated in this case by a correlation between potential classificatory behavior of a subject, on the one hand, and a microphysically constituted kind of object, on the other. As we have seen, the proposal has no fregean version, because it requires specification of a kind, and no such specification can be found in the introspectible content of color experience.

An Information-Theoretic Proposal

Here is an alternative way of preserving the first intuition. Imagine that a particular mental symbol is regularly tokened in response to visual encounters with objects of a particular kind, whose members belong to it by virtue of possessing some characteristic property. The symbol may then qualify as indicating—and thus, in a sense, as referring to—the kind with which it is correlated.[12] And tokenings of the symbol may consequently introduce its referent into the content of visual experiences, in such a way that objects are represented as members of the kind to which the symbol refers. Such an experience will naturally be described, on the one hand, as registering the similarity of its object to other members of the kind and, on the other, as attributing to its object the property characteristic of the kind. In a sense, then, the object will be seen as having a property by being visually associated with other objects that have it. A microphysical or microphysically realized property may thus be attributed to an object by way of the object's visually detected similarity to other objects.[13]

Introducing Qualia

Now suppose that the mental correlate of a color category were not some item of a subliminal mentalese but, rather, an introspectible sensation or quale. To begin with, this supposition could simply be appended to the foregoing russellian account. The visual sensation associated with the appearance of a particular object could then be treated like a numeral in a paint-by-numbers scene, assigning the object to a kind, and hence attributing to it an associated property, without characterizing the kind or property in any way. Which kind or property a particular sensation denoted would be fixed, as before, by causation or correlation.[14]

Once the mental correlate of a color category is imagined as accessible to introspection, however, the resources for a fregean theory become available. The content of a visual experience can then be imagined to invoke the accompanying sensation and hence to characterize its object under the description "having the property that is this sensation's normal or predominant cause."

Such an account of how colors are represented can be adopted by proponents of both identity- and realization-physicalism. An identity-physicalist can say that red is the property referred to within the proposed characterization—the property that tends to cause the accompanying sensation. A realization-physicalist can say that red is the higher-order property expressed by the entire characterization—the property of having a property that tends to cause the sensation. On the first reading, colors may turn out to be identical with microphysical properties; on the second, they may turn out to have microphysical realizations.

The Second Intuition: Causes of Visual Effects

At this point our development of the first intuition, that colors can be identified in terms of similarity classes, has brought us around to the second intuition, that colors can be identified in terms of their visual effects. Indeed, we have already canvassed the only plausible theories derivable from the latter intuition—namely, theories according to which colors are visually represented by, or by reference to, visual sensations that they cause.

These theories can be paraphrased as saying that colors are visually represented as the properties that normally cause objects to look colored. But such a paraphrase will make sense only if looking colored is understood to consist in giving a visual appearance that's accompanied by particular visual sensations, rather than in being visually represented as having colors. For if colors were represented as the properties that normally cause objects to be represented as having colors, the content of color experience would be viciously circular.

Now, some philosophers have denied that this circularity would be vicious. One philosopher has even claimed that it would be a virtue, in that it would account for the notorious undefinability of colors. Colors are indefinable, he says, precisely because their definitions are unavoidably circular.[15]

We think, however, that the proposed circular definition would imply that the content of color experience is vacuous. When one describes an object as having properties that would cause it to be visually represented as red, one is describing it in terms of the experiences that it is equipped to cause, and one is describing those experiences in terms of their content—namely, as experiences of seeing the thing as red. The content of one's description therefore includes, as a proper part, the content of the experiences that the thing is described as equipped to cause; and the content of one's whole description depends on that component. For this reason, the description cannot express the content of the experiences in question. If the content of seeing something as red were that the thing was equipped to cause experiences of seeing it as red, then the content of seeing something as red would include and depend upon the content of experiences of seeing it as red. The content of seeing something as red would thus include and depend upon itself; it would characterize the thing, in effect, as having a property that would cause experiences containing this very characterization; and hence it would fail to attribute any particular property to the object. Circularity in the content of color experience would render that content vacuous.[16]

Thus, the content of visually representing something as colored cannot be that the thing has whatever normally causes objects to be visually represented as colored. As we have seen, however, the content in question can still be that the thing has whatever normally causes objects to look colored, in the sense that it causes their visual appearances to be accompanied by a color sensation.

Outline of the Argument

We have now developed various proposals for ways in which visual experience might represent microphysically constituted color properties. We began with the Humean proposal that colors are directly denoted by the subject's classificatory dispositions. We then introduced an information-theoretic proposal, which says that colors are directly denoted by mental correlates, whether they be items of mentalese or introspectible qualia. We concluded with a fregean variant of the latter possibility, to the effect that colors are characterized descriptively as the properties that normally cause color sensations.

Despite the diversity of these proposals, we think that they are uniformly unsuccessful in showing that visual experience might represent microphysical or microphysically realized colors. Each of them fails to satisfy one of two fundamental requirements for an adequate theory of color vision.

First, we shall argue, a theory of color must respect the epistemology of color experience: it must be compatible with one's knowing what one knows about color properties on the basis of seeing them. The epistemological problem for physicalism is not that the microphysical nature of colors cannot be known on sight; it is rather that other things about colors are known on sight but could not be known in this way if physicalism were true.

Second, we shall argue that a theory of color must respect the phenomenology of color experience: it must be compatible with what it's like to see the world as colored. Mere reflection on what it's like to see colors does not reveal whether the properties being seen are microphysical, but it does yield various constraints on any theory of what those properties are. In particular, such reflection reveals that color experience is naive, in that it purports to acquaint us directly with properties of external objects. In our opinion, no physicalist theory can meet this phenomenological constraint while meeting those imposed by the epistemology of color as well. We consider these constraints in turn, beginning with the epistemological.

Epistemological Constraints

What do you know about colors, not as a student of physics or physiology, but simply in your capacity as a subject of visual experience? We think that you know, for example, that red and orange are properties; that they are different properties, though of the same kind—different determinants of the same determinable; that they are not as different from one another as they are from blue; and that they cannot simultaneously be instantiated in exactly the same place. Finally, you know that red and orange are properties that things visually appear to have, and you know when things appear to have them.

All but the last two items of knowledge are necessary propositions. Red and orange—that is, the properties that things appear to have in looking red and in looking orange—not only are distinct, similar determinants of the same determinable but are essentially so. A property that wasn't a determinate of the same determinable as red, or wasn't distinct from red, or wasn't similar to red—such a property simply wouldn't be orange. And vice versa.

What's more, mere reflection on color experience provides all the support that might ever be needed for all of the knowledge cited above. That is, you need only reflect on the experiences of seeing things as red and as orange in order to know that they are two distinct, incompatible, but rather similar determinates of a single determinable property; you need only reflect on particular experiences in order to tell which of these properties they represent; and there are no possible circumstances under which more evidence would be needed. We wish to remain neutral on the explanation for this phenomenon. The knowledge in question may be delivered in its entirety by introspection on the contents of the relevant experiences. Alternatively, it may require the recognition of relations among the contents of these experiences, so long as the relations are such as can be recognized *a priori*. It may even require empirical support, so long as the support required is no more than what's provided by the experiences themselves. All we claim is that the experiences of seeing red and orange provide whatever is necessary for this rudimentary knowledge about those properties.

Consider the consequences of denying that your knowledge about colors has this status. If the experiences of seeing red and orange didn't provide all of the support required for the knowledge that they're distinct but similar determinates of the same determinable, then your knowledge of these matters would be hostage to future empirical discoveries. You would have to consider the possibility of obtaining evidence that red and orange are in fact the same property or, conversely, that they aren't similar at all. And given how the references of "red" and "orange" are fixed, evidence that red and orange are the same property, for example, would amount to evidence that the property that objects appear to have in looking red is the same as the property that they appear to have in looking orange.

Does visual experience leave room for the hypothesis that things appear to have the same property in looking red as they do in looking orange? We think not. Nor does it leave room for the hypothesis that red and orange are less alike than red and blue, or that something seemingly seen as red on a particular occasion is being represented as having a property other than red. Your knowledge on these matters is such that nothing would count as evidence against it.

Meeting the Epistemological Constraints

Yet would such knowledge be possible if physicalism were true? We believe that the answer may be yes in the case of fregean realization-physicalism, but that in the case of all other versions of physicalism—that is, russellian theories and identity theories—the answer is no.

What sets the latter theories apart from fregean realization-physicalism is their implication that visual experiences like yours represent colors only as a matter of contingent fact. Under the terms of these theories, an experience internally indistinguishable from your experience of seeking something as red might fail to represent its object as having that color. The reason is that red is represented by your experience, according to these theories, only by virtue of facts incidental to the internal features of the experience.

Which facts these are depends on the physicalist's conception of visual representation. Under the terms of russellianism, they are the causal or correlational facts by virtue of which some mental item, or some behavioral disposition, introduces the microphysically constituted property red into the contents of experiences. Twin-earth examples, in the style of Putnam,[17] will readily demonstrate that the same mental item or the same classificatory behavior might have been correlated with objects of a different kind, sharing a different property—in which case, internally similar experiences would not have represented the property that, according to physicalism, is red.

Under the terms of fregeanism, the facts in virtue of which visual experience represents a microphysical property are the facts in virtue of which instances of that property uniquely satisfy the characterization by which things are visually represented as red. And these facts, too, are bound to be contingent if red is identical with a microphysical property, for reasons illuminated by the naive objection discussed above. Although the naive objection cannot defeat physicalism, it does force the fregean identity-physicalist to concede that the characterization by which things are visually represented as red does not represent what it is to be red. For as an identity-physicalist, he believes that to be red is to have a particular microphysical property, and yet the objection forces him to concede that things aren't seen under microphysical characterizations. The fregean identity-physicalist must therefore believe that things are seen as red by means of a contingent characterization—a characterization that is, in fact, uniquely satisfied by instances of the property red, but not because it represents what redness is. And twin-earth examples will once again demonstrate that such a characterization might not have been uniquely satisfied by instances of red or might have been uniquely satisfied by instances of another property. Just as a mental symbol might have tracked a different property, so the visual characterization "whatever causes this feeling" might have been satisfied by a different property; and in either case, your visual experiences wouldn't have represented red, under the terms of the corresponding theory.

Thus, fregean identity-physicalism is like russellian physicalism in implying that your experience of something's looking red might have been exactly as it is, in all respects internal to you, while failing to represent anything as red. And this consequence has the corollary that there are circumstances under which you couldn't tell, by mere reflection on the experience of something's looking red, whether it is being represented as having the property red.

The physicalist may object, at this point, that something's being contingent doesn't entail its being *a posteriori*. He will argue, more specifically, that the reference of "red" has been fixed for you by a description alluding to your visual experiences: red is, by stipulation, whatever property is attributed to objects by their looking red. That red is the property that something appears to have in looking red is therefore knowable *a priori*, even though it is contingent, just like the length of the standard meter-bar in Paris.[18]

This response misses the epistemological point. The term "red" has been stipulated as denoting the property attributed to objects by their looking red; but the phrase "looks red" has been stipulated as denoting experiences introspectively similar to some paradigm experience. The problem is that under the terms of the theories now in question, there is no introspectively recognizable kind of experience for which you can always tell by introspection whether the same property is represented in all or most experiences of that kind. These theories therefore imply, to begin with, that, for all you know by reflection on visual experience, the attempt to fix the referent of "red" as the property attributed to objects by their looking red may have failed, since there may be no property that predominantly satisfies that description. They imply furthermore that, even if there is a property represented by most instances of things' looking red, you cannot necessarily tell by reflection when a particular experience is representing that property.

This problem can best be illustrated by imaginary cases of context-switching.[19] Suppose that your environment were to change in such a way that your mental designator for red was correlated with, or your visual characterization of red was satisfied by, a new and different property that replaced the current property red wherever it occurred. At first the content of your visual experiences might remain the same, with the result that you saw objects as having a property that they no longer had. But gradually your visual designators or characterizations would come to denote the new property rather than the old. Tomatoes would therefore appear to have a new and different color property—appear to have it, that is, in the only sense in which a russellian or an identity-theorist can conceive of them as appearing to have any color at all. Yet in all respects internal to you, your experiences would remain unchanged, and so you would be unable to tell by reflection that you were no longer seeing tomatoes as having the color property that you had previously seen them as having.

Russellianism and identity-physicalism therefore entail that without investigation into the physical causes and correlates of your visual experiences, you cannot necessarily know whether tomatoes appear today to have a different color property from the one that they once appeared to have. You might know that whatever property they appear to have is likely to be the current holder of the title "red," if any property is. But you may not be able to tell when things have appeared to have that property in the past; and you may not be able to tell in the future when things appear to have it. Hence there remains a significant sense in which you don't necessarily know when things appear to be red.[20]

Indeed, these theories entail that you cannot always tell without investigation whether objects appear to have any color properties at all. For just as experiences internally indistinguishable from yours might represent different properties, so too they might simply fail to represent properties. Such a failure would occur if the characterizations applied to objects in visual experience were not satisfied, or if the corresponding mental designators were not systematically correlated with visual stimulation from objects of any particular kind.

Consider the russellian theories, which say that visual experience represents objects as colored by means of symbols or behavioral dispositions that designate microphysically constituted kinds. Reflection on such an experience wouldn't necessarily reveal whether the symbols being tokened, or the behavior being prompted, were correlated with objects sharing a common property and constituting a genuine kind. For all one could tell from having the experience, the objects associated with the symbol or behavior might be utterly miscellaneous, and so these purported designators might not indicate membership in a kind or possession of a property. Hence one would be unable to tell, when things looked red, whether there was a property that they thereby appeared to have. And if one didn't know whether things appeared to have a property in looking red, one wouldn't know whether there was such a property as red at all.

The same problem attends the fregean theory, in all but its realization-theoretic form. According to fregean identity-physicalism, as we have developed it, visual experience represents red by characterizing it as the property that normally causes a particular sensation. Yet reflection on a visual representation of this form would not necessarily reveal whether there was a property that normally caused the sensation, and so it wouldn't reveal whether the associated characterization succeeded in denoting a property.

Of course, the possibility of there being no colors represented in visual experience is only the most bizarre of many possibilities that introspection could not rule out if the present theories were true. A less bizarre possibility is that visual experience might represent only two color properties—one when things look either red, orange, or yellow, and another when they look either green, blue, or violet. The correlational or causal facts could certainly be arranged in such a way as to give these experiences one of only two contents, under the terms of russellian or identity-theoretic physicalism. These theories therefore imply that one cannot always tell without investigation whether red and orange are different colors, the same color, or no color at all.

Some Defenses and Replies

Now, physicalists sometimes admit that visual experience, as they conceive it, is compatible with the possibility that there are no colors.[21] We wonder, however, whether the full import of this concession is generally appreciated. The statement that there may be no colors sounds as if it should gladden the heart of an anti-realist, but it is in fact different from, and perhaps even incompatible with, the views that many anti-realists hold. What these anti-realists believe is that colors are properties that visual experience attributes to objects even though no objects instantiate them. What proponents of the present theories must concede, however, is that there may be no properties attributed to objects by their looking colored, and hence that there may be no such properties as colors, not even uninstantiated ones. They must allow that color experience not only may attribute properties to objects that don't have them, as the anti-realists claim, but may actually fail to attribute properties to objects at all, by failing to express any properties. If this possibility were realized, color experience would lack the representational competence required to be false, strictly speaking, whereas the falsity of color experience is what anti-realism is usually about. And in our opinion, the fact that color experience can at least be false is evident on the face of it.

A physicalist might respond that the designators and characterizations involved in color experience can be assumed to indicate some properties, since something or other is bound to be responsible for one's visual sensations, as specified in the characterizations, and something or other is bound to be correlated with the designators. But the liberal criteria of visual representation that would enable one to assume that some properties or other were being represented would simultaneously undermine one's claim to other items of knowledge about those properties.[22] For if one's experiences of things as red and as orange represented whatever properties in heaven or earth were correlated with two different designators, or responsible for two different sensations, then one would be even less able to tell by reflection whether those properties belonged to the same determinable, or required extension for their instantiation, or bore greater similarity to one another than to some third property. For all one could tell from seeing colors in the way imagined here, red might be an electrical charge, orange a degree of acidity, and blue a texture.

A physicalist might respond that if the similarities and differences among colors were conceived as relative to an observer, then they would indeed be revealed by reflection on visual experience.[23] Let the imperfect similarity between red and orange consist in the fact that they have distinct but similar effects on normal human observers, and any normal human observer will be able to detect their relation on sight.

The problem with this suggestion is that it can account only for our knowledge of contingent similarities and differences. Red and orange, as conceived by the physicalist, are properties that happen to have distinct but similar effects on human observers, but they might have had effects that were not distinct or were even less similar. Hence the similarity relation that would be accessible by reflection on visual experience, according to physicalism, is a relation that red and orange might not have had. In reality, however, reflection on the experiences of seeing red and orange tells us that if two properties didn't stand in precisely this relation, they wouldn't be the properties we're seeing.[24]

Smart's Analogy

Now, the epistemology of color similarities and differences has received considerable attention from some physicalists who are aware that their theories appear unable to account for it. Because these physicalists subscribe to russellian or identity-theoretic versions of physicalism, they are committed to the proposition that visual experience doesn't characterize objects in terms that would reveal wherein their color properties consist. The problem is that if visual experience doesn't reveal wherein colors consist, it cannot reveal wherein they are essentially alike or different. In order for visual experience to represent how being red is essentially similar or dissimilar to being orange, it would have to represent what it is to be red or to be orange—which it doesn't do, under the terms of the theories in question. These theories therefore seem unable to explain why the similarities and differences among colors can be known on sight.

Physicalists have attempted to meet this challenge by disputing its premise—namely, that visual experience would have to represent the nature of color properties in order to reveal their similarities and differences. They insist upon "the possibility of being able to report that one thing is like another, without being able to state the respect in which it is like."[25]

J. J. C. Smart once offered an analogy to illustrate this possibility. He wrote:

> If we think cybernetically about the nervous system we can envisage it as being able to respond to certain likenesses ... without being able to do more. It would be easier to build a machine which would tell us, say on a punched tape, whether or not ... objects were similar, than it would be to build a machine which would report wherein the similarities consisted.

David Armstrong quotes this passage in application to color similarities and concludes, "No epistemological problem, then."[26]

What Armstrong seems to be suggesting is that one detects the bare fact that red and orange are similar by means of a sensory mechanism that responds to their similarity and produces an awareness of it in one's mind. This similarity-detecting component of the visual sensorium is what corresponds, in Armstrong's view, to the similarity-detecting machine described by Smart.[27] Unfortunately, such a detector, though perfectly conceivable, would not yield the right sort of knowledge about color similarities. For if the similarities among colors were detected by sight, then one's knowledge of them would be defeasible, by evidence of an optical illusion or malfunction. The experience of seeing things as red and as orange would reveal that these colors looked similar, and hence that they were similar if one's eyes could be trusted; but one would have to acknowledge the possibility that their apparent similarity might be an illusion, and that they might not be similar, after all.

In reality, of course, the similarity between red and orange is known beyond question and could not turn out to be an illusion. One needs to have seen red and orange in order to know that they're similar, of course, but only because one needs to have seen them in order to know which properties they are. Once acquainted with them, one doesn't depend on visual evidence for one's knowledge of their similarity, since nothing would count as countervailing evidence.

Armstrong's Analogy

Armstrong has suggested that one's ability to perceive color similarities without perceiving their bases is analogous to the ability to perceive family resemblances:

> How can we be aware of the resemblance and the incompatibility of the colour-shades, yet be unaware of, and have to infer, the nature of the colour-properties from which these features flow? The answer, I take it, is in principle the same ... as for the cases where resemblance of particulars such as faces is observed but the respect of resemblance cannot be made out. Despite the fact that the respect in which the faces resemble one another is not identified, it can still act upon our mind, producing in us an awareness of resemblance.[28]

Now, if we follow Armstrong's instructions to interpret this analogy as comparing the perceived similarity of color properties to the perceived similarity of particular faces, then it does nothing to overcome our stated objection. Although one can often see that two faces are alike, one remains aware that the appearance of likeness may be illusory, and hence that the faces may turn out not to be alike, after all, whereas the appearance of similarity between red and orange is not subject to empirical refutation.

Yet Armstrong's analogy is open to a slightly different interpretation, which might seem to suggest a case in which knowledge of bare resemblance need not be defeasible, either. Let the similarity between colors be compared not to that between particular faces but, rather, to that between the contours that the faces appear to have, which are properties rather than particulars.[29] When the perception of family resemblance is thus interpreted as the perception of similarity between complex shapes, it no longer seems exposed to the risk of illusion. The faces may not have the shapes that they appear to have, of course, but the similarity between those shapes remains unmistakable, even though one may not be able to articulate the respects in which they're alike. Why, then, can't the similarity between perceived colors be equally unmistakable and yet equally unanalyzable?

The problem with this version of Armstrong's analogy is that one's ignorance of the respects in which perceived shapes are alike is not analogous to the ignorance that one would have of color similarities if russellian or identity-theoretic physicalism were true. Although one cannot say what's common to the contours that two faces appear to have, one sees those contours under modes of presentation that represent their nature, since shapes are spatial properties and are visually characterized in spatial terms.[30] Information about the aspects in which shapes are similar is therefore included in the introspectible content of their visual appearance. One may just be unable to isolate that information or extract it or put it into words. Under the terms of russellianism or identity-physicalism, however, one's inability to tell what colors have in common isn't due to the difficulty of processing information contained in their visual characterization; it's due to the absence of that information, since colors aren't characterized in terms that represent their nature.

The difference between these cases is like that between purely referential concepts, which have no sense, and concepts whose sense is difficult to explicate. If one has the concept of gold without being able to say what gold is, the reason may be that having the concept consists in nothing more than standing in the right causal relation to the appropriate objects. But if one has the concept of compassion without being able to say what compassion is, the reason is probably that one's concept has a *de dicto* content that one cannot immediately explicate. Thus, reflection on one's concepts of compassion and pity may not reveal how compassion and pity are alike, any more than reflection on concepts will reveal the relation between gold and silver—but not for the same reason. In the case of gold and silver, the reason will be that one's concepts simply don't reflect the basis of similarity; in the case of compassion and pity, it will be that a relation reflected in one's concepts isn't easy to articulate.

This difference is manifested by differences in one's authority about proposed accounts of the relevant objects or similarities. If someone proposes an account of what gold is, or how it is like silver, one cannot confirm his account simply by consulting one's concepts. But if someone proposes an account of what compassion is, or how it is like pity, reflection on one's concepts may indeed suffice to reveal whether he's right, even if it wouldn't have enabled one to formulate the account on one's own.

To judge by this test, the visual representation of shape is like a concept that's difficult to explicate, since one can indeed confirm an account of the resemblance between two faces by reflecting on how they look. There is thus good reason to believe that one's knowledge of family resemblance depends on visual information of a sort that is not contained in the appearance of colors, as understood by russellian or identity-theoretic physicalism. One does see the respects in which two faces are alike, although one may be unable to isolate or describe them, whereas the versions of physicalism under discussion imply that the respects of similarity between colors are utterly invisible. Hence one's ability to be certain about family resemblances is no indication that one could be equally certain about color resemblances if these versions of physicalism were true.

Explaining the Epistemological Intuitions Away

We believe that the foregoing epistemological objections rule out any theory that portrays visual experience as representing colors contingently—that is, without characterization that denote them necessarily. They thereby rule out russellian versions of physicalism and fregean identity-physicalism as well.

Although such theories cannot respect ordinary intuitions about the epistemology of color, some of them can attempt to explain those intuitions away. In particular, any physicalist who acknowledges the existence of distinctive color sensations, or qualia, can argue that we have mistaken introspective knowledge about those sensations for knowledge about the color properties that they help to represent. What the ordinary observer knows by reflection, this physicalist may claim, is not that there are distinct but similar properties that red-looking and orange-looking objects appear to have but, rather, that there are distinct but similar sensations that accompany these appearances. According to this response, we have displaced—indeed, projected—these items of knowledge from their true objects, which are color qualia, onto color properties.

But can the physicalist extend this explanation to our most fundamental knowledge claim, that color experience can be known on reflection to represent properties? He can try. For he can say that we have mistaken the introspectible presence of color qualia in visual experience for an introspectible *re*presentation of color properties. Because reflection on visual experience does reveal that things look colored in the sense that their visual appearances are accompanied by color sensations, the physicalist may argue, we have mistaken it as revealing that they look colored in the sense of being represented as having color properties.

But why would we commit this mistake in the case of color, when we have no tendency to commit it in the cases of other, equally vivid sensations? One isn't tempted to think that sensations of pain, for example, attribute any properties to the objects that cause them. Reflection on the experience of being pricked by a pin doesn't yield the conviction that the pin is being represented as having a pain-property. Why, then, should reflection on an experience accompanied by a color sensation yield the conviction that its object is being represented as colored?

Here again the physicalist may think that he has an explanation. For as Wittgenstein pointed out, sensations of pain, unlike sensations of red, are not regularly received from particular objects or surfaces; if they were, "we should speak of pain-patches just as at present we speak of red patches."[31] Perhaps, then, we believe that visual experience attributes color properties to objects because we've observed the regularity with which color sensations are associated with the perception of particular surfaces. According to this explanation, the knowledge that we have claimed to possess on the basis of mere reflection is in fact derived from observed patterns and correlations within visual experience.[32]

Unfortunately, the patterns and correlations cited here would provide no grounds whatsoever for believing that visual experience attributed color properties to objects in the ways required by russellian or identity-theoretic physicalism. From the fact that particular objects are individually associated in visual experience with a particular sensation, no conclusion can be drawn about whether the sensation has any normal or predominant cause, and hence about whether there is an external property that it can help to represent. Various objects regularly occasion sensations of red, but those objects are so various that they may not have any surface properties in common, for all one can tell from visual experience. Hence their observed association with one and the same quale provides no grounds for thinking that the quale has any informational potential.

What's more, the association of color sensations with particular objects is no more regular or reliable than that of pain with particular kinds of events. After all, pain serves its monitory function only because young children can learn that it regularly accompanies bumps, scrapes, punctures, encounters with extreme heat or cold, and so forth. Having obvious external correlates is essential to the evolutionary purpose of pain. If what led us to view a sensation as the representation of something external were its observed correlation with various external stimuli, we would have no more occasion to take this view of color than of pain.

Thus, the point of Wittgenstein's remark about pain patches cannot be that pain appears to have no representational content because it has no apparent external correlates. What, then, is the point? Surely, it's that sensations like pain (and color) involve qualities that we can easily think of as located in the external world, but that this thought is blocked, in the case of pain, by there being no particular places where it seems to be located. The external correlates of pain aren't places, and so pain isn't subject to the sort of displacement that the mind practices on other sensations.

Thus, what the association of sensations with particular surfaces produces, and what Wittgenstein was suggesting that it would produce even in the case of pain, is a tendency to perceive the sensations as located on those surfaces—an inducement, in short, to the projective error. But the result of this error is precisely that the qualia themselves, rather than microphysical properties, are attributed to objects in visual experience. Thus, if the patterns cited by the physicalist have their most likely result, they result in the falsity of physicalism as an account of the properties that visual experience represents.

The physicalist explanation of our basic epistemological intuition is therefore unstable. The physicalist wishes to claim that visual experience does not project sensations onto external objects, as their perceived properties, but that reflection on visual experience does project our knowledge about sensations onto objects, as knowledge about their perceived properties. What is cited as accounting for the latter projection doesn't really account for it, however, and would in fact account for the former projection instead.

Fregean, Realization-Theoretic Theories

Russellian and identity-theoretic versions of physicalism fail to cope with the epistemology of color because they must portray visual experience as representing color without a characterization that denotes it necessarily. Such visual representations would denote properties only contingently, and would therefore fail to provide the appropriate introspective knowledge of the properties denoted.

This problem does not affect fregean, realization-theoretic theories. A realization-physicalist can concede, in response to the naive objection, that red objects aren't visually characterized in microphysical terms, and yet hold a version of fregeanism according to which they are characterized in terms that express what it is to be red; for he doesn't believe that to be red is to have a microphysical property. His theory of visual representation may then enable him to account for the epistemology of color experience. For if visual experience represented red by means of a characterization that represented what it is to be red, then introspection on the content of such an experience would leave no doubt whether there was such a property, introspection on experiences containing the same characterization would leave no doubt whether they represented the same property, and introspection on experiences containing characterizations of various colors would reveal the relations of similarity among them—all because the introspectible content of each experience would reveal what it is to have the property therein represented.

We therefore turn to a consideration of fregean, realization-theoretic versions of physicalism. One such theory was already introduced, in our initial survey of physicalist theories. Before returning to that theory, however, we shall briefly introduce a new proposal, which is motivated by epistemological arguments of the sort considered above. This proposal has little intuitive appeal of its own; indeed, it would hardly have been intelligible before our epistemological arguments against the other proposals had been aired. As a response to those arguments, however, it has some apparent plausibility.

A New Proposal

The new proposal is an attempt to kill two birds with one stone.[33] It purports to explain at a stroke how colors are visually represented and how their similarities and differences are known. The explanation is that colors are visually characterized precisely as those properties which bear the appropriate similarities and differences to one another.

How could all of the similarities and differences among colors be included in their visual characterization? Here is how.

Let a *pigmentation* be any property of extended things that stands with its co-determinates in relations of similarity and difference representable by a spheroid space in which distance around the circumference, distance from the ends, and distance from the interior correspond to differences in three different respects (to be called, for our purposes, hue, lightness, and saturation). Then let coordinates be defined so that any determinate pigmentation can be labelled by three numbers specifying its longitude, latitude, and depth in the property space. The description "pigmentation xyz" will then have as its condition of satisfaction the presence of a determinate whose relation to its co-determinates corresponds to position xyz in a property space of this structure.

Now suppose that visual experience characterized surfaces as having pigmentations, specified by their coordinates in pigmentation-space.[34] Under the terms of fregeanism, such experiences would represent the surfaces as having some appropriately related determinates of some appropriately structured determinable. Under the terms of realization-physicalism, colors would be the second-order properties expressed by such characterizations—that is, the properties of having appropriately related determinates of an appropriately structured determinable.

We believe that this version of the proposal can account for all of the knowledge claimed in our epistemological intuitions. Reflection on the visual characterization of objects as having pigmentations xyz and qrs would yield the appropriate knowledge about the higher-order properties that the objects were thereby seen as having. That is, it would reveal that the experience represented its objects as having genuine, co-determinate properties, properties identical to those represented by internally similar experiences and differing from one another in degrees proportionate to $x-q$, $y-r$, and $z-s$. One would therefore know when one was seeing things as red or orange, and one would be able to tell their similarities and differences.

Unfortunately, this remedy for earlier epistemological problems only creates new ones. Once all of the requisite information has been encoded into the proposed visual characterization of colors, the resulting proposal—in any version—credits the subject of that experience with too much knowledge rather than too little. For it implies that the characterization of any one color encompasses that color's relations to all of the others, by locating it in a fully conceived color space. If color experience conformed to this proposal, the difference between red and orange would not only be evident from the experiences of seeing red and orange; it would be evident from the experience of seeing red alone, since that experience, by representing red as located in a property space of a particular shape, would already intimate the locations of co-determinate properties. The characterization of something as having a property located at longitude x, latitude y, and depth z in a space of co-determinate properties would already suggest the location of properties to the north or south, properties to the east or west, and properties above or below. Yet the experience of seeing something as red does not by itself reveal that the property now in view has a yellower neighbor (orange) and a bluer neighbor (violet), nor that it has more or less bright and more or less saturated neighbors, either. The current proposal has the unfortunate consequence that to see one color is, in a sense, to see them all.[35] The current proposal thus continues to get the epistemology of color wrong.

The Initial Fregean, Realization-Theoretic Proposal

We therefore return to the initial candidate for a fregean, realization-theoretic version of physicalism. This was the theory that objects are visually characterized as having properties that normally cause color sensations, and that colors are the higher-order properties expressed by these characterizations.[36]

The content that this theory assigns to visual experience, say, of red would be introspectively recognizable as representing a genuine property; for even if there is no property that's predominantly responsible for sensations of red, the property of having such a property is undoubtedly genuine. Furthermore, any internally similar experience would be introspectively recognizable as representing the same (higher-order) property, by virtue of containing the same characterization. And color properties, so defined, would stand in relations of similarity and difference generated by similarities and differences among the associated sensations. If one visual sensation differed from another in various respects, then the properties of being equipped to cause those sensations would differ isomorphically, by differing as to the sensations caused. Reflection on how it feels to see things as red and as orange would therefore be sufficient to reveal similarities and differences among those colors.

This fregean, realization-theoretic version of physicalism can therefore account for our knowledge of colors. Unfortunately, it does so at the expense of misrepresenting the *phenomenology* of color experience.

The present theory implies that the content of visual experience alludes to color qualia as properties distinct from the perceived colors of objects.[37] In order for one to see an object as having the property that causes visual experiences with a particular feel, one's experience would have to represent that feel as well as the property causing it. And one's experience would then lack the naiveté characteristic of vision.

Visual experience is naive in the sense that it doesn't distinguish between the perceived properties of objects and the properties of perceptions. Whereas the experience of pain, for example, distinguishes between an external cause (a pin's sharpness) and its sensory effect (a finger's pain), visual experience does not distinguish between color as it is in the object and as it feels to the eye: one feels sharp points as causing pains but one doesn't see colored surfaces as causing visual feels. The normal experience of seeing an object as red no more alludes to a sensation as distinct from the object's redness than it does to tomatoes or fire engines.

Thus, the only version of physicalism that gets the epistemology of color experience right gets the phenomenology wrong. In our opinion, any version of physicalism that acknowledges color *qualia* will commit the same phenomenological error, since it will imply that visual experience always has introspectible color qualities over and above the color properties that it attributes to objects. But this general thesis need not be defended here, since the only version of the second proposal that has survived our epistemological arguments is the fregean, realization-theoretic version, which portrays visual experience not only as having introspectible qualities but also as alluding to them in its representational content. This version of the proposal implies that visual experience not only involves color sensations but is also about those sensations, in addition to color properties—which is clearly mistaken.

Conclusion

We do not pretend to have proved that any physicalist theory of color must be inadequate, since we have not canvassed every possible theory. We think of our arguments as posing a challenge to any aspiring physicalist. We challenge the physicalist to explain how the physical properties that constitute colors, in his view, are represented in visual experience, and to explain it in a way that meets reasonable epistemological and phenomenological constraints.

One might think that the constraints that we have applied cannot be met by any theory of color, and hence that they must be unreasonable. The solution to the problems we have raised, one might conclude, is not to reject physicalism but rather to relax our epistemological and phenomenological constraints. In our view, however, there is a theory that satisfies these constraints, and it is one of the oldest and most familiar. It is the theory that colors are qualitative properties of visual experiences that are mistakenly projected onto material objects. A defense of that theory must be deferred, however, to another occasion.

Acknowledgements

For comments on earlier drafts of this paper, we are grateful to David Armstrong, C. L. Hardin, David Hills, Sydney Shoemaker, and Steve Yablo.

Notes

1. Our earlier paper contained a brief discussion of this theory [chapter 7, pp. 82–3]. The present paper can be regarded as expanding on that passage.

2. These remarks are intended to apply exclusively to expressions of the form "looks colored." Expressions of the form "seeing something as colored," "appearing to be colored," and so forth, will be interpreted compositionally.

Note that the problem discussed in this passage doesn't preclude "looks red" from *meaning* "visually appears to be red," in the sense of contributing that content to the statements in which it is used. If the kind of experience denoted by "looks red" is the kind that represents its object as red, then the phrase may indeed be used to introduce the content "visually appears to be red." The problem discussed here merely restricts the way in which the phrase may acquire its reference to that kind of experience. (See note 16, below.)

3. Here a further complication arises. We assume in the text that there is a single property represented by all or most instances of looking red. There will certainly be such a property if the way in which experiences qualify as instances of something's looking red is by representing the same property as the paradigm instance. In that case, the paradigm of something's looking red will define a kind of experience whose instances attribute the same property to their objects, and so all instances of looking red will represent the same property. The name "red" can then be fixed by the phrase "the property attributed to an object by its looking red."

But what if kinds of visual appearance are individuated differently? In that case, the kind of appearance defined by a paradigm case of something's looking red may include appearances representing different properties; and so there may be no property represented in most instances of looking red. Our attempt to attach the name "red" to the property attributed to an object by its looking red will consequently fail, since there will be no single property predominantly satisfying that description.

Physicalists who regard this outcome as a live possibility sometimes think that the reference of "red" cannot be fixed to a single property; and so they make a definition out of the description that we have treated as a reference-fixer. That is, they treat "red" as synonymous with the phrase "the property attributed to an object by its looking red," and they expect the term, so defined, to denote different properties in different circumstances. (See Frank Jackson and Robert Pargetter, "An Objectivist's Guide to Subjectivism About Colour," *Revue Internationale de Philosophie* 160 (1987), pp. 127–141, [chapter 6, this volume].)

These philosophers may find our usage strange, as we do theirs. But our linguistic differences with them will not prevent us from engaging them in argument. For they believe that red is a microphysical property in some circumstances, in the sense that a microphysical property is the one attributed to an object, in those circumstances, by its looking red. And we shall argue that an object's looking red never represents it as having a microphysical property, under any circumstances at all. Our arguments will therefore address their view, though not necessarily in their terms.

For a related problem, see the following note.

4. Some may contend that if there is a physical property that's distinctive of red-looking objects, then it will inevitably be the property that's attributed to objects by their looking red. But this contention simply assumes that the content of color experience is determined in a way that's conducive to the truth of physicalism about color—which should not be assumed from the outset. We shall consider at length whether the content of color experience is determined in this way. At the moment we are merely pointing out that until one has ascertained how colors are visually represented, one must allow for the possibility that their visual representation may have a content that is less useful for people to put into words that other facts correlated with color perception. One must therefore allow for the possibility that the content of color talk may diverge from that of color experience.

Some may argue that even if color experiences somehow represented properties other than external properties correlated with them, they would *also* represent those external properties, by virtue of the correlation. In that case, color experiences would attribute two different properties to their objects, and our identification of colors as the properties attributed to objects by color experiences would be ambiguous. (We owe this suggestion to Sydney Shoemaker.)

What is being imagined here—if it is indeed imaginable—is that visual experiences representing one property would be correlated with another property and would thereby come to indicate it, much as a Cretan's saying "It's raining" may come to indicate sunshine. If visual experiences representing one property could thus come to indicate another, the former property would still be identifiable as the one that they represented *in the first instance* (just as rain would be identifiable as what the Cretan was reporting in the first instance). Our identification of colors as the properties attributed to objects by their looking colored could therefore be easily disambiguated.

5. Note that in our terminology, identity-physicalism entails that colors have their microphysical natures necessarily. For in our terminology, the thesis "red = microphysical property x" is an identity statement whose arguments are rigid designators of properties.

As we explained in note 3, some physicalists treat "red" as synonymous with a non-rigid property description. These physicalists can therefore treat the thesis "red = microphysical property x" as a contingent truth.

6. For correlational theories of reference, see F. Dretske, *Knowledge and the Flow of Information* (Cambridge, Mass.: The MIT Press, 1981); D. Stampe, "Towards a Causal Theory of Linguistic Representation," *Midwest Studies in Philosophy* 2 (1977). We have reservations of a general nature about the prospects for correlational semantics, but we shall suspend these reservations for present purposes.

7. For a russellian view of how colors are visually represented, see Armstrong, in D. M. Armstrong and Norman Malcolm, *Consciousness and Causality: A Debate on the Nature of Mind* (Oxford, England: Basil Blackwell, 1984), p. 172: "A perception of something green will involve a green-sensitive element, that is to say, something which, in a normal environment, is characteristically brought into existence by green things, and which in turn permits the perceiver, if he should so desire, to discriminate by his behaviour the objects from things which are not green."

See also Jackson and Pargetter, "An Objectivist's Guide to Subjectivism About Colour," [pp. 68–9, this volume]:

> What is it for an experience to be the presentation of a property? How must experience E be related to property P, or an instance of P, for E to be the presentation of P, or, equivalently, for E to represent that P? One thing ... is immediately clear. A necessary condition is that there be a causal connection. Sensations of heat are the way heat, that is, molecular kinetic energy, presents itself to us. And this is, in part, a matter of kinetic energy *causing* sensations of heat. We say 'in part', because, for instance, the causation must be in the 'right way'.... For present purposes, however, the causal part of the story is enough. We can work with the rough schema: redness is the property of objects which causes objects to look red....

8. See J. J. C. Smart, "On Some Criticisms of a Physicalist Theory of Colors," in *Philosophical Aspects of the Mind-Body Problem*, ed. Chung-ying Cheng (Honolulu, Hawaii, University Press of Hawaii, 1975), pp. 54–63 [chapter 1, this volume]; D. M. Armstrong, "Smart and the Secondary Qualities," in *Metaphysics and Morality: Essays in Honour of J. J. C. Smart*, ed. Philip Pettit, Richard Sylvan, and Jean Norman (Oxford, England: Basil Blackwell, 1987), pp. 1–15 [chapter 3, this volume].

9. See Jackson and Pargetter, "An Objectivist's Guide to Subjectivism About Colour" [chapter 6, this volume]. This view also appears in Shoemaker, "Qualities and Qualia: What's In the Mind?" *Philosophy and Phenomenological Research* (1990), 50, suppl., pp. 109–131.

10. The only way to circumvent this problem would be to suppose that the redness of everything but tomatoes is seen as a surface similarity to tomatoes, whereas the redness of tomatoes is seen as a similarity to fire engines. Yet this supposition would imply that the redness of tomatoes looks different from that of other objects—which is false.

11. *A Treatise of Human Nature*, I.i.vii. This proposal may also be what Armstrong has in mind in some parts of *A Materialist Theory of the Mind* (London, England: Routledge and Kegan Paul, 1968), Chapter Twelve.

12. A full correlational theory would identify the referent of a mental item not with its actual causes or correlates but, rather, with the causes or correlates that it would have under counterfactual ideal circumstances. Different theories propose different sets of ideal circumstances, but these differences needn't concern us here. We shall gloss over these issues by saying simply that under such a theory, a mental item refers to its normal or predominant cause.

13. This account of how colors are visually represented follows the strict russellian line, in that it credits the mental symbol for a color with no meaning beyond a correlationally determined reference. There is some room here for liberalization. The mental symbol for red may have a very general sense, such as "a kind of object," and the visual representation of something as red may therefore characterize it, literally,

as of a kind. Which kind is being represented, however, will still be determined by the symbol's reference, since this account, like the preceding one, offers no resources for a descriptive characterization of the kind.

14. An identity-theoretic version of this account would say that color sensations denote microphysical properties. A realization-theoretic version would say that they denote higher-order properties that have microphysical realizations.

We do not wish to rule out either of these possibilities entirely. However, one realization-theoretic version of the current proposal can be excluded in advance. This version would be the russellian counterpart of a fregean theory that we shall introduce below. The fregean theory says that visual experience characterizes each color as the higher-order property of having some property that tends to cause a particular color sensation. The russellian counterpart of this theory would say that each color sensation is appropriately correlated with, and hence refers to, the higher-order property of having a property that tends to cause it.

The problem with the latter theory is that it would utterly trivialize the correlational semantics on which russellianism depends. Almost every property is correlated with the higher-order property of there being a property that tends to cause it. A semantics that allowed such a correlation to ground a relation of reference would be unable to draw a distinction between what has a reference and what doesn't.

15. John McDowell, "Values and Secondary Qualities," in *Morality and Objectivity: A Tribute to J. L. Mackie*, ed. Ted Honderich (London, England: Routledge and Kegan Paul, 1985), pp. 110–129.

16. We develop this argument at length in "Colour as a Secondary Quality," [pp. 86–90, this volume].

Note that the circularity at issue here is significantly different from the circularity at issue in our earlier discussion of the expression "looks red." There we were concerned with a circularity that could result from the structure of this expression. Identifying red in terms of things' looking red will be circular, we argued, if "looks red" gets its reference by logical composition, in a way that depends on the reference of "red." Here we are concerned with a circularity in the content of a visual representation, irrespective of which symbols bear that content or how they are structured. We argue that if the content of representing something as red is that the thing has the property that causes objects to be represented as red, then that content will be embedded in itself. The former circularity can easily be resolved, since "looks red" can be restructured as a unitary expression referring directly to a kind of experience. The latter circularity cannot be resolved by any restructuring of symbols. (See note 2.)

17. Hilary Putnam, "The Meaning of 'Meaning'," in *Mind, Language, and Reality* (Cambridge, England: Cambridge University Press, 1975); see also Tyler Burge, "Individualism and the Mental," in *Studies in Metaphysics*, ed. P. French, T. Uehling, and H. Wettstein (Minneapolis, Minn.: University of Minnesota Press, 1979).

18. See Saul Kripke, *Naming and Necessity* (Cambridge, Mass.: Harvard University Press, 1980), pp. 54ff.

Of course, those who define "red" as synonymous with "the property attributed to an object by its looking red" will think that it is not only necessary but analytic that red is the property something appears to have when it looks red. They will therefore claim that their view is compatible with your ability to tell that something appears to be red, since things necessarily appear to be red whenever they look red, and a thing's looking red is (by stipulation) an introspectively recognizable kind of experience.

True enough. But what these philosophers describe as the ability to tell that something appears to be red is less than meets the ear. It's the ability to tell that whatever property the thing appears to have is to be called red on this occasion. It's not the ability to tell when something appears to have that property.

Our claim that you can tell when something appears to be red means that there is a property, red, such that you can tell when something appears to have it. And this claim cannot be accommodated by these linguistic maneuvers.

19. Context-switching and its relevance to self-knowledge is discussed at greater length in Paul A. Boghossian, "Content and Self-Knowledge," *Philosophical Topics* (1989), pp. 5–26.

20. This problem is especially acute for the Humean proposal, according to which objects are represented as colored by being characterized as "one of *those*," where the reference of "those" is determined by the subject's classificatory dispositions. Not only would one be unable to tell by introspection whether the property characteristic of a particular set of objects was the same as it was previously; one would also be unable to tell whether an object was being assigned to the same set of objects as it was previously. In order

to tell whether the set to which tomatoes were visually assigned today was the same as the one to which they were assigned yesterday, one would have to investigate precisely which other objects one was disposed to include in that set on each occasion. Mere introspection would therefore fall even further short of revealing whether tomatoes appear to have the same color that they once appeared to have.

21. See, for example, Armstrong, *A Materialist Theory of the Mind*, p. 289.

22. Such liberal criteria are also unlikely to yield a plausible theory of representation. But as we said in note 6, we are ignoring such general problems in correlational semantics.

23. We owe this suggestion to Sydney Shoemaker.

24. Here, as elsewhere, a physicalist may reply that our sense of having introspective knowledge can be explained away. We shall consider this objection below.

25. These words are from J. J. C. Smart's "Sensations and Brain Processes." They are quoted in application to color by D. M. Armstrong in "Smart and the Secondary Qualities," [p. 44, this volume].

26. "Smart and the Secondary Qualities," [p. 44, this volume].

27. See Armstrong's *A Theory of Universals*, vol. 2 (Cambridge, England: Cambridge University Press, 1978), p. 127: "[W]hy should not the colour-properties act on our mind (or, rather, why should not states of affairs involving these properties act on our mind), producing awareness of resemblance and incompatibility, but not producing awareness of those features of the properties from which the resemblance and incompatibility flow?"

28. *A Theory of Universals*, vol. 2, p. 127, See also *A Materialist Theory of the Mind*, pp. 275–276.

29. Armstrong himself sometimes suggests that shapes rather than individuals are the relevant analogue. See *Consciousness and Causality*, pp. 178–179.

30. One might well have reservations about whether the spatial terms in which shapes are visually characterized fully capture their spatial nature. But such reservations tend to undermine Armstrong's claim that similarities of shape are evident on sight. In assuming that shapes are visually represented in terms that reveal their nature, we are simply taking Armstrong's view of the matter.

31. *Philosophical Investigations* (Oxford, England: Basil Blackwell, 1974), p. 312.

32. This suggestion, too, is due to Sydney Shoemaker.

33. The following remarks of Armstrong's sound like the theory developed in this section:

> The vital point to grasp here, I think, is that, with an exception or two to be noticed, our *concepts* of the individual secondary qualities are quite empty. Consider the colour red. The concept of red does not yield any necessary connection between redness and the surface of ripe Jonathan apples or any other sort of object. It does not yield any necessary connection between redness and any sort of discriminatory behaviour, or capacity for discriminatory behaviour, in us or in other creatures. It does not yield any necessary connection between redness and the way that the presence of redness is detected (eyes, etc.) in us or in other creatures. Finally, and most importantly, it does not yield any necessary connection between red objects and any sort of perceptual experience, such as looking red to normal perceivers in normal viewing conditions.
>
> There may be a conceptual connection between redness and extendedness.... There is certainly a conceptual connection between redness and the other colours: the complex resemblances and differences that the colours have to each other. But these conceptual connections do not enable us to break out of the circle of the colours ("Smart and the Secondary Qualities," [pp. 42–3, this volume]).

However, the rest of Armstrong's work makes clear that he does not subscribe to the theory developed here. In *A Theory of Universals*, vol. 2, he attributes such a theory to R. W. Church (pp. 108–111).

34. The use of numerical coordinates is not essential to this conception of color experience. Visual experience can be conceived as locating colors in the property space directly, without the use of coordinates; or it can be conceived as locating them in a network of similarity relations, without the use of any spatial analogy at all.

35. A proponent of this theory may reply that the complete conception of color space may be acquired gradually, as the subject of visual experience encounters new colors. But this reply isn't to the point, because our objection is not especially about the acquisition of color concepts. What refutes the present theory of color representation is not just that someone who has never seen orange cannot derive the concept of it from seeing red. It's also that someone who has seen both red and orange still does not have experiences of either color that, by themselves, would ground knowledge about the other.

What's more, the most plausible account of how a naive subject might discover color space is not compatible with the proposal under consideration. For according to the proposal, either one already sees colors in terms of their locations in a space of co-determinates—in which case the appearance of one color already alludes to the others—or one doesn't yet see colors in terms of their locations in color space—in which case, their appearances furnish no grounds for drawing the similarities and differences constitutive of such a space. One colored surface will appear to differ from another along three dimensions, according to the proposal, only if each surface is already seen under characterizations specifying three coordinates for its pigmentation. Hence the proposal doesn't allow for the possibility of *discovering* the dimensions of color space *on the basis of* what is seen in color experience. If one doesn't already see colors under characterizations locating them in such a space, then one sees nothing on the basis of which locations could be assigned to them.

36. Whether one regards realization-physicalism as equivalent to dispositionalism will depend on one's views on the relation between dispositions and their bases. For a dispositionalist theory of color that may be equivalent to realization-physicalism, see Christopher Peacocke, "Colour Concepts and Colour Experience," *Synthèse* 58 (1984), pp. 365–381 [chapter 5, this volume].

37. The following argument is developed more fully in "Colour as a Secondary Quality," [pp. 93–4, this volume].

9 How to Speak of the Colors

Mark Johnston

It seems to me that the philosophy of color is one of those genial areas of inquiry in which the main competing positions are each in their own way perfectly true.

For example, as between those who say that the external world is colored and those who say that the external world is not colored, the judicious choice is to agree with both. *Ever so inclusively speaking* the external world is not colored. *More or less inclusively speaking* the external world is colored.

What is it to speak *ever so inclusively* about the colors? There are many beliefs about color to which we are susceptible, beliefs resulting from our visual experience and our tendency to take that visual experience in certain ways. Some of these beliefs are "core" beliefs in this sense: were such beliefs to turn out not to be true we would then have trouble saying what they were false of, i.e., we would be deprived of a subject matter rather than having our views changed about a given subject matter. Contrast the more "peripheral" beliefs; as they change, we are simply changing our mind about a stable subject matter. However, what some call the lack of any sharp analytic/synthetic distinction means that there typically are many legitimate ways of drawing the core/periphery distinction. Let's say that we speak *more inclusively* about color as we underwrite more beliefs with some legitimate title to be included in the core. Then, speaking of color *ever so inclusively* is employing a conception of color which underwrites any belief included in the core on some one or other legitimate way of drawing the core/periphery distinction.

When the most inclusive way of talking about some phenomenon is either internally inconsistent or at odds with discovered facts, the question of elimination or revision of the talk arises. But when the question arises, the real issue is how inclusively we have to speak. In the case of color the interesting question is not "Is the external world colored?" but rather "How far short of speaking ever so inclusively do we have to fall in order to say truly that the external world is colored?"[1]

These remarks about the concept of color are quite general. Corresponding remarks apply to many if not all concepts. Color can in many ways function as an illustrative case of the systematic reasons which favor conceptual revision over elimination, reasons made more prominent and probative by the vagueness of the analytic/synthetic distinction.

Color Concepts as Cluster Concepts

Why does the external world fail to be colored ever so inclusively speaking?

Taking canary yellow as an example, beliefs with a legitimate title to be included in a core of beliefs about canary yellow include:

(1) *Paradigms*. Some of what we take to be paradigms of canary yellow things (e.g. some canaries) are canary yellow.

(2) *Explanation*. The fact of a surface or volume or radiant source being canary yellow sometimes causally explains our visual experience as of canary yellow things.

(3) *Unity*. Thanks to its nature and the nature of the other determinate shades, canary yellow, like the other shades, has its own unique place in the network of similarity, difference and exclusion relations exhibited by the whole family of shades. (Think of the relations exemplified along the axes of hue, saturation and brightness in the so-called color solid. The color solid captures central facts about the colors, e.g. that canary yellow is not as similar to the shades of blue as they are similar among themselves, i.e. that canary yellow is not a shade of blue.)

(4) *Perceptual Availability*. Justified belief about the canary yellowness of external things is available simply on the basis of visual perception. That is, if external things are canary yellow we are justified in believing this just on the basis of visual perception and the beliefs which typically inform it. (Further philosophical explication of this belief would come to something like this: if you are looking at a material object under what you take to be adequate conditions for perceiving its color and you take yourself to be an adequate perceiver of color then your visually acquired belief that the material object is canary yellow is justified simply on the strength of (i) the information available in the relevant visual experience and (ii) those general background beliefs about the external causes of visual experience which inform ordinary perception.)

(5) *Revelation*. The intrinsic nature of canary yellow is fully revealed by a standard visual experience as of a canary yellow thing.

Canary yellow is of course only an example. For each color property F, beliefs legitimately included in the core of beliefs concerning F will include the relevant instances of Paradigms, Explanation, Unity, Availability and Revelation.

The hardest of these beliefs to explicate is Revelation. Partly because of this, it is a quite controversial occupant of any core of beliefs about color. The content of Revelation was captured by Bertrand Russell in *The Problems of Philosophy* in these terms: "the particular shade of colour that I am seeing ... may have many things to be said about it.... But such statements, though they make me know truths about the colour, do not make me know the colour itself better than I did before: so far as concerns knowledge of the colour itself, as opposed to knowledge of truths about it, I know the colour perfectly and completely when I see it and no further knowledge of it itself is even theoretically possible."[2] Russell's view here is that one naturally does take and should take one's visual experience as of, e.g. a canary yellow surface, as completely revealing the intrinsic nature of canary yellow, so that canary yellow is counted as having just those intrinsic and essential features which are evident in an experience as of canary yellow. Hence, canary yellow is a simple non-relational property pervading surfaces, volumes and light sources. It is just this idea that visual experience is transparently revelatory which Descartes denied when he wrote of our visual sensations as arbitrary signs of the properties that cause them, employing the analogy of the sensations which a blind man receives of texture as a result of using a cane "to see".[3] Most recently, David Hilbert has stigmatized something very like Revelation as "'the fallacy of total information," suggesting that it is a philosopher's imposition on common sense.[4]

Other contemporaries take a different, more Russellian, view. There are those who think that no family of properties whose natures are not wholly revealed in visual experience could deserve the name of the colors. Thus, for example, Galen Strawson, in a vivid and tantalizing paper, writes "color words are words for properties which are of such a kind that their whole and essential nature as properties can be and is fully revealed in sensory-quality experience given only the qualitative character that that experience has."[5] Strawson's claim is not only a lucid statement of Revelation, but also in effect a denial that there is any negotiating with Revelation when it comes to speaking of the colors. You must either completely endorse Revelation or cease to speak of the colors.[6]

What follows is for those who find the positions of both Hilbert and Strawson unsatisfying. Our visual experience is the occasion of our making a cognitive error, the error of taking features of our experience to transparently reveal the nature of certain external features, so that, as against Hilbert, we are ordinarily inclined to feel the pull of Revelation. Nonetheless, as against Strawson, properties which satisfy Paradigms, Explanation, Unity and Availability could still deserve the names of the colors even if their natures were not fully revealed by sight.[7]

Before we consider such a compromise, why should we admit that the external world is not colored ever so inclusively speaking? Well, given what we know from the psychophysics of perception it follows that Revelation and Explanation cannot be true together. For when it comes to the external explanatory causes of our color experiences, psychophysics has narrowed down the options. Those causes are either non-dispositional microphysical properties, light-dispositions (reflectance or Edwin Land's designator dispositions[8] or something of that sort) or psychological dispositions (dispositions to appear colored) with microphysical or light-dispositional bases. Explanation therefore tells us that we must look among these properties if we are to find the colors. Revelation tells us that the natures of the colors are, in Gregory Harding's useful idiom, *laid bare* in visual experience.[9] The nature of canary yellow is supposed to be fully revealed by visual experience so that once one has seen canary yellow there is no more to know about the way canary yellow is. Further investigation and experience simply tells us what further things have the property and how that property might be contingently related to other properties.

However, the natures of the non-dispositional microphysical properties and the surface reflectance properties in play in visual perception are not revealed or laid bare by our visual experience. It is not even evident in visual experience that such properties are implicated in its production. In any case, visual experience certainly leaves us with a lot more to know about the nature of both the categorical microphysical properties of surfaces and the reflectance properties of surfaces. So those properties do not satisfy Revelation. Hence, ever so inclusively speaking, no such property can be the property canary yellow. Mutatis mutandis for the other colors.

The remaining surface property which is a standard explanatory cause of visual experience as of canary yellow things, and hence the remaining candidate to be canary yellow, is the disposition to look canary yellow. Now the nature of a disposition to look a certain way *may* be revealed by a visual experience if that experience is appropriately construed. For when it comes to the disposition of objects to produce a certain experience, it is plausible to hold that if one has an experience of the kind in question, *and takes that experience to be a manifestation of the disposition in question*, one thereby knows the complete intrinsic nature of the property which is the disposition. Consider this example: twenty five years ago I felt nausea when I tasted a juicy apricot during a rough sea-crossing. I had the experience of nausea and I took it to be a manifestation of the power or disposition of juicy apricots to produce nausea in me during rough sea-crossings. What more was there to know about this dispositional property? Only certain extrinsic matters, matters concerning not the nature of the dispositional property of being nauseating for me on rough seas but rather its relations to other things. I did not know which things in general had the property, nor did I know the property's relations to other properties such as the chemical and biological properties responsible for the nauseating effect of juicy apricots on a susceptible subject. But so far as knowing the *intrinsic* nature of the dispositional property, i.e. knowing that property in the sense relevant to Revelation, experiencing nausea and taking it to be a manifestation of the disposition sufficed. When a disposition is a disposition to produce a certain subjective response then a subjective response of the kind in question may indeed reveal the nature of the disposition so long as the subject takes his response to be the manifestation of that disposition. So the disposition to look canary yellow can be revealed by sensory experience if that sensory experience is appropriately construed.

That is, although we can immediately show that the colors-as-Revelation-represents-them-as-being are neither categorical microphysical properties nor light-dispositional properties on the grounds that we had more (in fact almost everything) to understand about what these properties were like even after having encountered the colors, the same point cannot be decisive against identifying the colors-as-Revelation-represents-them-as-being with dispositions to look colored.

The decisive consideration is rather that *steady* colors, as opposed say to highlights, do not appear to be relational properties and hence do not appear to be dispositions to look colored.

A basic phenomenological fact is that we see most of the colors of external things as "steady" features of those things, in the sense of features which do not alter as the light alters and as the observer changes position. (This is sometimes called "color constancy".) A course of experience as of the steady colors is a course of experience as of light-independent and observer-independent properties, properties simply made evident to appropriately placed perceivers by adequate lighting. Contrast the highlights: a course of experience as of the highlights reveals their relational nature. They change as the observer changes position relative to the light source. They darken markedly as the light source darkens. With sufficiently dim light they disappear while the ordinary colors remain. They wear their light- and observer-dependent natures on their face. Thus there is some truth in the oft-made suggestion that (steady) colors don't look like dispositions; to which the natural reply is "Just how would they have to look if they were to look like dispositions?"; to which the correct response is that they would have to look like colored highlights or better, like shifting, unsteady colors, e.g. the swirling evanescent colors that one sees on the back of compact discs.

But if this is a good way of making the point that colors don't look like dispositions then it cannot be right to follow Paul Boghossian and David Velleman, and conclude that the external world is not colored because colors do not look like relations and so do not look like dispositions.[10] For some colors do look like relations. Within our visual experience there is a phenomenal distinction between steady and shimmering color appearances, and the latter appear as relational qualities in just this sense: a course of experience of such qualities reveals their dependence on the perceiver's position and the light source.[11] Given that the relational nature of the "unsteady" colors is apparent in visual experience, it is hard to motivate the claim that *they* look non-dispositional.

Nor is a version of the Bohossian-Velleman thesis restricted to the steady colors very appealing. The restricted thesis would be that nothing in the external world is colored except the backs of compact discs, highlighted spots, holographically colored patches on credit cards, and a few other odd exceptions. These very qualifications weaken the phenomenologically based denial that the external world is colored, for they count some overt dispositions as colors of external things. We should then want to know why the covert dispositions, dispositions to look steadily colored, do not also count as colors.

Even so, Boghossian and Velleman seem to me completely right to emphasize the disparity between *steady* colors-as-they-naively-seem-to-be and colors conceived of as dispositions. A property cannot appear as a disposition unless it appears as being a relation of the bearer of the disposition to the manifestation of the disposition and the circumstances of manifestation. Given that, Revelation is at odds with taking the steady colors to be dispositions. We have already concluded that Revelation is at odds with taking the colors to be either non-dispositional microphysical surface properties or light-dispositional surface properties: such properties can't have their natures laid fully bare to us in visual experience.

Barring a bizarre pre-established harmony of redundant causes of our visual experience, a harmony in which the colors-as-Revelation-represents-them are extra causes of our visual experience on top of the causes that psychophysics recognizes, it follows that the colors-as-Revelation-represents-them-as-being are not among the external causes of our visual experience. That is, assuming both Revelation and what we know from psychophysics, it follows that Explanation is violated. So, ever so inclusively speaking, the external world is not colored (or at least not steadily colored.)

It would however be an instance of the characteristic fallacy of many Eliminativists in many areas of philosophy to draw the conclusion that the external world is not really (steadily) colored.

For we are not bound to speak ever so inclusively. Speaking ever so inclusively can seem like speaking strictly and so can seem demanded by philosophical seriousness. But it turns out to be just speaking under the aegis of one among several conceptions of color; indeed, the most belief-laden and incautious of these conceptions. Such is the shadow cast across Eliminativist projects by the vagueness of the analytic/synthetic distinction.

Any serious philosopher tempted by Eliminativism or Irrealism about color (more generally, about Xs) must consider this question: how far short of speaking ever so inclusively must we fall in order to say truly that the world is colored (or includes Xs)? The prospects of various accounts of color *more or less* inclusively speaking, accounts which abandon or weaken Revelation, need investigating.[12] The investigation begins at a familiar conceptual juncture.

Are Color Concepts Primary or Secondary?

As between those who say that the world is colored because colors are primary qualities and those who say that the world is colored because colors are secondary qualities the judicious choice is first to agree with neither, then to agree with both and finally to agree with the friends of the secondary qualities.

Agreeing with neither might be a way of registering the fact that there is a salient, "intuitively based" conception of color which they both fail to underwrite, namely the conception of the colors-as-Revelation-represents-them-as-being. But it might also be a way of highlighting the fact that the very distinction between primary and secondary qualities has itself the dubious distinction of being better understood in extension rather than intension. Most of us can generate two lists under the two headings, but the principles by which the lists are generated are controversial, even obscure. Of course, on one well-known criterion, secondary qualities are supposed to be dispositions to produce a sensory response. Yet, even if we adhere to the dispositional criterion we still lack an adequate understanding of what dispositions are and what their exact relations to their bases might be. As we shall presently see, this means that we lack precisely the understanding which would allow us to appreciate what would *count* as an argument for taking canary yellow either to be a disposition to look canary yellow or to be the microphysical or light-dispositional basis of such a disposition.

One way to show that would be to show that a full-dress account of dispositions invalidates most of the standard arguments against the dispositional or secondary quality theory of color. Fortunately, even the first steps in an account of dispositions—all that can be given here—suffice to show that *many* of the popular arguments against dispositional theories of color are better taken as arguments against an over simplified conception of dispositions.

Let us say that the concept of the property F is a concept of a dispositional property just in case there is an a priori property identity of the form

(6) The property F = the T disposition to produce R in S under C.

A T disposition is some specified type of disposition, e.g. an invariable disposition, a probabilistic disposition, or a standardly mediated disposition (more on these later). R is the manifestation of the disposition; S is the locus of the manifestation and C is the condition of manifestation.

Let us then say that the concept of the property F is a response-dispositional concept when something of the form of (6) is a priori and (a) the manifestation R is some response of subjects which essentially and intrinsically involves some mental process (responses like sweating and digesting are therefore excluded), (b) the locus S of manifestation is some subject or group of subjects, (c) the conditions of manifestation are some specified conditions under which the specified subjects can respond in the specified manner. Moreover, we shall require (d) that the relevant a priori identity does not hold simply on a trivializing "whatever it takes" specification of either R or S or C, e.g. "the F-detecting response, whatever that is" or "the F-detecting subjects, whoever they are" or "the F-detecting conditions, whatever they are". In a manner of speaking these would not be specifications at all since in offering them one would not be evidencing any real knowledge of *who* the subjects or *what* the responses or conditions of response are.

According to one well-known criterion secondary quality concepts are response-dispositional concepts of *sensible* qualities.[13] Primary quality concepts are categorical concepts of sensible qualities. We may follow Locke and further distinguish concepts of Tertiary qualities, i.e., concepts of dispositions to produce effects other than subjective responses, e.g. dispositions to reflect light.

Hence, someone who alleges that it is a priori that

(7) the property red = the standardly realized disposition to look red to standard perceivers under standard conditions

is claiming that the concept of red is a response-dispositional concept of a sensible quality, i.e., a secondary quality concept. But the following are also secondary quality accounts, if the identities are understood as true a priori:

(8) The property of being red = the disposition to look red to standard perceivers as they actually are under standard conditions as they actually are.

(9) The property red for subjects S_i under conditions C_i = the disposition to look red to the S_is under conditions C_i.

Talk of response-dispositions immediately provides useful consequences. As (8) indicates, it is not an objection to all secondary quality accounts of color concepts to observe that in a possible world in which the standard perceivers saw things differently in the standard conditions of the world, the colors of things need not be different from what they actually are. (8) allows just that. As (9) indicates, it is not an objection to all secondary quality accounts of color concepts to observe that for many or all of the things we take to be colored there are no standard perceivers or standard viewing conditions, so that the best we can do is talk about the color relative to this kind of perceiver or that kind of viewing condition. (9) allows just that.

Furthermore, the explicit focus on dispositions as opposed to mere counterfactual conditionals serves to show that many of the other sorts of arguments which have led philosophers to abandon the secondary quality account of color concepts do not in fact succeed. We can now see why they are better taken as arguments against an all too simple account of dispositions.

Case 1. There might have been a ray emitted from the center of green objects, a ray which acted directly on our visual cortices so that green objects always would look red to us in any viewing situations. But this would not be enough to make them green.

Case 2. There might have been a shy but powerfully intuitive chameleon which in the dark was green but also would intuit when it was about to be put in a viewing condition and would instantaneously blush bright red as a result. So although in the dark the chameleon is green it is not true of it in the dark that were it to be viewed it would look green. It would look bright red. (Although this seems like a bizarre case from the philosopher's wax museum, it turns out that we have something rather like shy chameleons in our eyes! For consider rhodopsin, the photoreactive chemical in the rods on the surface of our retinas. Before it is hit by enough photons to trigger electrical impulses in the rods, rhodopsin is crimson. Photons bleach rhodopsin so that it first becomes yellow and then transparent. But since the rods function as a backup system to the retinal cones to enable us to see under very poor lighting conditions, any good viewing condition is probably a condition in which the rods are firing as a result of their constituent rhodopsin having undergone a photochemical change with its resultant color change. How do we know that rhodopsin is crimson in the near dark? Well, we can in fact view it under very poor light, i.e. insufficient light to produce the photochemical change. So rhodopsin is not utterly "shy" in the manner of the chameleon.)

Case 3. Consider a transparent object whose surface is green but never looks and almost never would look surface green because the object's interior *radiates* orange light at such an intensity that the greenness is masked or obscured. It is nonetheless surface green even though it would never look so, as is shown by the fact that it *reflects* just the same kind of light that some other surface green things reflect.

These sorts of cases would constitute good objections if a secondary quality account had to assert things like

(10) It is a priori that x is red for S_i in C_i iff x would look red to S_i's under C_i.

However, to assume that is to assume that something having a disposition to produce R in S under C is equivalent to the holding of the corresponding dispositional conditional: if the thing were to be in C it would produce R in S. That this is not so, that the relation between the holding of a disposition and the holding of its corresponding dispositional conditional is more complex, is shown by cases which precisely parallel those just discussed.

Case 1* Mimicking. A gold chalice is not fragile but an angel has taken a dislike to it because its garishness borders on sacrilege and so has decided to shatter it when it is dropped. Even though the gold chalice would shatter when dropped, this does not make it fragile because while this dispositional conditional is not bare, i.e. the breaking when struck has a causal explanation, something *extrinsic* to the chalice is the cause of the breaking. Mutatis mutandis for the ray-bedeviled green surface. Even though the surface would look red if viewed, this does not make the surface itself disposed to look red.[14] For while this conditional is not bare, i.e. the surface's looking red when viewed has a causal explanation, something extrinsic to the surface is the cause of its looking red.

Case 2* Altering. The glass cup is fragile but an angel has decided to make the cup shatterproof if it begins to fall to the ground or if it is about to be hit by a hammer, or enter any other condition of being struck. Even though the conditional corresponding to fragility does not hold, i.e. the cup would not break if struck, the cup was fragile before the angel did its work. Were it not for the extrinsic activities of the angel prior to the cup being struck then the cup would have broken when struck. Mutatis mutandis for the shy but intuitive chameleon. In the dark, there is an extrinsic property of the chameleon's skin, i.e. the property of being the skin of a chameleon with a shy and intuitive psychology, which leads the chameleon's skin to change color before it goes into a viewing condition. Were it not for these extrinsic features, if the chameleon's skin were to be viewed then it would look green.

Case 3* Masking. Consider a fragile glass cup with internal packing to stabilize it against hard knocks. Packing companies know that the breaking of fragile glass cups involves three stages: first a few bonds break, then the cup deforms and then many bonds break, thereby shattering the cup. They find a support which when placed inside the glass cup prevents deformation so that the glass would not break when struck. Even though the cup would not break if struck the cup is still fragile. The cup's fragility is masked by the packing which is a) something extrinsic to the glass cup and b) causes the glass cup when struck to withstand deformation without breaking. Were it not for such an extrinsic masker the cup would break when struck. Mutatis mutandis for the green thing which intensely radiates orange from its interior. Were it not for the masking properties extrinsic to the surface, if the surface were to be viewed then it would look surface green.

In order to say when something has the disposition to R in S under C let us first provide a general characterization of mimicking, altering and masking.

In the mimicking of x's disposition to R in S under C, something extrinsic to x and the circumstances C is the cause of the manifestation R. This includes the case of veridical mimicking, where e.g., x has the disposition to break when struck but a deranged guardian angel has decided to break x when struck in a way that is independent of its fragility.

In the case of altering with respect to the disposition to R in S under C, there are intrinsic changes in x before[15] x goes into the circumstances of manifestation C such that these changes are or include a cause of x's R-ing, and if x had not changed intrinsically in such ways then x would not have R-ed.

In the masking of x's disposition to R in S under C, something extrinsic to x and the circumstances C is a cause of a manifestation inconsistent with the manifestation R.

We are now able to present one (inevitably somewhat stipulative) notion of a disposition. A thing x has the disposition to R in S under C iff one or other of the following cases hold—

The (Possibly Vacuous) Case of the Bare Disposition

x would R in S under C and no intrinsic feature of x or of anything else is the cause of x's R-ing in S. (Because bare dispositions by definition lack a constituting basis there seems little to be made of the idea of a bare disposition being masked, altered or mimicked.)

The Case of the Constituted Disposition

There are intrinsic features of x which masking, altering and mimicking aside, would cause R in S under C. These intrinsic features of x are the "constituting basis" of x's disposition to R in S. *We may therefore think of a constituted disposition as a higher-order property of having some intrinsic properties which, oddities aside, would cause the manifestation of the disposition in the circumstances of manifestation.*[16]

The dispositional thesis which many find in Locke,[17] may now be understood as the thesis that color concepts, like the concepts of the various sounds, tastes and smells, are concepts of *constituted* response-dispositions. In so far as Locke believed that redness was a power or disposition he did not believe that redness was a bare power or disposition but rather, in our terms, a constituted disposition.

Explanation

Clarifying the Secondary/Primary distinction as a restriction of the dispositional/categorical distinction and recognizing some complexity in our concept of a disposition implies that the difference between Secondary and Primary accounts of color concepts must really be quite subtle. The Secondary account treats canary yellow as a constituted disposition to appear canary yellow, i.e. as the higher-order property of having some (lower-order) intrinsic properties which, oddities aside, would cause the appearance as of a canary yellow thing. The Primary account treats canary yellow as a disjunction of such lower-order intrinsic properties, or at least ends up doing this once it assimilates the fact that the standard causes of the appearances of canary yellow are surprisingly disparate.[18]

Frank Jackson and Robert Pargetter suggest that when it comes to Explanation, i.e., counting a thing's having the property canary yellow as an explanatory cause of its appearing canary yellow, Primary Quality accounts do better because the Primary Qualities are more basic explainers of the canary yellow appearances than the dispositions are.[19] On their view, if dispositions are explainers at all, then they are explainers at one remove and by courtesy; as it were on the back of the explanatory role of the underlying, categorical Primary Qualities.

Given the present account of dispositions and the point that any Primary Quality account will have to make do with identifying canary yellow with a disjunction of those disparate properties responsible for (standard, veridical) appearances as of canary yellow things, there is no room for an invidious distinction when it comes to Explanation. Primary and Secondary Quality accounts of color are on all fours with respect to Explanation.

For consider Zinka the canary and a lifelike color photograph of her. The canary yellow appearance produced when one looks at Zinka is due to a physical property very different from the physical property responsible for the canary yellow appearance of the relevant part of the photograph. Call the relevant physical properties P1 and P2 respectively. The fact that Zinka's feathers have P1 explains the canary yellow appearance that occurs when one looks at Zinka. But P1 is not canary yellowness according to the Primary Quality Account. On that account, canary yellowness is what canary yellow things have in common and so is a disjunctive property which includes as disjuncts P1, P2 and so on. That disjunctive property is a property which standardly explains the occurrences of appearances as of canary yellow things. So we may also explain the appearance one has when one looks at Zinka in terms of Zinka's having the disjunctive property. However this appeal to the disjunctive property is as much an explanation at one remove from P1, an explanation by courtesy, as the explanation that the canary yellow appearance of Zinka is due to the property of having some property, in Zinka's case P1, which, oddities aside, causes the manifestation of the disposition to appear canary yellow. We get from P1 to the Primary Quality of canary yellow by moving, as it were, sideways to the disjunction. We get from P1 to the Secondary Quality of canary yellow by moving, as it were, upwards to the disposition, i.e., to the higher-order property of having some property which, oddities aside, would cause the appropriate visual experience in the appropriate viewing condition.

Hence the theoretical mood which prompts the remark that as between those who say that the external world is colored because colors are Primary Qualities and those who say that the external world is colored because colors are Secondary Qualities the judicious choice is to agree with both. Having understood better what constituted dispositions are, considerable subtlety is required to discern any advantage had by one theory and not the other. Is canary yellow a disposition constituted by different properties in different cases or simply a disjunction of these different properties? As a result of so clarifying the issue one might well have the feeling that here, as elsewhere, a vigorous dispute is simply fed by indeterminacy, i.e., that there is no fact of the matter between the disputants, so that the disputed positions simply represent roughly equally good styles of argumentative bookkeeping.

Contrary to such metaphilosophical ennui, there is really nothing intrinsically wrong with considerable subtlety. And indeed, with just a little subtlety, we can discern a significant weakness in the Primary Quality account of the colors, a weakness that ultimately turns on the fact that the account implies that vision does not acquaint us with the colors but only gives us knowledge of the colors by description.

Unity and Availability

Recall the requirement of Unity. The family of similarity and difference principles holding among the colors includes the principle that canary yellow is not a shade of blue, i.e. that canary yellow is not as similar to the blues as they are among themselves.[20] The Primary Quality account of color has it that the shade canary yellow is the non-dispositional (and probably disjunctive) property which standardly explains the canary yellow appearances. Mutatis mutandis for the various shades of blue. Suppose that color science ends up discovering this: the non-dispositional property which standardly explains the canary yellow appearances and the various non-dispositional properties which standardly explain the various appearances of the shades of blue are not, when taken together, as similar among themselves as are the various non-dispositional properties which standardly explain the various appearances of the shades of blue. On the simplest version of the Primary Quality account, this would be the discovery that canary yellow is not a shade of blue, i.e., not to be counted among the blues.[21]

But is it really a matter of scientific discovery that canary yellow is not a shade of blue? No: such similarity and difference principles surely have a different status. We take ourselves to know these principles just on the basis of visual experience and ordinary grasp of color language. No one had to wait until the end of the second millennium A.D. to find out whether or not canary yellow is a shade of blue.

That, of course, is just a first move against the Primary Quality account. The friend of the account should be allowed to answer that indeed it is not a matter of scientific discovery that canary yellow is not a shade of blue. Rather, he might say, such a principle, along with other unity principles, must be held true as a condition on any family of properties deserving the color names. So the principle that canary yellow is not a shade of blue turns out to be relatively a priori after all. More exactly what is a priori is a biconditional: P deserves the name "canary yellow" just in case (i) P is the categorical surface property standardly responsible for the appearances as of canary yellow things and (ii) this property stands in the right similarity relations to other standardly explanatory categorical properties.

On the envisaged account, a given property turns out to count as canary yellow only if a complex similarity condition on that property and a host of others is discovered to hold. For example, the candidate properties to be the blues have to show a natural or genuine similarity among themselves, a similarity which they do not share with the candidate to be canary yellow.

Suppose color science discovers this condition holds along with the other unity conditions which the Primary Quality theorist regards as central. Then some (complex, disjunctive) physical properties turn out to be canary yellowness, teal, turquoise, sky blue and so on. And particular things turn out to have these properties. But what then gives one the right to say that there are canary yellow things is not simply visual perception and the very general background beliefs which inform visual perception, but also and crucially, recherche facts from color science. That is, on this version of the Primary Quality account one is not justified in believing that some things are canary yellow unless one knows that color science finds that among the causes of our experiences of color are physical properties which stand in certain complex similarity and difference relations. For this is a central precondition which this version of the account lays down on any property characterized in color science turning out to be canary yellowness, and hence on particular things turning out to be canary yellow. The unwelcome consequence is that the colors are not perceptually available.

The conclusion for which we are aiming is this: when the Primary Quality account is adjusted to accommodate Unity, it violates Availability, i.e., it will follow that the colors of things are not perceptually available. Given the adjusted account, we are not justified simply on the basis of visual perception and the background beliefs which characteristically inform perception in believing that Zinka is canary yellow. For we are evidently not justified simply on this basis in supposing that the non-dispositional surface causes of our visual experiences exhibit the relevant similarities and differences.

However, to successfully argue that on the present version of the Primary Quality account the colors of things are not perceptually available we must engage with a complication familiar to epistemologists. This is the idea that by a convenient "failure of deductive closure" we could still be perceptually justified in believing that there is a property, canary yellow, had by Zinka even though we are not perceptually justified in believing that any property satisfies the similarity condition for being the property canary yellow. Whatever the general merits of the idea that one need not be justified in believing all the deductive consequences of what one is justified in believing, the idea of failure of deductive closure has its limits, and it can be shown that the conclusion for which we are aiming cannot be plausibly evaded by an appeal to a convenient failure of deductive closure. For on the present version of the Primary Quality account, the requirement that a host of microphysical similarity and difference relations hold is not just a collateral consequence of there being colors in general and canary yellow in particular. Instead, the present account has it that the claim that there are colors is conceptually equivalent to the claim that the categorical surface properties standardly causally responsible for our experiences as of colored things exhibit the required similarities and differences.

The relevance of this last point may be brought out in the following way. Imagine a sophisticate who took the alleged conceptual equivalence to heart and found himself therefore hesitating in concluding just on the basis of the way Zinka the canary looks that Zinka is canary yellow. "Zinka certainly looks the way something would have to look to count as canary yellow" he thinks "but we must wait and see if color science discovers the similarities and differences required for there to be such a property as canary yellow." Given his lucid understanding of the Primary Quality concept of canary yellow the sophisticate would not be justified in concluding just on the strength of perception that there is such a property as canary yellow. Hence he is not justified just on the strength of perception in taking Zinka or anything else to be canary yellow. Yet on the present account the sophisticate has the correct understanding of the concept canary yellow. So we in our turn can hardly be justified in concluding just by looking that Zinka (or anything else) is canary yellow. For we gain no global advantage with respect to justification by failing to be conceptually lucid. Thus the Primary Quality account is at odds with Availability.

To be sure, there are well-known cases in which more *empirical* knowledge would put one at a comparative disadvantage with respect to empirical justification—cases

in which one "knows more by knowing less"—and we can invent conceptual analogues of such cases.[22] However such cases never show the kind of *global* disadvantage with respect to justification from which our sophisticate suffers. If conceptual
lucidity is not enough in itself to produce a global epistemic disadvantage and the
Primary Quality account is true, then we can be no more perceptually justified in
believing that things are canary yellow than is the conceptual sophisticate apprised
of the Primary Quality account. Conclusion: on the Primary Quality account the
colors of things are not perceptually available. The upshot is that in trying to secure
the right status for the unity principles, and so avoid allowing that canary yellow
might turn out to be a shade of blue, the Primary Quality account ends up violating
Availability.[23]

Does the Secondary Quality account fare any better? First, does it secure the right
status for the unity principles, allowing for example that we can know just on the
basis of perception and ordinary understanding of the color terms that canary yellow
is not a shade of blue?

The problem may be reduced to its simplest form: take teal and turquoise. They
are similar color properties. Indeed they are essentially and intrinsically similar. That
is to say teal and turquoise exhibit a kind of similarity that is not a similarity in the
other properties to which they are related, nor a mere similarity in their causes and
effects, nor a similarity in the properties upon which they supervene. Rather, the
similarity between teal and turquoise with which we are concerned is to be found in
any possible situation no matter how their instances, effects or contingent relations
with other properties (including lawlike relations) vary. This is what I mean to focus
upon by saying that teal and turquoise are essentially and intrinsically similar. Suppose one could spell out the nature of teal and the nature of turquoise, i.e., the
higher-order features these properties have in any possible situation. Then that specification of features would list some common features of teal and turquoise. That is
the way in which teal and turquoise are similar. They are not similar simply in virtue
of being (even nomically) related to similar consequences or similar bases. They are
similar in virtue of what they essentially and intrinsically are.

If teal and turquoise were categorical microphysical properties then any essential
and intrinsic similarity between them would have to be a similarity in some higher-
order microphysical respect. What we know simply on the basis of perception is not
sufficient to know that there is such a similarity.

However, if teal is essentially the disposition to manifest a certain appearance Te
and turquoise is essentially the disposition to manifest the appearance Tq then teal
and turquoise will be essentially and intrinsically similar if these two manifestations
are similar. *That these dispositions have similar manifestations is a fact available to us*

in visual perception. For it is evident in visual perception that the appearance Te is similar to the appearance Tq. That these manifestations are more similar to each other than either is to the manifestation of the disposition canary yellow is also a fact available to us in visual perception. By a simple extension of these considerations, the fact that canary yellow is not a shade of blue, i.e., the fact that canary yellow is not as similar to the blues as the blues are among themselves, is guaranteed by the claim that these properties are dispositions and by the evident fact that the appearance of canary yellow is not as similar to the appearances of the blues as those appearances are among themselves.

Notice that the different status of color similarities on the Primary and Secondary Quality accounts derives exactly from the central difference between the two accounts. It is precisely because the Primary Quality account treats the color appearances as merely the standard effects of the microphysical properties it identifies as the colors that the account cannot allow for perceptual knowledge of intrinsic and essential similarities among the colors. On the Secondary Quality account the color appearances are not merely the standard effects of the dispositions whose manifestations they are. Since they are also the manifestations cited when attributing the relevant dispositions, we know something intrinsic and essential to these dispositions when we know their manifestations.

The Secondary Quality account provides no threat to Unity. But does it secure Availability? Are the dispositions to appear colored perceptually available?

Someone who has no reason to suppose that he is an inadequate color perceiver or is in bad viewing conditions is such that his spontaneous visually acquired belief about the color of a thing he is seeing is typically justified. He acquires the belief by perception and typically nothing he believes warrants his suspending this belief. Suppose then that Sam's belief that Zinka is canary yellow is a belief of this kind. We considered the epistemic situation of a sophisticate who lucidly accepted that version of the Primary Quality account, an account which has it that conditions involving similarities among the categorical causes of color experience are a priori constraints on anything turning out to be canary yellow. Such a person would not be justified in concluding just by looking that Zinka or anything else is canary yellow. But then, *given that one cannot be in a (globally) worse epistemic condition just as a result of conceptual lucidity, if the Primary Quality account in question is true then Sam cannot be perceptually justified in believing that Zinka is canary yellow.*[24]

Can a similar argument be run against a Secondary Quality account? Such an account treats colors as constituted dispositions to present color appearances. So if the fact that Zinka is canary yellow is to be perceptually available then perception must be able to justify the belief that Zinka has a constituted disposition to appear canary yellow. Otherwise a sophisticate who accepts the Secondary Quality account would not be perceptually justified in concluding that Zinka (or anything else) is canary yellow. That is to say that perception must provide the materials to justify the claim that Zinka has the property of having some intrinsic property which, oddities aside, would cause the relevant appearance in the relevant circumstances. These materials do seem to be provided by having the relevant appearance in the relevant circumstances and employing the background beliefs on which perception feeds. These are beliefs about our perceptual experience being by and large the effects of our perceptual capacities, the circumstances of perception and the intrinsic properties of the things perceived. On the strength of having the appearance and enjoying these background beliefs we are justified in believing that the object perceived has some intrinsic properties which would typically cause the appearance in the circumstances. But that means that on the strength of perception one can be justified in believing that the object has the constituted disposition to appear so in the circumstances.

Indeed one can perhaps be justified in believing slightly more on this basis. It is a perceptually available fact that certain colored things standardly block out the colors of things behind them in the line of sight; while others, color volumes or filters, standardly transform those colors; while still others, transparent volumes such as unpolluted air, clear water or colorless glass, in no way obscure or transform those colors. Therefore, visual perception supports the hypothesis that transparent but not opaque bodies allow to pass through them some standard conveyor or class of standard conveyors of information about the colors of external things. That is, a course of experience as of opaque and transparent bodies encourages the belief that there is some standard conveyor or class of standard conveyors of information about color.[25] Since it is perceptually evident that there are some standard conveyors of information about color, it is therefore perceptually evident that there is some standard process or processes mediating between the dispositions to appear colored and their effects, viz. the various color appearances. But then, if a Secondary Quality theorist were to identify colors with such standardly mediated dispositions, he would not threaten the ordinary perceptually based justification which we have for taking things to be the color they seem to be. Let us now turn to the motives for just such an identification.

Which Response-Dispositional Concepts are the Color Concepts?

Just what form should the Secondary Quality account take? The reasonable choice emerges from a critical version of the method of cases. We look to our intuitive judgments in both real and imaginary cases, we examine to what extent these intuitions are influenced by a bogus conception of colors driven by Revelation and then try to save the undebunked intuitions.[26]

Rigidification

Is it really so that in a possible world in which ripe tomatoes are chemically as they actually are but standardly look violet, they are nonetheless red because they standardly look red in the actual world? For a dispositionalist this is the question of whether to rigidify, i.e., fix on actual responders and actual conditions. Whichever way one is drawn, the main point is that the rigidified and the unrigidified response-dispositions are equally response-dispositions. If a case can be made for the colors being rigidified response-dispositions then so be it. However, we may run into indeterminacy here even if our intuitions initially favor the idea that in a possible world in which ripe tomatoes are chemically as they actually are but standardly look violet they are nonetheless still red. For this intuition may be influenced by a conception of color driven by Revelation. In imaginatively picturing the relevant possible world to ourselves we slap onto the tomato surfaces redness-as-Revelation-represents-it-as-being, thereby providing an independent standard of correctness by which to criticize the counterfactually standard appearances. As a result, a simple reliance on intuition might here make things seem more determinate than they could in fact be.

Standard Mediation

As well as the consistent fancy of the strange ray from the *center* of a red-surfaced ball masking the redness of the surface by acting directly on the visual cortex to produce an impression of a green surface, we have the equally consistent fancy of such a strange ray emanating from the *surface* to likewise obscure the redness of the surface by directly producing the appearance of a green surface. In this second case it is utterly implausible to deny that the surface itself has the constituted disposition to look green. Yet it is not green but red.

Fatal for the dispositional theory? No; a dispositionalist who identifies the colors with standardly mediated dispositions need not count the surface as green. For the strange ray bypasses the eye. This is sufficient to make the processes involving it non-standard causes of visual experiences. But then the disposition of the red ball to look green, based as it is in such a process, will not be a standardly mediated disposition to look green. So although the red surface is disposed to look green, the right sort of dispositionalist need not count it green.[27]

No doubt this use of the modifier "standardly" to qualify the way in which the target dispositions are to be mediated or realized will prompt the question as to just what might or might not count as the processes involved in the standardly mediated dispositions to appear colored. The processes of refraction-influenced reflection frequently involved in producing the appearances of the shimmering colors may be counted standard enough, even if the processes of reflection without refraction involved in producing the appearances of the steady colors are more commonly in play. There will of course be a region of indeterminacy, in which there is no fact of the matter as to whether or not a given process is common enough to be a standard mediator. But there will also be clear cases on the other side, where the disposition to appear colored is not standardly mediated, as with the case of the rotating Benham disc.

The top of one typical kind of Benham disc is divided along a diameter into black and white regions. If the disc is rotated at a rate of about seven cycles per second and viewed under bright tungsten light various colored bands will appear on the top of the disc. But it feels very strained to say that while rotating the top of the disc changes color. Contrast a disc whose surface is chemically prepared so that the air rushing by as the disc rotates sets off a color-affecting chemical change on the surface.

Psychologists call the colors which appear during the rotation of Benham discs "subjective" colors, thereby registering a conviction that these discs only seem to change color while rotating. The intuition to be captured is thus that these achromatic discs remain achromatic throughout rotation. How is the dispositionalist to capture that intuition? In his informative discussion of Benham discs, C. L. Hardin supposes that the best move for the dispositionalist bent on excluding such subjective colors is to insist that the real colors are those that appear to standard perceivers under standard *viewing* conditions and then to claim that movement with respect to the eye is not a standard viewing condition. Hardin rightly rejects this last claim and consequently rejects dispositionalism. He writes

There are at least three difficulties with this initially plausible restriction 'on movement'. First we need not move the black-and-white stimulus at all. It is the pulsed sequence of presentations which matters. One stillborn proposal for color television derived a chromatic effect from a suitably pulsed set of black-and-white signals. The "Butterfield encoder" gave a fairly good color rendition including skin tone.... One can in fact see faint, desaturated subjective colors by looking closely at the noise pattern of an unoccupied channel on a black-and-white television set.... The second difficulty with the restriction is that the eye moves involuntarily and incessantly in a random series of drifts and jerks, and these are sufficient to generate "subjective" colors on a stationary black-and-white pattern.... The third difficulty is the mate of the second: if all relative motion between target and eyeball is prevented, both the outline and the colors of the object soon disappear.[28]

Surely these are effective considerations against the idea that the standard viewing condition for color rules out movement. Many things constantly move relative to us, indeed rotate relative to us, without this in any way undermining our confidence that we have seen them in their true colors. We cannot capture the intuition that the colors of rotating Benham discs are "subjective" by stipulating that only color appearances which arise under standard viewing conditions are veridical. The thing to do is not to require that the viewing condition be standard but that the processes which mediate the relevant dispositions to produce color appearances be among the processes which are standard or typical when it comes to seeing color.

Hardin's example of the Butterfield encoder and his emphasis on pulses suggests just this idea. In the case of an encoder beginning to work at some time t, if d is the time taken for light from a given region of the encoder's screen to reach the observer's eye and e is a period just shorter than the resolution time of the human eye, i.e., the time required for the eye to process light, then the light arriving from that region at $t + d + e$ will be light that is very different in its subjective effects from light that arrived at $t + d$. When these conditions are satisfied let us say that the light is temporally *inhomogeneous*. In such cases very different kinds of light "bunch up" in the eye forcing the receptors to integrate across such inhomogeneities. Now the finite resolution time of the receptors in the eye means that there is always "bunching up." That is to say that where d is the time light takes to reach the eye from the viewed region, the light from the region that the eye is responding to at $t + d$ is never just the light that left the region at t. Rather it includes the light that left the region during the period between t and $t - e$. But standardly this does not matter, for the bundle of light that left the region at t is light with the same subjective effects as the bundle of light that left the region at $t - e$. What bunches up is more or less the same sort of light. In the case of temporal inhomogeneity this last condition is not met. This makes for a non-standard process mediating the appearances and hence realizing the dispositions to appear. The eye is forced to integrate across temporally inhomogeneous packets of light coming in swift sequence from the same region of the scene before the eyes.

Hence a dispositionalist has the resources to say that despite the fact that the screen of the Butterfield encoder is disposed to look yellow, green and blue, it is really achromatic. And he will say the same about the process mediating the subjective colors of the Benham disc. They too are produced by the eye integrating in a case of temporal inhomogeneity. The light coming from a given region of the scene before the eyes is temporally inhomogeneous thanks to the rotation of black and white portions of the disc through that region. The eye is forced to integrate across inhomogeneous packets of light coming in swift sequence from the same region of the scene. This is a non-standard process mediating the visual appearances. So although various hues are disposed to appear across the Benham disc during rotation they are not standardly so disposed. The Benham disc remains achromatic through-out rotation.

Let us now turn to a spatial analog of temporal inhomogeneity; the case of poin-tillism. Pointillism or the optical fusion of small adjacent regions of different color arises because the eye also integrates over spatial inhomogeneities. One need not think that there is a deep ontological divide between space and time to think that while integrating over temporal inhomogeneity is non-standard, integrating over spatial inhomogeneity is on the way to becoming standard. The standard technology of four-color printing means that most of the printed colors other than cyan, magenta, yellow and black which we now see are the products of the optical fusion of a mixed selection of dots of these four colors. It is a bit too severe to say that the only veridical colors that we now see on the pages of magazines are white, black, cyan, magenta and yellow, the rest being illusory color appearances. But it is not obvious that a dispositionalist is required to say this. "Standardly mediated" is not equivalent to "naturally mediated" but rather to "typically mediated," and the pointillistic realization of printed color has arguably now become typical or stan-dard. Again the dispositionalist may happily admit that indeterminacies may well arise when we consider cases in which a mode of realizing color appearances is *becoming* standard. The dispositionalist should not be disturbed by the fact that this admission is at odds with a naive conception of color, i.e., a conception which con-forms to Revelation and as a result thinks of surfaces as wrapped in phenomenally revealed features which will always make it a determinate fact what the real color of the surface is. (For we have shown that such a conception is not coherent, not con-sistent with the idea that we *see* colors.)

Relativized Colors

It is one thing to say that there are indeed red patches of color on the pages of many magazines. But it would be strange to deny what the closest viewing of some of these patches reveals: that these patches are made up of small magenta and yellow dots, that therefore these patches are motley in color. How can the same patch be red and motley yellow and magenta? Relativism to the rescue: the patches are standardly disposed to look red to the naked eye from a normal reading distance and standardly disposed to look motley yellow and magenta to the closest view. They are, according to the best kind of dispositionalist, red for perceivers employing the naked eye at reading distance, and motley yellow and magenta for perceivers at the closest view-ing range. The best kind of dispositionalist is a color relativist.

It is not widely recognized that a color relativist can consistently find some truth in many remarks about "real" colors. Chromatic lights are said to obscure the real colors of patches viewed under them. The color relativist avoids one kind of invidious distinction between the standard disposition of a cloth to look pinkish-blue in daylight and the standard disposition of the same cloth to look simply pink under pink light. For the relativist, both are equally *veridical* colors. But the second color is, as things ordinarily go, the color associated with the more transient and interrupted appearance of the cloth. If we mean by "real color" the least transient veridical color then daylight and ordinary indoor light *do* typically reveal the real colors of things. When the colored thing is something whose color appearance changes as the quality of the daylight changes, e.g. the sea, there may be no simple answer to questions which seek to pinpoint the real color. Is the sea *really* green or grey or blue? Or greenish-blue or bluish-grey or grayish-bluish-green? Again we should not be too perturbed by indeterminacy.

Hence we arrive at the following account of when a surface has a relative color

X is hue H for perceivers P under conditions C iff X is [?actually?] *standardly* disposed to look H to perceivers P [?as they actually are?] under conditions C [?as they actually are?].

What is standard in the way of the processes mediating a visual response-disposition will vary from possible world to possible world. Once again some may feel the temptation to rigidify or fix on what is actually standard in the way of causally mediating between visual response-dispositions and visual responses. And once again there is the question of how much of the alleged intuitive privilege of the actual world's mechanisms is due to picturing the imagined alternatives as exemplifying the colors-as-Revelation-represents-them-as-being. Were there such colors then they could be systematically misrepresented in any alternative world by that world's standardly mediated appearances. But there cannot be such colors. Perhaps that saps much of the temptation to rigidify or fix on the processes that are actually standard. In any case it would be odd to do this once it is allowed, as in the case of four-color printing, that what is standard may vary over time. For we can imagine our world evolving in the direction of what is standard in some other world. What was always standard there becomes standard here.

If one wants to avoid the consequences of not rigidifying on the actually standard processes mediating the color appearances one had probably better understand "standard mediating processes" as "natural mediating processes" and so disparage pointillism and therefore accept the slightly odd view that the pages of magazines are filled with occasions for color illusions. Neither choice is wholly comfortable, but either way the resultant and, I think, relatively mild discomfort *is not peculiar to the Secondary Quality account.* Recall that the Primary Quality account picks out its favored properties as the non-dispositional properties standardly or normally responsible for the relevant color appearances. Similar discomfort arises when this account gets explicit about what it means by "standard" or "normal". The discomfort is mostly an aftershock of the inevitable denial of Revelation.

Kripke's Reference-Fixing Account

In order to justify the claim that such a Secondary Quality account of the colors allows us to speak more inclusively of the colors than any Primary Quality account allows, it must be shown that the kind of problem illustrated by the fact that we know in advance that canary yellow could not turn out to be a shade of blue arises because of the central idea behind the Primary Quality account, and not just because the argument concentrated on a determinate shade like canary yellow rather than on the determinable hue that is yellow.

Someone might think that if we began with a Primary Quality account of the hues—red, blue, green, yellow, etc.—then we could just stipulate that canary yellow is a yellow and not a blue, thereby getting round the problem of canary yellow threatening to turn out to be a shade of blue.

Indeed, when one of the most inventive advocates of the view that colors are Primary Qualities gives his account of the color properties he naturally treats the hues and not the shades. Thus in *Naming and Necessity* Saul Kripke writes of yellow, not canary yellow, claiming that the hue term "yellow" is akin to a natural kind term.[29] On that account, the term "yellow" has its reference fixed in terms of the description "the manifest (i.e., non-dispositional) surface property which is normally responsible for things appearing yellow". Of course, something will then count as yellow only if this description denotes, so that the reference fixing account for "yellow" will treat the following conditional as having a priori status.

(10) If there is a unique manifest surface property normally responsible for things appearing yellow, say Y, then yellowness is Y, otherwise "yellow" does not denote.

This account yields its own paradoxical consequences. To see why, recall that hue is just one color determinable, along with saturation and brightness. Let us focus on brightness and its determinates—being (quite) bright, being dark and being intermediate in brightness. These stand to the determinable brightness as yellow stands to hue. If "yellow" gets a reference-fixing treatment then so should the names for these brightness qualities.[30] So we have

(11) If there is a unique surface property normally responsible for things looking bright, say B1, then brightness is B1, otherwise 'brightness' does not denote.

(12) If there is a unique surface property normally responsible for things looking dark, say B2, then darkness is B2, otherwise 'darkness' does not denote.

(13) If there is a unique surface property normally responsible for things looking intermediate in brightness, say B3, then the property of being intermediate in brightness is B3, otherwise "the property of being intermediate in brightness" does not denote.

One of the things we know about yellow just on the basis of sight and without relying upon information about scientific discoveries is that there cannot be a yellow with no brightness quality whatsoever, a yellow which is neither bright nor dark (i.e., brownish) nor intermediate in brightness. However, on the reference-fixing account so far adumbrated this is at most a matter of scientific discovery—a discovery to the effect that everything that has Y also has at least one of B1 or B2 or B3. For all we know now it might actually turn out that there are things with Y but none of B1 or B2 or B3. On the present account such things would be a shade of yellow that was neither bright nor dark nor anywhere in between on the scale of brightness. Were there such shades, they could not be the object of fully veridical perception, since any visual perception would present some brightness quality. So in that sense they would be not be fully visible shades of yellow.

Furthermore, on the reference-fixing account it is at most a matter of scientific discovery that everything that has Y has at most one of B1 or B2 or B3. For all we know now it might actually turn out that there are things with Y and both B1 and B3. On the account under discussion, such things would be a shade of yellow that was at once bright and dark, e.g., as bright as the yellow on the disc of the moon and as dark as a dark brown. (Dark yellow get called brown.)[31]

As against all this we know in advance that there cannot be such strange yellows just as we know in advance that canary yellow is not a shade of blue. Or rather, to put the point in a way that takes proper note of the vagueness of the analytic/synthetic distinction: any account which has it coming out true that we know these things in advance thereby better deserves the name of an account of the *colors*.

What about the strategy of conditionalizing on what we know in advance? What about articulating in an antecedent of a conditional just the requisite relations between hue and brightness. An example of the required "frontloading" (Peter Railton's nice term) would be—

(14) IF Y is the property normally responsible for the yellow appearances and B1 is the property normally responsible for the bright shade appearances and B2 is the property normally responsible for the dark shade appearances and B3 is the property normally responsible for the appearances of intermediate shades AND it is

a consequence of the laws of color science that anything that has Y has one and at most one of B1 and B2 and B3 THEN yellowness is Y, otherwise the term "yellowness' does not denote.

Once again a problem about the perceptual availability of the colors arises. Suppose that in the year 2000 as a result of discoveries in color science we come to know that the antecedent of (14) is satisfied. Then the account employing (14) implies that some parts of the external world were colored yellow all along. But we were not justified in believing this all along. For until 2000 we were ignorant of a central precondition on things being yellow. Indeed, even after the year 2000 we can only know that surfaces are yellow by relying upon knowledge of what holds up as a lawlike statement of color science. As against this, we have Availability: if there are yellow surfaces, good perceivers can be justified in believing this just by looking at them and without relying upon exotic scientific discoveries. Once again, the properties alleged to be the colors are not perceptually available, and this is because the account which identifies or conditionally identifies the colors with the non-dispositional, microphysical properties talked about in color science thereby concerns itself with properties one step too remote from the appearances—the microphysical bases of dispositions to appear colored rather than the dispositions themselves.

The dispositional account fares better with the internal relations among hue, saturation and brightness. Beginning again with the fully determinate shades, notice first that every color experience is an experience of some shade of color. That is to say that every color experience is simultaneously an experience of a certain hue quality, a certain saturation quality and a certain brightness quality. Each appearance of a shade is an appearance of something with a specific value along these three dimensions. So to be disposed to produce an appearance with some single hue quality is ipso facto to be disposed to produce an appearance with some single saturation quality and is ipso facto to be disposed to produce an appearance with some single brightness quality. Hues with no brightness quality, saturationless hues and so on are no more possible than *experiences* of shades devoid of hue, saturation or brightness are possible. This is just because of the intimate connection between the experiences and the colors according to the dispositional view.[32]

The perceptual availability of the colors; our being able to tell there are colors, and what colors things are, just on the basis of perception, has played an important role in the argument so far. It has not been assumed that an account which violates Availability could not deserve the name of an account of the colors, but only that ceteris paribus, an account which does *not* violate this principle better deserves the name of an account of the colors. Mutatis mutandis with Unity. Our conclusion should therefore not be that the Primary Quality account is hopeless as an account of the colors. Rather we should conclude that while we can speak of the colors as response-dispositions and still speak more or less inclusively, we must speak less inclusively if we speak of the colors as the categorical bases of such dispositions. For we must then give up either Unity or Availability.

There is a reply in the offing. As against this attempt to produce a contradiction among Unity, Availability and the Primary Quality account, the friend of the account may urge that we treat "similar" wherever it occurs in the formulation of a unity principle as simply short for "looks similar" so that the unity relations are indeed knowable just on the basis of visual perception. Then canary yellow would be a shade of blue only if it looked as similar to the blues as they look among themselves. We know just on the basis of visual perception that this last condition is not satisfied. The Primary Quality theorist may thus hope to escape our arguments so far by replying that Unity is much less demanding than we thought.

I think it can be shown that the reply falsifies the contents of the unity principles which are central to our beliefs about the colors. For the reply entails that in knowing on the basis of vision that canary yellow is not a shade of blue we simply know that canary yellow does not look as similar to the blues as the blues do among themselves. That implies that what we know on the basis of vision leaves it open that canary yellow may nonetheless be as similar to the blues as they are among themselves. But that means that vision tells us almost nothing about what canary yellow, teal, turquoise, sky blue are like. And that is to say that on the Primary Quality account, vision merely gives us knowledge of the colors by description, i.e., allows us to know the colors just as the properties, *whatever they might be like*, which are standardly causally responsible for the color appearances. However, if vision gives us only knowledge by description of the colors, if vision does not acquaint us at all with the way the colors are intrinsically, then the colors can hardly be said to be visible properties.

On the other hand, vision can acquaint us with the natures of the color properties if these properties are dispositions to produce visual responses. The similarities that color vision reveals will then be visually apparent similarities among the colors, not mere similarities among the visual appearances which the colors, whatever they might be like, cause. There will be, after all, a grain of truth in Revelation—visual experience taken, not naively, but as a series of manifestations of visual response-dispositions, can acquaint us with the natures of the colors. (Despite this grain of truth, Revelation as it stands is still false on the Secondary Quality account, for Revelation implies that if colors are dispositions then all colors, even the steady colors, look like dispositions.)

Revelation Revisited

The Secondary Quality account can recognize a grain of truth in Revelation. This grain of truth is important when it comes to accounting for the value of vision. The faculty of vision either represents itself as (or is spontaneously taken by its possessors as) a mode of revelation of the natures of certain properties of visible things, viz. their colors and Euclidean shapes. A particular counts as visible only if it has visible properties and it has visible properties only if it has properties with whose natures vision acquaints us. That is to say that although it is a necessary condition of a property F being visible that something's having F at some time explains a visual experience, this is not sufficient. For many fundamental physical properties satisfy this necessary condition while nonetheless not being visible properties. They fail to count as visible properties because vision does not acquaint us with the nature of these properties but only with their effects.[33]

The notion of acquaintance with a property, equivalently of knowing the nature of a property, is somewhat obscure. We do not want to follow Russell's line in *The Problems of Philosophy* and say that when one is acquainted with a property one has nothing more to know about it except which particulars in fact have it. For then, as we have seen, it would follow that *no* causes of our experience are visible.

In lieu of Russell's all too demanding account, we might offer the following operational consequence of being acquainted with a number of properties. If you know or are acquainted with the nature of properties F1, F2, ... FN then you can know a family of similarity and difference relations (unity principles) holding among F1 through FN and know these without relying upon knowledge of the laws in which the properties are implicated or upon knowledge of which particulars have the properties. Obviously acquaintance can be a matter of degree on this view. So we do not need a complete revelation of the nature of a property to be acquainted with the property. Vision can thus acquaint us with the response-dispositions that are the colors of the Secondary Quality account, even though vision fails to represent them as dispositions. Contrast Kripke's Primary Quality account of the colors as properties picked out by reference-fixing descriptions which mention mere effects of the properties: on this view since vision gives us only knowledge by description of the microphysical causes of our experience of colors, and those causes are the colors, vision gives us only knowledge by description of the colors.

Return now to the defensive suggestion of the Primary Quality theorist to the effect that the only unity conditions worth underwriting are similarity and difference conditions among appearances. Notice that this maneuver and our operational account of acquaintance together imply that we are not at all acquainted with the colors but only with their visual effects. Given that visible properties are the properties with which vision can acquaint us, it follows that the colors are invisible.

The Primary Quality theorist can of course allow that the colors are visible in a less demanding sense, namely that they are properties which in a standard and systematic way explain our visual experience. So the whole issue ultimately turns on this question: "Why is it so bad if we are not acquainted with the colors and with other visible qualities by vision but know them only by description?"

This is a question about the comparative interest and point of concepts of the colors and of other visibilia. And I think that the question has an interesting answer which favors the Secondary Quality account. For I believe that our implicit cognitive values favor acquaintance with objects, people, places, and hence with their properties. If that is so than we have reason to want vision to be a mode of access to the natures of visible properties. But then we have reason to refigure our concepts of the colors along the lines suggested by the Secondary Quality theorist.

That our implicit cognitive values favor acquaintance with things emerges if we consider what would be so bad about the situation which the skeptic claims we are actually in. Consider two familiar philosophical cartoons by which the traditional skeptical problem of the external world is typically presented—the case of the eternal movie buff and the case of the brain in the vat. The eternal movie buff has spent all his life in a dark room watching images on a screen before his eyes. Never having left his room he has no idea whether the images correspond to anything outside his chamber. The brain in the vat is fed a full sensorium by fiendishly clever neural stimulation. A computer coordinates the pattern of stimulation so that the brain has a complete and consistent sensory illusion, say as of living an ordinary life in Boise, Iowa. These bizarre predicaments are employed to highlight a skeptical worry about our own predicament. The eternal movie buff cannot be justified in holding any visually generated beliefs about the external world, restricted as he is to mere images which he cannot check against external reality. He can only check experience against experience. But this is also our predicament. We also can only check our experiences against other experiences. It is no more possible for us to attempt to match our experience against external reality as it is in itself, as it is independently of how it is experienced by us. The case of the brain in the vat deflates the natural thought that we have an epistemic advantage over the eternal movie buff by possessing a number of potential windows on the world which we can use to triangulate to an external reality as it is in itself. The triangulations of the envatted brain lead it to beliefs about a life lived in Boise, Iowa. But all these beliefs are false.

Whatever the force of these cartoons in presenting the traditional problem of the justifiability of our beliefs about the external world, and even if their force is undermined by noting that a spontaneous and utterly natural belief is justified in the absence of a good case against it, the cartoons also serve to illustrate a deeper epistemic anxiety about our own condition.

This deeper problem of the external world is the problem of acquaintance, the problem of how we could be acquainted with anything given the nature of information transmission. The nature of any signal received is partly a product of the thing sending the signal and partly a product of the signal receiver. We cannot, it seems, separate out the contribution of our own sensibility to our experience from the contribution of the objects sensed. The case of the brain in the vat shows that our experience does not discriminate between many different kinds of external objects so long as their effects on our sensibility are isomorphic in certain ways. But that suggests that relative to the problem of acquaintance, even if we are not brains in vats things are as bad as they would be if we were brains in vats.[34] We cannot take our experiences to reveal the natures of external things. No sensory experience could at the same time reveal two things so intrinsically unalike as the nature of life in Boise and the nature of the inner working of the vat computer. But for all that could be revealed in a fully coherent experience either could be the cause of that course of experience. Conclusion: sensory experience does not reveal the nature of its causes.

In both cartoons sensory experience is clearly depicted as simply an effect of external causes whose natures are in no way revealed by the experiences they cause. Sensory experience in no way acquaints the brain or the buff with the nature of the external causes of that experience. In this respect, sensory experience is unsatisfyingly like Morse code transmission: both involve interpretable effects at the end of an information-bearing process or signal. But the intrinsic natures of the originators of the signal are not manifest in the signal. This is a very depressing comparison. Perception represents itself as (or is at least spontaneously taken by its possessors as) a mode of access to the natures of things. When I see the sun setting against the magenta expanse of the sky, I seem to have something about the nature of the sky and the sun revealed to me. I seem not just to be partly under their causal influence in a way that leaves completely open what their natures might be like. The acquaintance with external features which vision seems to provide is something we very much value, or so it seems to me.

The general problem of acquaintance is a difficult one, but we have already accumulated the materials for a solution to that problem as it arises for vision and color. Part of my pleasure in seeing color is not simply the pleasure of undergoing certain experiences but the pleasure of having access to the natures of those features of external things that are the colors. This need not be a pleasure founded in a false belief, a pleasure which philosophical reflection would have me see through. For suppose the colors are response-dispositions. These are genuine, albeit relational, features of external objects. Their manifestations are the various experiences in various subjects as of the various colors. These sensory manifestations are not simply the effects of the dispositions they manifest. They are or can be manifestations in a more interesting sense. About any disposition of objects to produce a given experience, it is plausible to hold that if one has an experience of the kind in question and takes that experience to be a manifestation of the disposition in question, one thereby knows the complete intrinsic nature of the disposition. Of course one does not thereby know the facts concerning how in general the disposition is specifically secured or realized. But these are facts concerning the disposition's contingent relations to other properties. They do not concern the intrinsic and essential nature of the disposition. So, as claimed earlier, I take myself as having come to understand the complete nature of the property of being nauseated one afternoon twenty five years ago when I tasted a juicy apricot on a ferry crossing from Melbourne to Hobart. Similarly, if I conceive of the magenta of the sunset as a (constituted) disposition to produce a certain visual response in subjects like me, and I now discover myself to be responding just so, I can be in possession of all there is to know about the essential nature of the dispositional property that is magenta. I do not thereby know the contingent details of how magenta might be physically realized here before my eyes or anywhere else. But that is ignorance of the relation between the disposition and the other properties which happen to realize the disposition. I do seem to know everything intrinsic and essential to the response-disposition that is magenta. Mutatis mutandis for the other colors. Vision can be a mode of revelation of the nature of visual response-dispositions. It cannot be a mode of revelation of the properties which the Primary Quality Theorist identifies with the colors. Since we are inevitably in the business of refiguring our inconsistent color concepts, we should make the revision which allows us to secure an important cognitive value—the value of acquaintance with those salient, striking and ubiquitous features that are the colors.[35]

The point here is not simply that the Primary Quality Account does not satisfy even a qualified form of Revelation. What is more crucial is that as a result, the account does not provide for something we very much value: acquaintance with the colors. The ultimate defect of the Primary Quality View is therefore a practical one. From the point of view of what we might call the ethics of perception, the Secondary Quality Account is to be preferred. It provides for acquaintance with the colors.

I began by indicating that the possibility of speaking more or less inclusively about the colors is a typical consequence of the vagueness of the analytic/synthetic distinction. But that means that the vagueness of the analytic/synthetic distinction will typically have this consequence: without clearly changing the topic we will always face a choice of precisely which concepts to use. Such a choice is not dictated by the natures of the things under discussion. For those natures, admit of many types of true descriptions. (For example, there is no doubt that colored objects have both the features favored by the Secondary Quality theorist and the features favored by the Primary Quality theorist.) What should guide such conceptual choices? Surely here, Pragmatism is entirely vindicated: it is human interests, broadly construed, which make it reasonable to confront the world armed with these concepts rather than those.

So although the philosophy of color may be one of those genial areas of inquiry in which the main competing positions are each *in their own way* perfectly true, *it may also be that given what we value only one account is the right one for us to employ.*[36]

Acknowledgments

Thanks to Paul Boghossian, C. L. Hardin, David Lewis, Peter Railton, David Velleman and Stephen Yablo. An earlier draft of this paper was delivered as an invited paper at The Eastern Division of the American Philosophical Association, December 1989. An outline of many of these ideas was presented at the 1989 Spring Colloquim of the University of Michigan Philosophy Department, although then I was more favorable towards the Primary Quality account than I am now. I am told that Charlie Martin discussed mimicked and masked dispositions thirty years ago in his classes at Sydney University.

Notes

1. If one wants a reason for being interested in the answer, the quick reason is that unless the external world is colored it is invisible. For if the external world is not colored then we do not see the colors of external things. They are not visible. Now the surfaces of material objects are visible if they are either visibly translucent, visibly transparent, visibly opaque or visibly reflective. Determinables like transparency, opacity, etc. are visible only if their determinates are visible. The various volume colors are the determinate ways of being transparent and translucent, the various barrier colors are the determinate ways of being opaque, and the various colors of virtual images in mirrors are the determinate ways of being reflective. So if colors are not visible then no surface of a material object is visible. But if no surface of a material object is visible, then no material object is visible. Such is the consequence of denying that nothing corresponds to external color, the proper sensible of sight. Unless the external world is colored we do not see it and that means we do not see, period. If the world is not colored, we may get some kind of schematic propositional knowledge about our environment by sight but sight does not acquaint us with the natures of any external things. Our question might as well be "How far short of speaking ever so inclusively do we have to fall in order to say truly that we see?" or "In what sense do we see external things?" The last section of this paper addresses, in a preliminary way, the question as to why we should care about seeing external things in one or another sense of "seeing".

2. See *The Problems of Philosophy* (London, OUP, 1912) p. 47.

3. For this analogy, see the first few pages of part one of Descartes' *Optics*.

4. See David R. Hilbert *Color and Color Perception* (CSLI, Stanford, 1987) pp. 29–42.

5. " 'Red' and Red" *Synthèse* 78, 1989; p. 224.

6. I cannot help thinking that it is this conviction which is driving some of the provocative arguments of Paul Boghossian and David Velleman to the conclusion that the external world is not colored. When for example they discuss Christopher Peacocke's version of the dispositional theory their main point is that if colors were that kind of disposition then visual experience could be convicted of misrepresenting the nature of the colors. To which a friend of the Peacocke account should reply "Just so! Revelation is a bit of an overstatement. We can't completely save the phenomenology of color experience." Nor do Boghossian and Velleman themselves completely save the phenomenology of color experience, for that experience represents the external world as colored. See Paul A. Boghossian and J. David Vellman "Color As A Secondary Quality" *Mind* 1989 [chapter 7, this volume].

7. The same point about the relevant error can be made in the terms allowed by those, like Gilbert Harman, who take what others regard as sensational features of perceptual experience to be none other than further representational features of perceptual experience. The error in question involves taking these further representations as indicating the complete nature of sensory qualities. See Gilbert Harman "The Intrinsic Quality of Experience" *Philosophical Perspectives* 4, pp. 31–52.

8. The reflectance of a surface is given by a set of proportions of reflected light to incident light for each wavelength of visible light. For the original version of Land's theory see *Scientific American*, 237, Dec 1977. In the latest version of the theory Land shows how the color appearance of an illuminated patch is associated with a triple of "designators." A designator is a weighted proportion of the light of a given wavelength coming from the colored patch to the light of that wavelength coming from a given surround. When we have a designator for each of the long, medium and short wavelengths coming from and around an illuminated patch, we have enough physical information to determine the color appearance of the patch to normal perceivers. So we could identify colors with dispositions to give off light conforming to an appropriate set of triples of designators. This would be a complex and scientifically realistic light-dispositional theory.

9. See Harding, G. 1991. Color and the mind-body problem. *Review of Metaphysics* 45, 289–307. As I understand him Harding completely endorses Revelation and builds his ontology around the result.

10. See "Color as a Secondary Quality" op. cit.

11. For the distinction between steady and unsteady or "shimmering" colors see Hazel Rossotti *Color: Why the World Isn't Grey* (Princeton University Press, 1983) chapters 3 and 4. Rossotti uses "stable colors" for what I am calling "steady colors". "Stable" sounds to me to be the opposite of "transient" and there can be transient colors that are nonetheless steady, e.g. the greyness of the sky when it is overcast.

12. Why abandon or weaken Revelation rather than Explanation? The answer turns on the fact that Explanation is also a very plausible condition on colors being visible. It would be perverse to allow that the colors are indeed properties satisfying Revelation but that they are invisible.

13. Sensible qualities are qualities that are visible, audible, testable, etc.

14. Some tell me that their intuition is that something extrinsic to the ray-bedeviled surface disposes it to look red, so the surface is indeed disposed to look red. I do not so much want to deny the intuition as to separate out a conception of dispositions which requires an intrinsic basis for the disposition. Maybe the ordinary notion of a thing's power or capacity tends to carry this implication of there being in the thing an intrinsic basis for the disposition that is the power. At least it seems more strained to say that the ray-bedeviled surface *itself* has the power to look red. That seems to suggest that it would continue to have that power were the surface hived off from the ray-emanating core.

The related case of the strange ray emanating from the surface is discussed below in the main body of the text.

15. Why not also allow the case where x changes intrinsically as x goes into the circumstances C? Because this would rule out an absolutely straightforward case of the manifestation of a disposition, a case in which putting x in C changes x in precisely the way that is causally responsible for the manifestation.

16. This is not, of course, an analysis of the notion of a disposition, since it does not tell us the conditions for attributing dispositions when the oddities are in play. I attempt a full-blown analysis in "Dispositions: Predication with a Grain of Salt" unpublished manuscript.

17. For reasons to hesitate in attributing the dispositional thesis to Locke see A. D. Smith "Of Primary and Secondary Qualities" *The Philosophical Review* XCLX, 1990.

18. On the disparate nature of the standard causes, even of appearances of the same shade, see C. L. Hardin *Color For Philosophers* (Hackett, 1988) pp. 1–52.

19. "An Objectivist's Guide to Subjectivism About Color" *Revue Internationale de Philosophie* 1987 [chapter 6, this volume].

20. Since similarity is always similarity in some respect it is a fair question as to what respect I have in mind here. The answer is similarity in respect of hue, the most salient of the similarities among the shades.

21. Or at least it would be that discovery if the similarity in question was plausibly identified with a similarity in respect of hue. For more on what this involves see the discussion of Saul Kripke's view below.

22. Suppose that I am a waif brought up in a monastery. As a matter of strict monastic rule no married male is allowed to enter the gates of the monastery. I have a highly predictive stereotype associated with the concept of a bachelor inhabiting the monastery, viz. that of a male inhabiting the monastery. Now as a result of monkish gossip it is widely but wrongly suspected that Brother Bernard, who we all know to have been a man of the world, has a wife or two in Tuscany. I know of the gossip and accept it, but because of my stereotype of a bachelor as a male inhabiting the monastery, I adhere to my true and well-grounded belief that Brother Bernard is a bachelor. In rhetoric class I am finally taught the definition of "bachelor" and I conclude that Brother Bernard is not a bachelor. As a result of conceptual lucidity I know less by knowing more.

Nonetheless the crucial point is that even in such cases being conceptually lucid does not confer a **global** disadvantage when it comes to justified applications of the concept in question. When it comes to applying the concept bachelor outside the monastery, where there are indeed married males, I am not disadvantaged as a result of what I learned in the rhetoric class. Nor is this so within the monastery when it comes to the bachelorhood of the other monks beside Bernard. And there are many *possible* cases in which thanks to my newly acquired conceptual lucidity I would be better placed when it comes to having justified belief about who the bachelors are. The thing that it is hard to believe about our color sophisticate is that in every actual and possible case he is worse off than we as a result of his conceptual sophistication, so that he never could be justified simply on the basis of perception in judging the colors of things, while we are almost always so justified. This is not made any easier to believe by examining cases in which one ignores a misleading defeater thanks to a conceptual mistake.

23. By the way, it is tempting to see here the form of a general worry about any natural kind account of concepts for which analogues of Unity and Availability hold. Most observational concepts seem to me to have such analogues.

24. The strategy of considering the epistemic position of the relevant philosophical sophisticate has wide application. It also has at least three attractive features. It does not assume what is anyway crazy, i.e., that *ordinary* subjects' possession of justified belief depends upon their employing implicitly or explicitly the right philosophical account of those beliefs. Secondly, the strategy provides a way around all too convenient appeals to the failure of deductive closure—to one's not having to know all of the consequences of what one knows. Thirdly, the strategy does not entail the paradox of analysis because it does not depend upon supposing that we can always substitute into belief contexts on the basis of the conceptual equivalences that make up philosophical accounts. It is enough to warrant suspension of the perceptually based belief that canary yellow is not a shade of blue if this belief is conceptually equivalent to a belief for which one could possess no perceptual justification, *viz.*, that the microphysical causes of the appearances of canary yellow are not as similar microphysically to the microphysical causes of the appearances of the blues as this latter class of causes are similar among themselves.

25. However, as against Goethe, who suggested that we can see that the colors are the deeds and vicissitudes of light, it is *not* perceptually evident whether light is such a standard conveyor or simply a medium of ambient brightness which allows such standard conveyors to propagate. Hence Newton's Tertiary Quality account of being red as being such as to give off light which is "Rubrifick", light which is such as

to cause in perceivers the appearance of a red thing, goes beyond what is perceptually evident about the relation between color and light. Thus the persistence among astute phenomenologists of vision of the classical doctrine of "visual rays"—the doctrine that seeing is achieved by exploratory rays which in illuminated conditions go out from the eye to the object perceived. Avicenna in his *Treatise on Meteorology* written in the first half of the 11th century still finds the need to argue against this classical theory of vision by pointing to the implausibility of supposing that the eye has something that extends into the celestial spheres. See David C. Lindberg *Theories of Vision From Alkindi to Kepler* (University of Chicago, 1976) pp. 44–49.

26. Compare the method employed in the paper "Human Beings" *Journal of Philosophy* 1987; where the strict analogue of the Revelation-driven conception of color is the Bare Locus view of personal identity, according to which we are subjects of reflective consciousness capable of surviving any amount of psychological and physical change, however abrupt. This view comes about as a result of taking the simple way in which we are presented to ourselves in conscious experience as the presentation of a simple subject of that experience. To adequately theorize about personal identity in the wake of this error we must examine the extent to which our judgments about cases are driven by this error.

27. Notice that we have in this case, as with the first sort of ray-bedeviled red surface, an example of a persistent color illusion: fool's green, if you like. On the dispositionalist view we are here developing, fool's green can arise in at least two ways: either by the mimicking of the disposition to look green or as a result of the non-standard nature of the processes involved in the disposition to look green.

28. See *Color For Philosophers* op. cit. p. 72.

29. *Naming and Necessity* (Harvard University Press 1980) fn71, p. 140. This footnote offers a very clear formulation of a straightforward reference-fixing account of the hue concepts. In a Spring Colloquium held at the University of Michigan in 1989, Kripke presented a much more detailed treatment of these issues in which color concepts did seem to be turning out to be more like cluster concepts.

30. This assumption simply makes things neater. I leave it to the reader to verify that the problem that follows would apply even to a mixed account which treated the hues as Primary and the brightness qualities as Secondary.

31. Once again, since visual experience cannot present a shade with incompatible brightness properties such shades would not be fully visible. Notice that the Primary Quality theorist is badly placed to rule out such not-fully-visible shades. First his account implies that there are such shades. But secondly, on his account it is a natural assumption that not all the properties importantly associated with the causing of a visual experience are manifested in that visual experience.

32. The astute reader may be thinking of the possibilities opened up by allowing the masking of dispositions. Even with a perpetually masked disposition to look, say, surface green, the masked manifestation will be an appearance of a green surface. Such an appearance will ipso facto be the appearance of a surface with some saturation and some brightness quality.

33. The physical properties associated with sound could also have been the dominant cause of our visual experiences. But we would not then have seen sound in the relevant sense. The trouble with the idea that we could have seen the sound properties is that vision could tell us nothing about the natures of such properties, it could not acquaint us with the way these properties intrinsically are, it could only acquaint us with their effects. So in the bizarre possible world in which similar physical processes are causally responsible for both the appearances of canary yellow and the sound of B-flat it would be wrong to say that we see B-flat as we see canary yellow. It would have been equally wrong to say this if the actual world had turned out to be bizarre in just this way.

The composer Alexander Scriabin (1872–1915) had synesthesia and so "saw" B-flat in the sense that he had, thanks to neural cross-wiring, certain visual experiences when he heard B-flat. It is an interesting question what it was like to be Scriabin, in particular whether the visual experiences he had when he heard B-flat presented themselves as revelations of the nature of B-flat, a nature missed by all great musicians except Scriabin, or whether these experiences simply seemed to Scriabin to be the "visual signatures" of B-flat. Even if the former, it is hard not to imagine Scriabin then going on to think of B-flat as a sensible complex with two sides to its nature, the one which all people with perfect pitch knew, and the other reserved for him and a few other select souls. What he couldn't have coherently thought is that B-flat was a simple quality whose nature was as much revealed by vision as by hearing. That would be the absurd thought that he saw the sound B-flat, the thought ruled out by our intuitive condition on visibilia.

34. In *Reason, Truth and History* (Cambridge, 1983) Ch 2, Hilary Putnam claims that if we were brains in vats then we couldn't mean the standard thing by "WE ARE BRAINS IN VATS" so that we could not formulate to ourselves the traditional problem of the external world. Notice that even if this were so it would not in anyway deal with the deeper epistemic anxiety.

35. It may be worth noting how the distinction between Primary and Secondary Qualities looks for someone who appreciates that response-dispositions can have their natures revealed by their manifestations. As well as the dispositional criterion, Locke had another way of demarcating Secondary from Primary Qualities. Our experiences of Primary Qualities "resemble" their causes in external things. This resemblance thesis is notoriously difficult to coherently fill out. But if the resemblance thesis implies that we can come to know the nature of certain sensible properties on the basis of our experience of them then there is an interesting consequence to be drawn. Since response-dispositions but not their bases have their natures revealed by their manifestations, the qualities that are Secondary by the dispositional criterion are Primary by the resemblance criterion and the qualities that are Primary by the dispositional criterion are Secondary by the resemblance criterion.

36. For more on this Pragmatic approach to concept employment see "Objectivity Refigured: Pragmatism minus Verificationism", in *Reality, Representation, and Projection*, eds. J. Haldane and C. Wright. New York: Oxford University Press, 1993.

POSTSCRIPT: VISUAL EXPERIENCE

So the colors are best construed as dispositions to produce certain visual experiences in us. What are visual experiences? Is it true, as some have suggested, that one can make sense of Revelation

the intrinsic nature of a shade is fully revealed by a standard visual experience as of a thing having that shade

only if one construes visual experience as awareness of sense data; so that the appeal of Revelation depends upon either mistaking some of the properties of sense data for the color properties of external things or at least supposing that there is a nature-revealing match between some of the properties of sense data and the color properties of external things? If so, wouldn't visual experience here be tempting us into a particularly crude form of projective error, i.e., either the sheer mistaking of a mental feature for a physical feature or at least the odd belief that a mental feature could "match" a physical one? And, as Sydney Shoemaker and Michael Tye have urged, wouldn't such a crude projective account itself be an implausible story about visual experience?

Yes it would. But fortunately, Revelation is not tied to this account of visual experience. The first thing to see is that Revelation can be perfectly well explicated on the Intentionalist View which denies that visual experience involves the direct awareness of a mind-dependent item or sense datum. On the Intentionalist View, visual experience is a sui generis propositional attitude—visually entertaining a content concerning the scene before the eyes. Visually entertaining a content to the effect that p is to be distinguished from believing that p and indeed even from having the suppressed inclination to believe that p. When I have a visual experience of a stick half submerged in water the stick looks separated, but I do not believe that the stick is separated. David Armstrong's suggestion is that such cases show that experiencing is the acquisition of a possibly suppressed inclination to believe things about the scene before the eyes. As against this, the acquisition of a disposition seems to be only a regular effect of the event of experiencing. It is conceptually possible that the cause occurs without the effect, so that the acquisition of a disposition to believe is not a necessary condition of experience. Nor is it sufficient. One could acquire a suppressed disposition to believe, say, that the scene before the eyes is poorly lit—in ways that bypassed experience—latent depression, hypnotism, etc. One would not thereby be experiencing a poorly lit scene. We have no accurate statement of what the right way of acquiring the suppressed disposition to believe is unless we require that it is by way of visual experience. That is to say that seeing or visually experiencing is not believing. Still, visually experiencing might be the acquisition of a sui generis propositional attitude, which I have chosen to dub "visually entertaining a content."

How would Revelation work given this view of visual experience? If we think of visual experience as the entertaining of contents concerning the scene before the eyes, then it is natural to take the contents that are visually entertained to be layered. First there are contents to the effect that such and such objects have such and so colors and shapes. Then there is a level of content concerning what these colors and shapes are like, what their natures are. This could be understood as the attribution of higher-order properties to the color and shape properties themselves. Visual experience seems to tell us not just that things are canary yellow but just what canary yellow is like.[1] That is why vision seems to give us a particularly intimate contact with the visible aspects of visible things, why it seems to lay the natures of these aspects bare.[2] Unfortunately, we lack the vocabulary to well articulate the content of these higher-order attributions. Some talk of the dissectiveness of the colors, their particular "grain," the way red and yellow come toward you while blue and green discreetly "hang back," the way we can see red and blue in purple, and so on and so forth.

In any case, it is clear how Revelation could be explained within this framework. Given that visual experience involves entertaining contents layered in this way, Revelation is the claim that the higher-order content which attributes properties to the colors itself fixes what it is to be this or that color.

But as I have argued, none of the candidate properties which are causally relevant in the production of our visual experience fit anything like the profiles which are plausibly taken to be part of the higher-order content of visual experience. So the external world is not colored or at least is not colored in the way visual experience represents it as being.

There is a obvious worry at this point. Surely, when it comes to the concept of canary yellow—the profile a property would have to fit in order to count as canary yellow—the *visual* concept of canary yellow, or equivalently the profile associated with canary yellow by visual experience, has a special privilege. If there is such a thing as the visual concept of canary yellow and nothing in the external world fits that concept, then nothing in the external world is canary yellow. We might, as in "How to Speak of the Colors," find some surrogate property or properties which fit most of our central beliefs about canary yellow, but this is not much of an achievement if there is a visual concept of canary yellow, a concept deployed in visual experience itself, and that concept fits no property of external things. Visual experience's own concept of canary yellow dominates and minimizes the relevance of these other beliefs. The worry is then that if we explain Revelation in terms of the Intentionalist View augmented with the account of layered content, then the only thing to say will be that the external world is not colored. Whereas on the Sense Data Theory we have a veil of mental items between subjects and external objects, on the Intentionalist View visual experience is the entertaining of systematically false content.

However there is still a third account of visual experience, which seems to me to be compatible with the doctrine of "How to Speak of the Colors." This is the so-called Multiple Relation Theory of visual experience.[3]

Visual experience is a type of awareness. Awareness is a relation between a subject and an object. What is characteristic of visual experience is that it is the type of awareness in which an object phenomenally looks a certain way to a subject. As on the Intentionalist View, an object *phenomenally* looking a certain way to a subject is distinct from and prior to the object producing in the subject the belief or the inclination to believe that it is that way. (Hence the familiar contrast between phenomenal and epistemic uses of "looks," where an epistemic use is one in which the subject is expressing his belief or possibly suppressed inclination to believe that something is some way.) As against the Intentionalist View, an object's phenomenally looking a certain way to a subject is not to be analyzed as the object's causing the subject to visually entertain the content that it is that way. As against the Sense Data Theory, an object's phenomenally looking a certain way to a subject is not to be analyzed as the object's causing in the subject a sense datum which is that way. According to the Multiple Relation Theory both the Sense Data Theory and the Intentionalist View go wrong in trying to analyze the primitive notion of visual awareness, equivalently, the notion of an object phenomenally looking a certain way to a subject.

So what then goes on when Zinka the canary looks canary yellow to me? I have a certain visual experience which involves Zinka's phenomenally looking canary yellow to me. At this level of experience there is no room for error because there is as yet no judgment, no belief, and indeed no content entertained. A particular relation holds between Zinka and me. Then in immediate reflection upon my visual experience, I mistakenly abstract out from Zinka's phenomenally looking a certain way to me a certain way which I take Zinka to be. It is this kind of immediate belief, e.g. that Zinka is, as it were monadically, the way she phenomenally looks that is the locus of error in visual perception. (This is not the mistaking of a mental feature for a physical feature but the mistaking of a relational feature for a non-relational feature. Is this the mistake one unlearns in art school?)

Visual experience itself is not poisoned by concepts of colors which could never find application to external objects. Visual experience is not a conceptual matter. But visual experience does prompt immediate beliefs which take things to be colored in ways they could never be. Nonetheless these beliefs are not our only central and important beliefs concerning the colors. Hence, even if these immediate beliefs are false it could still turn out in an interesting sense that the external world is colored.

A bonus of adopting the Multiple Relation Theory is that we can then reply to the familiar objection that the dispositional account of the colors is inevitably circular, and circular in a way that is either self-defeating or at least unhelpful.

The dispositional account had it that

x is canary yellow for O in C iff x is (standardly) disposed to look canary yellow to O in C.

The term "canary yellow" appears on the left- and right-hand sides of the biconditional. This raises questions about circularity.[4] However this dispositional account analyzes a relational property—being canary yellow to O in C—as the power or disposition to produce the holding of another relation between x and O in C. That relation is x's phenomenally looking canary yellow to O in C. This latter relation is not x's looking canary yellow for O in C to O in C. Hence it is not x's looking standardly disposed to look canary yellow to O in C, whatever that could be.

The dispositional account is unmysterious. It treats the colors as dispositions of objects to produce certain types of visual awareness (equivalently, certain phenomenal looks). Perhaps it is just asking for trouble to partially characterize those types of visual awareness with terms which are the same as the names for the colors themselves. So, to be less misleading,

x is canary yellow for O in C iff X is (standardly) disposed to produce a certain kind of visual awareness of x by O in C.

Which kind of visual awareness? We can introduce the kind of awareness in question to an appropriate subject by experiential paradigms and foils. A visual experience of Zinka would be among the paradigms, a red afterimage would be among the foils. In learning to attend to such a kind of visual experience, the subject learns to neglect differences among experiences which do not make for a difference in respect of the experiential kind in question. We can thus make our concepts of the dispositional colors as coarse-grained or as fine-grained as we like.

Notes

1. Mike Thau, who is writing a dissertation on perception and from whom I have learnt much on these issues, believes that I should instead think of perception as attributing to surfaces both colors, which surfaces do have, and another set of colorlike properties which surfaces could not have. I find no evidence for this double attribution on the part of perception. In coming to master color terms we never find ourselves confused as between which of the two kinds of colorlike properties which visual perception represents a surface as having is supposed to be denoted by the term we are mastering. The best explanation of this is that there is only one kind of colorlike property, the kind we know as the colors.

2. This way of putting the point is due to Greg Harding from whose deep work on color perception I have learnt much.

3. For detailed treatments of this theory see chapter 4 of Frank Jackson's *Perception* (Cambridge University Press, 1977) and Harold Langsam's "The Theory of Appearing Defended" forthcoming in *Philosophical Studies*.

4. See Paul Boghossian and David Velleman, chapter 7, pp. 86–90.

10 A Simple View of Colour

John Campbell

I

Physics tells us what is objectively there. It has no place for the colours of things. So colours are not objectively there. Hence, if there is such a thing at all, colour is mind-dependent. This argument forms the background to disputes over whether common sense makes a mistake about colours. It is assumed that the view of colour as mind-independent has been refuted by science. The issue, then, is whether the view of colour as mind-independent is somehow implicit in the phenomenology of colour vision. I want to look at the background argument which controls this dispute.

We can see this argument at work in the dispute between Mackie, who presses the charge of error in the phenomenology, and McDowell, who resists the charge. They take the issue to be the characterization of colour experience. For Mackie's Locke, 'colours as we see them are totally different ... from the powers to produce such sensations'.[1] Further, if we take the appearances at face value, we will not take colours to be microphysical properties of things: they do not appear as microphysical properties. Still, if we take the appearances at face value, we will take it that we are seeing the properties of objects in virtue of which they have the potential to produce experiences of colour. The perception reveals the whole character of the property to us. Since it is not just a power to produce experiences in us, there is a sense in which this property is mind-independent; and according to Mackie, the mistake of common sense is to suppose that there are any such non-physical mind-independent properties. McDowell, on the other hand, insists that vision presents colours as dispositions to produce experiences of colour. After all, he asks, '[w]hat would one expect it to be like to experience something's being such as to look red'—that is, as having the dispositional property—'if not to experience the thing in question (in the right circumstances) as looking, precisely, red?'[2] For Mackie and McDowell, the legitimacy of our ordinary talk about colours turns on this issue about phenomenology. They agree that we do have colour experiences, and that objects have the powers to produce these experiences in virtue of their microphysical structures. They agree there is no more going on than that. The only issue between them is whether this is enough to vindicate the phenomenology. The question is whether it seems that there is more to colour than dispositions to produce experiences of colour, whether it seems that colour is mind-independent.

I shall take the view of colours as mind-dependent to find clearest expression in the thesis that they are powers of objects to produce experiences in us. I shall not be concerned with more rarefied theses of mind-dependence, which might be applied to properties quite generally.

The view of colours as mind-independent must acknowledge some role for colours in colour-perception. I shall equate this view with the thesis that they are to be thought of as the grounds of the dispositions of objects to produce experiences of colour. This is not a kind of physicalism about colours. To suppose that it must be is to assume an identification of the physical and the objective which the thesis may question. It may instead be that the characters of the colours are simply transparent to us. Of course, we often have to consider cases in which the character of a property is not transparent to us; but there may also be cases in which transparency holds.

The background argument with which we began needs elaboration. It does not as it stands provide a convincing argument for the assumption that colours are mind-dependent. A simpler view of colours thus remains in play. On this view, redness, for example, is not a disposition to produce experiences in us. It is, rather, the ground of such a disposition. But that is not because redness is a microphysical property—the real nature of the property is, rather, transparent to us. This view of colours would be available even to someone who rejected the atomic theory of matter: someone who held that matter is continuous and that there are no microphysical properties. The view of colours as mind-independent does not depend upon the atomic theory. Nevertheless, without there being a commitment to any thesis of property identity, someone who holds this simple view may acknowledge that colours are supervenient upon physical properties, if only in the minimal sense that two possible worlds which share all their physical characteristics cannot be differently coloured. It is usually supposed that if common sense accepts this position, it is mistaken: to defend common sense is to clear it of the charge of accepting the view. But we shall see that we do not have any reason to abandon this Simple View.

II

The central line of objection to the Simple View depends upon a particular conception of what is required for a property to be mind-independent. This attack depends on supposing that a mind-independent property must be one that figures in an 'absolute', or 'objective' description of the world. The defining feature of such a description of reality is that understanding it does not require one to exploit anything idiosyncratic about one's own position in the world.

Colours, conceived as the Simple View conceives them, cannot figure in any such description. The Simple View acknowledges that to understand ascriptions of colour, one must have, or have had, experiences of colour. There is no other way of grasping what a particular colour-property *is*. The character of the property is, though, transparent to this way of grasping it.

This is a forceful line of argument for the mind-dependence of colours. But it proves too much. If it were correct, it could be extended to show more than that colours are mind-dependent. We could also use it to show that *particularity*—a physical thing's being the *particular* thing that it is—is mind-dependent. It is much easier to see what is going wrong when we apply the above line of thought to the case of physical things. So I shall spend most of this section on this case, returning at the end of it to draw the comparison with colour.

The possibility of massive duplication shows that the subject can never fade out of the picture in singular reference. There is no 'absolute' or 'objective' conception which refers to particulars. The point needs some glossing, though. The possibility of massive duplication makes it vivid that we use spatiotemporal locations to differentiate things—that is what makes the difference between identifying particulars, and identifying types. But we can identify spatiotemporal locations only by appeal to their relations to things. How then does the apparatus of singular reference get off the ground? The possibility of massive duplication rules out its being by purely qualitative singling-out. One answer is that one uses one's own location, as what ultimately anchors one's singular reference to *this* sector of the world rather than to a duplicate. Yet this cannot be right. One cannot locate all other objects by reference to oneself, for one's own location is itself identified by appeal to the objects one perceives. One is not oneself somehow a uniquely firmly anchored spatial thing. In fact, the conclusion is correct, that the subject can never fade entirely out of the picture in singular reference, but not because one has always to identify things by appeal to one's own location. The point is rather that the demonstratives we need to get reference to physical things off the ground invariably *introduce* the subject: his identifications of objects always provide a frame of reference by which the subject can triangulate his own location, or else they depend upon a range of identifications of objects by references to which the subject can triangulate his own location.

One might conclude from this that particularity is mind-dependent. One might conclude that what makes a physical thing the *particular* thing that it is, is, ultimately, its relation to a mind. If we want to resist this conclusion, we have to explain how particularity can be mind-independent even though there is no 'absolute' or 'objective' way of identifying particulars.

The mind-independence of particularity is what explains a modal datum. Intuitively, it would seem that I can make sense of the idea that all the things around me might have existed, and might continue to exist, even if I simply had not been around to think about any of them. But in thinking this thought, I am, of course, using the fact that I am demonstratively linked to those things: for the thought I have is a thought about *those very* objects. This also, however, provides room for the thought of my own location with respect to them: so what makes it possible for me to abstract away from that? At this point one might appeal to the existence of other thinkers than oneself, who can identify those very objects whether or not I am around. But we surely want to underwrite the possibility that many of the particular things around us might have existed even if there had been no sentient beings. It is here that it can seem so appealing to invoke ways of identifying those particulars from *no* point of view. Yet there is no such way of identifying a particular thing.

We have to abandon the notion of an 'absolute' or 'objective' description of reality, which identifies particular things. We need another tack. We have to appreciate how fundamental in our thinking is our grasp of a simple theory of perception. This theory provides us with the idea that our perceptions are caused by a pair of factors: by the way things are in the environment, and by one's meeting the enabling conditions of perception—being in the right place at the right time, suitably receptive, and so on. The problem about the mind-independence of particularity is the result of operating as if we had a range of thoughts relating to what is there anyway, which we can as it happens employ in a simple theory of perception. Operating in this way, we naturally have some difficulty in explaining how it is that we find it intelligible that things are thus and so anyway. The correct response is to acknowledge that *what makes it the case* that our thoughts concern what is there anyway, is that they are embedded in a simple theory of perception. This embedment is internal to those thoughts: it is what constitutes them as being the thoughts they are.

Simple predicates of physical things are themselves explained in terms internal to this theory. The *stability* of predications of enduring objects, and the framework of expectations into which they fit, make sense only in the context of this simple theory.

This simple theory, being so fundamental, has an autonomous role to play in controlling our grasp of modal truth. It is this simple theory that makes it intelligible to us that our perceptions concern a world of objects which are there independently of us. The independence of the particulars is grasped once the subject understands that perception of them requires not just their existence, but the meeting of these further, enabling conditions of perception. The existence and character of the particulars is quite independent of whether these further conditions are met.

Of course the theory is *corrigible*, and it is always open to us to make new discoveries about the essential character of the world. The fact remains that our grasp of modal truth, including our conception of what sorts of things there are, is controlled by our developing grasp of this theory.

This point about spatial thinking marks a contrast between it and thought of abstract objects. For abstract objects in general, it is plausible that there is a canonical level of singular thought which controls our grasp of modal truth. Thus for numbers we have the numerals: modal truths about numbers are ultimately responsible to what is transparently conceptually possible at the level of thought expressible using numerals. The reason why it is not essential to any number that it be the number of the planets is that it is transparently conceptually possible that 9, for example, should not be the number of planets. The reason why 9 is essentially greater than 7 is that it is transparently conceptually necessary that 9 is greater than 7. As Quine once put it, making sense of modality here means 'adopting a frankly inequalitarian attitude towards the various ways of specifying the number'.[3] In the spatial case, however, there is no level of singular thought which can play this role. The position of a number in the number series individuates it, and is essential to it, if anything is, and that is precisely what the numerals capture. In contrast, what individuates a physical thing is its location at a time: and that is the very paradigm of a contingent property. How is it that individuation and essence can come apart like this? The reason for the asymmetry is the role which is played by a simple theory of perception in the spatial case, in controlling our grasp of modal truth. This simple theory has no parallel in the case of abstract objects.

What holds for spatial things here, holds for their properties. The mind-independence of a property of physical things is just a different issue to whether it can figure in an 'absolute' or 'objective' conception of reality: it has to do rather with the embedment of the property in a simple theory of perception.

We can put the point by asking how we are to explain the modal datum for colours, that objects might have been coloured exactly as they are even had there been no sentient life. The proponent of the dispositional analysis takes it that in explaining this datum we have to appeal to an 'absolute' or 'objective' conception of the world, which can only be a physical characterization of it. And there is also an appeal to the global supervenience of colour on the physical, so that the datum is explained as amounting to the fact that the world might have had just the physical structure it actually does even had there been no sentient life: and that structure is one which has the power to produce particular colour-experiences in us, as we actually are. On this approach, the modal datum would simply not be intelligible to someone who rejected the atomic theory, taking matter to be continuous. But there is an alternative way of explaining the modal datum. The alternative is to point out that the experience of a colour is characteristically the joint upshot of the operation of a pair of factors: the object's having that colour, on the one hand, and on the other, the satisfaction of a whole range of enabling conditions of perception: for example, that the lighting is standard, the percipient is appropriately situated and oriented, and so on. All the modal datum comes to is that this pair of factors is genuinely distinct. Whether the object has the colour is one thing, and whether anybody is in a position to see it—indeed, whether anybody is there at all—is another. Grasping this point does not require an acquaintance with the atomic theory of matter. At this point, though, it may be said that colours, conceived as the Simple View conceives them, can play no role in the causation of perception.

III

One line of argument against the Simple View is that on it, colours become epiphenomena. We can put the point in terms of the intuitive notion of an 'explanatory space'. The suggestion is that common sense and science are jostling for the same 'explanatory space'. They are attempting to give causal explanations of the same phenomenon: perception of colour. One explanation we might give of colour perception is in terms of wavelengths and physiology. But on this view, to suppose both explanations are correct would be to suppose that the colour-experience is causally overdetermined. The only reasonable alternative is to take the colours to be epiphenomena.

The dispositional analysis is an attempt to resist this conclusion while hanging on to the idea that the two ways of explaining colour perception can be driven, in an easily understood way, into a single 'explanatory space'. On the dispositional theory, the relation between the two accounts is analogous to that between an explanation of the dissolution of salt in terms of its solubility, and an account of the underlying chemistry of salt and water. These two accounts do not compete; rather, the explanation of dissolution by solubility merely holds open the place for the scientific account. So too, on the dispositional analysis, the explanation of colour perception in terms of colour does not compete with the scientific account, but more modestly, just holds open the place for it.

The obvious response to this whole line of thought is to question whether talk of colours and talk of wavelengths really do occupy the same 'explanatory space'. We have, on the one hand, the causal explanation of colour perception by colour, and on the other, the explanation of visual processes by wavelength. The obvious model for the relation between the two accounts is the relation between the following two types of causal explanation: the explanation of one psychological state by appeal to others—the explanation of a desire by appeal to a further belief and desire, for instance—and the explanation of one neural state by appeal to others. There is surely some connection between these two types of explanation, but it is not easy to characterize, and it is not evident that we should think of them as occupying a single 'explanatory space'.

Another line of attack on the role of colour in causal explanation comes from Locke. In some moods, he held that causal explanation must be mechanistic. The transmission of motion by impulse is inherently intelligible, and all other phenomena are rendered intelligible by being shown to be merely complex cases of the operation of impulse. An attempt at causal explanation which did not reduce the phenomena to contact phenomena would, on this view, have failed to render them intelligible. So it would not explain. If we think of colours on the Simple View, as the grounds of dispositions to produce experiences of them, we must acknowledge that they have no role to play in this type of explanation. They have no role in mechanistic science. This criticism, though, is not devastating. There is a wide range of causal explanations which are not themselves given at the level of basic physics—in zoology, in economics, in meteorology, and by common sense, for instance. And we have abandoned the view that basic physics must be mechanistic.

The obvious model is, again, causation in the mental. Many philosophers would want to view psychological explanations as causal, while acknowledging that they are not given at the level of basic physics. There is, of course, a problem about how psychological explanation is related to description of the world in terms of physical law. The very same problem arises for the simple view of colour properties as non-dispositional causes of our perceptions. The problem is how causation at this level is related to descriptions of the phenomena in terms of basic physics. But the problem here is no worse than in the case of causation in the mental, and it can surely receive a parallel solution.

Just to illustrate, a simple, familiar solution in the case of the mental would be to hold that mental events are physical events, and that the nomological character of causation shows up at the level of description of these events as physical. Just so, one might hold that a thing's being red is a physical event, an experience of redness is a physical event, and that the nomological character of the causation between them shows up at the level of physical description.

It is sometimes charged that this view allows for a systematic relation between explanations at the level of the supervening properties—psychological properties of colours—and genuinely causal explanations, but that it does not show how explanations at the level of the supervening properties can themselves be causal explanations. Another way to put the point is to ask how there can be more than one 'explanatory space', if all causation is physical causation.

This is a problem for all causal explanations given by the special sciences and common sense. We are certainly not in the habit of proceeding as if the only causal explanations are those given in terms of basic physics. Nor does it seem that any causal explanation not given in terms of basic physics must be one which appeals to properties which are dispositions, or properties which are functionally defined. Suppose, for example, that a round peg fails to enter a round hole. We explain this by saying the peg and board are made of a rigid material, and that the diameter of the peg is greater than that of the hole. This is not explanation in terms of basic physics, but it is causal explanation. And there is no reason to suppose that the roundness and size of the peg are anything other than categorical properties of it. Equally, when we explain an experience of redness by appeal to the redness of the object seen, this may be causal explanation though it is not at the level of basic physics, and even if the redness is not a disposition or a functionally defined property of the object.

There are many models which might be given for the relation between the two 'explanatory spaces'. Here is one. A thing's possession of a higher-level property can be related to a range of physical properties like this: in each nearby possible world in which the thing has the higher-level property, it also has some one or another of that range of physical properties. Suppose now that we causally explain someone's having an experience of redness, by appeal to the redness of the object seen. In each nearby world in which the object seen is still red, it has one or another of a range of microphysical properties. In each such nearby world, the particular structure the object has in that world initiates a causal sequence ending, so far as we are concerned, in a physical event which is also an experience of redness. So the explanation in terms of redness adds modal data to a description of the physical sequence. It says that in nearby worlds in which the physical character of the thing was varied but its redness maintained, an experience of redness was still the upshot. This is, of course, only a sketch. But there seems to be no difficulty of principle about providing such a picture of the relation between the 'explanatory spaces'.[4]

IV

One source of resistance to the Simple View is suspicion of the idea that colours can have any substantive role in causal explanation, suspicion grounded on their lack of what we might call 'wide cosmological role'. The argument is that even if the causal relevance of colours stretches somewhat beyond the explanation of perception, it certainly is not possible to state laws concerning colour which have the sweeping generality of laws concerning mass. As it stands, this line of argument is quite unconvincing. The special sciences make copious reference to properties which do not have a wide cosmological role, but they are none the less engaged in causal explanation.

We might in particular remark that we appeal to the colours of things not just in explaining particular perceptions of them, but also in explaining the evolution of the mechanisms of colour vision. The reason why our visual system was selected for just was, in part, its utility in identifying the colours of things. That is the point of the system. Of course, it is rarely helpful to know the colour of a thing simply for its own sake: an interest in colour is typically serving some further end of the organism. But it is precisely the identification of *colour* that has this instrumental value. There is, then, a rich role for the appeal to colours, conceived as the Simple View conceives them, in explaining the development of the mechanisms of colour vision.

It might be noted further that, even in explaining the perceptions of a single individual, there is a certain richness in the structure of our appeal to colours. It is not just that we explain an individual perception of redness by the redness of the thing perceived. We also explain the relations between our experiences by the relations between the colours of the things seen. For example, the similarity between two experiences of redness may be causally explained by the similarity in colour of the objects seen. The similarity and difference between an experience of light red and an experience of dark red are explained by the similarity and difference of the colours seen: by the fact that the objects seen have the same hue combined with varying quantities of white and black. And so on.

There is, though, a further question lying behind this suspicion about the Simple View. The challenge is the more extreme one, not merely that colours simply lack wide cosmological role, but that the attempt to use colours in framing causal hypotheses yields only pseudo-hypotheses.

We can begin by putting the point as a sceptical problem. On the dispositional analysis, there is no question but that objects have the colours we ordinarily take them to have. Looking red in ordinary circumstances just is being red, so there is no room for doubt about whether something that ordinarily seems to be red is red. It might be charged against the Simple View, though, that precisely because it rejects the identification of redness with the power to produce experiences of redness, it has to regard the sceptical question as posing a real problem. The problem is exacerbated by the fact that colours lack 'wide cosmological role'. We can bring this out by contrasting the case of shapes. Suppose someone asks whether objects really have the shapes we ordinarily take them to have, on the strength of their appearances. For example, suppose he asks whether bicycle wheels, though they look circular, might not in fact be triangular. The question can be dealt with by attempting to ride the bicycle: for ordinary motion, only circular wheels will do. Triangular wheels would give a very different effect. In contrast, consider the case in which someone asks whether this bicycle, though it looks white, really is white. Here there is no such auxiliary test we can use. Colour has no effect on the motion of the bicycle. The dispositionalist may hold that rejecting the dispositional analysis gives one a quite unreal sceptical problem, which one is forced to take seriously: do things have the colours they ordinarily seem to?

The proponent of the Simple View cannot evade the problem by saying that he takes whiteness to be whatever is the ground of the disposition to produce experiences of whiteness. That would indeed finesse the sceptical question—but it would also yield a view on which ordinary colour vision leaves us in the dark as to *which* property whiteness is. On this view, colours are hypothesized causes of our perceptions, rather than properties with which ordinary observation directly acquaints us.

As I have explained the Simple View, though, it holds that the characters of ordinary colour properties are transparent to us, and that ordinary colour vision is enough for us to know *which* property blueness is, for example. The charge is that on the Simple View, the ordinary percipient is left in the position of knowing which property blueness is, without having any guarantee that that property is the usual cause of his, or anyone's, perceptions of blueness.

The sceptical problem might be pursued by constructing an alternative explanation of ordinary colour perceptions, and asking whether the Simple View has the resources to rule it out. For example, it might be proposed that we live in an environment in which blueness is the ordinary cause of our perceptions of redness, greenness the ordinary cause of our perceptions of yellowness, and so on. To complete the construction of the alternative explanation, we should have to include stipulations about how the relations between the colours affect the relations between experiences of them. For instance, it might be said that one object's being bluer than another is the usual reason why an experience of it is an experience as of a redder object than is the experience of the second thing. And so forth. The dispositional analysis can rule out the proposal as absurd. We have yet to see whether the Simple View can do so.

The line of objection certainly ought to be pressed by someone who holds an error theory about ordinary colour vision. Someone like that takes the Simple View to be implicit in the phenomenology, but insists that the Simple View is entirely mistaken: nothing like colour figures in the causal explanation of perception, only the microphysical properties of things. If it is not only intelligible, but true, that our ordinary explanations of colour experience are altogether wrong, then it is legitimate to invite the proponent of the Simple View to consider various alternatives to his own preferred line of explanation, including deviant coloration.

At this stage, though, the objection to the Simple View need no longer be put in terms of scepticism. The problem can be reformulated as an attempt to construct what is sometimes called a 'switching objection' to the causal hypotheses offered by the Simple View, with the intention of showing them to be pseudo-hypotheses.[5]

It may help to make the strategy clearer if I first give an example of a 'switching objection' from a quite different area, and then show how a problem of that form is here facing the Simple View. The example I have in mind is the objection raised by Strawson's Kant to Cartesian dualism. The Cartesian assumes that one is immediately acquainted with one's own enduring soul. The objection is that whatever constitutes this 'immediate acquaintance', it is equally consistent with a whole series of hypotheses, for example: (i) that there is a sequence of momentary souls, each of which transmits its psychological states to the next in the sequence, as motion might be transmitted along a series of elastic balls, and (ii) that at any one time, one's body is connected up to a thousand qualitatively indistinguishable souls, all of which speak simultaneously through the same mouth.[6] This is not at all a sceptical problem. The strategy is rather to discredit the Cartesian by showing that the conceptual materials he introduces enable us to generate a variety of incompatible hypotheses, all of which must be acknowledged, by his own standards, to be equally legitimate.

The suspicion is that a parallel strategy can be used to discredit the causal hypotheses offered by the Simple View. Given the conceptual materials it introduces, the argument runs, it is possible to introduce a whole variety of causal hypotheses, all of which must be acknowledged, by the standards of the Simple View, to be equally legitimate. And, this line of thought concludes, that shows that these causal hypotheses are merely pseudo-hypotheses. We have already seen the kinds of alternative hypotheses that might be introduced, in which perceptions are said to be caused by quite unexpected colours, and the relations among the perceptions explained by quite unexpected relations among the colours of the objects seen.

This whole line of objection rests on the supposition that perceptions have their contents, as experience of this or that property, quite independently of which properties of things in the environment they are responses to. That assumption is questionable.

Again, the analogy with particulars is instructive. Recall the thesis that what makes a thing the particular thing that it is, is its relation to a mind. Consider how a proponent of this view might go about constructing a 'switching' objection to the assumption that particularity is mind-independent. The argument would be that, on that assumption, the course of one's experiences is consistent with a wide range of hypotheses as to *which* things are causing one's perceptions. The point could be stated as being, in the first instance, a sceptical problem: how can I be sure the very things I take to be causing my perceptions are causing them, rather than it being some range of qualitatively indistinguishable duplicates? There is obviously a variety of individual rival hypotheses that could be stated here. The 'switching' objection then is that by the standards of the view of particularity as mind-independent, all of these hypotheses have to be viewed as on a par with each other, and with the ordinary supposition that the things which seem to be causing my experiences are causing them. The only way out, the objection runs, is to suppose that particulars are individuated precisely by their relations to minds: that what *makes* a thing the *particular* thing it is, is the way it is related to the minds which apprehend it, so that there is no possibility of those minds being wrong about which particular thing it is.

This line of argument is not persuasive, and it seems evident that what has gone wrong is the supposition that one's experiences of things have their contents, as experiences of those *particular* things, independently of the question of which things they are responses to. That is what makes it possible for the question to arise, whether the experiences really are brought about by the things they are experiences of. But this is a mistake: the experience's being an experience of *that* thing is made so by its being brought about by that thing. So even though particularity is mind-independent, there is no possibility of the experiences being in general brought about by things other than the things they are experiences of. The answer to the 'switching' point is not that particularity is mind-dependent, but that experience is particular-dependent.

A parallel response can be made to the use of a 'switching' argument to show that colour is mind-dependent: namely, that what constitutes experiences being experiences of the particular colours they are is their being responses to just those features of the environment. Of course, it is not that illusion is impossible. It is rather that an experience's being an experience of a particular depends upon the subject's being able to use his colour vision to track that particular colour. So there is no possibility of setting up alternative causal hypotheses to explain colour vision: they simply bring with them changes in the characterization of the experiences to be explained.

V

Colour predicates seem to be in some sense 'observational'. I want to end by sketching a way of bringing this out. The point I want to make is that in the case of 'observational' predicates, there seems to be an epistemic dimension in the way the phrase 'looks φ' operates. In some cases, part of the effect of saying that a thing looks, for instance, round to someone is to say that if that person took the appearances at face value, without engaging in any reasoning, he would think that the thing is round. The phrase is connected to what one would judge without reflection. This certainly seems to hold for a whole range of 'looks φ' predications, such as 'looks old', 'looks expensive', 'looks efficient', and so on. But in the case of 'observational' predicates, there seems to be an epistemic aspect to the phrase 'looks φ'. It is possible for something to look old to a person who is in fact very bad at judging how old things are—someone whose unreflective judgements of age never constitute knowledge. In contrast, consider the phrase 'looks round'. Someone to whom a thing looks round must be someone who has the ability to tell whether things are round, unreflectively, on the strength of perception alone. It is not that such a person must be immune to illusion. Rather, the point is that without the capacity to tell, on occasion, unreflectively, that a perceived object is round, there is no basis for supporting that things ever look round to the subject. A parallel point seems to hold for colour predicates. Someone to whom things sometimes look green is someone who has a capacity to track greenness.

This line of thought can be pressed further, to resolve a dilemma over the characterization of colour experience. On the one hand, one may feel reluctantly compelled to acknowledge the possibility of inverted spectra—systematic differences between the qualitative characters of different people's colour experiences which do not show up in verbal or other behaviour. On the other hand, recoiling from this possibility, one may, in effect, deny the qualia and insist that if two percipients agree extensionally when they discriminate and group objects by colour, then their experiences just are the same, and there is no further question about qualitative similarity or difference. The Simple View allows a different approach. On it, we can say that the qualitative character of a colour-experience is inherited from the qualitative character of the colour. It depends upon which colour-tracking capacity is being exercised in having the experience. So if you and I are tracking the same colours, our colour-experiences are qualitatively identical. This view does not allow for the hypothesis of spectrum inversion; nor does it deny the qualitative character of colour vision.

Acknowledgments

I am indebted to Bill Brewer, Justin Broackes, Quassim Cassam, David Charles, Bill Child, Adrian Cussins, Philippa Foot, Elizabeth Fricker, Michael Smith, and Timothy Williamson. My focus on these issues was changed by Barry Stroud's John Locke lectures in 1987.

Notes

1. J. L. Mackie, *Problems from Locke*, p. 14.
2. J. McDowell, 'Values and Secondary Qualities', in T. Honderich (ed.), *Morality and Objectivity*, p. 112.

3. W. V. Quine, 'Reply to Professor Marcus', in *The Ways of Paradox*, p. 184.

4. This adapts the account of 'programme explanation' given in F. Jackson and P. Pettit, 'Functionalism and Broad Content', *Mind* 97, pp. 381–400, and 'Structural Explanation in Social Theory', in D. Charles and K. Lennon (eds.), *Reduction, Explanation and Realism*.

5. For a helpful taxonomy of such arguments, see C. Peacocke, 'The Limits of Intelligibility', *Philosophical Review* 97.

6. P. F. Strawson, *The Bounds of Sense*, p. 168.

11 The Autonomy of Colour

Justin Broackes

This essay takes two notions of autonomy and two notions of explanation and argues that colours occur in explanations that fall under all of them. The claim that colours can be used to explain anything at all may seem to some people an outrage. But their pessimism is unjustified and the orthodox dispositional view which may seem to support it, I shall argue, itself has difficulties. In broad terms, section 2 shows that there exist good straight scientific laws of colour, constituting what one might call a phenomenal science. Section 3 offers a larger view of what we are doing when we attribute colours to things, a view which makes it a case of holistic explanation, similar in many ways to psychological explanation. Section 2 emphasizes the model of scientific explanation, and section 3 the holistic model found in rational explanation; but it will emerge that colour explanation in different ways fits both models, as it also does the two principal notions of autonomy that the first section identifies.

1 Are Colours Explanatorily Idle?

Philosophers often say that colours are explanatorily idle. As McGinn has put it:

First, these qualities are not ascribed to things as part of the enterprise of explaining the causal interactions of objects with each other: colour and taste do not contribute to the causal powers of things. Primary qualities are precisely the qualities that figure in such explanations ... Secondly, secondary qualities do not explain our perception of them; primary qualities are what do that.[1]

On the other hand, some philosophers have thought the contrary,[2] and they have painters[3] and much of everyday speech on their side. We regularly hear claims like these:

(1) The red paint turned pink because he added white to it.

(2) The house gets hot in summer because it is painted black.

(3) The orange light of the evening sun made the façades of the buildings seem to glow.

(4) The yellow of a life-jacket caught his eye as he looked across the water into the distance.

(5) He stopped at the traffic lights because they were red.

Colours are invited to explain the appearance of things (3), human perception (4), action (5), and even the characteristics of non-sentient items, like the colour of a paint (1) and the temperature of a house (2).

Why then deny that colours explain what they seem to? Of course they are not fundamental physical properties, like mass and charge. But we should not need reminding that good explanation is not always explanation in the terms of basic physics. As Putnam has said, we can explain why a square peg will not fit into a round hole, by saying the board and the peg are rigid, and the round hole is smaller than the peg. An 'explanation' in quantum mechanics, or whatever other basic terms, would miss the relevant features. For 'the same [higher-level] explanation will go in any world (whatever the microstructure) in which those *higher level* structural features [rigidity and size] are present. In that sense *this explanation is autonomous.*'[4]

Why shouldn't colours occur in explanations that are autonomous in a similar way? Autonomy means different things to different people, and it may be helpful to clarify the two main senses I shall be giving it. The first involves no more than is introduced in the last quotation from Putnam: the same explanation would go through in any world where the same higher-level properties were present. It is no part of an autonomy claim in this sense, therefore, that properties invoked in an autonomous explanation are in every way independent of properties at other levels. The squareness of the peg is, for example, supervenient on the basic physical properties and arrangement of the peg's constituent parts. Colours similarly will be supervenient upon physical properties. In this usage, therefore, interdependence is not, as it is for Patricia Churchland, 'autonomy's opposite'.[5] Colour explanations will be autonomous in this sense if they are indifferent to the underlying realization of the property—if the same explanation would go through if the object's redness, for example, were realized in some microstructurally different way. But that does not imply that the explanation is independent of other properties in every way. It means that it is independent of microstructural variations that would result in the same macroproperty.

In what is probably a different sense, explanations are autonomous if they rule themselves, in that they are responsible to, and to be judged by, criteria internal to that style of explanation—and not by criteria from another domain. On this understanding, an autonomous explanation will typically (though not necessarily) be 'epistemically independent' of other explanations, in that knowledge that it meets the appropriate internal standards of success will be independent of knowledge concerning any other form of explanation. But it may still (and typically will) be the case that the explanation fails to be 'ontologically independent', in the sense that the higher-level causal relations would hold even if the underlying lower-level causal relations did not. In between these two senses of independence there is a third issue, of whether for any higher-level *classification* there has to be at a lower level a classification that corresponds (a type-identity, or restricted type-identity); and a fourth issue, of whether every higher-level *causal generalization* must correspond to (or be reducible to) one or more lower-level causal generalizations. But to claim that a property figures in autonomous explanations in the sense explained at the start of this paragraph is not to claim independence in any sense stronger than the first of these four.

I shall be exploring the prospects that colours figure in explanations that are autonomous in these two senses. Why should one resist the idea? Localized error, so to speak, is of course unavoidable: individual explanatory claims are bound sometimes to turn out false—as I shall later suggest is actually the case with (4). But some people may still suspect a global error—a mistake in the very idea that colours can occur in 'autonomous explanations'. The resistance must have a theoretical source, and I shall briefly consider four.

One might suspect that colour explanation, if there were such a thing, would compete for space with physics, and each would crowd the other out. The obvious reply is that explanatory schemes at different levels may peacefully coexist if they stand in appropriate relations. It is widely believed that mental and physical schemes of explanation can peacefully coexist if mental phenomena are supervenient upon physical phenomena. Could not colour explanation in a similar way coexist with the physical sciences, if a corresponding supervenience relation held there too?[6] The suggestion is plausible. My present perception of blue, for example, would be explained by the blueness of the mug in front of me, while the underlying visual processes were explained by whatever physical features are relevant. There will be no competition between the explanations, if the colour, as seems plausible, supervenes on the physical features.

One might worry about the fact that the putative effects of colour are primarily on humans, or, if on other things, on their colour, rather than on, say, their size and shape.[7] But that is hardly a reason to deny them causal efficacy: the primary effects of economic factors like an increase in the money supply are also on humans and other economic factors (rather than directly on the size and shape of physical objects); but we do not treat that as a reason to say they are causally idle.

A third worry might be that colours are parochial: there are totally colour-blind humans, and if they had been the only ones around, then they would hardly have felt they were missing something. But we can admit the parochiality of something without denying it causal efficacy. Economic factors, again, are parochial (there are societies without money, and a view of our own existence that makes money an irrelevance); but that does not make us deny the reality of economic causes.

Perhaps the most serious concern is that colours are dispositions, and dispositions neither cause nor explain. The issues are too complex to discuss properly here,[8] but there are problems at each stage of the argument. First, one may doubt whether colours are in fact dispositions. I shall later be giving reasons to deny the orthodox view of them as dispositions to produce experiences in us, while suggesting that they are dispositions of a different kind. But we can certainly not simply presume that colours are dispositions of any kind, in the face of the substantial body of philosophers who have recently argued that they are not.[9] Secondly, it is doubtful whether dispositions are explanatorily idle. There is a tradition of scoffing at explanations in terms of *virtus dormitiva*. But dispositions are not all like dormitive virtue (what about the engineer's properties of capacitance, inductance, resistance, and elasticity?), and even dormitive virtue has its explanatory uses. (The man fell asleep at the controls of the machine because he had drunk too much of a cough mixture with a dormitive virtue.) The issues can hardly even be aired here, but even if colours are dispositions, we cannot assume that they are explanatorily idle for that reason, any more than for the other reasons I have considered.

2   Colour Laws and Colour Science

What are the prospects of finding good straight scientific explanations that employ colours? What can colours be used scientifically to explain? We might distinguish three possible uses of colours: to explain (1) the effects of bodies (and light) on humans and other animals (notably in perception), (2) the effects of bodies (and light) on the colour properties of other bodies, and (3) the effects of bodies (and light) on the non-colour properties of other bodies (like their temperature, motion, or size).

The last category is the least promising. The most conspicuous cases where colour affects the non-colour properties of non-sentient things are cases where they do so only by affecting sentient beings, who in turn produce the effects in the non-sentient things. (The colour of the traffic-lights affects the motion of the cars, but only as it is seen by the drivers.) These cases therefore reduce to the first category. There may seem to be cases where colour is directly responsible for the non-colour properties of something: the warehouse walls, we may say, are heating up in the sun because they are painted black. But on closer inspection, the explanation seems to be invalidated by lower-level facts. The walls, we find out, are really heating up because they fail to reflect the infra-red light from the sun, rather than because they fail to reflect the visible light in the way that makes us call them black. It is not the blackness proper than explains the effect. Black things commonly absorb infra-red as well as visible light, so we naturally say 'if it hadn't been black, it wouldn't have heated up like that'. But the counterfactual is strictly false: the house could well have been some other colour and still heated up like that (if, say, it was painted in a green paint that also absorbed in the infra-red); and it could well have been black and not heated up like that (if the paint absorbed light in the visible range but not in the infra-red). The threat of invalidation by lower-level explanation may well be endemic to purported explanations of this kind. We have reason to believe that non-colour physical phenomena can in principle be explained in physical terms; we know (particularly from the existence of metamerism, described below) that colours are (often quite strikingly) variably realizable in physical terms; so it seems likely that for any physical effect produced by an object of one colour, there could be another object of the same colour that did not have that effect. The prospects, therefore, of finding laws by which colours could be treated as causes of the instantiation of other physical properties (other than via perception) seem remote—though the argument does not rule out the possibility in principle.

The initial prospects look better of giving scientific explanations on the basis of colour for the other two ranges of phenomena: human perceptions and the colours of things. Here a similar challenge arises, but in this case I think it can, at least often, be met. Quite aside from any general prejudice that the only decent explanation is explanation in the terms of physics, there is a worry that these phenomena are simply (as a matter of fact) better explained in terms of physical properties more basic than colour. The main reason for saying this is the existence of metamerism. Because of the limited sensitivity of the eye, two lights may have the same colour though their spectral composition is different. Two objects may look the same colour though the light coming from them is spectrally different, and their spectral reflectance profiles are different. This in itself is no reason to say that colours are unexplanatory: so far it seems a standard case of variable realizability. But many of the effects that we commonly ascribe to the colours turn out too to be determined not by the colours but rather by their realizations. We may say that the tomato looked brown because it was in green light. But it turns out that the *colour* of the object and the *colour* of the light are not sufficient to determine the object's appearance: it is the *spectral reflectance* of the object and the *spectral composition* of the light that determine the character of light reflected from the object, and hence its appearance. As is well known, a shirt and a pair of trousers may match in the midday sun, but differ in fluorescent lighting. Clearly, therefore, the appearance of the objects in the fluorescent light cannot be determined by the *colour* of the light and the *colour* of the objects.[10] The threat is not that there is lower-level explanation which goes deeper than the higher-level account (that in itself would not invalidate the account), but rather that the lower-level explanations show us that the purported higher-level account rests on claims that are just not true. It is simply *not true*, the challenge runs, that the reason the tomato looked that shade is that it was in green light of just that colour: for that shade of green illumination is neither necessary in the circumstances nor sufficient for the thing with that shade of red to look that shade of brown. A proper explanation will have to refer to the lower-level spectral characteristics of the object and the light. This threat, that the variable realizability of colours will invalidate purported colour explanations, I shall call 'the challenge of metamerism'.

If the threat seems to be realized in the case just described, that does not mean that it is in all colour explanations. Maybe some colour explanations can defeat the challenge of metamerism, and some cannot. This will be so if some but not all colour explanation is 'autonomous' in Putnam's sense: 'the same explanation will go in any world (whatever the microstructure) in which those *higher level* . . . features are present'.[11] Some explanations do seem to meet this condition. The mug looks blue to John because it is blue and John is looking at it in decent lighting, and he has good colour vision. The claim cannot be undermined by considering objects whose blueness is realized in a different spectral reflectance profile: whatever its spectral profile, as long as the mug is blue, then it will look blue to John in the circumstances described. It is the blueness that nomologically correlates with the effect, not just some lower-lying property that happens to be coinstantiated with the blueness. Other candidates for autonomy status come to mind: the object is opaque because it is white;[12] the paint is this particular green because it was mixed from paints of this blue and this yellow, in these particular proportions; the yellow book looks brown because it is in violet light. But are all these explanations in fact autonomous? Are they in fact immune to the challenge of metamerism? To see which are and which aren't, it will help to review some of the attempts of colour theorists to come up with serious laws.

I shall put aside the theory of the aesthetic qualities of colours in various combinations. Working often to develop a discipline parallel to those of harmony and counterpoint in music, Alberti, Goethe, Munsell, and Itten, to name only some of the more prominent, have tried to set out principles of the harmony of colours.[13] Some of the attempts have bordered on the fanatical: Munsell, trained as a painter, conceived his system of colour notation, with its numerical measures of hue, chroma, and value, as a prerequisite for the proper statement of the principles of colour harmony. 'COLOR ANARCHY IS REPLACED BY SYSTEMATIC COLOR DESCRIPTION,' he exclaimed in capital letters.[14] The status of such principles of harmony is a matter of such complexity that I shall set it aside for another time.[15]

In the field of straight experimental science, there is a fine body of explanation of colour phenomena. The work straddles areas which are otherwise often separated, like optics, quantum electrodynamics, chemistry, psychology, and psychophysics. The best-known work—like that of Newton in optics, and of Helmholtz and Max-

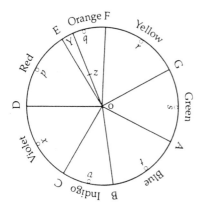

Figure 11.1
Newton's colour wheel: to predict the colour of mixtures of light. The circumference *DEFGABCD* represents "the whole Series of Colours from one end of the Sun's colour'd Image to the other." Let *p, q, r, s, t,
v, x* be the "Centers of Gravity of the Arches" *DE, EF, FG, GA, AB, BC*, and *CD*, respectively; "and
about those Centers of Gravity let Circles proportional to the Number of Rays of each Colour in the given
Mixture be describ'd." "Find the common Center of Gravity of all those Circles, *p, q, r, s, t, v, x*. Let that
Center be *Z*; and from the Center of the Circle *ADF*, through *Z* to the Circumference, drawing the Right
Line *OY*, the Place of the Point *Y* in the Circumference shall shew the Colour arising from the Composition of all the Colours in the given Mixture." The ratio of *OZ* to the radius of the circle gives the relative
saturation of the colour. (From Newton, *Opticks*, 154–5.)

well in psychophysics—is on the explanation of colour phenomena in terms of
physics. The kinds of explanation and law that are our present concern, on the other
hand, are those that explain colour phenomena in terms of other colour phenomena.
From a wide possible range, I shall consider five types of law, as developed in the
work of the nineteenth-century colour theorists Grassmann, Chevreul, and Rood.

One might take Newton's 'centre of gravity' law of additive colour mixing to be
the first straight scientific law where colours are among the explanantia.[16] Newton
claims that if the colours of the spectrum are arranged in a circle, with white in the
centre, then if you know the colours of the component spectral lights out of which a
compound light is composed, then you can predict the colour of the mixture. If you
consider the points on the colour circle representing the spectral lights in the mixture,
and assign to each of them a weight proportional to the intensity of light of that
kind, then the centre of gravity of the resultant figure will represent the colour of
the mixture of lights, as illustrated in figure 11.1. But though Newton talks of pre-
dicting the colour of the mixture from 'each Colour in the given Mixture'; he is using
'colour', I think, really for refrangibility or, as we would now say, wavelength. He is
giving a rule to allow us, from the relative amounts of light at each *wavelength*, to
predict the colour of the result. It was only with Grassmann's Third Law 150 years

later that it became clear that the explanantia in this kind of colour mixture law could be colours rather than wavelengths.[17] For, as a matter of empirical fact, the results of mixing a green light and a blue light of a particular hue and saturation will be perceptually indistinguishable, whatever the spectral composition of the two lights—however the green and blue are 'realized'. In the laws on the results of mixing coloured lights, the 'challenge of metamerism' can be met: in so far as Grassmann's Third Law is true (and that is within wide limits) variation in the spectral composition of the lights which does not change their colour will not change the colour of the mixture. Explanation of the colour of the mixture in terms of the *colour* of the lights combined is, in Putnam's terms, autonomous.

In the mid-nineteenth century, Chevreul, a chemist working at the Gobelins tapestry factory, tried to formulate other scientific laws of colour. Out of the many which he offered in his *Principles of Harmony and Contrast of Colours*,[18] I shall consider three important types: laws on the mixing of coloured pigments; laws for what appearance is produced when light of one colour falls on objects of a second colour; and laws of colour contrast, either simultaneous or successive. Two of these turn out, I think, not to meet the initial challenge of metamerism.

The mixture of coloured pigments is today called subtractive mixing, because each pigment may be thought of as subtracting a certain amount from the incident light in the process of (only partially) reflecting it. Crudely considering only red, green, and blue components of light, we may say that a yellow object reflects only the red and the green (and filters out the blue), a blue object reflects only the green and the blue (and filters out the yellow). If we paint, therefore, a layer of blue paint on top of a layer of yellow on some white paper, then the only light that is reflected is the light that can pass so to speak through both filters, namely, the green light. The effect of mixing two pigments subtractively is the same as that of superimposing two filters, so we seem to have an explanation here of why, when we mix yellow and blue paint, we get green.[19]

The trouble is, however, that this kind of explanation is not well equipped to resist the challenge of metamerism. It turns out that the colour of a pigment mixture is not determined solely by the *colours* and quantities of the components, but also by their spectral reflectance characteristics. It was a simplification to think of the filtering action of a blue pigment as simply removing the yellow. Two pigments of different spectral characteristics may look the same colour in a certain form of daylight. But now imagine we also have a coloured celluloid filter, and look at the metameric samples through it. It may well happen that, through the filter, the samples now look different from each other.[20] And the situation is essentially the same if, instead of having a celluloid filter in front of the eyes, we paint a layer of colour on top of the sample, as in subtractive mixing of pigments. The result is, then, that we cannot pretend that it is colour alone that determines the outcome of subtractive mixing: there may be differences between the result of mixing one yellow paint with blue and the result of mixing another yellow paint with it, even if the two paints look the same colour in daylight. In this area, it seems, rough-and-ready generalizations are all we can hope for.[21]

Chevreul extensively studied the effects of seeing an object of one colour in light of another colour. Pages of his *Principles of Harmony and Contrast* are filled with experimental generalizations like these:

Yellow rays falling upon a Black stuff, make it appear of a Yellow-Olive.

Yellow rays falling upon a White stuff, make it appear of a light Yellow....

Yellow rays falling upon a Blue stuff, make it appear Yellow-Green, if it is light, and of a Green-Slate if it is deep.

(Chevreul, *Principles*, 92)

Violet rays falling upon a Yellow stuff, make it appear Brown with an excessively pale tint of Red.

(Ibid. 94)

Unfortunately, these laboriously-collected generalizations are simply not reliable. Recognizing some of their shortcomings, theorists later in the nineteenth century (like Ogden Rood) tried to amend them. But there is a problem of principle: the existence of metamers makes it impossible to predict accurately the apparent colour of an object of one colour seen in light of another. There will be metameric yellow objects, for example, that in daylight are indistinguishable in colour, but in the same violet light no longer match each other. It therefore cannot be simply the *colour* of the object and the *colour* of the light that determine the appearance. I shall return to the question whether this conclusively scotches claims of lawlike autonomous status for all colour generalizations of this sort, but the initial challenge of metamerism has not been met.

The third category of colour law in Chevreul which I shall consider is laws of colour contrast. The appearance of a region of colour is affected both by the colours of objects that were in the field of view a short time before, and by the colours of other objects which are in the field of view at the same time. After-images are dramatic examples of the first phenomenon. Leonardo noted cases of the second: 'white garments make the flesh tints dark, and yellow garments make them seem coloured, while red garments show them pale.'[22] The phenomena were studied widely in the eighteenth century,[23] but it was Goethe and Chevreul who made them famous. Goethe explained that in both cases, it is 'the colours *diametrically opposed* to each other which reciprocally evoke each other in the eye' (*Farbenlehre*, §50, my emphasis). Each colour evokes its complementary—hence the names *successive contrast* and *simultaneous contrast*.[24] An object seen as red will leave a green after-image, one seen as turquoise will leave a yellow one.[25] 'A grey building seen through green pallisades appears ... reddish.' (Goethe, *Farbenlehre*, §57.)

The laws here are precisely ones of colour: the colour of the after-image is the complementary of the colour of the original appearance, and is not affected by the spectral realization of that colour.[26] The robustness of these laws is easy to understand given a knowledge of the causal processes involved; given that the cones in the retina respond in indistinguishable ways to two metameric red objects, and that our after-images and simultaneous contrast effects causally depend on our retinal responses, we would expect metameric red objects to be indistinguishable in their contrast effects. The challenge of metamerism in this case is therefore fully met.

Now for the final type of law. Ogden Rood worked on all forms of colour science at Columbia in the 1870s, and his *Modern Chromatics*[27] is still well worth reading. He offers one type of causal colour generalization that we have not considered before: describing how hue changes with saturation. One of several tables details 'the effects of mixing white with coloured light':

Name of colour	Effect of adding white
Vermilion	More purplish
Orange	More red
Chrome-yellow	More orange-yellow
Pure yellow	More orange-yellow
Greenish-yellow	Paler (unchanged)
Green	More blue-green
Emerald-green	More blue-green
Cyan-blue	More bluish
Cobalt-blue	A little more violet
Ultramarine (artificial)	More violet
Violet	Unchanged
Purple	Less red, more violet

(p.197)

The general formula covering these effects is this: 'when we mix white with coloured light, the effect produced is the same as though we at the same time mixed with our white light a small quantity of violet light.' (p. 197.) And this generalization again seems able to meet the challenge of metamerism. The process of mixing white with a coloured light is one of additive mixing, which we have seen already is unaffected by change of spectral composition. So if one orange of one spectral type turns redder on the addition of white, then a metameric orange of another spectral type will do so too.

Of the five types of law considered, three immediately meet the challenge of metamerism: the laws of additive mixing, of colour contrast, and of change of hue as a colour is desaturated. Only the first is readily expressed in mathematical terms (when developed for example in connection with a CIE x, y diagram). But they are all of them robust in the sense that substitution of metamers will not invalidate them. We can accept without worry, therefore, the autonomy in Putnam's sense of a wide variety of explanations that invoke colour.

Two of the types of law considered fail the test for robustness. Laws of subtractive mixing and of the appearance of objects seen in light of another colour are at risk of being invalidated by substitution of metamers. But the challenge may be being exaggerated. The existence of metamers certainly means that we will not be able to find absolutely precise and indefinitely refinable generalizations on these issues that are also true. But that does not mean that there cannot in this area be broad generalizations which are quite literally *true* and *lawlike* in the sense that they are supported by their instances and support counterfactuals. (There is a difference between a narrow claim that is only partly true, and a broad claim that is precisely true.) Though the appearance of a yellow object in violet light may not be determined exactly by the colours of the object and the light, it may still be determined roughly by them, for example, to lie somewhere in the brown region. Similarly, even if we cannot predict the exact appearance of a mix of yellow and blue paint, we may none the less be able to predict that it will be some form of green. And if this is so, then explanations that use precisely these deliberately broad terms will still be autonomous in Putnam's sense.[28]

How far exactly this objection is valid is an empirical matter. If we employ sufficiently broad colour classifications, then it will be fairly easy to find true generalizations about them. If we employ colour classifications that are too narrow, then it will be easy to find metameric counter-examples. How broad the classifications must be in order to be 'sufficiently broad' is an empirical question to which I do not know the answer. But the apparent availability of broad generalizations suggests that the challenge of metamerism is not an objection in principle to the idea of lawlike colour generalizations, even in those cases where colour does not determine *all* the colour properties at issue in the outcome. Even if the generalizations are broad and intrinsically incapable of indefinite refinement, they may still be lawlike, unobvious, and non-trivial.

In this section we have considered the prospects of good scientific laws about colours. The challenge to be met was not that lower-level explanation would be available as well (for that is innocuous), but that the proposed colour laws would actually be invalidated by metamerism: colour effects could only be explained in terms of information at the level of wavelengths, rather than colours. We considered five types of law as examples. Three of them conclusively meet the challenge: laws of additive mixture, of colour contrast, and of change of hue with saturation. Two of them on the other hand do not: laws of subtractive mixture, and of how objects of one colour appear in light of another. But even in these cases, there are still prospects at least of broad generalizations that are lawlike, and of correspondingly broad causal explanations. The case for the autonomy of at least some scientific colour explanations seems complete.

3 Colour Interpretation

We raised earlier the possibility that colours might have their home in a holistic interpretative scheme like that of rational explanation. The scheme might even be an extension of the scheme of rational explanation. This would certainly seem right if the traditional dispositional thesis were correct. If colours were dispositions to produce experiences in us, and if experiences were ascribed to people in the course of interpreting them as (more or less) rational creatures, then colours would figure in an extension of rational explanation. One striking consequence would be that a second form of *autonomy*, mentioned in section 1, would then seem to attach to ascriptions of colour. On one familiar picture, the ascription of psychological states is autonomous in the sense that it is responsible only to assessment by standards internal to that form of explanation. In one form of this view, set out by Davidson and developed by McDowell, psychological explanation is explanation of a special sort, namely 'rational explanation', which has different aims from those of broadly 'physical' explanation.[29] The ascription of psychological states has 'its proper source of evidence' only 'in terms of the vocabulary of the propositional attitudes'.[30] If colours were simply dispositions to produce psychological occurrences, then we might expect the former to inherit the same sort of autonomy as attaches to the latter—though the line of inheritance might not be direct. Though of course colours would not themselves be psychological states, they would in a sense be 'offshoots of the psychological'.

This is a powerful picture, but things are not that simple. Though the main figures are already recognizable, much will need to be repainted. The traditional dispositional thesis fails to make sense of some of our colour attributions, and this shows, so I shall argue, that we have a deeper conception of the nature of colours—namely, as (in the case of surfaces) ways in which objects change the light. This might threaten to remove any essential connection of colour with the psychological, but that depends on how exactly we characterize the 'ways' in which objects change the light. The ascription of colours does indeed prove to be part of the implementation of a scheme of explanation of everyday experience. That, by itself, might be said equally of other characteristics of external objects, like their size and shape, and does not guarantee that the qualities ascribed are themselves interestingly 'psychological'. None the less, it will turn out to be not just a prejudice that there is something both 'relative' and 'subjective' about colours which puts them in a different position: they really are connected with the psychological in a way that size and shape are not. The view of psychological ascription as the employment of a scheme of *rational* interpretation will turn out to need qualification; but the claim to autonomy in the special sense of this section will survive.

3.1 *Away from the Dispositional Thesis*

I shall set aside criticisms of the dispositional thesis on grounds of circularity or triviality, since these are not, I think, conclusive against versions that make no pretence at a reduction of colour. There is a more telling criticism that touches even the truth of the coextensiveness claim that something is red, yellow, or whatever iff it would look red, yellow, or whatever to normal observers under normal circumstances.[31] The problem is this. There are, we may imagine, killer yellow objects that kill anyone who looks at them.[32] Far from having a disposition to produce experiences of yellow in normal observers, they have a disposition to end all experience in them whatever. A defender of the dispositional thesis might insist: 'Such an object would still look yellow *if only it could be seen* by normal observers under normal circumstances.' But this does not need to be true: there is a difference between the nearby possible worlds in which an object is visible, and the nearby possible worlds in which it is visible and also has its actual present colour. Imagine a situation where there are a lot of killer yellow objects around, but we have learnt to deal with them: they tend to be small, they emit a distinctive bleeping sound, and (taking care not to look at them) we can easily cover them with thick black paint which the death-rays cannot penetrate. In such a situation the sentence 'If only the object could be seen ... then it would look yellow' will be false, simply because, if only the object could be seen, it would be covered in black paint.

The natural response is to plug the gap: instead of saying 'If only it could be seen ... ', the dispositionalist will say 'If only it could be seen *without changing its colour* ...'. This is progress, but not enough. There will be situations where an object can be seen and its colour is unchanged, but the colour itself cannot be seen. It may be a very short and faint flash of light; it may put our cones out of order but not the rods; it may be visible but only through a dark filter (and otherwise the death-rays get us). It looks as though we have to ensure not only that the object is visible and its colour unchanged, but that *the colour itself is visible*. We seem to have arrived at this:

(D1) x is yellow iff if only x's colour could be seen by a normal observer y, then x would look yellow to y.

This is true but trivial. It is tantamount to:

(D2) x is yellow iff if only a normal observer y could see what colour x is, then y would see x to be yellow.

And the same of course could be said of other properties too:

(D3) x is a dog iff if only a normal observer y could see what kind of animal x is, then y would see x to be a dog.

and even:

(D4) x is a piece of platinum iff if only a normal observer y could see what kind of substance x is, then y would see x to be a piece of platinum.

Of course there is a difference between these claims. The 'if only' clauses become progressively harder for humans to satisfy: we can often tell at sight whether something is yellow, perhaps less often whether it is a dog, and very seldom whether it is platinum. But by the time the dispositional thesis has been reduced to (D1), the interest lies not in what it says, but in any surrounding commentary that can be given to explain what part it plays in our thought about colours, and what else plays a part in addition.

   A deeper problem should also be evident. The puzzle cases are ones in which a normal observer *cannot* in fact see the colour (or chemical composition) of the object, but (struggling to maintain a version of the dispositional thesis) we insist on talking about how he *would* see the object if only he *could* see its colour (or chemical composition). But obviously if we take a view on this issue in any particular case, this can only be because we have already—quite independently of these dispositional theses—taken a view on what is necessary for an object to count as yellow or whatever. (In the parallel case, if we say 'if only he were able to see what substance it is, he would see it as platinum', then this can only be because we know already, for reasons other than its appearance, that the sample really is platinum.) If, therefore, we make sense of these cases of killer yellow, it can only be because we have—

independently of the dispositional thesis (D1)—a view on what it takes for something to be yellow. We must have, therefore, a conception of the nature of colours, just as we have a conception of the nature of platinum and of other chemical substances.[33]

What is this conception? What is the common factor between a visibly yellow object and one that is yellow but not visibly so? We cannot say simply: the primary qualities of the objects and their parts. Something that had exactly the same primary qualities (of all constituent parts) as a killer yellow object would kill people just as surely as the killer yellow object does. (Interestingly, even an ordinary yellow object in the dark cannot be said to have exactly the same primary qualities as a similar object in the light: a yellow book cover, for example, will in the light be absorbing photons and emitting photons, which it will not be doing in pitch darkness. If in the dark it were literally in the same primary quality state as it is normally in when illuminated, then it would be glowing!) If it has to be some physical property, then the common factor to all yellow objects will at best be some subset of primary qualities, or some relatively complex high-level primary quality. This of course is the physicalist proposal of Armstrong,[34] much criticized in the recent writings of Hardin and Westphal. It turns out that it is much harder to find a physical property common and peculiar to yellow things than one might imagine. There plainly is no one structural property responsible for the yellowness of all yellow objects. Neither is there any simple physical characteristic common to the light they give off, even when normally illuminated. (They will not, for example, merely give off light from the 'yellow' part of the spectrum: something that only reflected light of wavelengths from 565 to 575 nanometres would look so dark it would be black.) But on the other hand the suggestion that there might well be no physical property at all common and peculiar to yellow things is an odd one: for more than a century, psychophysics has investigated the physical characteristics of things that look yellow without obviously wasting its time. The idea of building a machine to tell the colour of any object from a 'purely physical' specification of it is hardly in the same class as the idea of building one to identify sentimental poems or baroque façades.

There are both phenomenal and non-phenomenal elements in our conception of colours; the difficulty is to see their interconnection. At one extreme there is the temptation to recognize only the phenomenal element: to say for example, as the dispositional thesis does, that being yellow is solely a matter of how a thing looks to people. But we know from killer yellow that this is not true. At the other extreme there is the temptation to recognize only the non-phenomenal element: to say for example that being yellow is solely a physical property.[35] But apart from the difficulty of saying how ordinary observers could (on this conception) have any confidence in their own ability to tell the colour of something at sight (why should unaided perception be a reliable guide to a 'physical property' of yellowness any more than it is to alkalinity, or to being made of platinum?), there is the difficulty of identifying the 'physical property' in question, and in offering an account of why we should wish to dignify with the title 'yellow' the items that have that physical property. A promising compromise is to make colour a non-phenomenal property identified phenomenally: 'yellowness is picked out and rigidly designated as that external physical property of the object which we sense by means of the *visual impression of yellowness*.'[36] This instantly accommodates killer yellow: killer yellow objects have the same underlying non-phenomenal property as those which produce impressions of yellow, though they do not themselves produce that impression because of the death-rays they give off as well.

But we should not let our minds be narrowed by the thought that the only range of properties available for our fundamental conception of colour is the range of physical properties. There are, at least at first sight, many properties that are not physical properties: mental, economic, functional, aesthetic, and moral properties, to cite only a few of the more striking (and perhaps overlapping) categories. Of course philosophers will take different attitudes to the apparent diversity: some will accept it whole-heartedly; others will deny it outright, insisting that there are no genuine classifications other than those of physics. In the middle will be people who accept certain ranges and try to reduce the others. To assure one's title to any of these views is not the task of a paragraph or two. The pressure towards a pluralism of types of property will be great for anyone impressed with Strawson and Grice's observation[37] that where there is agreement on the use of expressions with respect to an open class, there must necessarily be some kind of distinction present—unless one also believes that every distinction made with any predicate can be identified with a physical distinction, quite unrestrictedly[38] and without massaging the extensions of the terms. The arguments that this kind of physicalist property-identity is unlikely to be available are known well enough from the works of Davidson and Fodor not to need repeating here. Accepting a pluralism of properties, the principal challenge is then, I think, to show how this pluralism is compatible with a belief in the fundamentality of physics. Again, I think the essential moves have been made by Davidson and Fodor, showing that the irreducibility of, for example, mental to physical classifications is no obstacle to a broader physicalism that treats the former as supervenient upon the latter.

None of these views is uncontroversial. But given the prima facie availability of a view of mental properties of this general type, the possibility is open of regarding colours in a similar way: as properties that figure in an autonomous explanatory space (or subspace), irreducible to physical science, but supervenient upon it. Colours would figure in a distinctive form of colour explanation. The concerns of colour attribution would be different from those that govern the attribution of other ranges of property, though there would no doubt be points of contact.

3.2 Colour Interpretation

To say this is not to be relieved of the burden of doing something more to characterize the nature of the properties that colours, thus conceived, are, or to characterize the scheme of explanation which equips us thus to conceive them. I shall take the latter question first, and the former in the section that follows.

On the present suggestion, colours are in some ways parallel to mental properties, figuring in their own explanatory discourse. It may help, therefore, to employ some of the same techniques to elucidate colour discourse as have been used elsewhere to characterize mental discourse. In Davidson, and in a different way, in functionalists like Lewis and Shoemaker, one can find the suggestion that psychological discourse is the employment of an explanatory theory governed by certain constitutive principles. To characterize that discourse, we need to articulate some of the constitutive principles, and make clear how the overall explanatory scheme is applied to empirical cases.[39]

In Davidson's procedure of holistically interpreting either aliens or fellows, we make use of a priori principles which, for example, link belief, desire, and action, or (in another famous example) belief, meaning, and holding true. In Lewis and Shoemaker, there is a parallel idea that each psychological state can be characterized by the role it plays in a functional organization implicit in the platitudes and other a priori claims of common-sense psychology. What will be the parallel principles for colour explanation? Some of them will indicate relations between the various colour concepts; others will indicate their relations to the phenomena which they are used to explain.

Perhaps the fullest articulation of such principles is provided in Wittgenstein. In the *Remarks on Colour*, he considered a variety of propositions which seem to characterize a kind of 'logic' of colour. 'Pure yellow is lighter than pure, saturated red, or blue.' (III. 4.) 'A *shine*, a "high-light" cannot be black.' (III. 22.) 'Yellow is more akin to red than to blue.' (III. 50.) '[We don't] speak of a "pure" brown.' (II. 60.) 'Grey is between two extremes (black and white), and can take on the hue of any other colour.' (III. 83.) 'Black seems to make a colour cloudy, but darkness doesn't' (III. 156.) The source of many of the most interesting remarks is the letter from the painter Runge, which Goethe reproduced in his *Farbenlehre*—which in turn Wittgenstein had before him as he wrote some of the *Remarks*.[40] 'If we were to think of a bluish orange, a reddish green or a yellowish violet, we would have the same feeling as in the case of a southwesterly north wind.' 'Both white and black are opaque or solid.' 'White water which is pure is as inconceivable as clear milk.' (Runge's letter, §§2 and 11; cp. Wittgenstein, *Remarks* III. 94.) 'Black makes all colours dirty, and if it also makes them darker, then they equally lose their purity and clarity.' (Runge's letter, §5.) 'The opaque colours lie between white and black; they cannot be either as light as white or as dark as black.' (Runge's letter, §12, my translation.) A particularly important claim in Wittgenstein links the notions of surface colour and film colour: 'Something white behind a coloured transparent medium appears in the colour of the medium, something black appears black.'[41]

Wittgenstein's *Remarks* contain a fascinating discussion of the ways in which our mastery of such principles depends upon our natural capacities and our innate endowment—as also, we might add, does our mastery of parallel principles connecting psychological states. A fuller account of colour classification than my own would have to investigate this issue. But for present purposes, it will be sufficient to draw out other types of parallel between colour explanation and psychological explanation.

The ascription of psychological states to people is part of the holistic explanation of behaviour; similarly, the ascription of colours to things is part of the holistic explanation of our perception. To describe just one small element in the picture: rather as beliefs and desires (in a certain context) produce action, the colours of objects, the lighting conditions, and the presence of observers together (in a certain context) produce perceptions of colour. The explanation is holistic: one and the same perception may have been produced by say, a blue object in white light, or by a white object in blue light, just as one piece of behaviour may be caused by alternative combinations of beliefs and desires; and only the accumulation of evidence can allow us to choose between such alternatives. Most importantly, the mastery of the holistic scheme depends on mastery of a range of a priori principles which together constitute a kind of theory. It is of course a posteriori that any particular system can be interpreted as having beliefs and desires, but it is a priori that if a system has beliefs and desires, then they relate in various particular ways to each other, and to inputs and outputs. (In the hackneyed example, if someone desires that p and believes that her ϕing will bring it about that p, then other things being equal, she will tend to ϕ.) In similar fashion, though it is a posteriori that any particular region of the universe is coloured, it is a priori that colours relate in various ways to each other, and to things that they cause and are caused by. (For example: 'Nothing can be red and green all over.' 'If there is something blue at place p, and a person is present with p in front of her, conscious and with a normally functioning perceptual system, then (subject to various provisos) she will have an impression as of a blue object in front of her.'[42])

Most interesting is the way the parallel lends support to both the subjectivity and (in a different sense) the objectivity of colour. We are used to the idea that the states we ascribe to people when we employ the psychological scheme are 'subjective' in the sense not just that they are states *of* subjects, but also that the states are themselves perspective-dependent: only a theorist who has a particular point of view (embodied in his grasp of the a priori theory) will so much as comprehend the states thus ascribed. (Martians might make nothing of our talk of jealousy, through lacking the constitution necessary to grasp the theory, or to feel jealous.)[43] And yet the ascription of such states is perfectly objective in the sense that those ascriptions can perfectly well be really (and not merely 'apparently' or 'for practical purposes') true. (It may be a perfectly objective fact that person *a* is jealous.) In a similar way, the employment of colour terms is subjective in the sense that it embodies a particular point of view, inaccessible to certain perfectly rational people. At the same time, the colour ascriptions of people who have that 'point of view' are objective, in the sense of being assessable as genuinely true or not.[44]

Of course there is more than merely a parallel between the psychological scheme and the colour scheme. There are direct connections between them, because of the fact that colours give rise to experiences of colour, and (to put the matter carefully) variations in physiology determine simultaneously variations in the colours of which we are capable of being aware, and variations in the perceptual experiences in which we are aware of them.

How exactly does this picture of colour explanation relate to the issue of autonomy? In the second usage which I have distinguished, the term 'autonomy' is used for the status of a discipline or explanatory scheme which is self-governing, in the sense that it sets its own standards of correctness and is open to critical assessment only from within the discipline or explanatory scheme. In this sense, everyday classification of metals recognizes its own non-autonomy: we recognize that, on whether something is gold, common-sense judgements make claims that can only be fully justified (and may in fact be overturned) by going outside everyday methods of judging and turning to the metallurgists. Whether an explanatory scheme is autonomous or not is highly sensitive to the delimitation of the explanatory scheme: taken together, everyday classification of metals and metallurgy might count as autonomous, though the first alone did not. The notion is not easy to apply: psychological explanation might be presented as autonomous, in the sense that it sets its own standards; but yet it may turn out that those standards themselves make essential reference to physical and externalist considerations. So autonomy in this sense does not mean 'independence of the physical'. A claim of autonomy in itself carries no anti-scientific bias either: the physical sciences themselves could be described as autonomous. But what autonomy does mean is that if the *internal standards* of a field leave no place for criticism on scientific grounds of judgements in that field, then there is no place *simpliciter* for criticism of such judgements on those grounds. The claim of autonomy in itself is usually a trivial one, a demand to recognize an explanatory scheme for what it is: to recognize the relevance of certain kinds of consideration to judgements made in it, and the intrinsic irrelevance of other kinds of consideration. Whether the claim is news to anyone will depend on what kinds of consideration exactly are mentioned when the claim is developed in detail.

The role of colours as properties used in interpretation suggests that they occur in explanations that are autonomous in this second sense. How exactly? The most important point is that nothing outside the methods of colour discourse can force us to abandon a colour judgement: if on looking at an object in a variety of circumstances and checking with other people, we conclude that it is red, then there is no place provided for correction of this judgement on other grounds. So far, this is a pretty high-grade form of self-government. What we have also provided for, however, is the possibility that on occasion it may be impossible to tell by looking what colour something is (for example, because it would kill you first), and then it will often only be information about the physical (for example, the object's spectral reflectance curve) that can conclusively underwrite a colour attribution. Is this a departure from 'autonomy'? It is a little hard to know how to answer. Not if the internal rules on colour ascription themselves provide for this. It is only possible to apply colours to objects that cannot be seen if you already have a view on what colours *are*. I would suggest that it is now an integral part of colour ascription that anything which has the property that underlies our ordinary perceptions of red will itself be red. It is of the nature of a discovery, though a fairly obvious one, that the property in question, in the case of surfaces, is a way of changing the light (as I shall argue in the next subsection); but which spectral reflectance curves correspond to this way of changing the light will be a piece of *recherché* information. On this view, it is integral to colour explanation that there will be cases where the colour of something can only be determined by means other than simple perception: so colour explanation is autonomous precisely by itself making provision for reference to the areas outside superficial perception. By now this is a fairly modest claim of autonomy; but less turns on the employment of the label than on the understanding of the reasons for which it is employed.

Two further issues are worth a few quick comments. To describe colour explanation and psychological explanation as forms of 'interpretation' should not be taken as suggesting (as it does sometimes in Davidson) an instrumentalist or anti-realist view of the items ascribed in such explanation. Unless the occurrence of a term in a theory used to explain or interpret phenomena automatically forces an anti-realist understanding of that term, then the use of the word 'interpretation' here will not do so. Secondly, I have sometimes used the term 'rational explanation' where 'psychological explanation' would in some respects have been less misleading. I used the former term to allude to a view of the nature of psychological explanation found in Davidson and McDowell, which I wished to use as a model for colour explanation. But the term may have shortcomings even in its original context. The domain of psychological explanation seems to be wider than that of rational explanation, if the latter is defined by the 'constitutive ideal of rationality'. We may on occasion explain what people are doing by saying they are playing football, doodling, or dancing. The explanations are perspective-dependent (and may be impenetrable to the Martians), but it is not clear that the concept of *rationality* is central either to the activities or to our recognition of them. One might well say that we can describe people as engaging in such activities only if we treat them *also* as subjects of belief and desire, that is, as subjects of explanation that really is governed by the constitutive ideal of rationality. But even if this is true, it concedes that rationality is only one dimension of assessment of the distinctive lives of sentient beings. Even if the 'constitutive ideal of rationality' is the clearest source of the combination of subjectivity, autonomy, and realism that we find in psychological explanation, it is not to be assumed that it is the only one.

If this section has described some of the nature of colour discourse, it leaves us with the unfinished business of describing the nature of the items that this discourse actually equips us to talk about—that is, the nature of colours themselves. A recent suggestion is that of Jonathan Westphal: the colours of surfaces are ways in which they change the light.[45] The suggestion is immensely valuable, but it needs care to develop it in a satisfactory way.

3.3 *The Colour of a Surface as a Way in Which it Changes the Light*

There is a difference between the light reflected from a surface and the light incident on it. At or around any one wavelength the surface will reflect a certain proportion of the light, transmit a certain proportion, and absorb the remainder. And it is a high-level empirical fact about objects in our environment that these proportions, for any one surface, usually stay roughly constant from one time to another, regardless of how much light is falling on the object.[46] It is therefore usually possible to describe how a surface changes the light by giving a 'spectral reflectance curve' for it, showing the proportion of light it reflects at each wavelength (see figure 11.2). The

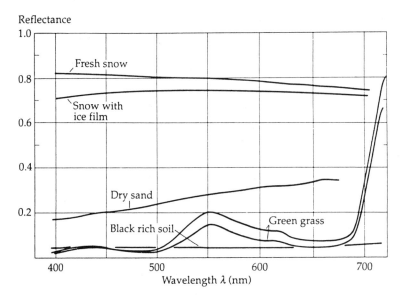

Figure 11.2
Spectral reflectance curves of some typical natural objects. (From Wyszecki, G., and W. S. Stiles, 1967/
1982. *Color science—Concepts and methods, quantitative data and formulae,* 2nd ed. New York: Wiley,
p. 63.)

spectral reflectance curve for a surface determines its colour, on at least one natural
understanding of that term, according to which the colour of, for example, a British
post-box is red—even if it is being mistaken for brown because the light is bad, or
for green by a person who is colour-blind or a recent victim of spectrum-inversion,
or it is invisible because there is no light on it at all.

Though spectral reflectance curves determine colours, they are not identical with
them. There are two problems. First, the space of spectral reflectance curves differs
from colour space: spectral reflectances vary in an infinite number of dimensions
(corresponding to the proportion of light reflected at each of an infinite number of
wavelengths of visible light), whereas on a natural interpretation, colours vary in just
three dimensions of hue, saturation, and brightness or lightness. The loss of dimensions corresponds to the fact that there are only three kinds of cone in the retina, and
objects with physically different spectral reflectances may be indistinguishable in colour. Secondly, the phrase 'the colour of the object' is indeterminate: the object may
be at one and the same time red, vermilion, a highly saturated vermilion, and also
R10Y 3080 (to pick a figure out of the air for the object's coordinates in the Natural
Colour System). The colour of an object is like its position, which may be at one and

the same time: in the house, in the bedroom, in the top drawer of the bedside table, and at such-and-such a coordinate position. Plainly at best there is going to be a many-to-one relation between spectral reflectance and even a colour coordinate position like R10Y 3080; and it will be even more many-to-one between spectral reflectance and a colour classification like *red*.

This does not mean that the colours of surfaces are not ways in which they change the light; it means only that ways of changing the light can be individuated in ways other than those of physics. Westphal's suggestion in his book *Colour* has two distinctive features; my own will emerge in discussion of them. First, Westphal seems to think we can characterize the colour of an object by taking its spectral reflectance curve and 'phenomenalizing' it—that is, reading it so that 'the *x*-axis is illuminant colour, not wavelength' (p. 32). (A surface colour itself might then be characterized by a certain *type* of thus phenomenalized spectral reflectance curve.) Secondly, following a suggestion of Wilson and Brocklebank, Westphal says that the significant property of objects 'is not the colour ... of the light they reflect, but rather the colour of the light they *don't* reflect' (p. 80). So a green object will be one which 'refuses to reflect a significant proportion of red light' (p. 81); a yellow object will be one that refuses to reflect much blue light (p. 80). When defining the colour of lights, Westphal mentions how lights of different colours will 'darken' objects—that is, I think, make them appear dark (compared with other objects illuminated with the same light). Thus a red light is one that is 'disposed to darken green objects' (p. 85), and a blue one that will darken yellow objects. Putting the two types of definition together, we have a medium-sized if not small circle: objects are green if they refuse to reflect red light, and light is red if it darkens green objects.

Neither of the two distinctive features of Westphal's suggestion will quite do. First, if we simply read the *x*-axis of a spectral reflectance graph as illuminant colour, then it is most unlikely that for any one *x*-value a single *y*-value can be recorded as the proportion of light of that colour which the object is disposed to reflect. For, given the facts of metamerism, it is quite possible for an object to reflect, say, 85 per cent of incident light of 570 nm, but only 75 per cent of a mixture of light of 550 and 600 nm which looks (and is) exactly the same colour. Secondly, specifying kinds of light which an object fails to reflect is not enough to determine its colour, unless we add that those are the *only* kinds of light which it fails to reflect[47]—and that of course would then be equivalent to telling us that it does reflect significant amounts of other kinds. So I cannot see any advantage in talking of the kinds of light that objects *fail* to reflect rather than the kinds that they succeed in reflecting.[48]

But this should not discourage us from working for a conception of colours as ways in which objects change the light, which is phenomenal but not quite in the way that Westphal suggests. Abandoning the two-step procedure that defines surface colour in terms of the (complementary) colour of light which such surfaces refuse to reflect, we might talk instead of the light that the surfaces succeed in reflecting. Holding to the aim of characterizing colour phenomenally, we might say: the red surfaces are those that when illuminated with normal white light tend to reflect light that is, phenomenally, red (whatever the spectral composition of that light)—where for accuracy that must be interpreted: the surfaces tend in normal white light to reflect light that results in normal people when normally affected by it having a perception as of a red material object.[49] But by then it seems no less illuminating to say, quite non-reductively, that red things are ones that change the light in a certain way, and that way is the way in which red things change the light. Does this make a pointless detour? No: for the route brings to light the fact that surface colours are ways of changing the light. What red surfaces have in common is *what they do* to the light: a factor that remains constant, however the character of the incident and reflected light vary individually. It is like the elasticity of a spring, a constant factor characterizing the way the length varies with the force to which the spring is subjected.[50]

Are there other ways to characterize this way of changing the light? We can say a lot within the everyday language of colour, employing either a priori or a posteriori connections: red things look darker than yellow ones; red is a deep colour; the most saturated reds seem more saturated than the most saturated yellows; red shades into orange in one direction and into purple in the other; a lightened red becomes a pink; red is a 'unique' hue: there are reds that seem to contain no hint of any other colour; nothing can be red and green all over. We can produce samples: *these* things are red, we may explain, and *those* are not, and there are borderline cases like *these*—though the samples will only be of use to people who can perceive pretty much as non-colour-blind humans do.

Can red be characterized in non-colour terms? We can clearly go a long way. We can characterize it as the colour corresponding to spectral light of approximately wavelengths 650 to 750 nanometres. But that of course uses the predicate 'colour'. We can do better: psychophysics and colorimetry have, I think, put us in a position where we can tell of any newly presented object what colour it is, simply from its spectral reflectance curve (together with standard data culled from human subjects).[51] It should therefore be possible to find a 'physical' property coextensive with 'red'. The questions remain whether this physical property will be *necessarily* coextensive with the colour, and whether it will be identical with it—and I cannot pretend to answer these here. But it must be obvious that the view of colours as introduced by a distinctively subjective scheme of explanation, and as phenomenally characterized ways of changing the light (as the present section has suggested), does nothing to rule out the idea that they might be characterizable a posteriori in other ways as well.

The attractions of taking colours as ways of changing the light are tremendous. I shall mention several.

First, consider a red car on a bright day. It clearly looks red. But you will also be able to see in it the reflections of other things around, from the road and the other cars to the sky above. The surface in one sense looks a perfectly uniform colour, but almost every point on it is, in another sense, presenting a different appearance. What is it that it constantly looks to be, when in this sense it constantly looks red? Why does it 'look the same'? Because there are in the visual array cues[52] that enable us to recognize it as a presentation of an object across whose surface there is a constant *relation* between incident and reflected light: there is a constant *way in which the surface changes the incident light.*

Secondly, this conception explains how it is that in order to tell what colour an object is, we may try it in a number of different lighting environments. It is not that we are trying to get it into one single 'standard' lighting condition, at which point it will, so to speak, shine in its true colours. Rather, we are looking, in the way it handles a variety of different illuminations (all of which are more or less 'normal'), for its constant capacity to modify the light.

Thirdly, this makes sense also of what might otherwise be thought a strange phenomenon: aspect-shift in colour perception. I have had the experience of looking at a book cover from just one angle, uncertain whether it is dark blue or black. At that point I can see it alternately as dark blue, and then as black, shifting at will between appearances. The effect goes as soon as I turn the book at a new angle to the light: it is suddenly clear that the object is dark blue. To count a transient perception as a perception of a dark blue object is to be prepared to count some different perceptions as perceptions of the same enduring object with the same colour; if such different perceptions do not in fact materialize as expected, then the object after all is not dark blue.[53] To be dark blue is not crudely to have a disposition to present a single appearance in a single kind of lighting; it is to present a variety of appearances in a variety of kinds of lighting, according to a constant pattern. And if it is puzzling how a *dynamic* property can make itself manifest in a *static* perception ('how can a disposition to present a variety of appearances be visible in a single appearance?'), then we already have, in familiar discussions of aspect-shift, the theoretical apparatus for a solution. It is because there is 'the echo of a thought in sight':[54] our perception of an object as having a certain colour is 'soaked with or animated by, or infused with'—the metaphors are Strawson's—'the thought of other past or possible perceptions of the same object'.[55] If it is a shock to find even colour appearances treated as soaked with thought—rather than being the brutely given *qualia* of today's descendants of sense-data—then that is a shock worth undergoing.[56]

A remarkable related phenomenon occurs with various forms of partial colour-blindness. The impression is often given that people classed as 'red-green colour-blind' (namely, the roughly 8 per cent of men and 0.5 per cent of women who have impaired colour discrimination of reds and greens, usually in the form of deuter-anomaly) have one and the same type of perception when looking at red, green, and grey objects.[57] Nothing could be farther from the truth. I myself have red-green deficiencies of vision, according to the Ishihara colour tests.[58] I confuse certain reds and greens in certain circumstances. But I do not have a single kind of perception from red, green, and grey things in general. I have no difficulty in seeing the red of a post-box, or the green of the grass, and my identification of their colour is not due to knowing already what kind of thing I am looking at. (I am equally good on large blobs of paint.) So I plainly do not have just one *concept*, applicable equally to red, green, and grey things. My problem is that occasionally I take something to be red (or brown) which turns out later to be green. What is interesting is that, when told of my mistake (or recognizing it myself, for example after trying the object in slightly different lighting), I can usually come to see the object *as* having its true colour. This involves what I earlier called an aspect-shift: the object actually comes to *look different*, even when the physical sensory stimulation is the same. Even in the lighting situation where I originally took the object to be brown, I do not 'get one and the same impression' as before if I later take the object to be dark green.

This makes perfectly good sense if colours are ways of changing the light. The person with red-green deficiencies is simply less good at telling from one viewing what is the object's *way of changing the light*; but by getting a variety of views of it, he may none the less recognize that property. There is no reason to say he lacks proper colour concepts; he is simply less good in applying them. His experience is, so to speak, ambiguous where other people's is not—in rather the same way as the experience of a person who sees with only one eye will be ambiguous, where that of a person who sees with two eyes is not. Most of the time those with monocular vision have no difficulty in recognizing the three-dimensional shape of objects around them—resolving cases of ambiguity by seeing the object from different angles. We certainly have no temptation to say that they lack a concept of shape in three dimensions.[59] And something parallel can be said of people with anomalies of colour vision.

This conception of colour also makes good sense of how colour perception could have evolutionary significance: the ways in which a surface changes the light will be a constant factor the tracking of which can easily be of benefit to an organism that is tracking that surface.[60]

The attractions of regarding colour as a way of changing the light are clear, though (particularly in the case of evolution, ecology, and colour-blindness) they raise questions that demand attention at much greater length. None the less, this cannot be a full conception of colour, simply because colours apply not only to objects that change the light, but also to objects that emit light. 'Yellow' is not simply ambiguous, as applied to surfaces, lights, illumination, films, after-images, and so on. But in at least some of these cases, the colour plainly cannot be a 'way of changing the light', so if yellow is a single feature, it cannot strictly ever be literally a way of changing the light.

The beginnings of a solution of the problem are not hard to find. There are a number of links between the yellowness of light and the yellowness of a surface. Yellow light falling on a white object will make it look yellow or yellowish, depending on the degree of adaptation possible to the light. Yellow light shining through a white translucent glass (like the globe of an old station waiting-room) will look similar to white light shining through a yellow globe. The exact connection of the two categories (surface colour and light colour), however, is complex, as Wittgenstein has taught us. Why is there no brown light? Why are there no grey lights?[61] What exactly are the parallels between the two areas of colour application? My own answer, which I think is also Wittgenstein's, involves both language and innate endowment, including physiology. To put the answer schematically: it is part of our language that some terms and not others apply to both lights and surfaces; someone who failed to grasp this would count as using different concepts from us. Other species might act differently from us in this, but then they would be using colour-concepts that were at best analogues of our own. But what we are here characterizing as similarities embedded in the language cannot be separated from our innate predispositions: it may, for example, be necessary to have a certain kind of neurophysiology in order to be capable of learning a language of this type. As always with rule-following, the ability to 'go on' in a certain way, given a certain training, is something that depends upon a certain natural endowment (and incidentally also upon environmental conditions, like certain kinds of constancy in the objects around us). Human beings to a large extent share with other humans these natural endowments, but there are conspicuous cases where, for example in the case of colour-blindness, a person is unable to learn a concept that others try to teach him.

The suggestion is that colours of surfaces are ways in which they change the light. The colours of lights are intimately connected with them: at one level, we may say, the same colours apply in parallel cases 'because such cases look similar'; but if pushed to say *in what respect* the cases look similar, we could only say 'in colour', and that was the very similarity we were (perhaps misguidedly) trying to explain. If on the other hand we say only 'the cases strike us similarly' then that is clearly correct: the very fact that we react by applying the same term shows that. But it is not a deep explanation of why the colour applies as widely as it does. Changing levels, we may indeed look at neurophysiological characteristics that are similar between human perception of the two cases. But in the most general terms, we may say that the similarity resides as much in our reactions to the things as in the things.

Section 2 defended autonomy in Putnam's sense: independence from mode of realization. The present section has defended autonomy in a second sense. A third sense might come to mind: explanatory independence from the objects of other explanatory schemes. I should make clear that I am not claiming autonomy in this third sense, either for colours or for psychological states. Psychological states do not form an explanatorily closed system, and the defence of psychological explanation as a form of holistic explanation autonomous in the other two senses does not need to pretend otherwise. There are a mass of psychological phenomena that are not explicable by the methods of rational explanation. 'Why do human beings forget as much as they do?' 'Why is a person who has just lost his job more susceptible to illness than one who hasn't?' 'Why do people become schizophrenic?' 'Why do people with Alzheimer's disease lose their mental faculties?' Maybe part of the answer to these questions will involve rational explanation invoking psychological states like imagining and desiring. But in most cases, what explanation is available will cross into other areas, like (at different levels, more than one of which may be relevant to a single puzzle) physiology, evolutionary biology, scientific psychology, and others.

In similar fashion, colour phenomena, though sometimes explained by other colour phenomena, will not always be. A mass of questions come to mind the answers to which force us to turn to other disciplines. 'Why do colours fade?' 'Why does red seem to advance in front of green?' 'Why is the sky blue?' 'Why is grass green?' 'Why do colour contrast effects occur?' 'Why do blue objects come to seem relatively brighter *vis-à-vis* red objects as the light goes in the evening?' (The Purkinje phenomenon.) 'Why does hue change with brightness?' (The Bezold-Brücke effect.) Only physics, physiology, chemistry, and various forms of scientific psychology can tell us. But the admission that colour phenomena form anything but an explanatorily closed set is perfectly compatible with claims of autonomy in the other two senses.

Acknowledgments

For discussion and comments on earlier versions of this paper, I am grateful to David Bell, Quassim Cassam, William Child, Larry Hardin, Kathleen Lennon, Michael Martin, Peter Smith, Paul Snowdon, Helen Steward, and Tim Williamson, as well as to other members of audiences where I have presented it. I owe a special debt to John Campbell: without his own writings on colour this would have been very different work, and without our many discussions, it would have been a good deal less enjoyable. To David Charles I am grateful for criticism and encouragement that go way beyond those of a generous editor.

Notes

1. C. McGinn, *The Subjective View: Secondary Qualities and Indexical Thoughts* (Oxford: Oxford University Press, 1983), 14–15. Cf. J. Bennett, *Locke, Berkeley, Hume: Central Themes* (Oxford: Oxford University Press, 1971), 102f.; J. McDowell, 'Values and Secondary Qualities', in T. Honderich (ed.), *Morality and Objectivity: A Tribute to J. L. Mackie* (London: Routledge & Kegan Paul, 1985), 118.

2. 'Colours have characteristic causes and effects—that we do know' (Wittgenstein, *Remarks on Colour*, ed. G. E. M. Anscombe, trans. L. L. McAlister and M. Schättle (Oxford: Blackwell, 1977), III. 82).

3. The painter Philipp Otto Runge said in a letter to Goethe: 'This has driven me on at least to study the characteristics of the colours, and whether it would be possible to penetrate so deeply into their powers, that it would be clearer to me what they achieve, or what can be produced by means of them, or what affects them'. (Runge, as quoted in Goethe's *Farbenlehre*, in the *Zugabe* that follows §920, my translation; J. W. Goethe, *Sämtliche Werke*, ed. K. Richter, H. G. Göpfert, N. Miller, and G. Sauder (Munich: Carl Hanser, 1989), x. 266). There is a translation of virtually all of the *Didaktischer Teil* (Didactic Part) of the *Farbenlehre*, by Charles Eastlake (Goethe, *Theory of Colours* (London: John Murray, 1840), repr. with intro. by D. B. Judd (Cambridge, Mass.: MIT Press, 1970)). Unfortunately Runge's letter is not translated by Eastlake.

4. H. Putnam, 'Philosophy and our Mental Life', in H. Putnam, *Philosophical Papers*, ii: *Mind, Language and Reality* (Cambridge: Cambridge University Press, 1975), 296.

5. P. S. Churchland, *Neurophilosophy* (Cambridge, Mass.: MIT Press, 1986), 380.

6. Though no definition of supervenience is uncontroversial, a first approximation would be: f-properties supervene on g-properties iff it is metaphysically necessary that situations indiscernible in g-terms are also indiscernible in f-terms, but not vice versa. The case for peaceful coexistence of mental and physical discourses has been made in different ways by Davidson, Fodor, and Dennett. Therre are people who have argued for the elimination of the mental. But the most notable proposals (like that of Churchland, *Neurophilosophy*, esp. chs. 7–9) attack the mental scheme of discourse not on the a priori ground that different levels of discourse can never coexist peacefully (Churchland is herself a defender of a plurality of levels of scientific discourse—see p. 358), but rather on the a posteriori ground that 'folk psychology' is not the best candidate for the job it is intended for, and looks set to be replaced by an ideally developed neuroscience (see e.g. p. 396). So the belief in a plurality of legitimate levels of discourse is I think not a contentious one. The second issue—raised by the claim that folk psychology should be replaced by neuroscience—is not one which I can pretend to discuss properly here. But since the issue lurks in the background of discussions later in this paper, it may help to say now that my own response would be to call into question Churchland's view of what the aim of mental discourse *is*. If its aim is not to 'explain and predict' in the manner of the physical sciences, then failure *at that job* is not a reason to abandon it. (For alternative views of the domain and methods of rational explanation, see e.g. Davidson, 'Mental Events' and 'Psychology as Philosophy', repr. in D. Davidson, *Essays on Actions and Events* (Oxford: Clarendon Press, 1980); J. McDowell, 'Functionalism and Anomalous Monism', in E. LePore and B. McLaughlin (eds.), *Actions and Events: Perspectives on the Philosophy of Donald Davidson* (Oxford: Blackwell, 1985); K. Lennon, *Explaining Human Action* (London: Duckworth, 1990).) A third and different matter is Churchland's claim that 'cognitive psychology' looks unlikely to succeed in isolation from neural science (or if it persuades itself that it is 'autonomous with respect to neuroscience' (p.362)). On this issue, Churchland's view seems completely persuasive, if the domain of cogitive psychology includes such questions as why we

sleep, and why we forget as much as we do. But that does not immediately lend support to the second claim, unless the aims of ordinary mental discourse and 'folk psychology' are the same as those of cognitive psychology. For the comparison between the relation of mental and physical explanations and that of colour explanation and physical explanation, see J. Campbell, 'A Simple View of Colour', in J. Haldane and C. Wright (eds.), *Realism and Reason* (Oxford: Oxford University Press, forthcoming), §3 [chapter 10, this volume]. I urged the same point in J. Broackes, 'The Identity of Properties' (D. Phil. thesis, Oxford University, 1986), 228. Not being able to argue all points at once, the succeeding discussion presumes the peaceful coexistence of the first pair, and considers the suitability of using that as a model for the relation of the second pair.

7. The effect of the black paint on the temperature of the house seems an exception to this. But we will shortly have reasons to doubt whether the claim is strictly true.

8. I discuss them more fully in my book *The Nature of Colour* (Routledge, forthcoming).

9. e.g. P. M. S. Hacker, *Appearance and Reality* (Oxford: Blackwell, 1987), chs. 3 and 4; Campbell, 'A Simple View of Colour'; and Barry Stroud in his John Locke lectures in Oxford.

10. Cf. R. M. Evans, *An Introduction to Color* (first pub. 1948; New York: Wiley, 1965), 59: 'The whole key to the solution of any *color* problem lies in a knowledge of what has happened to the relative *energy* distribution of the light ... Two light sources having completely different energy distributions may look exactly alike to an observer and yet may produce entirely different colors if the light from them falls on the same object. It is apparent that no description of these lights in terms of *colors* can ever explain the situation, but knowledge of the energy distributions may make it entirely obvious' (my emphasis in the first sentence).

11. 'Philosophy and our Mental Life', quoted above.

12. Cf. J. Westphal, *Colour* (Oxford: Blackwell, 1987), 37–8.

13. Alberti, for example writes: 'Grace will be found, when one colour is greatly different from the others near it ... This contrast will be beautiful where the colours are clear and bright. There is a certain friendship of colours so that one joined with another gives dignity and grace. Rose near green and sky blue gives both honour and life. White not only near ash and crocus yellow but placed near almost any other gives gladness. Dark colours stand among light with dignity and the light colours turn about among the darks. Thus, as I have said, the painter will dispose his colours' (Leon Battista Alberti, *Della Pittura*, book II, near end; in J. R. Spencer's translation, *On Painting*, rev. edn. (New Haven, Conn. and London: Yale University Press, 1966), 84–5). (John Spencer's reference in his notes to 'the colour chords' of 'the Albertian colour system' (p. 130 n. 83, cf. p. 105 n. 23), however, finds more systematicity in Alberti's comments than I can find there.) Goethe's *Farbenlehre*, pt. 6, esp. §§803 ff., sets out principles of colour harmony, and traces them to the eye's 'tendency to universality' (§805). The same tendency as he uses to explain contrast effects (when the eye 'spontaneously and of necessity ... produce[s]' the complementary colour) is responsible also, he thinks, for our finding combinations of complementary colours harmonious (§§805–7, cf. §61). Munsell carefully distinguishes the aesthetic characteristics of three typical paths one may take from a given colour: the 'vertical' path (taking lighter and darker values of the same hue), the 'lateral' path (changing the hue without changing either value or chroma) and the 'inward' path (towards the centre of the colour solid and beyond to the opposite hue). Describing their uses, he adds that the third is 'full of pitfalls for the inexpert' (A. H. Munsell, *A Color Notation*, 8th edn. (The Munsell Color Company, 1905, 1936), 38).

14. Munsell, *A Color Notation*, 24.

15. One point, however, may be worth raising. There is a tendency to think that aesthetic responses to colour are direct and unaffected by reasoning, training, and cultural influence. But this (like the 'tingle-immersion' view of aesthetic response in general) will not survive scrutiny. Aesthetic judgement, with respect to colour as anything else, is always open to revision, at least in its details, as a result of aesthetic experience of other situations, reflection, and *thought*. None the less, it is remarkable that there is such a discipline as harmony and counterpoint at all—and it seems therefore that, at least with respect to what might be called a strictly delimited aesthetic language, it is possible to make rough-and-ready aesthetic judgements on the basis of rules: 'this is not (for the language of Haydn and Mozart) discordant', 'the chord progressions of this chorale harmonization are more or less in the style of Bach'. Something similar

in the case of colour seems promising: you cannot tell in advance that this particular colour combination will never, in any context, look good. (Maybe the four colours look terrible together on the walls of a room, and awful used in a particular textile design for a dress. But when employed in a particular way on a book jacket, they suddenly look right.) It is a matter of continual artistic discovery that things that people once assumed would never look right or sound right can suddenly begin to do so, employed in a new way—a way which may itself change the artistic or musical language. But we can none the less come up with limited rules of thumb: for example, that any employment of this combination of colours, if seen pretty much with present eyes, will look a bit unpleasant.

16. Isaac Newton, *Opticks* (first pub. 1704, 4th edn. 1730; New York: Dover, 1979), book I, pt. 2, prop. vi, prob. ii (pp. 154–8).

17. 'Two colours, both of which have the same hue and the same proportion of intermixed white, also give identical mixed colours, no matter of what homogeneous colours they may be composed.' (H. G. Grassmann, 'Theory of Compound Colours', *Philosophical Magazine*, 4 (1854); repr. in D. L. MacAdam (ed.), *Sources of Color Science* (Cambridge, Mass.: MIT Press, 1970), 60.) Some qualifications should be noted. Maxwell's triangle and the subsequent empirical research leading to the 1931 CIE x, y chromaticity diagram showed that in place of Newton's circle, the locus of spectral points in this kind of mixing diagram needs rather to be in the shape of a plectrum or tongue. Secondly, each point on a modern chromaticity diagram represents a certain hue and saturation, but brightness is not taken into account, as it needs to be in a full explanation of additive mixing. (For further details, see e.g. R. W. G. Hunt, *Measuring Colour* (Chichester: Ellis Horwood, 1987), 58–60.)

18. M.-E. Chevreul, *The Principles of Harmony and Contrast of Colours, and their Applications to the Arts*, 2nd edn. (1st French edn. 1838; trans. Charles Martel (London: Longmans, 1855)).

19. Some forms of colour mixing are neither precisely subtractive nor precisely additive. In colour printing, if dots of different colours are printed *on top of* one another, the mixing can be considered subtractive; if dots too small to be individually seen are printed *next to* one another, then the mixing can be considered additive.

20. Mathematically, to get the character of light reaching the eye we would (at each wavelength λ) multiply the power of the illuminant at λ by the reflectance of the sample at λ and then by transmittance of the filter at λ. Now (as far as the character of light reaching the eye is concerned) it does not make any difference whether the filter comes between the illuminant and the object, or between the object and the eye. (The two cases may be perceptually different, if the context results in different adaptation.) Since we already know that two metameric samples may become distinguishable in colour when the illumination is varied, it is not surprising then that the same happens when the samples are seen through a filter.

21. F. W. Billmeyer and M. Saltzman, *Principles of Color Technology*, 2nd edn. (New York: Wiley, 1981), 130, gives a remarkable CIE diagram (after Johnston, 1973) showing the results of mixing various paints with increasing amounts of titanium dioxide white. The colour changes often show up as lines that are anything but straight, and in some cases the result of adding a small quantity of white is to move the colour not in the direction of white but at 90° to it. In certain circumstances, there will also be chemical reactions in colorant mixing, and then clearly no mixing rule that attended only to the colours of the colorants and not to their chemistry could hope to account for the results.

22. *The Notebooks of Leonardo da Vinci*, ed. I. A. Richter (Oxford: Oxford University Press, 1952), 136.

23. Chevreul (*Principles*, pt. 1, sect. 2, ch. 2) acknowledges that Buffon (1743) noticed examples of both types, and also mentions Scherffer (1754), Œrpinus (1785), Darwin (1785), and Count Rumford (1802).

24. Chevreul gives the impression that he invented the terms. (In *Principles*, p. 374, he talks of earlier writers who lacked 'the fundamental distinction which I had made between two sorts of contrast under the names of *simultaneous contrast* and *successive contrast* of colours'.) But Goethe had grasped the distinction quite clearly (e.g. in the *Farbenlehre*, §56). I have not seen any reference in Chevreul to Goethe's work, and I do not know what the relation between them was. But there is a fundamental agreement between them, notably on the universality of these contrast effects (Chevreul: '*every* colour seen simultaneously with another, appears with the modification of an accidental colour' (*Principles*, p. 376, my emphasis); Goethe, *Farbenlehre*, §51) and in the view that an understanding of contrast is the foundation for understanding the laws of colour harmony (Chevreul, *Principles*, 376–7; Goethe, *Farbenlehre*, §§60–1, §§805–7). This is why

both of them attack earlier writers' descriptions of contrast effects as 'accidental colours' or 'adventitious colours' (Goethe, *Farbenlehre*, §§1–2, Chevreul, *Principles*, p. 376), whereas in fact 'they are the foundation of the whole doctrine' (Goethe, *Farbenlehre*, §1).

25. One description of the phenomenon in the *Farbenlehre* is almost as remarkable as the event it describes: 'I had entered an inn towards evening, and, as a well-favoured girl, with a brilliantly fair complexion, black hair, and a scarlet bodice, came into the room, I looked attentively at her as she stood before me at some distance in half shadow. As she presently afterwards turned away, I saw on the white wall, which was now before me, a black face surrounded with a bright light, while the dress of the perfectly distinct figure appeared of a beautiful sea-green' (Goethe, *Farbenlehre*, §52, p. 22).

26. It is worth noting however, as Goethe and Chevreul did not, that after-image complementaries are not always the same as mixture complementaries: the colour of the after-image produced by a coloured light may not be the same as the colour of a second light that when mixed with the first yields white. Perhaps unfortunately for Goethe, the eye's 'tendency to universality' (*Farbenlehre*, §805) is not entirely precise. See M. H. Wilson and R. W. Brocklebank. 'Complementary Hues of After-Images', *Journal of the Optical Society of America*, 45 (1955), 293–9.

27. (London: C. Kegan Paul, 1879.)

28. Davidson makes a telling admission when discussing psychophysical generalizations. He admits that, notwithstanding his denial of psychophysical laws, it would be embarrassing to deny that there are any 'inductively established correlations between physical and psychological events' ('The Material Mind', in his *Essays on Actions and Events*, 250). 'The burned child avoids the flame' is his example; one even less susceptible of counter-example might be: 'A conscious person with no otherwise detectable abnormality, holding a hand in a flame, will begin to feel pain'. Davidson's comment is that such generalizations 'are lawlike in that instances make it reasonable to expect other instances to follow suit without being lawlike *in the sense of being indefinitely refinable*' ('Mental Events', 224, my emphasis). If what Davidson says here is right, then the broad generalizations about colour contemplated at this point in the main text will be 'lawlike' only in the weaker of two senses of the term. But Davidson's stronger sense of 'lawlike' may itself be anomalous. Why should being lawlike in any sense be a matter of being 'indefinitely refinable' or 'sharpen[able] without limit'? Davidson's original explanation of the notion was that 'Lawlike statements are general statements that support counterfactual and subjunctive claims, and are supported by their instances' ('Mental Events', 217). But it is not clear that this notion of law has any internal connection with that of indefinite refinability. If this is right, then Davidson's denial of psychophysical laws is rather weaker than at first appears (strictly all it denies is *indefinitely refinable* psychophysical laws, *sharpenable without limit*); and his argument for the identity theory would require not just the Nomological Character of Causality as naturally interpreted, but the stronger principle that 'events related as cause and effect fall under strict deterministic laws, *indefinitely refinable and sharpenable without limit*' ('Mental Events', 208, amended by the addition of the words in italics). A further difficulty with Davidson's view comes to the surface here: if on his view there are two senses of 'lawlike', and it is in only one of these that he wishes to deny the existence of lawlike psychophysical connections, then it is odd that the argument for that denial actually seems to make no play with the difference between those two senses. To rephrase the point: if the criterial and evidential differences between the nature of mental and physical discourse do not rule out the existence of lawlike psychophysical connections in the weaker sense, it is not clear that they can rule out the existence of lawlike psychophysical connections in the stronger sense—given that Davidson's argument for the latter claim shows no obvious sensitivity to the difference between these two senses.

29. 'To recognize the ideal status of the constitutive concept [of rationality] is to appreciate that the concepts of the propositional attitudes have their proper home in explanations *of a special sort*: explanations in which things are made intelligible by being revealed to be, or to approximate to being, as they rationally ought to be.' By contrast, what might roughly be called 'physical' explanation is characterized as 'a style of explanation in which one makes things intelligible by representing their coming into being as a particular instance of how things generally tend to happen' (McDowell, 'Functionalism and Anomalous Monism', 389, my emphasis).

30. Davidson, 'Mental Events', 222, 216.

31. There are good reasons for adding 'actually' and perhaps also 'now' operators to this. But I shall not go into these here, and they are independent of my present concerns.

32. I have heard the killer yellow example ascribed to Saul Kripke and Michael Smith. I do not know how either of them has used the example, however, and I can only apologize if I have distorted it or omitted the best bits.

33. I bracket here questions of what Putnam has called the 'division of linguistic labor'. It may be that individual users do not need such a conception, if others in the community, to whom they are prepared to defer, have one. So I talk here of what 'we' need. Our conception may itself be 'obscure and relative'—like a definite description of which we only later identify the satisfier.

34. See D. M. Armstrong, *A Materialist Theory of the Mind* (London: Routledge & Kegan Paul, 1968), ch. 12.

35. Abstracting from a number of contentious issues, I shall offer as a first elucidation of the notion of a physical property: 'a property that can be introduced in the language of physics'.

36. S. Kripke, *Naming and Necessity*, rev. edn. (Oxford: Blackwell, 1980), 128 n. 66. I take it here that Kripke means by 'physical property' a property introduced by the predicates of physics. He also says, however, that yellowness is 'a manifest physical property of an object' (128 n. 66; cf. 140 n. 71), and it would be possible to take 'manifest physical properties' to be something other than properties of physics: perhaps physical in a broad sense (part of the natural world) but also 'manifest' in the sense *fully open to view, fully grasped by anyone who understands the term*, so that colour would be a phenomenal property rather than one of physical science. This would make the view closer to the 'simple view' of John Campbell, the non-reductive realisms of Hacker, Stroud, and Putnam, and the view which I defend myself.

37. See P. F. Strawson and H. P. Grice, 'In Defence of a Dogma', *Philosophical Review*, 65 (1956), 141–58.

38. Note that even those who (like Lewis) advocate restricted type-identity must (if Grice and Strawson are right) allow that there is some property common, say, to Martians in pain and humans in pain, even if it is not what these theorists call 'pain'. This may be the property of being in a physical state which plays the role of pain for that kind of organism, and we can call it a second-order physical property if we like. But it should be noted that it is not definable in the language of physics alone, unless the specification of the higher-level *functional role* is itself definable in the language of physics—which there is reason to doubt. Some would take refuge at this point in a metaphysically charged use of the word 'property', designed not to apply to just any classification that people are capable of coherently effecting. But that still leaves the problem of making sense of a plurality of classifications, to replace that of making sense of a plurality of properties.

39. There are of course notable differences in these philosophers' attitudes to the constitutive principles. Lewis and Shoemaker, for example, believe that the significant interrelations between psychological states can be captured in *topic-neutral* causal terms (which yet are sufficient to form an individuating description of each such state), whereas Wittgenstein would not: the constitutive principles might themselves embody a particular 'point of view', the grasp of which was not available to just anyone. The idea of treating colour discourse in parallel to mental discourse can be found in Wittgenstein: 'The colour concepts are to be treated like the concepts of sensations.' (*Remarks on Colour*, III. 72.)

40. It is a great pity that the letter is omitted from Eastlake's translation, and even from some German collected editions of Goethe's works. The letter follows §920 of the *Didaktischer Teil* of Goethe's text (Munich edn., 264–71).

41. *Remarks on Colour*, III. 173; cf. Goethe, *Farbenlehre*, §582. Wittgenstein may have unconsciously remembered Goethe's comment, or he may have independently rediscovered it. In general Wittgenstein seems to have paid more careful attention to Runge's letter than to the rest of Goethe's text.

42. For parallels between the explanation of action and the explanation of perception (though he is not talking of colour in particular) see C. Peacocke, *Holistic Explanation* (Oxford: Clarendon Press, 1979), esp. ch. 1.

43. A further form of subjectivity lies in the fact that, in the case of ordinary psychological descriptions, the scheme employed by the theorist is also a scheme employed by the object of the theory: persons are in a special sense self-interpreting systems. This form of subjectivity clearly does not have a direct parallel in the case of colour.

44. Of course there are other senses of 'subjectivity' and 'objectivity' of which I am not here speaking. The particular combination of forms of subjectivity and objectivity which I propose receives a fuller defence in McDowell, 'Values and Secondary Qualities', and D. Wiggins, 'A Sensible Subjectivism?', in D. Wiggins, *Needs, Values, Truth* (Oxford: Blackwell, 1987).

45. A physical colour is defined by Westphal as 'the alteration of a complete spectrum'. A green object, for example, is 'an object which will absorb or darken almost all of any incident red light and reflect or not darken higher proportions of light of the other colours' (*Colour*, 84).

46. Exceptions include objects that change colour with temperature, those that fade in the light, and things like light-sensitive sunglasses. Fluorescent, iridescent, and glossy surfaces also need special treatment.

47. This is significant, for example, for Westphal's project of explaining why nothing can be red and green all over. The incompatibility is only a straight logical incompatibility, as Westphal wishes, if it is the incompatibility of an object's reflecting a low proportion of green light *but not of red light*, and also reflecting a low proportion of red light *but not of green light*. Without the italicized clauses, it would be open to someone to think an object could be both red and green, by being black.

48. Westphal's motive, I think, is that the results of subtractive colour mixing are more directly predicted from the former kind of information than from the latter (though, as we have seen in section 2, they will not be exactly predictable from colour information at all without recourse to spectral data). This of course does not show how ordinary people (as opposed perhaps to dyers) *think* of colours; and if Westphal is not making a claim at the level of thought (or Fregean sense), then there seems no reason for preferring his kind of characterization to an equivalent one in terms of colours reflected. As a matter of fact, grass actually reflects what one might well think a significant proportion of red light: approaching 80% at the extreme red end of the spectrum, as figure 11.2 illustrates. It none the less looks green partly because of the relatively low sensitivity of the eye at that point, and also because the effect of increasing by just a small amount the reflectance of the complementary colour red will only be to *lighten* or desaturate the green.

49. I talk of 'normal' white light, to count out, for example, light that is composed of two very narrow complementary bands around, say, 480 and 580 nm. Such light is phenomenally detectable for the reason that coloured objects illuminated by it look quite different from normal. A defence of the employment of the notion of normality must wait for another occasion.

50. I should perhaps make clear that the claim is that (all) surface colours are ways of changing the light, not that (all) ways of changing the light are surface colours. There will be some objects that change the light in ways that preclude our ascribing any simple colour to them—e.g. mirrors, highly metameric objects, oil films—except perhaps relative to a particular angle or position of view, or of illumination.

51. I describe the method to be employed in *The Nature of Colour*.

52. Here and elsewhere I employ some of the language and the doctrine of Gibson's ecological optics. See e.g. J. J. Gibson, *The Ecological Approach to Visual Perception* (first pub. 1979; Hillsdale, NJ: Lawrence Erlbaum, 1986), ch. 5 and pp. 97–9.

53. Cf. Strawson: 'there would be no question of counting any transient perception as a perception of an enduring and distinct object unless we were prepared or ready to count some different perceptions as perceptions of one and the same enduring and distinct object … To see [a newly presented object] as a dog, silent and stationary, is to see it as a possible mover and barker, even though you give yourself no actual images of it as moving and barking' ('Imagination and Perception', in P. F. Strawson, *Freedom and Resentment and Other Essays* (London: Methuen, 1974), 52–3).

54. The phrase is Wittgenstein's (*Philosophical Investigations*, II. xi., p. 212). Strawson makes much of it in 'Imagination and Perception'.

55. 'Imagination and Perception', 53.

56. There are some interesting consequences of applying this outlook to the inverted-spectrum puzzles, but I cannot go into these here.

57. 'To about 5 per cent of all men, green and red are both indistinguishable from grey' (Hazel Rossotti, *Colour* (Harmondsworth: Penguin, 1983), 123). Such people have 'an inability to discriminate red, green and grey' (Hacker, *Appearance and Reality*, 151).

58. These are the cards devised by Shinobu Ishihara, Professor of Ophthalmology at the University of Tokyo, in 1917. Each card carries a circle made up, like a *pointilliste* painting, of small blobs of different colour. Normal trichromats will see one numeral in the pattern of blobs; the colour-blind, according to their pattern of non-discrimination, will see a different numeral, or sometimes none at all. More sophisticated tests are available now, though I have not seen them myself, and the Ishihara test is still rated as efficient in detecting red-green defects. My own deficiency is, I think, deuteranomaly.

59. There is another source of difficulty for the view that those with red-green anomalies lack normal colour concepts. They are said to be capable of recognizing variation in saturation and in brightness (obviously enough in, for example, the case of yellow and blue objects); they also (if they are not deuteranopes) see a full variation of spectral hues. But in that case, putting together the concepts of saturation, brightness, and hue, they ought to have a full conceptual grasp of the variation of colour within the red and green regions too—whatever their difficulties may be in recognizing it. There are more serious deficiencies of colour perception which result in certain spectral lights being seen as achromatic—which one would naturally suppose was bound to result in misapprehension of the hue circle. But there is still, even with such people, a real question (and I mean just that) whether they may none the less have learned our own colour concepts properly, by appreciating the abstract structure of colour space (which other people in the community can tell them about) and recognizing as much of their colour perception as is sound as the (more than usually fallible) presentation of *certain* colours in restricted regions of that space—which can serve as points of reference allowing them to 'place' other colours which they actually cannot see.

60. By contrast it is hard on the orthodox dispositional view to see any reason why colour-vision should have had adaptive value. Why on earth should our ancestors have evolved so as to be good at tracking the disposition of objects to cause a sensation of red in normal humans under normal circumstances? Human beings didn't even exist then!

61. And remember: 'If we taught a child the colour concepts by pointing to coloured flames, or coloured transparent bodies, the peculiarity of white, grey and black would show up more clearly.' (Wittgenstein, *Remarks on Colour*, III. 240.)

12 Phenomenal Character

Sydney Shoemaker

I

I have opposed, in various places, what I call the object-perceptual model of introspection (see Shoemaker, 1986). This is the view that introspective knowledge should be thought of as analogous to the sort of perceptual knowledge, in particular visually based knowledge, in which we know whatever facts we know by perceiving one or more objects and observing the intrinsic properties of these objects and their relations to one another. On this view of introspective awareness, awareness of mental particulars is primary and awareness of mental facts derives from this. I would like to hold, in opposition to this, that introspective awareness is awareness of facts unmediated by awareness of objects; awareness *that* unmediated by knowledge *of*.[1] In part, although by no means entirely, my opposition to the object-perception model is my opposition to the act-object conception of sensations and sensory experiences.

This issue is not, directly, the subject of the present paper. I mention it because it provides part of the background for the issues I shall be discussing. As will soon be apparent, there is a prima facie strain between my opposition to the object-perception model of introspection and my being what Frank Jackson calls a "qualia freak."

If we had only such intentional states as beliefs and desires to deal with, the view that introspective awareness is awareness of facts unmediated by awareness of objects would seem phenomenologically apt. My awareness of a belief just comes down to my awareness that I believe such and such. This goes with the fact that the properties of beliefs that enter into the content of such awareness seem to be primarily intentional or representational properties—the property of being a belief that such and such is the case—and include few if any of the "intrinsic" properties which, on the object-perception model, objects of perception ought to be perceived as having. But in the case of sensations, feelings, and perceptual experiences things seem to be different. While a few philosophers have recently maintained that the only introspectively accessible properties of these are intentional ones, I think that the majority view is still that these have a "phenomenal" or "qualitative" character that is not captured simply by saying what their representational content, if any, is.[2] There is, in the phrase Thomas Nagel has made current, "something it is like" to have them. It is commonly held, and has been held by me, that the introspectible features of these mental states or events include non-intentional properties, sometimes called "qualia," which constitute their phenomenal character and determine what it is like to have them. While these qualia are taken to be themselves non-intentional, or non-representational, they are held to play a role in determining the representational content of experiences; *within* the experiences of a single person, sameness or difference of qualitative character will go with sameness or difference of representational contents. But it is held to be conceivable that in different persons, or the same person at different times, the same qualitative character might go with different representational contents. Then we would have a case of "inverted qualia." The classic case of this is John Locke's example of spectrum inversion, in which one person's experiences of red are phenomenally like another person's experiences of green, and vice versa, and likewise for other pairs of colors.

Qualia are often taken as paradigms of *intrinsic* properties. And insofar as our introspective awareness of sensations and sense experiences involves awareness of qualia, it may seem to satisfy one of the requirements of the object-perception model of introspection that is not satisfied by introspective awareness of beliefs and other intentional states, namely that it is in the first instance awareness of intrinsic properties of objects of the awareness. And there is in fact one conception of qualia which presupposes the object-perception model. Philosophers sometimes give as examples of qualia properties they call by such names as "phenomenal redness." This suggests a view according to which for each "sensible quality" S which we can perceive an external thing to have there is a property, phenomenal S-ness, such that perceiving an external thing to be S involves "immediately" perceiving, or in some way being directly aware of, an internal "phenonomenal object" which is phenomenally S. This is the much reviled sense-datum theory of perception. If we reject this, we are left with the question of what conception of qualia, and of introspective awareness of them, we can accept if we do not accept the version that goes with the sense-datum theory.

But this question is inextricably bound up with others. There are questions about the relationship between the phenomenal or qualitative character of experiences and their representational content. And, closely related to these, there are questions about the status of, and the nature of our awareness of, the so-called "secondary qualities" of external objects—for the identity of the latter seems in some way bound up with the phenomenal character of our perceptual experiences of them. These collectively make up what I shall call the problem of phenomenal character.

II

Wittgenstein said that "It shews a fundamental misunderstanding, if I am inclined to study the headache I have now in order to get clear about the philosophical problem of sensation" (Wittgenstein, 1953, I, 314). This is, I am afraid, an inclination I frequently have when I think about philosophy of mind. But I am not entirely repentent about this. Wittgenstein was certainly right if he meant that studying one's headache is not likely to provide one with the solution to any philosophical problem about sensation. But while providing oneself with examples of the phenomenal content of experience won't provide the solution to the problems, it can help to make vivid what the problems are.

Another passage in Wittgenstein is pertinent here. He talks about the "feeling of an unbridgeable gulf between consciousness and brain process," which occurs when I "turn my attention in a particular way on to my own consciousness, and, astonished, say to myself: THIS is supposed to be produced by a process in the brain!—as it were clutching my forehead" (Wittgenstein, 1953, I, 412). The sense of mystery is all the greater, I think, if we replace "be produced by" in Wittgenstein's expostulation with "consist in," getting "THIS is supposed to consist in a process in the brain." Wittgenstein goes on to comment on how queer this alleged business of "turning my attention on to my own consciousness" is. But we can get much the same puzzle without any attempt to turn our attention inwards. I look at a shiny red apple and say to myself "THIS is supposed to be a cloud of electrons, protons, etc., scattered through mostly empty space." And, focussing on its color, I say "THIS is supposed to be a reflectance property of the surface of such a cloud of fundamental particles." Here we have, of course, the seeming disparity between what Wilfrid Sellars called the "manifest image," the world as we experience it, and what he called the "scientific image," the world as science tells us it is (see Sellars, 1963). How, one wonders, can the color one experiences be any part or aspect of what the best scientific theory tells us is out there?

And it is not only in the case of such properties as color that we can generate perplexity about this disparity without any problematic turning of attention onto one's own consciousness. For return to the case of pain. The headache, after all, is experienced as being in one's head, a part of one's body. To counteract any tendency to confuse the head and the mind, let's change our example—instead of attending to a headache, attend to the pain in a stubbed toe. One may well be inclined to say to oneself, incredulously, "THIS is supposed to be a neural process in the brain!" For many of us the perplexity this generates is not dissipated by Wittgenstein's attempt to show that such remarks are, in a philosophical context, a case of language gone on a holiday.

In the first instance, then, the problem of phenomenal character isn't really a problem about the objects of *introspective* awareness. At least in the case of color, taste, smell, etc. it is about the objects of *perceptual* awareness. The case of pains, itches, tickles, etc., is tricky. There is a well established tradition of regarding these as mental entities, and that may make it seem that the awareness of them must be introspective. Yet, as I observed, we experience these items as being in one place or another in our bodies. Since the seventeenth century, at least, a prominent subtheme in discussions of these matters has been that despite differences in the way they are treated in ordinary language, pain and the secondary qualities are metaphysically on a par. In a few philosophers this has led to attempts to objectify pains—to construe them as states of the body which we perceive in having pain experience (See Graham and Stephens, 1985, and Newton, 1989). More commonly it has led to attempts to subjectify the secondary qualities—to construe them as features of sensations.

I will assume here that colors are where the contents of our visual experiences and our ordinary ways of talking place them—on the surfaces of physical objects, or in expanses of sky or water. Grass is green, the sky is blue, ripe tomatoes are red. But reflection on the disparity between the manifest and the scientific image makes inescapable the conclusion that, to put it vaguely at first, the phenomenal character we are confronted with in color experience is due not simply to what there is in our environment but also, in part, to *our* nature, namely the nature of our sensory apparatus and constitution. The intuition that this is so finds expression in the inverted spectrum hypothesis—it seems intelligible to suppose that there are creatures who make all the color discriminations we make, and are capable of using color language just as we do, but who, in any given objective situation, are confronted with a very different phenomenal character than we would be in that same situation, and it is not credible that such creatures would be misperceiving the world. But I think that the intuition is plausible independently of that. How *could* the phenomenal character we are confronted with be solely determined by what is in the environment, if what there is in the environment is anything like what science tells us is there? At the very least, the way things appear to us is determined in part by limitations on the powers of resolution of our sensory organs. And it seems obvious that it depends on the nature of our sensory constitution in other ways as well. There is good reason to think, for example, that the phenomenological distinction between "unique" and "binary" hues (e.g., ones like "pure" red, on the one hand, and ones like orange, on the other) is grounded in a feature of our visual system, and has no basis in the intrinsic physical properties of the objects we see as colored (see Hardin, 1988).

I have deliberatedly used the vague phrase "the phenomenal character we are confronted with," which leaves it unspecified what is supposed to *have* this phenomenal character—the external objects perceived, or our subjective experiences of them. And the problem is, in part, about how to eliminate this vagueness. Looking at the matter one way, the obvious solution is to put the phenomenal character in the experiences. This gets us off the hook with respect to the problem of reconciling the manifest image with the scientific image, as the latter applies to the external objects—although it still leaves us, if we are materialists, with the problem of reconciling the manifest image, i.e., the phenomenal character, with what we think about the real nature of the mind itself. But, putting this latter problem on the side for now, locating the phenomenal character in the experiences seems to fly in the face of the phenomenology. For what seemed to pose the problem was the experienced character of redness, sweetness, the sound of a flute, and the smell of a skunk. And *these* are not experienced as features of sensations or sense-experiences; they are experienced as features of things in our environment.

If we insist on saying that the phenomenal character really belongs to experiences or sensations, it is hard to avoid the conclusion that our sense-experience systematically misrepresents its objects in the environment—that it represents them as having features that in fact belong to the experiences themselves. This is the view I have called "literal projectivism"—that we somehow project onto external objects features that in fact belong to our experiences of them.[3] But this seems, on reflection, to be unintelligible. I am looking at a book with a shiny red cover. The property I experience its surface as having, when I see it to be red, is one that I can only conceive of as belonging to things that are spatially extended. How could *that* property belong to an experience or sensation? Remember that an experience is an experiencing, an entity that is "adjectival on" a subject of experience. It seems no more intelligible to suppose that a property of such an entity is experienced as a property of extended material objects than it is to suppose that a property of a number, such as being prime or being even, is experienced as a property of material things. The literal projectivist view may seem more palatable if the projected properties are said to be properties of portions of the visual field (see Boghossian and Velleman, 1989). But that, if taken literally, amounts to a resurrection of the sense-datum theory, with all of its difficulties.

A different view is what I have called "figurative projectivism." This concedes that qualia, understood as properties of experiences, are not properties that could even seem to us to be instantiated in the world in the way in which colors, for example, are perceived as being. But it says that associated with each quale is a property that can seem to us to be instantiated in the world in this way—and that when an experience instantiates a quale, the subject perceives something in the world as instantiating, not that quale itself, but the associated property. The property is in fact not instantiated in the external object perceived, or in any other object—its seeming to be instantiated there is a result of how the perceiver is constituted. That is what makes the view projectivist. But the property also is not instantiated in the experiences of the perceiver—that is what makes the projectivism figurative. In fact, on this view, the "secondary qualities" that enter into the intentional content of our experiences are never instantiated anywhere. They live only in intentional contents; in Descartes' terminology, they have only "objective" reality, never "formal" reality.[4]

This view has its own set of unattractive consequences. Like literal projectivism, it implies that our perceptual experience is incurably infected with illusion—that we cannot help but perceive things as having properties that they do not and could not have. In addition, while we can make sense of the idea of there being properties that are in some way represented in our experience but never instantiated in anything— e.g., the property of being a ghost—it is difficult, to say the least, to make sense of the idea that experienced color could be such a property. Granted that there are in fact no ghosts, we at least have some idea of what would *count* as someone veridically perceiving an instantiation of the property of being a ghost. But if we ourselves do not count as veridically perceiving the instantiation of redness-as-we-experience-it, I think we have no notion of what would count as veridically perceiving this.

Although it seems to me clearly unacceptable, figurative projectivism has some of the features which I think an acceptable account ought to have. It holds that the phenomenal character we are presented with in perceptual experience is constituted by some aspect of the representational content of our experience, thereby acknowledging the fact that we focus on the phenomenal character by focusing on what the experience is *of*. It holds that the properties that enter into this representational content, and in that way (i.e., by being represented) fix this phenomenal character, are not themselves features of our experiences—are not themselves qualia. But it holds that the qualia instantiated in an experience do determine the representational content that fixes the phenomenal character. Indeed, it holds that it is of the essence of any given quale that its instantiation by an experience makes a certain determinate contribution to that experience's representational content. But this is not to say that all aspects of the representational content of an experience are among the features that determine its qualitative character. For suppose Jack and Jill are spectrum inverted relative to each other. When both are looking at a ripe tomato, their experiences will be markedly different in phenomenal character, and so in one sense different in representational content—given that phenomenal character is determined by representational content. Yet I would want to say, and a figurative projectivist could agree, that the experiences of both represent the tomato, and represent it correctly, as being red. So the figurative projectivist need not say, and I think should not say, that redness is among those properties represented in our experience but not instantiated anywhere in the world, although he may want to say this of "redness-as-we-experience-it," on some understanding of that phrase. Further, the figurative projectivist would say, and I would agree, that despite the differences in phenomenal character, and representational content, between the experiences of Jack and Jill, there is no sense in which the experience of one of them is more or less true to the objective nature of what is experienced, namely the tomato, than the experience of the other. They experience the tomato differently, but not in a way that makes the experience of one of them more or less veridical that the experience of the other. All of this I agree with. The question is how one can hold all this without going all the way with figurative projectivism and holding that the experiences of *both* Jack and Jill, each in a different way, misrepresent the tomato by representing it as having a property it does not have, and that, more generally, every visual experience represents its object as having properties that *nothing* in this world has?

Once these desiderata for a solution to the problem have been made clear, it begins to be clear what sort of solution it must have. How can the experiences of Jack and Jill represent the tomato differently and yet neither of them misrepresent it, given that the same information about its intrinsic nature is getting to both? This can only be because the different properties their experiences attribute to the tomato are *relational* properties. So the bare bones of the solution is this. Let Q1 be the quale associated with redness in Jack, and let Q2 be the quale associated with redness in Jill. There is a relational property consisting in producing or being disposed to produce experiences with Q1. And there is one that consists in producing or being disposed to produce experiences with Q2. Jack's experience represents the tomato as having the first of these relational properties, and Jill's experience represents it as having the second of them. And in fact it has both. Neither property is the property of being red, which is also attributed to the tomato by the experiences of Jack and Jill. So while the contents of their experiences have something in common (both represent the tomato as being red), they also differ in a way that does not involve either of them misrepresenting the tomato.

What, more specifically, are these relational properties? There are in fact a number of candidates. One pair that might seem to qualify consists of the property something has just in case it is producing in Jack an experience with Q1 and the property something has just in case it is producing in Jill an experience with Q2. Another consists of the property something has just in case it is apt to produce in Jack, under certain conditions, an experience with Q1, and the property something has just in case it is apt to produce in Jill, under these conditions, an experience with Q2. Other pairs are defined not with respect to the experiences of Jack and Jill specifically, but with respect to creatures having the sorts of sensory apparatus, or sensory constitutions, Jack and Jill have. Finally, there is a pair which consists in the property something has just in case it is currently producing an experience with Q1 in a subject appropriately related to it, and the property something has just in case it is currently producing an experience with Q2 in a subject appropriately related to it. Our tomato has properties of all of these kinds, and each of these pairs of properties is such that Jack's experience could represent the tomato as having one member of the pair and Jill's experience could represent it as having the other member of the pair, without either experience misrepresenting it. If we give the name "phenomenal properties" to those properties of external things the representation of which constitutes the "phenomenal character" of experiences, then these different kinds of relational properties are candidates for being phenomenal properties; I shall return later to the question of which of them is the best candidate for this.

But it is bound to be objected that it cannot possibly be the representing of such *relational* properties as these that constitutes the phenomenal character of perceptual experiences. We do not, at least ordinarily, experience things *as* affecting our experience in certain ways, or *as* being apt to affect our experience in certain ways. The content of our experience is not relational in this way. Insofar as the difference between the experiences of Jack and Jill lies in what properties they ascribe to the tomato, it surely consists in what *monadic* properties they ascribe to the tomato.

But the way properties are represented in our experience is no reliable guide to what the status—as monadic, dyadic, etc.—of these properties is. Reflection shows that the relation *to the right of* is, at least, triadic, but do we experience it as such? And consider being heavy. What feels heavy to a child does not feel heavy to me. Reflection shows that instead of there being a single property of being heavy there are a number of relational properties, and that one and the same thing may be heavy for a person of such and such build and strength, and not heavy for a person with a different build and strength. But when something feels heavy to me, no explicit reference to myself, or to my build and strength, enters into the content of my experience. Indeed, just because one is not oneself among the objects of one's perception, it is not surprising that where one is perceiving what is in fact the instantiation of a relational property involving a relation to oneself, one does not, pre-reflectively, represent the property as involving such a relation. Thus it is that one naturally thinks of *to the right of* as dyadic.

Just as one's self is not among the objects one perceives, so the qualia of one's experiences are not among the objects, or properties, one perceives. And so these too are not explicitly represented in the content of one's experience. Does this mean that we are not introspectively aware of the qualia? Well, if I am right in my rejection of the perceptual model of introspection, we don't in any sense *perceive* them. But neither do we in any sense *perceive* the representational content, and the phenomenal character, of the experience. Introspective awareness is awareness *that*. One is introspectively aware that one has an experience with a certain representational content, and with the phenomenal character this involves. And if one reflects on the matter, and has the concept of a quale, this brings with it the awareness that one's experience has the qualia necessary to bestow that content and that character. But it would be wrong to say either that one is aware of what the qualia are like or that one is not aware of what the qualia are like. In the sense in which there is something seeing red is like, there is nothing qualia are like (just as, in that sense, there is nothing electricity is like, and nothing apples are like). What is "like" something in this sense is an experience, sensation, or whatever, or perhaps the having of an experience or sensory state, and being like something in this sense is a matter of having phenomenal character, which in turn is a matter of having a certain sort of representational content. The relation of qualia to this phenomenal character is not that of *being* it, and not that of *having* it, but rather that of being constitutive determiners of it. The qualia are determiners of it in two ways. It is partly in virtue of having the qualia it does that the experience represents what it does; the qualia serve as "modes of presentation." And part of what it represents is the instantiation of a property, a "phenomenal property," which is in fact, although it is not explicitly represented as, the relational property of producing, or being apt to produce, experiences having these qualia.

This account needs qualia because it needs a way of typing experiences which not does consist in typing them by their representational contents. It needs this because only so can there be properties whose identity conditions are given by saying that things share a certain property of this type just in case they produce, or are apt to produce under certain conditions, experiences of a certain type. Such types can be called phenomenal types. Sameness of phenomenal type, and likewise phenomenal similarity, is a functionally definable relation (see Shoemaker, 1975a, 1975b, 1982 and 1991). Roughly speaking, the similarity ordering amongst the experiences in the repertory of a creature corresponds to the similarity ordering amongst the associated stimuli that constitutes what Quine calls the creature's "quality space"; it is shown behaviorally by what discriminations the creature can make, by what sorts of conditioning it is subject to, what sorts of inductions it makes, and so on. Qualia will be the features of experiences in virtue of which they stand in relations of phenomenal similarity and difference, and belong to phenomenal types. It is usual to characterize qualia as being, among other things, nonintentional features of experiences. But if, as I have suggested, the properties represented by our experiences include ones that are constituted by their relations to the qualitative character of the experiences, qualia will be very intimately related to a kind of intentional property. If, for example, an experience having quale R represents its object as having a phenomenal property, call it R*, which something has just in case it is producing or apt to produce R-experiences, then R will be necessarily coextensive with the intentional property an experience has just in case it represents something as having R* in a way that involves having R.[5]

To at least one reader there has seemed to be a "whiff of circularity" here. It is true that a particular phenomenal property is defined in terms of a particular quale—in my example, R* is defined in terms of R. And since it belongs to the functional role of the quale that it serves as a mode of presentation for the phenomenal property, there is a sense in which R is defined in terms of R*. But this seems to me an innocent circularity of the sort we can get around by what David Armstrong calls a "package definition," or, more technically, by the use of the Ramsey-Lewis method for defining theoretical terms. Certainly there is no circularity involved in saying that there is a pair of properties x and y such that the possession of x by an experience represents the possession by something of y, and the possession by something of y consists in its producing, or being apt to produce, an experience with x. By itself this will not provide a basis for defining any particular pair of properties, since there will be indefinitely many different pairs satisfying this description. But we can pin down one of these pairs by building more into the description. E.g., given the notion of phenomenal similarity, we might pin it down by saying that the experiences having x are phenomenally like those I have when I see a ripe tomato. There is no vicious circularity here. And while it is true that in virtue of having R an experience represents a property, R*, which is in fact a relational property that is defined in terms of R, this property is not represented as a relational property, and no reference to R enters into the content of the experience. Compare literal projectivism. According to it, an experience having R thereby represents an external object as having R; but although R is in fact a property of experiences, and is the very property whose possession by the experience gives it its representational content, it is not represented as being such. If, as I think, there is no circularity here (just implausibility), there is none in my account.

It is an important part of this view that what in the first instance we are introspectively aware of, in the case of experience, is its representational content. In this respect my view is similar to that of Gilbert Harman, who claims that the only introspectible features of experiences are their intentional or representational ones (see Harman, 1990). Harman does not recognize the special class of intentional features which according to me determine the phenomenal character of experiences, namely those that represent relational properties that an object has in virtue of producing or being apt to produce experiences with certain qualia. But let me focus for a moment on the point of agreement between him and me, namely that in the first instance introspective awareness is of representational content, or what comes to the same thing, of intentional features. What are the reasons for saying this?

One reason is phenomenological. As I have said already, if asked to focus on "what it is like" to have this or that sort of experience, there seems to be nothing for one's attention to focus on except the content of the experience. Indeed, it may seem at first that there is nothing to focus on except the external object of perception—e.g., the tomato one sees. Initially it may seem as though the question of what seeing the tomato is like can be none other than the question of what the visually detectable aspects of the tomato are. But then reflection makes one realize that one could be having the experience one does even if there were no tomato, and that there could be creatures whose experience of the tomato is different but who don't misperceive it. Even after this realization, however, one's attention remains fixed on the tomato—although now with the awareness that it doesn't matter, to the "what is it like" question, whether the tomato one sees is really there or is merely an intentional object. If one is asked to focus on the experience without focusing on its intentional object, or its representational content, one simply has no idea of what to do.

But this phenomenological fact goes with a fact about what our representational faculties are *for*, and what they presumably evolved to enable us to do. The most central fact about minded creatures is that they are able to represent aspects of their environment, both as they take it to be and as they want it to be, and to be guided by these representations of their environment in their interactions with it. In intellectually more sophisticated creatures the control over the world that is bestowed by this representational capacity is enhanced by a second order representational capacity—a capacity to represent their own first order representational states. But what this is in aid of is still effective representation of the environment (including the subject's own body). So it is not surprising that introspective awareness is keyed to representational states, and to the contents of these states.

III

Although I have focused on the example of visual experience, and in particular our experience of color, I think that what I have said can be applied to other sorts of perceptual experience—smell, touch, taste, and hearing. In all of these cases the phenomenal character of the experiences consists in a certain aspect of its representational character, i.e., in its representing a certain sort of property of objects, namely "phenomenal properties" that are constitutively defined by relations to our experience.

I think that the same account can also be extended to the case of pains, itches, and the like. When, for example, I have the experience I describe as a pain in my foot, my experience represents my foot as having a certain property. What property? The best available name for it is "hurting." This really is a property of my foot. But what it is for my foot to have this property is for it to cause me to have an experience having certain qualia. It is therefore a relational property. But I am not aware of it *as* a relational property, just as in my visual experience I am not aware of a red object *as* having a relational property defined in terms of a color quale. And my awareness of the quale of the pain experience, insofar as I am aware of it at all, is of the same sort as my awareness of the color quale; if you like, it is knowledge by description. What is primary here is a case of *perceptual* awareness—awareness of my foot as having a certain phenomenal property, namely hurting. Normally this goes with perceptual awareness of the foot that goes beyond awareness of it as having this property—e.g., feeling that it is bruised or cut. Going with this perceptual awareness of the foot hurting is introspective awareness *that* one is having an experience of one's foot hurting. And this should not be thought of as an inspection by inner sense of the quale which gives the experience this introspective character. There is no such inspection. The kinds of awareness there are here are, first, perceptual awareness of the foot, second, introspective awareness (which is awareness *that*) to the effect that one is having an experience which if veridical constitutes such a perceptual awareness, and, third, the theoretically informed awareness that the experience has qualia which enable it to have the representational content it has.

I maintain that there is a sense in which our color experiences, our tactual, gustatory, etc. experiences, and our bodily sensation experiences have the same structure. This should not be interpreted to mean that color words, words for odors and tastes, and words like "pain" and "itch," all have the same sort of semantics, or express the same kinds of concepts. I doubt, for example, that "red" and "bitter" have the same sort of semantics. Consider Jonathan Bennett's example of phenol-thio-urea, which tastes bitter to three-quarters of the population and is tasteless to the rest (see Bennett, 1968). If as the result of selective breeding, or surgical tampering, it becomes tasteless to everyone, I say it has become tasteless. And if more drastic surgical tampering makes it taste sweet to everyone, I say it has become sweet. But I don't think that if overnight massive surgery produces intrasubjective spectrum inversion in everyone, grass will have become red and daffodils will have become blue; instead, it will have become the case that green things look the way red things used to, yellow things look the way blue things used to, and so on. I think that our color concepts are, for good reasons, more "objective" than our concepts of flavors. Here the semantics of our terms reflects our interests. Our dominant interest in classifying things by flavor is our interest in having certain taste experiences and avoiding others, and not our interest in what such experiences tell us about other matters.[6] With color it is the other way around; the evidential role of color dominates such interest as we have in the having or avoiding of certain color experiences.

Despite the differences between "red" and "bitter," both name properties of objects of perception, properties things can have when no relevant experiencing is going on. "Pain" does not name such a property. And probably "hurts" does not. If someone reports that there is a pain in his foot, we do not say that he is mistaken if there is nothing wrong with his foot and his feeling of pain is induced by direct intervention in his brain. And probably we do not say he is wrong in this case if he says that his foot hurts—although someone who said this would not seem wildly out of line. We could have had a usage in which the truth-value of a pain ascription depends on what is going on in the part of the subject's body in which she reports feeling pain; and there are recessive tendencies in that direction in our actual usage, as is shown by our uncertainty about how to describe cases of "phantom limb pain." But here again, the actual semantics reflects our interests. We have a strong interest in pain experiences, namely in avoiding them and getting rid of them, which is independent of our interest (which of course is not negligible) in what they reveal about the condition of our bodies. And this interest provides a reason for having an economical way of reporting and expressing these experiences—a way more economical than saying "I *seem* to feel a pain in my foot." But the phenomenology of pain experience, and the aspects of our usage of "pain" that reflect it (i.e., our speaking of pains as located in parts of our bodies), does not go comfortably with our truth conditions for pain ascriptions. The experience we report by saying that we feel a pain in the foot or the tooth does represent something about the foot or tooth; but we make the condition of the foot or tooth logically irrelevant to the truth of the pain ascription. In any case, what is important for my present purposes is that the differences in the semantics of "red," "bitter" and "pain" should not hide the similarities there are between the structure of our experiences of color, taste, and pain. The seventeenth century writers who were fond of comparing the status of the "secondary qualities" to that of pain were on to something right.

IV

I now want to return to the case of color, and to the question of what relational property it is the representation of which bestows on a visual experience its phenomenal character. In other words, the question of which relational properties count as phenomenal properties. Earlier I was casual about this; I mentioned several possibilities, and did not decide between them. The reason for my indecision is that none of the candidates is ideal. When I list my desiderata for a property the visual representation of which constitutes the phenomenal character common to my experiences of red thing, I find that some of the relational properties I mentioned satisfy some of these, and some satisfy others, but that none satisfies all.

What are these desiderata? First, the property should be one that can belong to the external objects we perceive as having colors. All of the candidates satisfy this. If we let R be the quale associated in my experience with redness, then the property of producing an R-experience in me, the property of being apt to produce an R-experience in me under such and such conditions, the property of being apt to produce an R-experience in someone with my sensory constitution under such and such conditions, and the property something has just in case it is currently producing an R-experience in a subject related to it in a certain way, are all properties that can belong to an external object and which normally *will* belong to an object I perceive as being red.

A second desideratum is that the properties should be of a kind such that where, intuitively, the color experiences of two subjects are phenomenally the same, the subjects are perceiving (or seeming to perceive) the same property of that kind, and that where the color experiences of two subjects are phenomenally different, they are perceiving (or seeming to perceive) different properties of that kind. Assuming the possibility of spectrum inversion, this would mean that the properties should be of a kind such that different perceivers can, under the same objective conditions, perceive the same objective thing, or things of exactly the same color, to have different properties of that kind, and perceive things having different colors to have the same property of this kind, this because of differences in their subjective constitutions. On the view of phenomenal character we are working with, these two differences are what the possibility of "spectrum inversion" comes to. Here a number of our candidates fail. Properties defined with respect to a particular subject, such as being disposed to produce R-experiences in me, cannot be perceived by other subjects in the way they can be perceived by that one; and so the perceiving of the same ones of these cannot go with having experiences the same in phenomenal character. Likewise, properties defined with respect to creatures with a particular sensory constitution cannot be perceived by creatures with other sensory constitutions in the way they can be by creatures with that constitution. Yet subjects who are spectrum inverted relative to each other will differ in their sensory constitutions—and such inversion requires that, for example, the experiences the one subject has in viewing red things be phenomenally like those the other has when viewing green things. Of our candidates, the only properties that satisfy this desideratum are the relational properties things have in virtue of actually causing experiences of certain sorts, e.g., the property something has just in case it is currently producing an R-experience in someone related to it in a certain way. Subjects who are perceiving the same properties of this kind will be having color experiences that are phenomenally alike.

Another desideratum is that the properties should be ones that one can perceive something *not* to have by perceiving it to have an incompatible property of the same sort, in the way one can perceive something not to be red by perceiving it to be green. The properties that failed the last test pass this one nicely—e.g., I can perceive that something is not apt to produce R-experiences in me in these conditions by perceiving that it is apt to produce G-experiences in me in these conditions (where G is the quale associated in me with the color green). But the properties that passed the last test fail this one. If I am not perceiving something to have the property *is producing an R-experience in a viewer*, and am instead perceiving it to have the property *is producing a G-experience in a viewer*, I am not thereby perceiving it to lack the first of these properties—for it may be producing G-experiences in someone else while it is producing R-experiences in me.

To make matters worse, there is another desideratum that is not satisfied by several of our candidates. This is that the properties should be ones that things can have when they are not being perceived. This is failed by the candidate that, all things considered, I prefer, namely *is producing an R-experience in a viewer*, i.e., the property something has just in case it is producing a R-experience in someone appropriately related to it.

So, unless I have overlooked something, there is no ideal candidate. What is to be done? Unless we decide that the whole approach I have been pursuing is off on the wrong foot, our best course would seem to be to see if we can maintain that some of the desiderata do not have to be honored. The first two desiderata seem to me not negotiable. But it is arguable that the last two seem compelling because we conflate two different elements in the representational content of our experiences, which we do because the experience itself does not distinguish these. If I am right, a color experience represents an object as having a "phenomenal" property that is constituted by a relation to sense-experience—and it is the representation of this property that gives the experience its phenomenal character. The experience *also* represents the object as having a certain color. The second of the represented properties, the color, does of course satisfy the last two desiderata—it is a property one can observe something to lack by observing it to have an incompatible property of the same kind, and it is a property something can have when unobserved. Conflating the first property with this one leads to the mistaken view that it ought to satisfy these desiderata; failing to distinguish the phenomenal property from the color, we think that the phenomenal property, like the color, should be such that we can perceive something to lack it, and such that something can have it when it is not being perceived. Once we see the need to distinguish these properties, we are free to take the phenomenal property to be what I say it is, namely the property of producing an experience with a certain quale in something related in such and such a way to the possessor of the property.[7]

I have just said that one's experience of, e.g., a ripe tomato represents it both as having a certain color and as having a certain phenomenal property, and that these two properties are conflated in the content of the experience. But these are not independent and separable aspects of the experience's content; rather, the experience represents the color *by* representing the phenomenal property. To put it otherwise, we see the color of a thing *by* seeing a phenomenal property it presents.[8] Since we are not in fact subject to intrasubjective spectrum inversion, in the experience of any particular person the seeing (or seeming to see) of a particular color invariably goes with the seeing (or seeming to see) of a particular phenomenal property. And since colors and their associated phenomenal properties go together in this way, it takes philosophical reflection, of the sort I have been engaged in here, to distinguish them.

Admittedly, the view that there is this two-fold character to the representational content of experiences is prima facie counterintuitive. But the alternatives are much worse. One alternative is to accept one of the versions of "projectivism" distinguished earlier: literal projectivism, which says that our color experiences ascribe to external things properties that in fact belong only to our experiences, and figurative projectivism, which says that our color experiences ascribe to external things properties that in fact belong to nothing. I have already said what I have against those views. Another alternative is to hold that the phenomenal character of experiences consists in their representational content, but that none of the properties they represent are in any way constituted by their relations to our experience. This view has no explanation to give of the seeming discrepancy between the world as we experience it and the world as science says it is. It makes no provision for cases in which experiences having the same "objective" representational content differ in phenomenal character. And it has the unpalatable consequence that the closest we can come to a case of spectrum inversion is a case in which someone systematically misperceives all of the colors. Another alternative is to hold that there are qualia which give experiences their phenomenal character, and that we have a direct, quasi-perceptual, introspective awareness of them. This, if divorced from literal projectivism, seems false to the phenomenological facts. As noted earlier, there seems to be no way to attend to the phenomenal character of one's experience other than by attending to putative objects of one's experiences—to the things one sees, hears, feels, etc., or at least seems to see, hear or feel, and to the properties one perceives, or seems to perceive, those things as having.[9]

As David Lewis likes to emphasize, every philosophical position has its costs. The costs of the views just surveyed seem to me far too much to accept. I have just been talking about one of the costs of my own view; in order to explain away its failure to satisfy one of the desiderata, we are required to say that our experiences represent different properties that they do not distinguish. This is similar in a way to another cost mentioned earlier: the account requires us to say that our experiences represent the instantiation of what are in fact relational properties, without representing these properties *as* relational properties. What are the benefits that outweigh these costs? First, the view is tailor made to fit the phenomenological facts. It puts the phenomenal character of experiences in their representational content. But it does this in a way that does justice to the intuition that how we experience the world is partly due to our sensory constitution, and the intuitions that have led philosophers to insist that there are qualia. And it does it without implying that our experience is systematically illusory.

Acknowledgments

Some of the material in this paper formed part of my Royce lectures, delivered at Brown University in October, 1993. Earlier versions of this paper were read at King's College, London, and Cornell University. I am grateful to the audiences on those occasions for helpful comments and suggestions. I am also grateful to David Robb, Michael Tye, and referees for *Noûs* for very helpful written comments.

Notes

1. A similar view is expressed in Dretske, 1993.

2. For the view that all introspectively accessible features of experience are intentional, see Gilbert Harman, 1990. There are similar views in William Lycan, 1987, and Michael Tye, 1991. The view advanced in the present paper can be seen as an attempt to reconcile the intuitions behind this view with belief in "qualia."

3. See Shoemaker, 1990. The view I call literal projectivism has recently been advocated in Perkins, 1983, and Boghossian and Velleman, 1989.

4. Such a view is suggested by Barry Stroud's formulation of the "theory of secondary qualities" in Stroud, 1977, pp. 86–87. It also seems to be the view of John Mackie in Mackie, 1976. Although in some passages the view Mackie attributes to Locke, with approval, seems to be literal projectivism, in the end it seems closer to figurative projectivism. For, on Mackie's reading, the resemblance thesis Locke affirms for primary qualities and denies for secondary qualities says, not that our ideas resemble things in the world with respect to their intrinsic natures (this is held to be false for the ideas of *both* sorts of qualities), but that the way external things are represented in our ideas resembles the way they actually are. Given that

the rejection of this thesis as applied to secondary qualities and their ideas does not reduce to the rejection of the first resemblance thesis (that which is rejected for secondary and primary qualities alike), it amounts to figurative projectivism. There is a more recent expression of figurative projectivism in Averill, 1992—the "sensuous colors" that he says our experiences attribute to objects are not, he says (p. 569), instantiated "in any physically possible world."

5. Suppose that someone has a remarkable perceptual sensitivity such that just by looking at someone viewing a red object she can see whether that object is producing in that person an R-experience, or just by looking at an object she can see whether it is apt to produce R-experiences in persons with a certain sort of perceptual system, even though she herself does not have that sort of perceptual system and is incapable of having R-experiences. It would seem that that person could have an experience with the intentional property *represents something as having R**, but lacking the quale R. If this case is possible, it will hardly do to say that it is the possession of this intentional property that confers on the experience its phenomenal character. (I owe this objection to Michael Tye.) What this example shows is the need to distinguish between intentional properties that are "reference-individuated" and ones that are "sense-individuated." (I make this distinction is Shoemaker, 1990). If Jack is someone whose experience represents something as being R* in virtue of having quale R, and Jill is someone with the remarkable perceptual sensitivity just imagined, then when both perceive something to be R* their experiences will share the reference-individuated property *represents something as having R**. But the senses, or modes of presentation, by means of which R* is represented will be different, and Jill's experience will not have the sense-individuated intentional property that Jack's experience has. It is those sense-individuated intentional properties whose possession essentially involves having certain qualia that confer phenomenal character.

6. Presumably our senses of taste and smell evolved, not to enhance the aesthetic quality of our lives, but to provide us with information about external objects that is pertinent to our survival. So if, as I suggest in the text, the semantics of our taste concepts and experiences is now tied more closely to the qualitative character of the experiences than to the objective information they provide, it would appear that the semantics has changed (here I am indebted to Bill Lycan). This does not seem to me an objection to my suggestion, but it does show that my suggestion is incompatible with the view that evolutionary function is the sole determiner of the representational content of experiences.

7. In virtue of what does an experience having a quale represent an object as having a particular phenomenal property, if phenomenal properties are what I say they are? It cannot do so in virtue of a causal relation between the experience and the property it represents—one cannot say that the causing of A by B is the (or a) cause of A (here I am indebted to David Robb). And of course I have ruled out the view that the content of the experience picks out the property by encoding a description, involving reference to the quale, which the property uniquely satisfies. I have no fully satisfactory answer to this question (which is hardly surprising, given that no one has a fully satisfactory account of how any experience has the representational content it has). But I think that my account fares well, in this respect, with its main competitors—literal projectivism and figurative projectivism. All three accounts hold that our color experiences represent properties that satisfy my "second desideratum": the properties are held to be of such a kind that where the color experiences of two creatures are phenomenally the same, the experiences represent the same property of that kind, and where they are phenomenally different they represent different properties of that kind. Neither sort of projectivism has any explanation to give of how it is that an experience represents the property which the projectivist theory says it represents. Literal projectivism says that the property represented is a quale belonging to the experience itself; but the fact that an experience *has* a property is certainly no explanation, by itself, of how it is that it is *that* property that it represents some other thing as having. Figurative projectivism says that the represented property is one that is instantiated nowhere; and so far as I can see, it offers no account of what makes an experience represent the particular uninstantiated property it does. Where my account has an edge over these theories is that the properties it says are represented satisfy the first desideratum as well as the second; they are properties the things represented actually have (in normal circumstances), even though the contents of the experiences do not tell the whole truth about them (in particular, do not say that they are relational). And if phenomenal properties as I construe them are the only properties that satisfy both of the first two desiderata, it seems to me that that should count as at least a partial explanation of how it is that our experiences represent these properties.

8. Here again I am indebted to David Robb.

9. As a referee pointed out, one can attend to a color without attending to what it is the color of, and can imagine a color without imagining any colored object. But even in these cases the property that is the object of the attending or imagining is external in the sense that to perceive or imagine it as being instantiated is necessarily to perceive or imagine it being instantiated in something external. I do not believe that after-images are a counterexample to this. If one "sees a red after-image" the property of redness enters into the intentional content of one's experience; but the experience is not veridical, and one is not perceiving the actual instantiation of redness in something, either external or internal.

References

Averill, Edward. (1992) "The Relational Nature of Color." *Philosophical Review*, 101, 3, 551–588.

Bennett, Jonathan. (1968) "Substance, Reality and Primary Qualities." In C. B. Martin and D. M. Armstrong (eds), *Locke and Berkeley, A Collection of Critical Essays*. New York: Anchor Books.

Boghossian, Paul, and Velleman, David. (1989) "Color as a Secondary Quality." *Mind*, 98, 81–103. [chapter 7, this volume]

Dretske, Fred. (1993) "Conscious Experience," *Mind*, 102, 263–281.

Graham, George, and Stephens, Lynn. (1985) "Are Qualia a Pain in the Neck for Functionalists?". *American Philosophical Quarterly*, 22, 2, 72–80.

Hardin, C. L. (1988) *Color for Philosophers: Unweaving the Rainbow*. Indianapolis, Indiana: Hackett Publishing Company.

Harman, Gilbert. (1990) "The Intrinsic Quality of Experience." In James Tomberlin (ed.), *Philosophical Perspectives, 4, Action Theory and Philosophy of Mind*, 31–52.

Lycan, William G. (1987) *Consciousness*. Cambridge, Mass.: Bradford-MIT.

Mackie, J. L. (1976) *Problems From Locke*. Oxford: Oxford U.P.

Newton, Natika. (1989) "On Viewing Pain as a Secondary Quality." *Noûs*, 23, 5, 569–598.

Perkins, Morland. (1983) *Sensing the World*. Indianapolis, Indiana: Hackett Publishing Company.

Sellars, Wilfrid. (1963) "Philosophy and the Scientific Image of Man." In *Science, Perception and Reality*, London: Routledge & Kegan Paul.

Shoemaker, Sydney. (1975a) "Functionalism and Qualia." *Philosophical Studies*, 27, 291–315.

——(1975b) "Phenomenal Similarity." *Critica*, 7, 20, 3–34.

——(1982) "The Inverted Spectrum." *Journal of Philosophy*, 79, 7, 357–381.

——(1986) "Introspection and the Self." *Midwest Studies in Philosophy*, X, 101–120.

——(1990) "Qualities and Qualia: What's in the Mind?" *Philosophy and Phenomenological Research*, 50, Supplement, 109–131.

——(1991) "Qualia and Consciousness." *Mind*, 100, 4, 507–524.

Stroud, Barry. (1977) *Hume*. London: Routledge & Kegan Paul.

Tye, Michael. (1991) *The Imagery Debate*. Cambridge, Mass.: Bradford-MIT.

Wittgenstein, Ludwig. (1953) *Philosophical Investigations*. Translated by Elizabeth Anscombe. Oxford: Blackwell.

13 Explaining Objective Color in Terms of Subjective Reactions

Gilbert Harman

I am concerned with attempts to explain objective color in terms of subjective reactions so I had better begin by saying what I mean by "objective color" and what I mean by "subjective reactions."

By "objective color" I mean the color *of an object*, in a very broad sense of "object" that includes not only apples and tables but also the sky, a flame, a shadow, and anything else that has color. So, objective color in this sense includes the red of an apple, the blue of the sky, the yellow of a flame, the purple cast of a shadow, and so forth.

By "subjective reactions" I mean a normally sighted perceiver's subjective impressions of color: how color looks. A person blind from birth might learn that objects have colors and might in some sense have subjective reactions to color, but not the sort of subjective reactions I mean.

I will be concerned both with the sort of explanation of color and the relevant subjective reactions to color that are available to normally sighted perceivers and with the sort of explanation that is available to others, including those who cannot have the relevant subjective reactions themselves.

1 Why Objective Color Should Be Explained in Terms of Subjective Reactions

Many salient facts about color cannot be explained purely in terms of properties of the surfaces of colored objects. We need also to appeal to the biology and psychology of color perception. These facts include red's being closer in color to blue than to green, even though the frequency of pure red light is farther from that of pure blue than from pure green. Related to that fact is the circular structure of hues, as opposed to the linear structure of relevant light frequencies. There is also the way in which colors can be organized in terms of three polar contrasts, white-black, red-green, and blue-yellow. These aspects of color are due to facts about the biology and psychology of color perception rather than to facts about the structures of surfaces.

Shepard (1992, 1993) offers an evolutionary explanation of the biological and psychological facts by noting that natural illumination from the sun varies in three independent respects: (1) in amount of total overall illumination, (2) in relative amount of longer red wavelengths (depending on the sun's angle), and (3) in relative amount of shorter blue wavelengths (depending on whether illumination is directly from the sun or indirectly from light scattered by the atmosphere). (If the red wavelengths are removed from sunlight, the remaining wavelengths center on green. If the blue wavelengths are removed instead, the remaining wavelengths center on yellow.)

Given these sorts of variation in natural illumination, a visual system structured like ours, in which light is analyzed in terms of white versus black, red versus green, and yellow versus blue, will be able to achieve a kind of constancy in colors attributed to objects, a color constancy that Shepard sees as having evolutionary benefits.

Shepard's evolutionary account contrasts with the suggestion in Dennett (1991) that human color perception and the colors of natural objects have evolved together. But Shepard's proposal explains facts of color perception not accounted for by Dennett's suggestion. In what follows, I will assume Shepard is basically right.

In any event, it would seem that we have to explain facts about objective color in terms of facts about perceivers (Gold 1993).

One simple way to do so identifies an object's being a particular color C with its tendency to be perceived as C by normal observers viewing it under standard lighting conditions. Various complications arise here, for example, concerning chameleons that change color when looked at (Johnston 1992). I want to disregard those (significant) issues in order to try to say more about the relevant subjective reaction, "perceiving something as C."

2   Color Sensations

Some authors call the relevant subjective reactions "color sensations." A normal viewer's perception of a red object in adequate lighting provides the viewer with "red color sensations." Some authors (Shoemaker 1981; Peacocke 1983) use the term "color qualia" in much the same way that other writers use the term "color sensations." I will argue below (section 4) that talk of color sensations is misleading in important respects, but let me use that terminology for the time being.

In these terms, a blind person does not in the normal way obtain color sensations from the perception of objects. Someone blind from birth may never have experienced color sensations. Such a person would normally not know what it is like to have such sensations.

Red color sensations are not red in the same sense in which red apples are red. We might say that red apples are red in the sense that they tend to produce certain reactions when viewed by perceivers. But red color sensations are not red in that sense. Red sensations cannot be viewed and they are (supposed to be) the relevant reactions, not the causes of the reactions.

To avoid possible confusion, some authors use a symbolism that distinguishes these senses of the word *red*, for example, distinguishing the word *red* from the word *red'* and saying we have *red'* color sensations rather than red color sensations (Peacocke 1983).

One problem is to say how these senses are related.

2.1 Objective Color Explained in Terms of Color Sensations

It may seem that the most obvious way to relate the two senses of color terms along the lines of the suggested reduction of objective color to subjective reactions is to try to define the colors of objects in terms of the color sensations they produce in observers: An object is red if and only if perception of it would give normal perceivers red' sensations under standard viewing conditions.

A number of issues arise here. What makes a perceiver a normal perceiver? What determines standard viewing conditions?

Circularity must be avoided. A normal perceiver cannot be defined as one who gets the right sensations from colored objects, nor can standard viewing conditions be defined as those in which normal perceivers get the right sensations.

One possible approach simply asserts that there are objective criteria of normalcy N and objective criteria of standardness S such that an object has color C if and only if perception of it by perceivers who are N in conditions that are S would produce C color sensations. Let us suppose for the sake of argument that such criteria exist. (A full account would have to investigate the criteria S and N.)

2.2 Color Sensations as Basic

A further issue concerns the nature of color sensations. What are they and what makes a sensation that sort of color sensation that it is?

Many authors (e.g., Nagel 1974) believe that no purely scientific account of color sensations is possible. In their view, the essence of such sensations is precisely their subjective "qualitative" character. They believe that there is no way to describe this qualitative character in purely scientific terms so that it would be fully understood by someone who had never experienced the sensation firsthand; someone who has never experienced a red' sensation cannot know what it is to have such a sensation.

In their view, the notion of a red' sensation is the notion of a sensation "like this," where "this" refers to a sensation that one is actually experiencing or imagining.

Since in this view the redness of an object is its power to produce red' sensations in perceivers, it follows that someone who has never experienced a red' sensation cannot fully understand what it is for an object to be red. A red object is an object with the power to produce sensations "like this" in perceivers. Someone who never experiences a red′ sensation is never in a position to be able to identify red objects as objects with the power to produce sensations "like this."

I postpone discussion of what conception of color and color sensations might be available to someone who has never had such experiences.

2.3 Variations in Color Sensations

It is interesting to consider the possibility that different people might have relevantly different sorts of sensations when perceiving objects that they call "red."

This possibility may seem quite likely, (1) if the relevant aspect of a sensation is its intrinsic qualitative character, (2) if the intrinsic qualitative character of a sensation depends on the exact nature of the underlying physical events in the brain giving rise to the sensation, and (3) if there are differences in these underlying physical events from one brain to the next (Block 1990, pp. 56–57).

The suggested analysis of objective color in terms of sensations implies that if there are relevant differences in people's color sensations, then different people have different concepts of the colors of objects and do not mean the same thing by their color terms. They do not mean the same thing by "red," "green," etc. even though they use the terms in exactly the same way of exactly the same objects, at least as far as their outer usage is concerned.

For George, an object is red if and only if it has the relevant power to produce sensations "like this" in normal perceivers, where George refers to the kind of sensation that he gets from viewing red objects. For Mary, an object is red if and only if it has the relevant power to produce sensations "like this" in normal perceivers, where Mary refers to the kind of sensation that she gets from viewing red objects. If George and Mary get different sorts of sensations from viewing red objects, they mean different things when they say that an apple is "red," in this view.

This is actually a pretty strange consequence: that people might mean different things by their words even though they use them in the same way with respect to objects in the world. But a further consequence is even stranger. Given the hypothesis that people do get different kinds of color sensations from objects they call "red," the suggested analysis implies that no objects have any colors (Block 1990, p. 56)!

According to the analysis, an object is red if and only if it has the power to produce sensations "like this" in normal perceivers viewing the object in standard viewing conditions. But, by hypothesis, no object has that power. A ripe tomato may have the power to produce sensations "like this" in me under those conditions, but it does not have the power to produce sensations of that sort in all other normal perceivers viewing the object in standard conditions. By hypothesis, viewing a ripe tomato produces different kinds of sensations in different, otherwise normal, perceivers. So, the analysis we are considering implies that a ripe tomato has no color, given that hypothesis.

So we have two absurd results. First, different people mean different things by their color terminology even when they use the terminology in the same way of external objects. Second, when people use color terminology to say that external objects are "red," "blue," or whatever, what they say is always false.

To avoid such absurd results, we must either abandon the suggested analysis of objective color or rule out the possibility that different perceivers get different sorts of color sensations from viewing objects called "red."

3   Functional Definitions of Color Sensations

The discussion so far has assumed that it is possible to fix on a kind of sensation by attending to it and intending to include in that kind of sensation anything "like this." But a sensation that occurs on a particular occasion can be classified in infinitely many ways and is therefore an instance of many different kinds of sensation. The sensation itself does not determine a single kind or type of sensation. Saying that red objects are objects with the power to produce sensations "like this" is not yet to say what type of sensations red objects have the power to produce, since there are infinitely many different ways in which sensations can be "like this." It is necessary also to say in what respect sensations have to be "like this" in order to count as "red′ sensations."

It would be wrong to say that a sensation has to share every aspect of "this sensation" if it is to be "like this," for then no other occurrences would count. There are always some differences among sensations: they occur at different times, have different causes, different effects, occur to different people, and so forth. Not all these differences are important. For example, the fact that "this sensation" is a sensation of mine distinguishes it from all sensations of other people, but that had better be irrelevant to its being a red′ sensation if anyone else is to be able to have a red′ sensation.

What is needed is a way of classifying sensations so that the sensations normal observers have on viewing a given color normally fall under the same classification, even if, according to some other way of classifying sensations, people have different sorts of sensations from viewing a given color.

One approach to solving the problem of type specification appeals to a "functional definition" of the relevant type of sensation in terms of typical causes and effects (Armstrong 1968; Lewis 1966). For example, the sensations classified as pains are those that are typically caused by tissue damage or extremes of pressure or heat applied to some location in one's body and that typically have as effects the belief that something undesirable is occurring at the relevant bodily location and the desire to be free of the occurrence.

A first stab at a functional definition of color sensations might suppose that they are typically caused by the perception of appropriately colored objects and that their typical effects are beliefs that perceived objects have the appropriate colors. So, a red' sensation would be a sensation that is typically caused by the perception of red things and that typically leads to the belief that one is perceiving something red.

Various worries can be raised about this account and more needs to be said. If it could be made to work, the suggested account would avoid some of the problems raised about the previous account. The account would not have to suppose that differences in the brain events that underlie color sensations mean that different, otherwise normal, perceivers have relevantly different sensations from the perception of the same objects. If you and I are both normal color perceivers, we will both receive red' sensations from the perception of ripe red tomatoes. What we mean by "red object" (namely, "object with the power to produce red' sensations ...") will be the same if we use the word in the same way of external objects, even if our red' color sensations differ in their detailed neurophysiological realizations.

However, when a functional account of color sensations is combined with an explanation of objective color in terms of color sensations, the resulting account of objective color is circular. It reduces to the claim that red objects are those that produce the sort of sensation that red objects produce. This is not only to explain the notion of objective color in terms of itself but to do so in a way that is almost completely empty.

4   Complication: There Are No Color Sensations

Before addressing the problem of circularity, it is necessary to clear up a point we have been so far ignoring, namely, that it is wrong to describe color impressions as color "sensations."

Normally, we use the term "sensation" for bodily feelings. Usually sensations have a more or less definite location in one's body—a headache, a pain in one's foot, butterflies in the stomach, etc. There are also other cases, such as a sensation of dizziness.

But the perception of color does not normally involve sensations in any ordinary sense of the term "sensation." When someone literally has visual sensations, they are pains or other feelings in the eye, resulting from overly bright scenes, perhaps, or itching from allergies or minor eye injuries. Color perception does not normally involve such sensations. On seeing what appears to be a ripe tomato, one does not feel a sensation of red in one's eye, nor is there literally a sensation or feeling at the location at which the tomato looks red.

How then should we think of perceptual experience, if not as involving visual sensations?

4.1 Representational Character of Perceptual Experience

One important point is that perceptual experience has a certain presentational or representational character, presenting or representing the environment in a certain way. When it looks to you as if you are seeing a ripe tomato, your perceptual experience presents or represents the environment as containing a red and roughly spherical object located at a certain distance and orientation "from here."

When you think about visual representation, it is very important to distinguish (a) qualities that experience represents the environment as having from (b) qualities of experience by virtue of which it serves as a representation of the environment. When you see a ripe tomato your visual experience represents something as red. The redness is represented as a feature of the tomato, not a feature of your experience.

Does your experience represent this redness by being itself red at a relevant place, in the way that a painting of a ripe tomato might represent the redness of the tomato with some red paint on the appropriate place on the canvas? No. That is not how visual representation works.

Does your experience represent this redness by having at some place some quality other than redness, a quality of red'ness, which serves to represent the redness of the tomato in some other way, different from the way in which a painting might use red paint to represent a tomato? Well, who knows? You have no conscious access to the qualities of your experience by which it represents the redness of the tomato. You are aware of the redness of the represented tomato. You are not and cannot become consciously aware of the mental "paint" by virtue of which your experience represents the red tomato.

It follows that your concept of a red object cannot be analyzed into your concept of a red' experience, meaning the specific quality that your perceptual experience has in order to represent objective redness, because you have no such concept of a red' experience. You have no idea what specific quality of your perceptual experience is used to represent objective redness. You only have the concept of objective redness!

4.2 The Concept of Color

In fact, your color *concepts* are almost certainly basic and not analyzable in causal terms. You perceive colors as simple primitive features of the world, not as dispositions or complexes of other causal features.

(Maybe some color concepts like *orange* can be analyzed in terms of concepts of primary colors, like *red* and *yellow*. And maybe some color concepts like *brown* can be analyzed in terms of hue, brightness, and saturation. I am not concerned with such internal analyses. I am concerned only with analyses of color in external terms, especially causal terms.)

Now, a scientific explanation may involve an analysis of something without claiming to be analyzing an ordinary concept. For example, when a scientific explanation of facts about the circle of hues treats color as a tendency to produce certain responses in perceivers, it is not offering that analysis of color as an account of the perceptual concept of color. The perceptual concept of color can be quite simple even if color itself is a complex phenomenon.

Of course, it would be useful to give an account of what it is *to have* a basic perceptual concept like the concept of redness, an account that might even be understood by someone lacking that basic perceptual concept. A congenitally blind person can understand that a normal color perceiver might have a basic perceptual concept of redness, for example. And normal color perceivers can understand that there may be animals or other alien creatures with basic perceptual concepts that humans do not have. To this end, we might try to provide a functionalist account of what it is for perceptual experience to have a given perceptual concept.

Now, in general, perceptual experience represents the environment in ways that enable a perceiver to negotiate paths among objects, to locate desired things and to avoid undesired things. Normally and for the most part, a perceiver accepts his or her (or its) perceptual representation, believing that things are as they appear, although the strong disposition to acceptance can be inhibited on special occasions.

The perceptual concept of red figures as part of the perceptual experience of red objects, enabling a perceiver to identify and reidentify objects as red. In other words, if a perceptual concept is a concept Q such that one has perceptual experiences of something being Q, then (roughly speaking) we can say that the concept Q is the concept of redness if perception of red things tends to produce experiences of something being Q.

But we must be careful to avoid circularity. Recall that we have been supposing that red is a tendency to produce perceptual reactions of a certain sort. We have seen that it is incorrect to describe the relevant reactions as sensations. Suppose then that we take the relevant reactions to be experiences with a certain representational or presentational content. If the relevant representational or presentational content is then identified functionally, we seem to be identifying redness as a property R, where R is a tendency to produce experiences that represent something as Q, where Q is the concept produced by perception of R things. That characterization is circular and does not distinguish red from green, for example.

Sosa (1990) points out that we can avoid circularity if we *use* the normally sighted person's primitive perceptual concept of red objects in our account. Then we can say that something is red if and only if it has a property R, where R is a tendency to produce experiences that represent something as Q, where Q is the concept produced by perception of *red* things, where here we are using the primitive perceptual concept *red*.

Of course, a person lacking that perceptual concept of *red* could not avoid circularity in the way Sosa suggests. Nor could normal human perceivers use that approach to provide noncircular accounts of animal or alien perceptual concepts that do not correspond to human perceptual concepts.

One noncircular account that might be useful to those lacking the relevant perceptual concepts would identify color in terms of *biological* mechanisms of color perception, perhaps via the evolutionary reasons for those mechanisms. In this view, for something to be red is for it to have a tendency to have a certain specific complex effect on a normal perceiver's sensory apparatus, in ways described by the scientific theory of color.

5   The Inverted Spectrum

Supposing this last account can be made to work up to a point, one might still worry that it seems to leave out an important aspect of color perception. As Block (1990) puts the objection, the functional account of what it is to have a concept of red captures the "intentional content" of the concept, but not its "qualitative content."

Qualitative content is what we imagine to be different when we imagine that one person perceives colors in a way that differs from the way in which another person perceives them. We seem even to be able to imagine the possibility of an inverted spectrum in the sense that the way things look to one of two otherwise normal color perceivers, George, might be qualitatively hue-inverted with respect to the way things look to the other, Mary (Shoemaker 1981).

It is not that (we imagine that) what looks red to George looks green to Mary. A given object looks green to both or red to both. That is, the colors their experiences represent the environment as having are the same. The imagined difficulty is that "what it is like" for George to see something as red is different from "what it is like" for Mary to see something as red.

The "what is it like" terminology comes from Nagel (1974). I am not convinced that this particular appeal to "what is it like" for a particular person to see something as green is in the end really intelligible. (I discuss what this might mean in section 7, below.) But let us assume that it is intelligible in order to explore the idea.

As I have argued, the difference in "what it is like" for George and Mary to see something as red cannot be a difference in visual sensations, so it has to be a difference in how George and Mary perceive objects to be. And it cannot be a difference in what colors they perceive objects to have, because they both count as correctly perceiving the colors of objects. The difference between them cannot be at that level.

So, the difference must be a difference in other qualities that objects are presented or represented as having. What we are imagining, then, seems to be something like this (Shoemaker 1994).

When George sees a red apple, his perceptual experience represents it as being Q. His experience also represents the apple as being red. Furthermore, the fact that his experience represents the apple as being Q makes it true in present circumstances that his experience represents the apple as being red. It seems we can imagine other circumstances in which neuronal connections leading from George's retina to his visual cortex were switched before birth in such a way that later, when his experience represents something as being Q, that constitutes representing it as being green, because, in these imagined circumstances, the perception of green things normally leads George to have perceptual experiences of those things as Q.

When we imagine normal perceivers like George and Mary with inverted spectra, we are then imagining something like this: A red object looks Q to George and T to Mary. A green object looks T to George and Q to Mary. An object's looking Q to George counts as its looking red to George. An object's looking Q to Mary counts as its looking green to Mary.

This may seem odd, so let me briefly review what led to this seemingly strange idea. We want to describe a case in which two people have inverted spectra with respect to each other. The difference between them has to be a difference in what they experience, but it cannot be a difference in properties they perceive their experience to have, because the relevant properties are perceived as properties of objects in the environment. The difference cannot be a difference in the colors they perceive these objects to be, because we are assuming that, as normal color perceivers, they attribute the same colors to external objects. So, it has to be a difference in other properties objects are experienced as having, properties we can identify as Q and T.

6 Worries About Inverted Spectra

I am not sure that the imagined possibility of inverted spectra is really coherent. (Please note: I am not sure.)

A red object supposedly looks Q to George and T to Mary. It would seem that an object cannot be both Q and T in the same place at the same time in the same way. That would be like an object's being both red and green at the same place and time in the same way. But then, either George's experience or Mary's experience or both of their experiences must be in some respect nonveridical, incorrectly representing the object seen.

Shoemaker (1994) observes that the best way to avoid this result is to suppose that the properties Q and T are radically relational, so that something can be Q to one person without being Q to another. Q and T would be incompatible only in the sense that an object cannot be both Q and T to the same person at the same place at the same time in the same way. On the other hand, an object could be Q to George and T to Mary at the same place at the same time in the same way.

What is it for an object to be Q to a given person? Shoemaker (1994) mentions two possibilities. First, it might be that an object is Q to a given person S if and only if S's perceptual experience currently represents the object as Q. Second, it might be that an object is Q to a given person S if and only if the object has a tendency to provide S with perceptual experiences representing that object as Q. In the first case, objects are Q to S if and only if S is experiencing them as Q. In the second case, objects can be Q to S even if S is not currently experiencing them if they are such as to produce relevant experiences under the right conditions.[1]

But either of these possibilities involves a serious circularity. In order to understand what the concept Q is, we need to understand what objects are Q to someone, but in order to understand what objects are Q to someone, we need to understand what the concept Q is.[2]

Recall Sosa's point, noted in section 4.2 above, that we might use the perceptual concept of color possessed by normal color perceivers to give a key part of a functional account of what it is to have such a concept: the perceptual concept of red is activated in perceptual experiences produced by the perception of *red* objects. Could we use the same idea here—experiences involving the concept Q are produced by perception of Q objects? That explanation would be satisfactory only if one had a firm grasp of the concept Q. But I do not find that I have a firm grasp of that concept.

If it is suggested that we try to break out of this circle as I suggested we might break out of our earlier circle with respect to actual color terms, like "red" and "green," by appeal to some tendency objects have to affect S's perceptual mechanisms, I find myself at a loss to know what aspects of perceptual mechanisms would be relevant.

Settling on something, for example, certain events in the visual cortex would seem simply to let the same problem arise all over again. For surely we can *imagine* even molecule-for-molecule identical people with the same events occurring in their visual cortex having inverted spectra with respect to one another. That seems to be just as imaginable as the previous case.

But this suggests the "problem" is really a pseudoproblem.

This makes me doubt that there is a concept Q of the claimed sort and so doubt that I have the relevant grasp of "what it is like for so and so to see red" that would allow me to suppose that red things might look different to different, otherwise normal, color perceivers.

But let me try to say more about "what it is like" to have an experience of a certain sort.

7   What Is It Like to See Red?

Terminology can become confusing here because different people seem to use similar terminology in different ways and people often use a variety of terminology. For example, philosophers talk about "what it is like" to have a given experience, about an experience's "phenomenological character," and about "qualia," as if these are different ways of getting at the same thing.

In fact, at least two different issues are involved. Let me explain by citing two different ways in which the term "qualia" has been used. First, qualia are sometimes taken to be experienced qualities of a mental experience, those qualities by virtue of which one's experiences represent what they represent (when they represent things), the mental paint of one's picture of the environment, one's mental sense-data. Philosophers who use the term "qualia" in this sense tend to hold that not all mental experiences involve qualia. They take qualia to be involved in perception and sensation but not always in relatively abstract beliefs and thoughts. In this sense of "qualia," it is at least a matter of controversy whether all experiences involve qualia.

On the other hand, qualia are sometimes identified with what it is like to have a given experience and it is supposed to be relatively obvious that all mental experiences involve qualia. Even with respect to a relatively abstract judgment, there is something that it is like to have that judgment—some qualitative character in this second sense.

Now, as I have indicated already, I am strongly inclined to deny that there are qualia in the first sense, the mental paint or sense-datum sense. In perception, all qualities of which we are aware seem to be presented to us as qualities of perceived things, external objects for the most part. Introspection does not support the claim that we are aware of mental paint. And, although arguments can be given for supposing that despite appearances we are aware of mental paint, these arguments seem to be uniformly fallacious through confusions over intentionality (Harman 1990a). So I see no reason to suppose that we are aware of mental paint.

With respect to qualia in the second sense, what it is like to have a given experience, I agree with Nagel (1974) that there is a distinctive kind of understanding that consists in finding an equivalent in one's own case. That is "knowing what it is like to have that experience." I have compared that sort of understanding with knowing what an expression used by someone else means. One understands it to the extent that one finds an equivalent expression in one's own language or by learning how to use the expression oneself. Even if use determines meaning, an external objective description of use need not provide the sort of understanding that comes from knowing the translation into one's own terms (Harman 1990b, 1993a).

Translation is a holistic enterprise. I map as much as I can of your language into mine in a way that tries to preserve certain constraints as much as possible (Harman 1993b). Similarly, in trying to understand what it is like for you to have certain experiences, I map as much as I can of your total experiential system into mine in a way that tries to preserve certain constraints as much as possible.

In either case, there is the possibility of "indeterminacy of translation" (Quine 1960). We can imagine that there are two different ways to map your color vocabulary into mine, or your color experiences into mine, preserving relevant constraints as much as possible. That is to imagine a genuine indeterminacy as to what it is like for you (or me) to see red, just as there is a genuine indeterminacy as to the best interpretation of numbers in set theory.

With respect to the color experiences of normal perceivers who are normal speakers of English, there is no such indeterminacy, because the relevant constraints on mapping one person's experiences into another's include taking into account what objects in the world give rise to those experiences.

So, what it is like for one normal color perceiver to see red is quite similar to what it is like for any other normal color perceiver to see red.

8 Conclusion

My tentative conclusion is that objective color is plausibly identified with a tendency to produce a certain reaction in normal perceivers, where the relevant reaction is identified in part with reference to the mechanisms of color perception.

The subjective response to color is constituted by perceptual experience presenting or representing the environment as relevantly colored. The concept of color as it figures in this representation is simple and unanalyzable in causal terms, because color is experienced as a simple basic quality, rather than a disposition or complex of causal properties. Possession of a perceptual concept of color is to be understood functionally: objective color leads to experiences in which the perceptual concept of color is manifested.

These causal accounts do not capture everything we seem to be able to imagine about color. In particular, they do not allow for possible inverted spectra in otherwise normal color observers. But it is far from clear that what we seem to be able to imagine is actually a coherent possibility.

Notes

1. I have oversimplied. Shoemaker's actual account supposes that an experience has a certain intrinsic phenomenal feature x that is responsible for its representing something as Q. For something to be Q is for it to be such as to produce experiences with feature x.

2. Shoemaker's attempted way out of this circle is to say, for example, that experiences of something as Q (i.e., experiences with feature x) are those experiences that "are phenomenally like those I have when I see a ripe tomato." That would help only if we already had the sort of account of interpersonal phenomenal similarity that would enable us to make sense of interpersonal inverted spectra. But we are in the process of trying to develop such an account. So that account would be circular if we adopted Shoemaker's suggestion.

References

Armstrong, D. 1968. *A Materialist Theory of the Mind.* London: Routledge & Kegan Paul.

Block, N. 1990. Inverted earth. *Philosophical Perspectives,* **4**, 53–79.

Dennett, D. 1991. *Explaining Consciousness.* Boston: Little, Brown.

Gold, I. 1993. *Color and Other Illusions: A Philosophical Theory of Vision.* Ph.D. dissertation, Princeton University.

Harman, G. 1990a. The intrinsic quality of experience. *Philosophical Perspectives,* **4**, 31–52.

Harman, G. 1990b. Immanent and transcendent approaches to the theory of meaning. In *Perspectives on Quine,* ed. R. Gibson and R. B. Barrett. Oxford: Blackwell, pp. 144–57.

Harman, G. 1993a. Can science understand the mind? In *Conceptions of the Human Mind: Essays in Honor of George A. Miller,* ed. G. Harman. Hillside, NJ: Erlbaum, pp. 111–21.

Harman, G. 1993b. Meaning holism defended. *Grazer Philosophische Studien* **46**, 163–71.

Johnston, M. 1992. How to speak of the colors. *Philosophical Studies,* **68**, 221–63 [chapter 9, this volume].

Lewis, D. 1966. An argument for the identity theory. *Journal of Philosophy,* **63**, 17–25.

Nagel, T. 1974. What is it like to be a bat? *Philosophical Review,* **83**, 435–50.

Peacocke, C. 1983. *Sense and Content.* Oxford: Oxford University Press.

Quine, W. V. 1960. *Word and Object.* Cambridge, MA: MIT Press.

Shepard, R. N. 1992. The perceptual organization of colors: An adaptation to regularities of the terrestrial world? In *The adapted mind: Evolutionary psychology and the generation of culture,* ed. J. H. Barkow,

L. Cosmides, and J. Tooby. New York: Oxford University Press [chapter 14, *Readings on Color, vol. 2*].

Shepard, R. N. 1993. On the physical basis, linguistic representation, and conscious experience of colors. In *Conceptions of the human mind: Essays in honor of George A. Miller*, ed. G. Harman. Hillsdale, NJ: Erlbaum.

Shoemaker, S. 1981. The inverted spectrum. *Journal of Philosophy*, **74**, 357–81.

Shoemaker, S. 1994. Phenomenal character. *Noûs*, **28**, 21–38 [chapter 12, this volume].

Sosa, E. 1990. Perception and reality. In *Information, Semantics and Epistemology*, ed. E. Villanueva. Oxford: Blackwell.

14 Colors and Reflectances

Alex Byrne and David R. Hilbert

1 Introduction

When we open our eyes, the world seems full of colored opaque objects, light sources, and transparent volumes. One historically popular view, *eliminativism*, is that the world is not in this respect as it appears to be: nothing has any color. Color *realism*, the denial of eliminativism, comes in three mutually exclusive varieties, which may be taken to exhaust the space of plausible realist theories. Acccording to *dispositionalism*, colors are *psychological* dispositions: dispositions to produce certain kinds of visual experiences. According to both *primitivism* and *physicalism*, colors are not psychological dispositions; they differ in that primitivism says that no reductive analysis of the colors is possible, whereas physicalism says that they are physical properties. This paper is a defense of physicalism about color.

We shall proceed as follows. After first making a useful distinction and some preliminary clarifications immediately below, we outline and motivate our own theory in section 2. Then, in section 3, we reply to three objections. The case for physicalism is summarized in section 4.

1.1 Green-Representing and Green-Feeling Experiences

If it looks to you as if something is green and square at location L, then your experience is veridical only if something is green and square at L. If in fact there is nothing green and square at L (perhaps there is only a green circle or a pink square at L, or perhaps there is only a pink circle, or even nothing at all) then your experience is (at least partly) illusory. Thus your experience is veridical only if the proposition *that there is something green and square at L* is true, and illusory otherwise. It may also look to you as if something is orange and round at location L'. Thus your experience is veridical only if the proposition *that there is something orange and round at L'* is true, and illusory otherwise.

Your experience, then, may be said to *represent* that there is something green and square at L, and that there is something orange and round at L'. If we take propositions to be sentence-like entities, we may define a conjunctive proposition C—the *content* of your experience—as follows. A proposition p is a conjunct of C iff p is represented by your experience (taking C to be a conjunct of itself, and "represents" to distribute over conjunction). Intuitively, the content of a visual experience is the complete way the experience represents the world as being.

Typically, you will accept "the testimony of your senses," and believe that there is something green and square at L. If you come to believe that the lighting conditions are abnormal (for example), you may change your mind, and not believe that the world is this way. But even so, it will continue to look as if there is something green and square at L—the proposition that there is something green and square at L will continue to be represented by your experience. There is no straightforward relationship, then, between the content of an experience and the content of beliefs formed on the basis of that experience.

Let a *green-representing experience* be a visual experience that represents the world as containing something green. Thus the content of such an experience will have as a conjunct a proposition that predicates the property green.[1]

Now, when people with normal vision look at grass, shamrocks, and jade, in daylight, they have green-representing experiences. These experiences are thus similar in respect of content. Assuming, as we shall, that "spectrum inversion" does not actually occur, such experiences are also phenomenologically alike: there is something obviously similar in respect of what it is like to undergo them. Let a *green-feeling experience* be a visual experience with this phenomenological character.

Whether green is a physical property or even whether anything *is* green, at least this much is true: typically, whenever someone has a green-feeling experience, she has a green-representing experience.[2] That is, the property green is a property that green-feeling experiences typically represent objects as having.[3] However, what is very much in dispute is whether this connection between green-feeling experiences and green-representing experiences is *necessary*. Many think, for example, that in some possible worlds green-feeling experiences represent, not that objects are green, but that they are red. We shall be taking up this question later.

So, let it be clear at the outset that our main interest is in properties that certain types of (human) visual experiences represent objects as having. We are not significantly concerned with the question of whether other animals see colors and, if so, what sort of properties these might be (on this latter topic, see Hilbert 1992). Neither are we significantly concerned with the semantics of color words. And we are not at all concerned with an "objective physical definition" (MacAdam 1985, p. 34) of color that can be employed in good conscience by color scientists irrespective of how matters stand with visual experience.

2   A Physicalist Theory of Color

Our physicalist theory of color has two main components. First, colors are types of surface spectral reflectances. Second, color content and color phenomenology necessarily go together. We shall discuss these in turn.

2.1 *Colors Are Reflectances*

The surface spectral reflectance (SSR) of an object is given by specifying, at each wavelength in the visible spectrum, the percentage of light the object reflects at that wavelength. As one of us has argued at length before, the most plausible version of physicalism about *surface* (or object) colors takes these properties to be types of SSRs.[4] For simplicity we will concentrate here on surface color[5]; the extension of our account to light sources and transparent volumes is a matter for another time.[6]

If two objects have the same SSR, in all visible illuminations they will reflect the same amount of light. If one object is substituted for another with the same SSR (assuming they are the same size) in the scene before the eyes, no visible color difference will result. The SSR of an object is (typically) an illumination-independent property: the SSR of an object does not change if the object is taken from a room to a sunny street, or if the lights are turned out. And this, arguably, is also a feature of color.

Let us assume that our visual experiences are, in normal viewing conditions, mostly veridical in respect of color. Certain frogs, iceberg lettuce, and dollar bills (say) are green. Is there an SSR that all and only green objects share? Given that our color perceptions are mostly veridical, the answer is no. Green objects differ widely in their SSRs. This is even true for particular shades of green, as is shown by the phenomenon of *metamerism*: the fact that some objects with different SSRs have perceptually indistinguishable colors in normal conditions of illumination. Two objects that differ in reflectance but have perceptually identical colors in a certain illumination are a *metameric pair* (with respect to that illumination).[7] Moreover, the difference in reflectance between the members of a metameric pair need not be small in the way that the difference in length between two lines of perceptually indistinguishable length is small. An object that reflects almost no light in the neighborhood of 540 nanometers (nm) could be indiscriminable in normal conditions of illumination from an object that reflects nearly all the incident light at this wavelength.

But is there a *physical property* that all and only (actual and possible) green objects share? Given our assumption about the general correctness of our color perceptions, the answer is (plausibly) yes. The property that all green objects share is a *type* of SSR.[8] Very roughly, this property—call it "SSR$_{GREEN}$"—is the type of SSR that allows an object in normal illumination to reflect significantly more light in the middle-wavelength part of the spectrum than in the long-wavelength part, and approximately the same amount of light in the short-wavelength part as in the rest.[9]

Obviously, particular reflectances meeting these specifications—for instance those of frogs, lettuce, and dollar bills[10]—may be otherwise very different.

The property green, if it is this type of SSR, is not a particularly interesting property from a physical point of view. Since we only find it salient because our perceptual apparatus is built to detect it, it might be called an *anthropocentric* property (cf. Hilbert 1987). Alien physicists lacking our visual apparatus would not need to single it out for special attention, unlike the property of having charge e, or spin $1/2$. (These aliens might likewise find the visible spectrum no more than an arbitrary segment of the entire electromagnetic spectrum.) But that does not at all impugn the status of an idiosyncratic type of SSR as a physical property that is "objective," in almost every sense of that protean word. Particular SSRs are not in any philosophically interesting sense dependent on human beings; neither is the type, "either SSR_α or SSR_β or SSR_γ, ...," where these particular SSRs seem from a physical standpoint to be a motley collection.

As for the hues, so for the other color categories. The determinable green has various determinate shades—olive green, lime green, and so on. And it is itself a determinate of the determinables chromatic color, and color. These are all types of reflectances.

Let SSR_{GREEN} be a set of SSRs, such that an SSR is a member of this set just in case it is of the type we sketched a few paragraphs back—SSR_{GREEN}.[11] And in general: for any color X (a type of SSR), a particular SSR will be of this type just in case the SSR is a member of SSR_X. If we like, we can call the individual SSRs the "maximally specific colors," although it must be stressed that this is simply a natural way of extending our everyday color talk. The reflectance-types that the human visual system represents objects as having are considerably coarser than the maximally specific colors. Hence, although of course *objects* having maximally specific colors are visible, the maximally specific colors themselves are not, because they are not properties that one can tell an object possesses simply by looking at it. That is why the terminology is an extension of ordinary usage.[12]

This set-theoretic apparatus gives us a nice way to explain the determinate-determinable relation. But first we need a distinction. A *color property* is simply a reflectance-type. Thus, assuming our version of physicalism, examples of color properties are red, bluish green, sky blue, purple-or-green, sky blue-or-bluish-green-or-pink, and the maximally specific colors.

Now some color properties are those that objects can look to have, and others are not. An object can look lemon yellow, yellow, chromatically colored, or simply colored, but to humans nothing can look purple-or-green, or to have a maximally specific color. (Admittedly, one can tell simply by looking that an object is purple-or-green, but that is not to say that the object *looks* purple-or-green; rather, it will look green, or look purple, and thus one may infer that the object is purple-or-green.)

Those color properties that objects can look to humans to have will be precisely those that human visual experience can represent objects as having. Say that such properties are *representable color properties*.

With this distinction between color properties (like green) that are representable and those (like purple-or-green) that are not, we can say that two color properties, X and Y, stand to one another in the relation of determinate to determinable just in case X and Y are representable color properties and SSR$_X$ is a proper subset of SSR$_Y$. So lime green is a determinate of green, because this property (and green itself) is a representable color property, and SSR$_{\text{LIME-GREEN}}$ is a subset of SSR$_{\text{GREEN}}$. But, although SSR$_{\text{PURPLE}}$ is a proper subset of SSR$_{\text{PURPLE-OR-GREEN}}$, purple-or-green is not a representable color property and hence, as desired, not a determinable of purple.

2.2   *Content and Phenomenology*

The relationship between the content and phenomenology of experience has recently been much debated.[13] Any adequate theory of color must take a stand on this question, at least as it concerns color experience.

Let us say that two experiences are *the same in color content* just in case they represent the same color properties instantiated at the same (viewer-centered) locations. And let us say that two experiences are *the same in color phenomenology* just in case (to put it loosely and intuitively) any phenomenological difference between them would not be described using color vocabulary. (So the phenomenological difference between seeming to see movement at the periphery of one's field of view and not seeming to see such movement is not a difference in color phenomenology.)

We may now put the thesis we wish to defend as follows:

NECESSITY
For all possible subjects S_1, S_2 and all possible worlds w_1, w_2, if S_1 is having a visual experience in w_1 and S_2 is having a visual experience in w_2, then these experiences are the same in color content iff they are the same in color phenomenology.

That is, we claim that the color content and color phenomenology of visual experience cannot come apart. (It is worth noting that Boghossian and Velleman's attack on physicalism in chapter 8 of this volume is largely directed against versions that hold color content and color phenomenology to be only *contingently* connected.[14])

NECESSITY is intuitively plausible, at least in straightforward cases of vision. The experience of seeing a ripe tomato does not seem to contain content and phenomenology as separable elements. Asked, first, to imagine having a visual experience that represents the world as containing a red tomato immediately before one and, second, to imagine having a visual experience whose color phenomenology is like *that*, the naive subject has only one way of responding to both questions.

Why think NECESSITY is false? There are a number of apparent counterexamples. Of these, only one—the case of "spectrum inversion"—requires extended discussion. The rest we shall relegate to a footnote.[15]

Imagine, then, that Invert and Nonvert are "spectrally inverted" with respect to each other, and have been since birth. Nonvert has normal vision, but Invert has red-feeling experiences when he looks at gooseberries, and green-feeling experiences when he looks at raspberries. First premise: this case is possible. Second (relatively uncontroversial) premise: Nonvert's experiences represent, by and large, the true colors of objects. Third premise: the same is true of Invert (cf. Shoemaker 1982; Block 1990). If these three premises are true (and we shall examine how the first and third might be supported shortly), then we have counterexamples to both the left-to-right and right-to-left parts of NECESSITY, as follows.

The left-to-right part. When Invert and Nonvert both look at a gooseberry, their experiences are both green-representing. Thus this is a case of same color content (the gooseberry is represented as having the property green), but different phenomenology (Invert and Nonvert have, respectively, red- and green-feeling experiences).

The right-to-left part. When Invert looks at a gooseberry and Nonvert looks at a raspberry, they both have red-feeling experiences that are, respectively, green- and red-representing: same phenomenology, different color content.[16]

Our response is this. First, we shall describe a hypothetical case of a subject—Fred—who is spectrally inverted in only one eye, using only assumptions that the inverted spectrum argument itself requires. Then we shall imagine that Fred is presented with a red raspberry, and looks at it first through one eye, and then through the other. His visual experience will change. If the inverted spectrum argument against NECESSITY is sound, then (it turns out) this change in Fred's experience is not a change in the color properties the raspberry is represented as having. We shall argue that this is not acceptable. Hence the inverted spectrum argument is unsound.[17] We shall finally discuss the question of which premise of the inverted spectrum argument should be denied.

To begin. Suppose that Fred is spectrally inverted in only one eye, his left. So, he has red-feeling experiences when he looks at green objects with his left eye, and green-feeling experiences when he looks at green objects with his right eye. Further imagine that Fred only uses one eye at a time (say the left on Monday, Wednesdays, and Fridays, and the right the other days of the week). He has been raised in an environment that changes color early on Monday, Wednesday, and Friday mornings, and changes back on Tuesday, Thursday, and Saturday. These changes amount to successive color inversions and reinversions: before dawn on Monday, gooseberries change from green to red, and raspberries change from red to green; before dawn on Tuesday gooseberries change back to green, and raspberries change back to red.

Gooseberries, then, produce green-feeling experiences in Fred any day of the week; likewise, mutatis mutandis, for other objects. So we may fairly suppose that Fred believes he is cyclopean, and has no inkling that his environment changes color in this systematic way.[18] It seems reasonable to presume that, if Invert's phenomenological inversion with respect to Nonvert is possible, Fred's case, as we have described it so far, is likewise possible.

Now, on the assumption that Invert's visual experience, when he is looking at a gooseberry, represents the gooseberry as having the property green, and so forth, what are we to say about the content of Fred's visual experiences?

Well, why is it supposed that Invert sees the true colors of objects? Here we should distinguish two reasons. First, it might be claimed that this is simply an intuitive judgment about the case—after all, Invert can use his color vision to navigate the world successfully, so why suppose he is systematically misperceiving it? If this is the reason, then it seems we may draw the same conclusion in Fred's case (perhaps, because of the additional complexity, a little more tentatively): so, for example, when Fred looks at a (green) raspberry on Monday with his left eye, his red-feeling experience is green-representing.

Second, it might be argued that Invert sees the true colors of objects from the theoretically motivated premise that color content is an *extrinsic* matter: it varies between subjects who are duplicates, and so can be affected by purely environmental changes.[19] Putnam's familiar Twin Earth story shows that this is so in the case of contents involving natural kind concepts, like the concept of water (Putnam 1975). On Earth Oscar believes that water is wet. On Twin Earth, where the clear potable fluid XYZ flows in the rivers and falls from the sky, and where H_2O is nowhere to be found, his perfect twin Twoscar does not have this belief. He believes that *twater* (the stuff XYZ) is wet.

For simplicity, let us suppose that the diagnosis of this difference in content is that an inner state-type of Oscar is reliably caused by the presence of water, not twater, and vice versa for Twoscar. If the moral of Twin Earth extends to Invert's case, then because his red-feeling experiences are reliably caused by the presence of green objects before his eyes, he has a green-representing experience when he looks at a gooseberry.

If all this is right, then it would seem that red-feeling experiences produced by Fred's left eye are green-representing. For they are reliably caused by the presence of green objects—Monday's raspberries, for instance. And we may suppose that the visual pathways leading from each of Fred's eyes do not causally interact. He thus has, in effect, two visual systems used on different days, and that is presumably enough to apply the simple externalist theory of content mentioned above to each individually.

(Of course, externalist theories of content may take other forms [see, for example, Millikan 1984; Dretske 1981, 1988; Fodor 1990]. But whatever the details, it seems very likely that we can have our desired result—that green-feeling experiences produced by Fred's left eye, and red-feeling experiences produced by his right, are red-representing—at the cost of complicating our example.)

The upshot, then, is that if Invert is not the victim of a systematic color illusion, by parity of reasoning Fred isn't either.[20]

So, if the standard inverted spectrum case is a genuine counterexample to NECESSITY, Fred's plight may be described as follows. He has his left eye phenomenologically inverted with respect to his right: red objects viewed with his left eye cause green-feeling experiences, and red-feeling experiences when viewed with his right. But Fred's green-feeling experiences produced by his left eye are red-representing, just like the red-feeling experiences produced by his right eye.

Now for the advertised change in Fred's experience that we say a proponent of the inverted spectrum argument must misdescribe. Suppose that we take a red raspberry and allow Fred to look at it first with his right eye, and then with his left (contrary to his usual practice). What will Fred's visual experience be like? Well, simply imagine a raspberry that changes color from red to green, and imagine looking at the raspberry through one eye, blinking just as the raspberry changes color. Assuming you have normal vision, that is what it will be like for Fred.

To Fred it will be as if the raspberry—part of the scene before his eyes—has undergone a change. If Fred thinks conditions are normal, and that his visual apparatus is functioning properly, he will believe, on the basis of his experience, that the raspberry has changed in respect of a salient surface property. That is, the raspberry first looks one way to Fred, and then *another* way.

But of course this is precisely what a defender of the inverted spectrum argument *cannot* say. The difference between Fred's first and second look is *not* a difference in the properties his experience represents objects as having. If the inverted spectrum argument is sound, the "testimony" of Fred's experience is that the world is exactly the same way both times, *that the raspberry has not changed at all*. Surely this cannot be correct. The fact is that the scene before Fred's eyes *looks to him to change* (it is irrelevant that the appearances are deceptive). But this just *is* a change in the content of his experience, at least if we are to retain any intuitive grip on that notion.[21,22]

The inverted spectrum argument is therefore unsound. According to the first premise, the phenomenology of Invert's color experiences is inverted with respect to Nonvert's. According to the second premise, Nonvert sees the true colors of objects. According to the third premise, Invert's visual experiences are likewise veridical. As we have indicated, in the present context the second premise may be taken for granted. We now need to examine what either denying premise one, or denying premise three, would involve.

As we mentioned, two reasons might be given for holding the third premise: that Invert's experiences represent raspberries as having the property red, gooseberries as having the property green, and so on. First, that this is more or less obvious just from the description of the case. Second, that color content is an extrinsic matter.

We may similarly distinguish two reasons for holding the first premise: that Invert's alleged long term phenomenological inversion is possible. First, that this is more or less obvious just from the description of the case. Second, that phenomenology is an *intrinsic* matter: it does not vary between subjects who are duplicates, and so is unaffected by purely environmental changes. According to this second reason, there is a certain intrinsic state that is sufficient for having a green-feeling experience, and Invert is hooked up to the world in such a way that a raspberry before his eyes causes him to be in it.

So there are two reasons—intuitive and theoretical—for each of the first and third premises. And therefore we need to deny both the intuitive and theoretical reasons for one of them. If it's the third premise, then we must say that (a) any intuition that Invert sees the true colors of objects is not probative, and (b) the content of color experience is intrinsic[23]—it does *not* vary between duplicate subjects. If it's the first premise, then we must say that (c) any intuition that Invert's phenomenological inversion is possible is not probative, and (d) the phenomenology of color experience is extrinsic—it *does* vary between (some) duplicate subjects.

And here, it might be thought, we face a dilemma, because (a), (b), (c), and (d) are widely taken to be very implausible. But each of thinks he can comfortably sit on one of these horns.[24] Although we concede that both premises have some measure of intuitive support, it is surely far from conclusive, and thus a case can be made for (a) and (c). (Admittedly, it would be nice to have an explanation of why intuition has led us astray.) What about (b) and (d)? First, however matters may stand with water-beliefs, it is quite disputable that color content is extrinsic. Not all theories of intentionality worth taking seriously exclude intrinsic content across the board.[25] To take a crude example, consider the theory that the mental symbol "red" refers to the property red because in ideal conditions instantiations of red *would* cause tokenings of the symbol "red," and similarly for the other colors. Provided that the specification of "ideal conditions" is wholly determined by the intrinsic properties of the subject, as it conceivably might be, twins will share color contents, and so color content will be intrinsic. We do not think that anyone is in a position to rule out all possible versions of such theories. Second, it is also quite disputable that phenomenology is intrinsic (for recent dissent, see Dretske 1995, 1996; Tye 1995; Lycan 1996).

3 Replies to Objections

So far we have set out, with some accompanying defence, the main lines of our own theory. In this section we reply to three objections. The first is (in effect) an objection to NECESSITY. The second two are common objections that are widely taken to be fatal to any sort of physicalism about color.

3.1 First Objection: Actual Variations in Phenomenology

When subjects with normal vision are asked to locate "unique" green on the spectrum—a green that is neither yellowish nor bluish—the variation in their responses is significant, at least covering the interval from 490 to 520 nm. And disputes about whether, say, a bluish green fabric is predominantly green or predominantly blue are common in everyday life.

Take two normal subjects, Ted and Alice, who disagree on the spectral location of unique green. Ted says it's 490 nm, Alice says it's 520 nm. It is natural to suppose that Ted and Alice have phenomenologically identical experiences when looking at, respectively, 490 and 520 nm lights. And it is equally natural to suppose that they have phenomenologically different experiences when they look at 490 nm lights. To avoid complications with the colors of light sources, let's switch attention to object color. There will be a patch that produces in Ted a unique-green-feeling experience, but produces in Alice a bluish-green-feeling experience.

By NECESSITY, since our subjects enjoy phenomenologically different experiences, the color contents of their experiences must differ. Ted's experience is representing the patch to be unique green, and Alice's experience is representing the patch to be bluish green. These are different properties, and (so the argument goes) they are contraries: if something is unique green, it is not also bluish green. So either Ted or Alice is misperceiving the color of the patch. This, it might be thought, is implausible.

According to us, unique green is a type of SSR—$SSR_{U\text{-}GREEN}$. And an SSR is of this type just in case it is a member of $SSR_{U\text{-}GREEN}$. Likewise, bluish green—let's pick

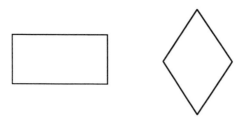

Figure 14.1

a particular shade—is a reflectance-type whose corresponding set is $SSR_{\text{B-GREEN}}$. So far, none of this helps. But suppose that $SSR_{\text{U-GREEN}}$ and $SSR_{\text{B-GREEN}}$ intersect—they have some members in common. Then although Ted and Alice's visual experiences represent the patch to have different properties, those properties are not contraries. Therefore, if this supposition is reasonable, there is no barrier to supposing that both Ted's and Alice's experiences are veridical. We cannot prove, of course, that this supposition is correct, but we do claim that it is a possibility to be taken seriously.

But is it reasonable? Surely nothing can be both unique green and bluish green! But why not? Of course, we are not denying that unique green and bluish green are *distinct* properties. Nor are we denying that nothing can *appear* simultaneously to one perceiver to be both unique green and bluish green. We are suggesting, though, that some ways of being unique green are also ways of being bluish green.

One way to show that this is an option is to find other perceptible properties that are partners in crime. Take the experiences of, on the one hand, something's looking rectangular and, on the other, something's looking diamond-shaped. When one enjoys the former type of experience, the symmetries about the bisectors of the figure's sides are salient. And when one enjoys the latter type of experience, the symmetries about the bisectors of the figure's angles are salient.[26] For an example of the types of experiences we mean, look at figure 14.1.

Now, although the property of being a diamond and the property of being a rectangle are *not* contraries, arguably nothing can *look* simultaneously to be a rectangle and a diamond. Squares, of course, are both diamonds and rectangles. But no square both looks to be a rectangle and a diamond simultanously. Not, at any rate, in the particularly obvious way illustrated by figure 14.2.

Here the left-hand figure looks rectangular, and the right-hand figure looks diamond-shaped. It is not perceptually obvious that the left-hand figure is diamond-shaped, or that the right-hand figure is rectangular. It would not be altogether surprising to find a perceiver on a restricted diet of shape perceptions who mistakenly thought that no diamond could ever be rectangular.

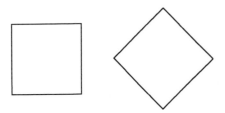

Figure 14.2

But isn't there this disanalogy with the color case? By physically rotating figure 14.2, or by rotating the corresponding mental image, one can readily see that the right-hand figure is rectangular. That is why the idea that the properties of being a square and of being a diamond are contraries does not survive informed reflection. But if a patch looks unique green, that's the end of the matter.

Not quite. If a patch looks unique green, it can typically be made to look bluish green by changing the viewing conditions slightly. Admittedly, there is nothing that is exactly parallel to the rotation of a mental image, but the analogy does not have to be perfect. The point is simply to show that two shape properties could *mistakenly* seem to be contraries, and hence that the corresponding claim in the color case is at least a possibility.

But even if bluish green and unique green are in fact contraries, this is not a disaster. That many of us misperceive unique green objects is certainly an unwelcome result; but at least (for all the objection says) we veridically perceive them as green, and perhaps that is enough.

3.2   *Second Objection: Red Is Really* More Similar to Orange than It Is to Green

Before stating this objection, we need to introduce two senses of similarity.

First, *relative* similarity. Let x, y, and z be distinct things ($x \neq y \neq z \neq x$). x and y are perfectly similar (or just plain similar) relative to a family of properties $\{P_1, \ldots, P_n\}$ just in case both x and y have each P_i. x is more similar to y than to z, relative to a family of properties $\{P_1, \ldots, P_n\}$ just in case x and y share more P_is than x and z do.[27]

So, for example, a square and a triangle are both similar relative to the family {having at least three angles}, and are also both similar relative to the family {being either a square or a triangle}. (This last relative similarity claim shows that *any* two things are similar relative to *some* property or other.[28]) Properties themselves have properties, and so, like particulars, stand in various relative similarity relations. For example, the property squareness and the property triangularity are similar relative to the family {being a geometrical property}.

Here are two examples of comparative relative similarity. A square is more similar to a circle than to a triangle, relative to the family {having at least fourfold symmetry, being a nontriangle, having exactly three angles}. A square is more similar to a triangle than to a circle, relative to the family {being angled, being a closed figure, having no straight edges}.

One might think that relative similarity is all the similarity there is, but this is arguably not the case. Think of perfect duplicates—this cube of sugar and a molecule-for-molecule copy of it. They share all their intrinsic properties. Isn't this a *natural* respect in which they are similar? Suppose we have cube, a tetrahedron, and a sphere. Isn't the first more similar, in a natural respect, to the second than it is to the third? Again, isn't squareness more similar, in a natural respect, to triangularity than it is to circularity? Assuming these questions are at least intelligible, let us call similarity in a natural respect, *natural* similarity.[29]

Let SIMILARITY be the claim that—in the natural sense—red is more similar to orange than to green. Now we can set out the objection in the form of an argument[30]:

(1) We know SIMILARITY solely on the basis of ordinary visual experience.

If the colors are physical properties—the argument continues—then we would need to find out which physical properties red, orange, and green are, in order to determine whether or not SIMILARITY is true. That is, we would need color science— ordinary visual experience wouldn't suffice. So:

(2) If physicalism is true, (1) is false.

Hence:

(3) Physicalism is false.

It must be admitted that the first premise appears to be in good shape. The first premise (and so SIMILARITY) seems true, perhaps even obviously so. Indeed, theses like SIMILARITY are often given as paradigmatic examples of natural similarity relations holding among properties.[31]

What about the second premise? We may well regard the above reasoning in its support with some suspicion. Admittedly, if colors are physical properties, then SIMILARITY is hostage to empirical fortune. Color science, we may fairly presume, reveals the nature of properties like reflectances, and thus reveals the natural similarity relations in which reflectances stand to each other. And there can surely be no guarantee that these similarity relations will be the ones we believe to hold on the basis of ordinary perception. However, the mere possibility of defeat does not generally overturn claims to knowledge—why should it do so in this case? To this there are two replies. First, it might be argued that there is no reason to suppose that ordinary perception is a reliable guide to natural similarity relations between *physical* properties. If so, physicalism implies, not just the possibility of defeat, but that we have no business believing SIMILARITY simply because red, orange and green look that way. According to this first reply, if physicalism is true, then we are not *justified* in taking SIMILARITY to be true solely on the basis of ordinary perception, and thus we do not *know* it by these means. Second, it might be argued that our claim to know SIMILARITY has a special status: it is simply not defeasible. According to this second reply, the first premise should be reformulated along these stronger lines. Then, since physicalism implies that our claim to know SIMILARITY *is* defeasible, the argument for the second premise is straightforward.

We need not pursue this any further, because if physicalism (our brand of it, at least) is true, some intuitively correct natural similarity claims in the style of SIMILARITY will be *false*. Perhaps SSR_{RED} *is* more similar, in the natural sense, to SSR_{ORANGE} than to SSR_{GREEN}; but it seems extremely doubtful that this relation holds between, for example, SSR_{BLUE}, SSR_{PURPLE}, and SSR_{GREEN}.[32] Hence the truth of (a variant of) the second premise is immediate. Physicalism implies that we couldn't know that blue is more similar to purple than to green without color science, for the simple reason that blue is *not* more similar to purple than to green, if physicalism is true. So it appears that we are in big trouble.

We deny the first premise. Visual experience, we think, does *not* tell us that the colors are naturally similar. Rather, visual experience tells us that colored *objects* in the scene before the eyes are *relatively* similar—relative to the color properties that one's experience represents the objects as having. This needs some explaining.

A certain colored chip looks to be a maximally determinate shade of red—call it "red_{21}." It also looks scarlet (say), red, chromatically colored, and colored. So the visual experience of the chip not only represents it as having red_{21}, but also as having, *inter alia*, the color properties scarlet, red, chromatic color, and color. Thus, assuming physicalism, the chip is visually represented as having various types of reflectances, ranging from the comparatively determinate $SSR_{RED_{21}}$ to the maximally indeterminate $SSR_{COLORED}$, where any object that falls under the more determinate reflectance-types also falls under the less determinate ones. (Recall the end of section 2.2. above.)

Now suppose that you see three chips—x, y, and z—together, and that x looks scarlet, y crimson, and z lemon yellow. You would judge that x is more similar (in respect of color) to y than to z. Why? An explanation is to hand if we make a natural assumption about the sorts of color properties that your experience represents the chips as having. Namely, there are more color properties that x and y are both represented as having than there are color properties that x and z are both represented as having. If that were so, then x would be seen as sharing more color properties with y than with z. And this would make your comparative similarity judgment intelligible.

That assumption seems right in this case. Indulging in some oversimplification, the color properties that x and y are both represented as having are: red, chromatic color, and color. The color properties that x and z are both represented as having are: chromatic color, and color. And there are more of the former than the latter.

So we propose that our judgments of color comparative similarity relations between objects are simply reflections of *relative* similarity relations holding between those objects. Let C_1, C_2, ... be all the color properties. Suppose x is judged more similar (in respect of color) to y than to z, on the basis of experience E. Then this judgment is explained by the fact that x is more similar to y than to z, relative to the family {being visually represented by E as having C_1, being visually represented by E as having C_2, ... }. But what is the *content* of the judgment that x is more similar (in respect of color) to y than to z? Let an E-*color property* be a color property that E actually represents either x or y or z as having. Then we may analyze—or, perhaps better, explicate—the judgment that x is more similar (in respect of color) to y than to z thus: x and y share more E-color properties than x and z do.

It is a good deal less clear what people are up to when they make similarity claims about color *properties*, for instance, that scarlet is more similar to crimson than to lemon yellow. Some of them, at least, will mean to be making a natural similarity claim. (In which case, according to us, sometimes they will speak falsely.) We have already explained why, when confronted with any three objects, looking scarlet, crimson, and yellow, respectively, a subject will judge the first more similar to the second than the third. Any reflective subject knows that any three such objects will elicit such a similarity judgment. And, without getting into the question of whether subjects speak truly when they say that scarlet is more similar to crimson than to lemon yellow, this is enough to explain why they say it.

To make this explanation of our similarity judgments between color properties quite general, it will be useful to define a relation between three color properties X, Y, and Z as follows:

X looks more similar to Y than to Z iff for all possible visual experiences E^{33}, and for all possible objects x, y, and z, if E represents x as having X, y as having Y, z as having Z, then:

There are more color properties that E represents x and y as having than there are color properties that E represents x and z as having.

Then we can say that our explanation of judgments of similarity between the colors is this: any *intuitively true* similarity claim of the form "X is more similar to Y than to Z" (setting aside whether it *is* true) corresponds to a truth of the form "X looks more similar to Y than to Z," and vice versa.

Now someone might object that this is not always so. For consider red, orange, and green. Suppose x, y and z are seen as having these colors, respectively. x is represented to be various more or less determinate shades of red, red, chromatically colored, and colored. y is represented to be shades of orange, orange, chromatically colored, and colored. z is represented to be various shades of green, green, chromatically colored, and colored. If this is the full story, then the color properties x and y are both represented as having *are* the color properties that x and z are both represented as having, viz. chromatic color and color. Thus, if we look back at how "red looks more similar to orange than it does to green" is defined, we see that it's false. But of course "red is more similar to orange than it is to green" is an intuitively true similarity claim. This looks like a difficulty for our account.

But it can be overcome. It is reasonable to suppose that there *is* a color property that x and y, but not z, are represented as having, and if so the above account of the color properties x, y, and z are represented as having is incomplete. The common property is *red-or-orange-or-purple*—"reddishness," for short (we are taking pink to be a kind of red and brown a kind of orange). Anything that's either red or orange or purple does look (as we say) reddish. Therefore the natural supposition is that there is a property that visual experience represents all red, orange, and purple objects (and no others) as having.

According to the proponent of the argument we have just been considering, visual experience tells us that red is more similar to orange than to green, in the natural sense. We say it tells us nothing of the sort. Visual experience simply tells us that red objects have certain color properties in common with orange objects, and certain color properties in common with green objects; and there are more of the former than the latter.

It must be emphasised that we are not explaining *why* or *how* the visual system represents objects as having this multitude of properties. That might be thought a disadvantage, but in any case we are not denying anything that is known at the neurophysiological level, or taking a stand on the details of opponent-process theory.

One advantage of our account is that it makes no appeal to the notion of natural similarity relations among properties. It is not so clear that the idea is intelligible, and in any case has proved very hard to analyze.[34] A fortiori, we do not need to suppose that visual experience can represent such relations.

3.3   Third Objection: Physicalism Cannot Account for Binary Structure

Hardin has claimed that even if physicalism is successful in accounting for the relations of similarity and difference among the colors, there still remains one crucial sort of chromatic fact that resists a physicalist treatment. As we have already noted, some colors, for example, orange, always look to be mixtures, whereas others, for example, red and yellow, do not. Any shade of orange appears, or at least will appear to a reflective perceiver, to be a mixture of red and yellow in varying proportions. In the case of yellow, however, there is a shade of yellow that does not appear to be a mixture of any other hues—unique yellow. There are exactly four unique hues (red, green, yellow, blue) and all the others are binary.[35] This distinction is deeply embedded in contemporary color science and is thought by many to reflect fundamental facts about the physiology of color vision.[36] Here, Hardin argues, we have a serious problem for physicalism:

> If we reflect on what it is to be red, we readily see that it is *possible* for there to be a red that is unique, i.e., neither yellowish nor bluish. It is equally apparent that it is *impossible* for there to be a unique orange, one that is neither reddish nor yellowish.... If yellow is identical with **G**, and orange is identical with **H**, it must be possible for there to be a unique **G** but impossible for there to be a unique **H**. If hues are physical complexes, those physical complexes must admit of a division into unique and binary complexes. No matter how gerrymandered the physical complex that is to be identical with the hues, it must have this fourfold structure, and, if objectivism [i.e. physicalism] is to be sustained, once the complex is identified, it must be possible to characterize that structure on the basis of physical predicates alone (1993, p. 66).[37]

Let BINARY be the claim that yellow is unique and orange is binary. The passage from Hardin suggests an argument paralleling the one in the previous section:

(1) We know BINARY solely on the basis of ordinary visual experience.

If—the argument continues—yellow and orange are "physical complexes," and if BINARY is true, "those physical complexes must admit of a division into unique and binary complexes." Hence, if the colors are physical properties, then we would need to find out which physical properties are yellow and orange, in order to determine whether or not BINARY is true. That is, we would need color science—ordinary visual experience wouldn't suffice. So:

(2) If physicalism is true, (1) is false.

Hence:

(3) Physicalism is false.

Unlike the previous argument, where SIMILARITY had a tolerably clear interpretation, the usual explanation of BINARY is more than a little opaque. Take orange. We say it is a binary color because it is, or appears to be, a mixture of red and yellow. But what does that mean? Is orange a combination of the two properties red and yellow? No: a "combination" of two properties A and B is presumably the property $A\&B$ (if it's not that, what is it?). Everything that has the property *red&yellow* is red, but (many) orange objects are not red. Is orange a mixture of red and yellow as a field of poppies and buttercups is a mixture of red and yellow? No, because an orange patch does not appear composed of separate red and yellow blobs. Is orange binary because any orange pigment looks as if it was formed by mixing red and yellow pigment? Well, given common experience with pigments, and a mildly theory laden account of perception, perhaps it does appear that way. But this can hardly be in what the binary/unique distinction consists.[38] If there is a sense in which orange pigment looks to be a mixture of red and yellow pigment, then presumably green pigment looks in this sense to be a mixture of yellow and blue pigment. If this explanation of the binary/unique distinction were right, green would be a binary color. But it isn't.

So it is really not at all obvious that there is a natural interpretation of BINARY such that its truth requires some physically motivated "division into unique and binary complexes."[39] In any case, we have an analysis of BINARY that shows that, even if physicalism is true, it may be known on the basis of ordinary visual experience. Thus we deny (2).

In the previous section we claimed that there is a color property—reddishness— that visual experience represents all and only red, orange, and purple objects as having. Therein lies the similarity between these colors. There is equal reason to believe that visual experience represents objects as having greenishness, blueishness, and yellowishness.

Setting aside color properties that are always represented in (chromatic) color experience—chromatic color and color—the four properties just mentioned are plausibly the *superdeterminables*: every other representable color property is a determinate of one of these properties.

Now any object that is visually represented as orange is also represented as having precisely two of these superdeterminables, reddishness and yellowishness (in fact, we may identify orange with *reddishness&yellowishness*). And any object that is visually represented as yellow is either represented as having greenishness and yellowishness, reddishness and yellowishness, or, in the case of unique yellow, only yellowishness. Thus, there is a shade of yellow such that any object represented as having that shade is represented as having just one superdeterminable, and no such shade of orange. This is our analysis of BINARY. And so there is no evident difficulty in knowing that yellow is unique and that orange is binary on the basis of ordinary visual experience. The objection from binary structure therefore fails.[40]

4   Conclusion: The Case for Physicalism

Physicalism about color has considerable attractions. Unlike eliminativism, it does not convict experience of widespread error. Unlike primitivism, it provides a reduction of the colors and, moreover, a reduction to properties that we are already committed to on independent grounds. The physicalist theory presented here has some additional advantages. Unlike the most popular version of dispositionalism, it gets by without suspect visual-field properties like Peacocke's red′ (see, for example, Peacocke, this volume, chapter 5). Further, it can accommodate our intuitive judgments of similarity relations among the colors, and the binary/unique distinction. But serious problems—although not peculiar to physicalism—remain. Two stand out. First, what makes it the case that visual experience has the representational content that it does? Second, what is the right account of the difference between the various sensory modalities? We are as yet far from satisfactorily answering these questions.

Acknowledgments

We are particularly indebted for comments on early drafts and much discussion to Ned Hall, Katie Hilbert, Jim Pryor, Judith Thomson, Robert Stalnaker, and Ralph Wedgwood. For comments on later versions, thanks to Justin Broackes, Fiona Cowie, Mark Crimmins, Daniel Stoljar, Sarah Stroud, and Mark Johnston.

Notes

1. The preceding remarks about the content of experience will pass for the purposes of this paper. But they are sketchy, and do not begin to do justice to the many complexities here (for some of these, see Peacocke 1992, chapter 3).

2. Why "typically?" Because, perhaps, some green-feeling experiences—for example, the experience of having a green afterimage—are not green-representing (see Boghossian and Velleman, this volume, chapter 7, section 2.3 of the Introduction, and note 15 below).

3. Athough relatively uncontroversial this claim is not universally accepted. Tolliver (1994) denies that visual experiences represent objects as having colors. Of course, the claim is also problematic if spectrum

inversion is supposed to be a live possibility (but here our assumption that it is not is largely for convenience).

4. See Hilbert 1987. Defenders of a similar account include Matthen 1988; Grandy 1989; and Tye 1995.

5. Also for simplicity, we shall ignore the fact that colors vary along dimensions other than hue.

6. For some remarks about light sources, see Hilbert 1987, pp. 132–4.

7. Metamerism is not just illumination-relative, but also observer-relative. The phenomenon is treated at greater length in Hilbert 1987; it is argued there that metamerism creates difficulties for some forms of dispositionalism.

8. It might be claimed that there are colored objects in a possible world where the laws are such that objects reflect and absorb certain ectoplasmic rays, and could not interact with light (and hence do not have reflectances). If so, then colors are not reflectance-types. Perhaps this alleged possibility is even clearly conceivable—at least in the sense in which philosophers' "zombies" are clearly conceivable. But it would be hasty to remove "alleged." Maybe all we can reasonably conclude is that objects could *look* colored in a world where objects do not have reflectances—and we can live with that. For some relevant discussion see Yablo 1993 and Tye 1995, chapter 7.

9. This will ensure that the hypothesized red-green opponent channel is negative (i.e., biased toward green) and the yellow-blue channel is more or less balanced. See Hardin 1993, chapter 1, and Hurvich 1981. For the graphical representation of an SSR of a typical green paint, see MacAdam 1985, figure 2.1. For present purposes, the details of the psychophysics and physics do not matter.

10. Of course, even the parts of a dollar bill that look green at arm's length are not uniformly green viewed close up. Thus the parts that look green and so are represented as having SSR_{GREEN} themselves have parts whose reflectances are not of this type. Does this mean that when dollar bills appear at arm's length to have large green regions this is an illusion? No. True, when a region looks uniformly green parts of it are represented as having SSR_{GREEN}, but not *arbitrarily* small parts. (Cf. Hilbert 1987, chapter 2.)

11. Taking SSR_{GREEN} to be well-defined is certainly an oversimplification, because of the vagueness of color categories. For an attempt, using fuzzy set theory, to accomodate such vagueness, see Kay and McDaniel 1978.

12. In Hilbert 1987 (chapters 5, 6) the maximally specific colors are called "maximally determinate colors," "individual colors," or simply "colors," and the fact that this is an extension of everyday talk is not explicitly discussed. For some criticism, see Watkins 1995, esp. pp. 3–4, 11–12.

13. *Loci classici*: Shoemaker 1982, Peacocke 1983, Harman 1990 and Block 1990. See also Block 1996, forthcoming; DeBellis 1991; Dennett 1991; Harman, this volume, chapter 13; Shoemaker 1990, 1991, 1994a, this volume, chapter 12; Tye 1992, 1994; Lycan 1987, 1996b; and many of the papers in *Philosophical Issues* 7, ed. E. Villanueva (Atascadero, CA: Ridgeview, 1996).

14. See especially pp. 118–21.

15. Here are three apparent counterexamples. The first two are directed against the left-to-right part of NECESSITY, the last against the right-to-left part.

First, a case suggested by some remarks of Peacocke's (this volume, chapter 5, p. 59). If you look through a sheet of green cellophane at a white sheet of paper, rather surprisingly it looks white. Without the cellophane, of course it still looks white. So, it might be argued, the color contents of the two sorts of experiences are the same—both represent the paper as having the property white—but there is a clear phenomenological difference between them. There is, as it were, a "green tinge" present in the first sort of experience but not in the second.

However, with the green cellophane in place, the scene before the eyes looks just as if the paper is white and the ambient illumination is green. It is therefore natural to propose that the first experience, but not the second, represents (falsely) that this is the case. Therefore the color content of the two experiences differs.

For the second case, consider the experiences of having, respectively, a red and a green afterimage. They differ, of course, in phenomenology. But, it might be argued, such experiences do not represent anything as having a color, and so they are trivially alike in color content. (Cf. Boghossian and Velleman, this volume, chapter 7, pp. 91–2.)

However, we think the experience of having a green afterimage represents that there is a green patch some indeterminate distance before the eyes, and hence it is green-representing (and nonveridical). Cf. Harman 1990, p. 40; Tye 1995, pp. 107–8; Lycan 1996a, p. 83. (And in fact, sometimes one mistakes afterimages for colored patches on the surfaces of objects.) So, as in the first case, the color content of the two experiences differs.

For the third case, consider blindsight. Blindsighted patients are, apparently, able to perform above chance when forced to choose the color of an object presented in their blind fields (see Hardin 1993, p. xxx). Two blindsighted patients, one of whom performs above chance (call her "S") and the other at chance, might enjoy visual experiences identical in phenomenology when a tomato is presented in their blind fields. This, it might be argued, is a case of a difference in the color properties represented by visual experience, with no accompanying difference in phenomenology.

However, although this may be a case of different content, it is not a difference in the content of *visual experience*. The tomato may be represented as having the property red by some part of S's visual system. But since there is certainly no ordinary sense in which the tomato *looks red* to S (she herself would deny it), the property red does not enter into the content of her visual experience.

16. Someone who is persuaded to deny NECESSITY on the basis of either the inverted spectrum argument or one of the first two cases given in note 15 above will think that there are (possible) green-feeling experiences that are not green-representing. So she owes us an account of what is common to all and only green-feeling experiences. It cannot be color content, so what is it? It is worth briefly examining Peacocke and Shoemaker's answers to this question.

First, Peacocke's answer: all green-feeling experiences present the "sensational property" *green'* ("green-prime") to the subject. Green' is, of course, *not* the property green, and not a property objects are *represented* as having. Rather, it is supposed to be a property of "regions of the visual field"—a property, that is, of something like sense-data. (See Peacocke 1983, chapter 1, 1992, pp. 7–8, and this volume, chapter 5.)

Although we shall not argue for this here, we think that once sensational properties like green' are admitted, an error theory of color experience is inescapable: the common person mistakenly takes green' to be a property of gooseberries and cucumbers (for precisely this view, see Boghossian and Velleman, this volume, chapters 7, 8).

Shoemaker's ingenious answer (this volume, chapter 12) is that while all green-feeling experiences do not share a *color* content, they all represent objects as having a "phenomenal property," which we may call "phenomenal-green." Phenomenal-green (not to be confused with green) is the property of "producing in a viewer" green-feeling experiences, and is thus a property things do not have when they are not being perceived (p. 241). But Shoemaker's view has, like Peacocke's, the disadvantage that it leads to an error theory, or so it seems to us. According to Shoemaker, when Invert and Nonvert look at a raspberry, their experiences each represent it as having two properties: phenomenal-green and red (Invert) and phenomenal-red and red (Nonvert). If Shoemaker is right that experience represents objects as having phenomenal-colors, then we think that the common person mistakenly takes objects to have these properties when they are not being perceived.

17. In fact, we think that Fred's case is simply an especially vivid way of making points that could be made using the standard inverted spectrum case, and is therefore a ladder that may be kicked away. But it does not seem fruitful to insist on this, because it seems most unlikely that our opponents would agree.

18. Fred's plight might be described as a case of partial intrapersonal spectrum inversion on Alternately Inverting Earth (cf. Block 1990). We should emphasize that we are not supposing that Fred *in principle* could not tell on the basis of his visual experience that something is awry. Given certain assumptions about his environment and the asymmetry of color space, perhaps he could. All we are supposing is that (perhaps due to limitations on his part) he is not able to notice any difference.

19. Of course, the conclusion that Invert sees the true colors of objects is not *entailed* by the premise that color content is extrinsic. What is true, rather, is this. Most, maybe all, *plausible* theories of extrinsic color content entail that Invert (or Invert as he appears in a more intricate example) sees the true colors of objects.

20. It might be objected that this is not right, because Fred and Invert differ in a crucial respect (here we are indebted to Robert Stalnaker). Fred remembers that some objects look the same (in respect of color) to him on Tuesday as other objects did on Monday (in Shoemaker's "qualitative sense" of "looks the

same"—see Shoemaker 1982). In particular, suppose that Fred is looking at a strawberry on Tuesday and recalls that it looks the same as a raspberry he saw on Monday. Now if our description of Fred's case is correct, the raspberry was represented by Fred's experience on Monday as *green*, while the strawberry is represented as *red*—yet he remembers that they look the same! And this, it might be thought, is not plausible. (Compare Invert's case: he remembers that a raspberry looked the same to him yesterday as a strawberry does today, but his experiences represent them as having the *same* color.)

We reply as follows. Cases where someone *undergoes* spectrum inversion and, after a while, sees the true colors of objects as before, are taken, by the proponents of the inverted spectrum argument, to be clearly possible. (Indeed, more so than cases of spectrum inversion from birth.) Thus the subject remembers that some objects (for example, gooseberries) looked the same to him before the inversion as others (for example, raspberries) do after the inversion, but even so gooseberries were represented as green, whereas raspberries are represented as red. If this is not problematic, why suppose Fred's case is?

21. It might be replied that although it appears to Fred that the world has not changed, he mistakenly *believes* that it appears to him that the world has changed. That is, Fred is the victim of an illusion with respect to his *experience*: he believes that his visual experiences differ in content, but in fact there is no difference. But this reply does not work, for at least two reasons. First, we may suppose that Fred, perhaps like many of us in normal circumstances, has no beliefs about his *visual experience*—he just has beliefs about the scene before his eyes. Second, we may alternatively suppose that Fred is apprised of his role in the Gedankenexperiment, and is a proponent of the inverted spectrum argument. He will then believe that his visual experiences are the *same* in content, but the world will still appear to him to change.

22. Another reply—requiring some stage-setting—is this. Return to Invert and Nonvert, both looking at a gooseberry. A proponent of the inverted spectrum argument will usually say that this is not just a case of same properties represented, but a case of same content *simpliciter*. Call this the "Same Content Claim" (see, for example, Shoemaker 1982, Block 1990). But there is another way of taking the inverted spectrum, equally inhospitable to NECESSITY, which we will call the "Fregean Response."

According to the Fregean Response, two visual experiences may differ in content despite representing objects as having the same properties. Visual experiences, on this account, represent properties under various "modes of presentation," akin to Fregean senses. And these modes of presentation are supposed to enter into the content of the experience.

The Fregean Response and the Same Content Claim both agree that Invert and Nonvert's experiences are the same in respect of what we are calling "color content": they both represent the raspberry as having the *property* red. But the Fregean Response, unlike the Same Content Claim, says that the experiences differ in their visual modes of presentation of this property, and thus in their content.

Now go back to Fred and the red raspberry. According to the Same Content Claim, the change in Fred's experience is not a change in content—it is solely a change in phenomenology. We complained that it *is* a change in content. So far, so good.

However, it might be objected that our complaint is of no force against the Fregean Response. According to it, the content of Fred's experience *does* change. When he takes his first look, the raspberry is represented as having the property red under one mode of presentation, and when he takes his second, the raspberry is represented as having this same property under a *different* mode of presentation.

But the Fregean Response does not do justice to the fact that the *raspberry* appears to Fred to change. The raspberry changes only if it gains or loses a property, and so the raspberry will *appear* to change only if it appears to gain or lose a property. If the difference between Fred's experiences were simply a difference in modes of presentation, then the raspberry would not appear to gain or lose a property, and so would not appear to change. That is, if the Fregean Response were right, then although *the way the raspberry appears* would change, *the raspberry itself* would not appear to change.

To see the difference, consider a case where modes of presentation might do useful work: distinguishing between sensory modalities (cf. Shoemaker 1990). Arguably, the very same property—shape—can be represented by both tactile and visual experiences. If that's right, it would be natural to appeal to modes of presentation to give a representational account of the phenomenological difference between seeing that an object is square and feeling that it is. To switch to a hypothetical example, suppose that Fred can taste colors. Red things have a distinctive taste that green things lack, and so on. The property red (we are pretending) is a property that certain of Fred's visual and gustatory experiences both represent raspberries as having. The experiences are different, it might be claimed, because they differ in content at the level of sense rather than reference; that is, Fred's visual and gustatory modalities represent the same property—red—under different modes of presentation. Here the appeal to modes of presentation, whatever its other defects, does not suffer from the problem just raised for the Fregean Response. When Fred successively sees and tastes a raspberry, the way the raspberry appears changes, but the raspberry itself does not appear to change.

23. Sometimes philosophers use "narrow content" to refer to what we have here called "intrinsic content." But "narrow content" is used ambiguously in a way that invites confusion. Some say that while Oscar and Twoscar do not share a belief with the content *that water is wet*, they *do* share some *other* mental state: a mental state that determines, together with the environmental facts, whether the subject believes that water is wet, or whether she believes that twater is wet. Such a state—the organismic contribution to believing *that water is wet* (and to believing *that twater is wet*)—is supposed to have "narrow content" (see, for example, Fodor 1987). Narrow content in this sense is at best some etiolated kind of content and at worst unintelligible (for some classic objections see Stalnaker 1989). This sense of "narrow content" is not what we mean by "intrinsic content": the latter is just familiar propositional content that is necessarily shared between duplicates.

24. We should record that one of us (DH) prefers to deny the first premise, while the other (AB) prefers to deny the third.

25. Hilbert 1987 implicitly assumes a correlational theory of content in the style of Dretske 1981, and Hilbert 1992 explicitly assumes a teleological theory in the style of Millikan 1984. These two theories do exclude intrinsic content.

26. See Peacocke 1992, pp. 74–6, from which the example is taken.

27. These definitions are inevitably somewhat stipulative. For instance, we might just as well have said that x and y are perfectly similar relative to a family of properties $\{P_1, \ldots, P_n\}$ just in case x and y either both have or both lack each P_i. And we might just as well have said that x is more similar to y than to z, relative to a family of properties $\{P_1, \ldots, P_n\}$ just in case x and y share some P_i that z lacks, and if x and z have some P_j, then y has P_j. But for the argument to follow, the (second) definition given in the text is the one we want.

28. We are here assuming that properties are "abundant" in Lewis's (1983) sense. To every set of possible things, no matter how diverse, each thing paired with a possible world it inhabits, there corresponds a property had by all and only those things in those worlds. Assuming, as Lewis holds, that possible individuals inhabit only one world, we can put this more cleanly as: to every set of possible things, no matter how diverse, there corresponds a property had by all and only those things.

29. For a defense of natural similarity (although not under this name) see Lewis 1983; and Armstrong 1978, 1989. Natural similarity is not usually left as primitive: Armstrong, for instance, analyzes simple cases of it as the sharing of certain special sorts of properties—universals—which are wholly present wherever they are instantiated.

30. Cf. Johnston, this volume, chapter 9, pp. 149–54; and Boghossian and Velleman, chapter 8, pp. 116–127.

31. See, for example, Armstrong 1989, p. 33.

32. See MacAdam 1985, figures 2.1, 2.2, and 2.6.
    Hilbert 1987 (chapter 6) can be understood as arguing that physicalism can accomodate SIMILARITY (although perhaps not our knowledge of it). There colors are identifed with certain triples of integrated reflectances. It is claimed that a certain space of such triples, with a physically motivated metric, is roughly isomorphic to color similarity space. But this is not right, or not right enough: the space of triples provides only a very loose approximation to similarity relations among the colors. See Thompson 1995, chapter 3, for detailed discussion.

33. Here (although not in the statement of NECESSITY) "possible visual experience" should be understood to be restricted to visual experiences that can be produced by the *human* visual system (as it actually is). On our view, we cannot rule out the possibility that some strange kinds of visual systems can produce an experience that represents three objects x, y, and z to be scarlet, crimson, and lemon yellow, but does not represent (for example) x and y to be red. (Although, of course, every scarlet object *is* red.) Dropping the

restriction to the human visual system would therefore imply that the defined three-place relation does not hold between any color properties.

34. See Armstrong 1978, chapters 21, 22; 1989, pp. 103–7.

35. If we wish to include the achromatic colors the list of unique hues should include black and white. Brown is a puzzling case (see Hardin 1993, p. 141). These complications do not affect our argument and will be ignored in what follows.

36. See *Readings on Color, vol. 2: The Science of Color*.

37. For endorsements of this complaint, see Varela et al. 1991, p. 166; Thompson 1995, pp. 135–9. (Thompson's endorsement is somewhat qualified: he thinks the argument shows that colors are not "nonrelational" properties.)

38. *Pace* Tye 1995, p. 148.

39. Hardin's official demand is that "those physical complexes must admit of a division into unique and binary complexes." On a uncharitable reading, this is easy to meet: just stipulate that the physical properties to be identified with red, green, yellow, and blue are to count as unique, and the rest binary. But we take it that Hardin thinks that (if physicalism is to be saved) the division must be physically motivated.

40. Our response to this objection also provides an account of the opponent structure of the hues. Red is opposed to green, and blue is opposed to yellow, because no object is represented by the human visual system simultaneously as having reddishness and greenishness, or yellowishness and bluishness. But we are not offering any explanation of this fact (see the end of 3.3 above).

References

Armstrong, D. M. 1978. *Universals and Scientific Realism*. Cambridge: Cambridge University Press.

Armstrong, D. M. 1989. *Universals: An Opinionated Introduction*. Boulder, CO: Westview Press.

Block, N. 1990. Inverted Earth. In *Philosophical Perspectives 4*, ed. J. Tomberlin. Atascadero, CA: Ridgeview.

Block, N. 1996. Mental paint and mental latex. In *Philosophical Issues 7*, ed. E. Villanueva. Atascadero, CA: Ridgeview.

Block, N. Mental ink. In *Anti-Individualism and Scepticism*, ed. M. Hahn and B. Ramberg. Cambridge, MA: MIT Press, forthcoming.

Boghossian, P. A., and J. D. Vellemen. 1989. Colour as a secondary quality. *Mind* 98, 81–103. Reprinted as chapter 7 of this volume.

Boghossian, P. A., and J. D. Vellemen. 1991. Physicalist theories of color. *Philosophical Review* 100, 67–106. Reprinted as chapter 8 of this volume.

DeBellis, M. 1991. The representational content of musical experience. *Philosophy and Phenomenological Research* 51, 303–24.

Dennett, D. 1991. *Consciousness Explained*. Boston: Little, Brown.

Dretske, F. 1981. *Knowledge and the Flow of Information*. Cambridge, MA: MIT Press.

Dretske, F. 1988. *Explaining Behavior*. Cambridge, MA: MIT Press.

Dretske, F. 1995. *Naturalizing the Mind*. Cambridge, MA: MIT Press.

Dretske, F. 1996. Phenomenal externalism. In *Philosophical Issues 7*, ed. E. Villanueva. Atascadero, CA: Ridgeview.

Fodor, J. A. 1987. *Psychosemantics*. Cambridge, MA: MIT Press.

Fodor, J. A. 1990. A theory of content, II: the theory. In his *A Theory of Content and Other Essays*. Cambridge, MA: MIT Press.

Grandy, R. E. 1989. A modern inquiry into the physical reality of colors. In *Mind, Value and Culture: Essays in Honour of E. M. Adams*, ed. D. Weissbord. Atascadero, CA: Ridgeview.

Hardin, C. L. 1993. *Color for Philosophers: Unweaving the Rainbow* (expanded edition). Indianapolis: Hackett.

Harman, G. 1990. The intrinsic quality of experience. In *Philosophical Perspectives* 4, ed. J. Tomberlin. Atascadero, CA: Ridgeview.

Harman, G. 1996. Explaining objective color in terms of subjective reactions. In *Philosophical Issues* 7, ed. E. Villanueva. Atascadero, CA: Ridgeview. Reprinted as chapter 13 of this volume.

Hilbert, D. R. 1987. *Color and Color Perception: A Study in Anthropocentric Realism*. Stanford: CSLI.

Hilbert, D. R. 1992. What is color vision? *Philosophical Studies* 68, 351–70.

Hurvich, L. M. 1981. Chromatic and achromatic response functions. In his *Color Vision*. Sunderland, MA: Sinauer Associates. Reprinted as chapter 3 in *Readings on Color, vol. 2: The Science of Color*.

Johnston, M. 1992. How to speak of the colors. *Philosophical Studies* 68, 221–63. Reprinted as chapter 9 of this volume.

Johnston, M. 1997. Postscript: visual experience. An appendix to chapter 9 of this volume.

Kay, P., and C. K. McDaniel. 1978. The linguistic significance of the meanings of basic color terms. *Language* 54, 610–46. Reprinted as chapter 17 in *Readings on Color, vol. 2: The Science of Color*.

Lewis, D. K. 1983. New work for a theory of universals. *Australasian Journal of Philosophy* 61, 343–77.

Lycan, W. G. 1987. *Consciousness*. Cambridge, MA: MIT Press.

Lycan, W. G. 1996a. Layered perceptual representation. In *Philosophical Issues* 7, ed. E. Villanueva. Atascadero, CA: Ridgeview.

Lycan, W. G. 1996b. *Consciousness and Experience*. Cambridge, MA: MIT Press.

MacAdam, D. L. 1985. The physical basis of color specification. In his *Color Measurement: Theme and Variations*. New York: Springer-Verlag. Reprinted as chapter 2 in *Readings on Color, vol. 2: The Science of Color*. References to the latter.

Matthen, M. 1988. Biological functions and perceptual content. *Journal of Philosophy* 85, 5–27.

Millikan, R. G. 1984. *Language, Thought, and Other Biological Categories: New Foundations for Realism*. Cambridge, MA: MIT Press.

Nassau, K. 1980. The causes of color. *Scientific American* (October), 124–54. Reprinted as chapter 1 in *Readings on Color, vol. 2: The Science of Color*.

Peacocke, C. 1983. *Sense and Content: Experience, Thought, and their Relations*. Oxford: Oxford University Press.

Peacocke, C. 1984. Colour concepts and colour experience. *Synthese* 58, 365–82. Reprinted as chapter 5 of this volume.

Peacocke, C. 1992. *A Study of Concepts*. Cambridge, MA: MIT Press.

Putnam, H. 1975. The meaning of 'meaning.' In *Language, Mind and Knowledge: Minnesota Studies in the Philosophy of Science* 7, ed. K. Gunderson. Minneapolis: University of Minnesota Press.

Shoemaker, S. 1982. The inverted spectrum. *Journal of Philosophy* 79, 357–81.

Shoemaker S. 1990. Qualities and qualia: what's in the mind? *Philosophy and Phenomenological Research* 50 (Suppl.), 109–31.

Shoemaker, S. 1991. Qualia and consciousness. *Mind* 100, 507–24.

Shoemaker, S. 1994a. Self-knowledge and 'inner sense.' Lecture III: the phenomenal character of experience. *Philosophy and Phenomenological Research* 54, 291–314.

Shoemaker, S. 1994b. Phenomenal character. *Noûs* 28, 21–38. Reprinted as chapter 12 of this volume.

Stalnaker, R. 1989. On what's in the head. In *Philosophical Perspectives* 3, ed. J. Tomberlin. Atascadero, CA: Ridgeview.

Thompson, E. 1995. *Colour Vision*. New York: Routledge.

Tolliver, J. T. 1994. Interior colors. *Philosophical Topics* 22, 411–41.

Tye, M. 1992. Visual qualia and visual content. In *The Contents of Experience*, ed. T. Crane. Cambridge: Cambridge University Press.

Tye, M. 1994. Qualia, content, and the inverted spectrum. *Noûs* 28, 159–83.

Tye, M. 1995. *Ten Problems of Consciousness: A Representational Theory of the Phenomenal Mind*. Cambridge, MA: MIT Press.

Varela, F. J., E. Thompson, and E. Rosch 1991. *The Embodied Mind: Cognitive Science and Human Experience*. Cambridge, MA: MIT Press.

Watkins, M. 1995. Dispositionalism in disguise: reply to Averill and Hilbert. Paper delivered at APA Central Division meeting.

Yablo, S. 1993. Is conceivability a guide to possibility? *Philosophy and Phenomenological Research* 53, 1–42.

15 Reinventing the Spectrum

C. L. Hardin

Even if Divine Revelation should tomorrow provide us with the definitive solution to the problem of color realism, we would still be faced with an even more difficult question of ontology: the nature and locus of the qualities of color experience. The question is hard to avoid; even those philosophers who would ultimately locate colors outside of organisms typically grant an important role to color experiences. Independently of philosophical proclivity, it is evident that color experience is intimately involved with the brain, and the appearance of at least some colors is inextricably bound up with brain function. The colors experienced in afterimages, colored shadows and simultaneous contrast, are explicable in terms of the operation of nervous systems and cannot plausibly be supposed to exist apart from them.[1]

Most philosophers would agree that the qualities of color experiences *supervene* upon brain function. But to say this is not to shed much light on the precise nature of the relationship. Is the supervenience necessary, or only contingent? Does the supervenience relationship in this instance simply reflect a causal relationship, or is the color experience–brain function connection more intimate than that? Are the qualities of color experience ultimately physical? If so, in what way? Are they perhaps physical, but not reducible to the properties and entities known to present-day physics? Or are they nonphysical denizens of Cartesian minds?

Mind-body materialists of a reductive stripe offer an ontologically parsimonious reply to these questions. According to such reductive materialists, experiencing color qualities is nothing more than having certain neural processes. However, there is a philosophical tradition, based upon some powerful intuitions, according to which even an explanatory relationship between qualitative experiences and brain processes—let alone an identity of one with the other—is unintelligible. Here is a famous passage from Leibniz:

It must be confessed, moreover, that *perception* and that which depends on it *are inexplicable by mechanical causes*, that is, by figures and motions. And, supposing that there were a machine so constructed as to think, feel and have perception, we could conceive of it as enlarged and yet preserving the same proportions, so that we might enter it as into a mill. And this granted, we should only find on visiting it, pieces which push one against another, but never anything by which to explain a perception. (*Monadology*, section 17)

More recently, Joseph Levine (1983) argues that although mental processes and physical processes might in fact be identical, we can never have scientific grounds for supposing them to be so:

Let's call the physical story for seeing red 'R' and the physical story for seeing green 'G'.... When we consider the qualitative character of our visual experiences when looking at ripe

McIntosh apples, as opposed to looking at ripe cucumbers, the difference is not explained by appeal to G and R. For R doesn't really explain why I have the one kind of qualitative experience—the kind I have when looking at McIntosh apples—and not the other. As evidence for this, note that it seems just as easy to imagine G as to imagine R underlying the qualitative experience that is in fact associated with R. The reverse, of course, also seems quite imaginable.

Levine is here suggesting that in the absence of an intelligible connection between seeing red and the R story and seeing green and the G story, we can never be entitled to take seeing red to be identical with having neural processes R. The very possibility that somebody could have had the same physical constitution and display the very same behavior that she does now and yet have seen as red what she now sees as green (and, generally, for the same set of stimuli, experiencing all colors as interchanged with their actual-world complements) is sufficient to show that no physical story can ever capture what it is to experience a color.

In what follows, I will contend that the prospect for a reduction of color experiencing to neural functioning is not so bleak. Reflection upon known facts will suggest that the possibility of an undetectable spectral inversion may be an illusion based upon our ignorance, and that if the facts were to be filled in further, the possibility of an undetectable spectral inversion would come to seem to be as fanciful as the possibility of a human being having Superman's x-ray vision. Specifically I wish to argue that:

• Primate surface-color space is asymmetric.

• The structure of this space reflects intrinsic characteristics of the colors.

• Rather than serving as a stumbling block for a program of neurofunctionalist reduction, color qualities are the natural expression of neurofunctional mechanisms.

• We have good reason to believe that two human beings with similar neurofunctional architectures will not have color qualities undetectably inverted with respect to each other.

• We ought to be disinclined to attach much theoretical weight to the claim that there are possible creatures who have both similar functional architecture and sensory qualities undetectably inverted with respect to each other.

I shall confine my attention to perceived surface colors, that is, the perceived colors of reflective objects with visual surrounds, in order to include both brown and black among the colors. The focus throughout is to be on the qualities of sensory experience, but I have no philosophical theory of "qualia" to offer here, and I shall try to avoid using that term in what follows.

Some features of the opponent scheme of color vision will be important for our discussion. The scheme calls for six phenomenally elementary colors, which I shall refer to as the *Hering primaries*, after the founder of opponent-process theory, Ewald Hering. Two of these, white and black, are achromatic colors, and the remaining four, red, yellow, green, and blue, are chromatic colors. Each of the Hering primaries is *unitary*, that is, contains no perceptible trace of any of the others, and this feature distinguishes them from the rest of the colors, such as the pinks, the maroons, the limes, the browns, and the oranges, which are *binary*, that is, perceptual mixtures of the elementary colors. The pinks, for example, are reds that are both whitish and bluish. Oranges are reddish yellows. Browns are blackish oranges or blackish yellows. To say that orange is a *perceptual* mixture of red and yellow is not to refer to the way that orange pigments or lights are physically generated. This point is important, so let's consider it in more detail.

Suppose we project onto a screen two overlapping beams of light, one red, one green. The region of overlap will look yellow. Now let one of the beams be red, the other yellow. The region of overlap will look orange. In both instances, we have physically combined lights to produce a mixed color. The difference is that whereas the orange spot *looks* like a mixture of red and yellow, the yellow spot does not *look* like a mixture of red and green—we would not, for instance, be inclined to describe it as a reddish green. The orange is both physically and perceptually mixed, whereas the yellow is physically mixed, but not perceptually mixed. In fact, if we choose our green and our red beams properly, the yellow will look pure, without any tinges of other colors. It will, in fact, look exactly the same as a monochromatic yellow, a yellow produced by light of a single wavelength of about 580 nm. The orange light, which we here produced by physically combining red and yellow beams, could also be matched precisely by light of a single wavelength, in this case, 590 nm. We may thus conclude that perceptual mixture is independent of physical mixture.

Orange is, then, a perceptual mixture of red and yellow. Its location midway between red and yellow in perceptual resemblance space is consequent upon its resembling red as much as it resembles yellow, but this is in turn consequent upon its perceptually containing the same amount of red as it contains yellow. The description of orange as perceptually *containing* a certain percentage of red and *containing* a certain percentage of yellow may sound bizarre, but it can be justified by the performance of human subjects. People who are presented with patches of light from a spectral source and then asked to estimate the percentage of a given hue *in* the patch can, with a little practice, do it easily and reliably. It is interesting to see what visual scientists Sternheim and Boynton (1966) discovered when they required their experimental subjects to use only a restricted set of hue terms to describe light samples drawn from the longwave end of the spectrum. If the subjects were permitted only the names 'red', 'yellow', and 'green', they were able to describe all of the samples in the longwave range, with the percentage totals for each wavelength sample adding to 100. The term 'orange' proved to be replaceable by terms for red and yellow, even at the wavelengths where those same subjects would in other experiments locate their best examples of orange. However, when the term 'yellow' was forbidden, and the terms 'red', 'orange', and 'green' permitted, the region surrounding 580 nm, where most subjects would locate their best yellows, was underdescribed, with total hue estimates falling well below 100 percent through most of the region, and typically going to zero for 580 nm, the spectral region which most subjects see as unitary yellow.

In a nutshell, whereas orange can always be described in terms of red and yellow, yellow cannot be described in terms of red, green, and orange. The same asymmetry holds between all of the Hering primaries on the one hand, and all of the remaining colors on the other. The Hering primaries are necessary and sufficient for naming all of the colors, a fact that justifies singling them out as perceptual primaries. One might wonder whether this is a fact about linguistic primacy rather than a fact about perceptual primacy. The answer to that question seems to be no, as we shall presently see.

But first, let us notice a consequence of the fact that orange is a perceptual mixture of red and yellow. Could it be otherwise? Could someone experience a color that would be orange but be neither reddish nor yellowish? Of course there could quite easily be a creature who readily discriminates patches of 590 nm light from a wide variety of surrounds without experiencing those patches as reddish or yellowish. But that's not the present question, which is whether such a creature would nevertheless experience those patches as *orange*. It seems perfectly plain that the creature's failing to see reddishness and yellowishness would *constitute* its failing to see orange.[2] To use an old-fashioned mode of philosophical speech, orange is *internally related* to red and yellow. Precisely because of that, any "spectral inversion" that would carry a binary color like orange into a unitary color like blue would be readily detectable. To distinguish binary from unitary colors, we would only need to run the Sternheim-Boynton procedure.

Nearly all of the hundreds of nameable colors are, like the orange colors, binaries, and therefore perceptually composite, specifiable by necessary and sufficient conditions, and thus nicely suited for pairing off with structured neural processes. There are but six colors that fail to be composite. We have thus severely constrained the possibilities for undetectable spectral shifts such as those that some philosophers have claimed might be brought about by small rotations of the hue circuit. Assuming that the circuit is so configured that unitary red, yellow, green, and blue are 90 degrees from each other, any rotation less than 90 degrees will carry some binary hues into unitary hues, and each unitary hue into a binary hue, a definitely detectable result. Although this is a useful consequence, we have not yet solved our problem. What we must next do is to show that the primaries are not interchangeable. This is a more difficult task, for there is nothing about the simple opponent-process scheme that forbids such an interchange of primaries. We must look into other aspects of color phenomenology to see if we might find deep reasons, based in the qualitative features of the colors themselves, for thinking that the colors of human experience are intrinsically not invertible.

To see whether there might be such reasons, it will be helpful to return to the question that was raised a moment ago, about whether the composite nature of orange and the noncomposite nature of yellow is really a matter of linguistic rather than perceptual primacy. Let us approach this question by comparing color categorization in human adults with color categorization in human infants, as well as with color categorization in our close primate relatives, chimpanzees and macaques.

Categories are equivalence classes of items that need not be identical. When we call a particular surface 'blue', we do not mean to say that it is identical in color to every other surface that is blue. Things that you take to be blue—your neighbor's car, your boss's dress, the sky, the sea—typically differ from one another in tint, shade, or hue. There are light blues, navy blues, electric blues, powder blues. Yet all of them resemble each other more than any of them resembles something that you see as yellow, or as red. It is important to understand that the resemblance that connects two instances of the same color category is not necessarily a function of the perceptual distance between them. It is not hard to find three color samples A, B, and C, which are such that B is separated from A on the one side and from C on the other by the same number of just-noticeable differences, and yet A and B are seen to belong to the same color category whereas C is seen to belong to a different color category. The rainbow looks banded, even though each of its constituent regions blends smoothly into its neighbors.

Are some categorizations of color continua more natural than others? We have already seen that adult speakers of English find that four hue names—'red', 'yellow', 'green', and 'blue'—are necessary and sufficient to describe the colors of the spectrum. Four-month infants know precious little English, and they cannot describe what they see. Nevertheless, by watching their eye fixations one can tell whether they see two stimuli as similar or different. Infants will lose interest in a stimulus that looks similar to its predecessor, but continue looking at a stimulus that they regard as different from what went before. This is the basis of a standard technique, used by

Spelke and others, to study categorization of various sorts among the very young. By exposing infants to sequences of colored lights whose dominant wavelengths are 20 nm apart, and recording their eye movements, Bornstein and his collaborators were able to map out their spectral color categories (Bornstein et al. 1976). These proved to line up rather well with the spectral categories of adults that are mapped with color-naming procedures. In a similar fashion, a macaque was trained to respond differentially to spectral lights that human beings would see as good representatives of their categories, and then presented with randomized sequences of lights that did not match the training lights. These lights were categorized by the macaque in pretty much the same way as adult human English speakers would classify them (Sandell et al. 1979).

We can now see that there must be innate mechanisms not only for detecting resemblances among colors but for categorizing them as well. We should not of course suppose that color categories are consciously or explicitly born in mind by monkeys or infants, but rather that their brains are so wired as to incline them to respond to certain classificatory demands in a characteristic fashion. This was strikingly demonstrated in a series of chimpanzee categorization experiments by Matsuzawa (1985).

In order to see what motivated Matsuzawa, we need to take a brief look at Berlin and Kay's famous work on basic color terms (Berlin and Kay 1969). Basic color terms are distinguished from nonbasic terms by their salience and their generality. Applying criteria based on these characteristics, Berlin and Kay were able to show that no language currently has more than 11 basic color terms, that each of the terms has a small set of best, or *focal* examples, that the focal examples from different languages cluster tightly in perceptual color space, and that, in consequence, basic color terms are readily translatable from one language to another. In English, the basic color terms are, as one might expect, the names for the Hering primaries, 'red', 'yellow', 'green', 'blue', 'black', and 'white', as well as 'brown', 'gray', 'orange', 'purple', and 'pink'. The stimuli in the Berlin and Kay work were a selection of Munsell color chips, a collection of color samples carefully scaled and reproduced to exacting standards. The sample consisted of maximally saturated chips taken from the outer shell of the Munsell color space. Using alternative color-order systems, other investigators, notably Boynton and Olson (1987) in the United States and Sivik and Taft (1994) in Sweden, have since carefully studied the ranges of these terms with very good overall agreement, exploring the interior of the color solid as well as its outer skin. Among other findings, they showed that some colors, such as blue and green, are seen over wide regions of the space, whereas other colors, such as red, orange, and yellow, are of much more restricted extent. We will look at the implications of this in a moment.

In the Matsuzawa experiment, to which I alluded above, the chimp, whose name was Ai, was trained on a set of 11 focal samples, learning to press the key that contained a contrived character for the appropriate basic color term. She was then presented with 215 of the Berlin and Kay chips that she had not seen. They were shown to her one at a time and in random order, and she was asked to name them. Following the sessions with the training chips, she did not receive reinforcement for her choices. The experimenter assigned a label to a chip when the chimpanzee gave it that label on at least 75% of the trials. The results were compared with those generated in a human color-naming experiment, again using the 75% consistency criterion. The outcomes were closely similar. The chimp had generalized from focal chips in essentially the same fashion as the human being.

This is a striking result, but what is its application to our problem? Think of it this way. Ai was presumably not doing what she was doing because of cultural bias, the grammar of color concepts, or any other such fancy hoo-hah. She was guided by what she saw, by what looked like what, by, if you will, the *intrinsic quality* of her sensory experience. The array of Munsell chips is scaled so that the samples are a constant number of just-noticeable-hue-differences apart, and a constant number of just-noticeable-lightness-differences apart. At one level of resemblance ordering, everything is smooth and orderly. But at the level of categorization, this is not at all the case, as we have already seen. (I might note parenthetically that other measures of perceptual distance are used in other color-order systems, but the results of categorization are essentially independent of this fact. The principles of scaling in the Swedish Natural Color System yield a solid of entirely regular shape, but the categorized areas are as irregular in shape and strikingly diverse in extent in the Natural Color System as they are in the Munsell solid.) If red occupies a small volume in the solid, and green a large one, what does this betoken but a substantial difference in phenomenal structure between red and green? Moreover, this difference is surely intrinsic to the qualities themselves. What else could serve as the basis for categorization? After all, the whole procedure only involves assessing the qualitative similarities and differences between one color and another.

I would next like to direct your attention to another categorical asymmetry, the strange case of the color brown. People differ in their sense of just how singular brown is. Nearly everybody agrees that brown has a certain affinity for yellow and orange, and if anyone is obliged to find the region of color space where it belongs, I would think that they would shove it down toward black, tucked underneath yellow and orange. But is brown just a blackened orange or yellow? Many people will hesitate to say so, for brown looks to have a very different quality from those two colors. People are surprised, and sometimes incredulous, to be told that, viewed in a bright light through a peephole, a chocolate bar looks to have exactly the same hue as an orange. They are surprised when they see a demonstration in which a projected orange spot is first dimmed, looking orange to the very edge of invisibility. The same spot is then blackened by surrounding it with an annulus of bright white light. When the blackening occurs, the orange spot is transformed into a rich brown. It is as if the original quality has been lost, and replaced by another. Performing a careful Sternheim-Boynton procedure shows that this brown is, indeed, none other than blackened orange (Quinn et al. 1988), but the sense of major qualitative alteration persists.

It is important to bear in mind that this appearance of strong qualitative differences is not a general characteristic of blackened colors, most of which resemble their parent hues. Blackened blues, such as navy blue, continue to look blue, and blackened greens—olive greens—continue to look green. Only oranges and yellows seem to lose the parental connection when blackened. If this is so, what would happen in the hypothetical case of spectral inversion in which hues are carried into their complements? The inverse of orange is turquoise, the inverse of yellow, blue. Therefore the inverse of the browns would be blackened turquoises and navy blues. If you are like most people, you find brown and yellow to be far more different from each other than light blue is from navy blue. It is worth remarking that in many languages, as in English, the difference between yellow and brown is marked by the use of two distinct basic color terms, but in no language whatever is the light blue–dark blue difference marked with distinct basic color terms and the yellow-brown difference left unmarked. In fact, with the possible exception of Russian, no language even has separate basic terms for light blue and dark blue.

It is thus fair to conclude that something has got lost in the inversion, and that if a human being were to be born with such an inversion, it would not go undetected. More to the point, since the blackness in a blackened yellow is the same as the blackness in a blackened blue, or, for that matter, red or green, there must be some characteristic of yellow that is not present in blue or in any of the other Hering primaries. We have here the mark of something we don't yet understand, probably having to do with the fact that yellow, unlike any other chromatic primary, is most pronounced only at high lightness levels. But couldn't there be a creature for whom the best yellow would exist at low lightness levels? I was once inclined to think so, but this is because I was insufficiently sensitive to the distinctions among yellow as hue, yellow as color category, and yellow as focal color, that is, the "best" example of a yellow. Although the *hue* yellow is to be found at all lightness levels, in brown, for instance, the *focal color* yellow is intrinsically light. The right thing to say about our hypothetical creature is that the very fact that its best example in the yellow hue category is at low lightness levels is the best of reasons for taking that to be a focal brown, rather than a focal yellow.

We of course want to understand why focal yellow is of intrinsically high lightness. This is basically to ask why its chromatic content should be highest at high lightness levels. The most helpful, indeed, I think, the *only* helpful explanation of this would be in terms of a neural mechanism. Recent neurophysiological evidence indicates that color-sensitive color cells in the cerebral cortex statistically "prefer" their yellows light and their reds dark (Yoshioka et al. 1996). This must of course be regarded as only the first step in a long journey that, if we are lucky, will bring us to a suitably rich mechanism to account for the properties of yellow. Finding such a mechanism would be the way to understand other facts about yellow, such as why it is that yellowish greens look as though they ought to be classified as greens, even though we judge the yellow content to be well above 50 percent. The very fact that the internal relations between yellow and its neighbors do not have the same form as the internal relationships between blue and its neighbors suggests that although yellow may be elementary with respect to phenomenal color mixing, it is not elementary simpliciter, any more than a proposition that is commonly used as an axiom for certain purposes is an axiom simpliciter. The only way to understand why the phenomenal structure of primary yellow is what it is, is to devise a good functional model, consistent with what we know about the underlying neurophysiology. Such models have already helped us to understand the unitary-binary and opponent structures of phenomenal color space (Hardin 1988). Irregularities in the structure of phenomenal color space not only render problematic the claim that colors are invertible, thus defusing an objection to a functional analysis of color perception, they positively cry out for explanation couched in terms of functional or neurofunctional mechanisms.

It would of course be nice at this point to produce a reasonable functional model that could account for the special phenomenal characteristic of brown. None is, alas, forthcoming. Indeed, for many of the asymmetries one finds in color spaces there is little in the way of available functional or neural mechanisms to explain them. But one never knows what tomorrow's mail may bring. For example, in an earlier version of this essay, I wrote the following:

There are several intrinsic irregularities in the phenomenal space of the colors. The *warm-cool* distinction is well-known, robustly cross-cultural, and still mysterious. There may be those who think that such mysteries are here to stay, and remain forever beyond the bounds of empirical inquiry. I do not share this pessimism. Furthermore, I think that nothing would be so helpful in making it unmysterious as a nice set of neurophysiological mechanisms that are otherwise confirmed and have built into them the images of the asymmetries that we find in the phenomenology.

Not long thereafter, there came to me a draft of a paper written by Betsy Katra and Billy Wooten of Brown University. Katra and Wooten asked 10 subjects to rate eight color samples as "warm" or "cool" on a 10-point scale, with 10 as "very warm." As one might have expected, the mean results gave the lowest rating (3.5) to the unitary blue sample, and the highest rating (6.75) to the orange sample. There was a high level of agreement among subjects. Katra and Wooten compared the group data with summed averaged opponent-response cancellation data, which can be interpreted as giving the level of activation of opponent channels. To quote Katra and Wooten's conclusion:

The remarkable correspondence between the obtained ratings of warmth and coolness and the activation levels in the opponent channels ... suggests that the attribution of thermal properties to colors may be linked to the low-level physiological processes involved in color perception. Higher ratings of warmth corresponded with levels of activation of the opponent channels in one direction, while cooler ratings corresponded with activation in the opposite direction. This suggests that a link to the activation level of the opponent channels, rather than the psychological quality of hue, drives the association of temperature with color, and that the association is more than simply a cognitive process.

They thus trace the connection between the warm-cool of temperature and the warm-cool of color to the corresponding activation levels of their respective neural systems rather than to stereotypical environmental associations such as red with fire and blue with water. This does not by itself warrant the conclusion that the respective *intrinsic* characters of the warm colors and the cool colors are a function of opponent activation levels, but it is consonant with that stronger claim. Furthermore, if one reflects on just how Katra and Wooten's subjects could gain information about the state of activation of their visual opponent cells, it becomes clear that it could *only* be by experiencing the colors of which these cells are the neural substrate. In other words, the color qualities themselves are the natural expression of neural activation, and we implicitly read them as such.

Now let us sum up these considerations. Color space has an irregular structure. The structure of color space is arrived at entirely by comparing the colors with each other, so the irregularity of structure is intrinsic to the domain of colors. Experiments with nonhuman primates strongly suggest that this irregular, intrinsic structure is of biological rather than cultural origin. The peculiarities of chromatic structure invite explanation in terms of biological mechanisms, and in some cases it is possible to produce such explanations, at least in outline. The details of the chromatic structural irregularities prohibit putative undetectable interchanges of color experiences: small rotations of the hue circuit carry unitary into binary hues; interchanges of warm and cool colors carry negative opponent-channel activations into positive ones, and vice versa; interchange of yellows with blues exchanges dark blues and cyans with browns; interchange of reds with greens maps a small categorical region into a large one, and a large region into a small one.

Some proponents of the possibility of an inverted spectrum (Shoemaker 1984) who have thought about these empirical data have conceded that human color space may not be invertible. They have, however, urged that this does not show that no creature could possibly have inverted sensory qualities, and some of them (e.g., Levine 1991) go on to argue that the mere possibility of inverted sensory qualities is sufficient to make any functionalist account of the qualities of experience suspect.

In one respect, they are right. Empirical arguments cannot (nontrivially) yield necessary truths. We philosophers rather tenaciously cling to this truism, perhaps because we sense that the independence of our discipline depends upon it. But we must beware of letting it bear too much weight. That we can in some fashion imagine that water is not H_2O, or that heat is a fluid, or that there exists a perfectly rigid body, does not license us to suppose that any of these things is possible in any scientifically interesting sense. At our present state of knowledge, to regard any of them as genuinely possible is to exchange hard-won intelligibility for a murky mess of imagery. Given as background what we now know about fluids and heat, it becomes much harder for us even to *imagine* that heat is a fluid. Granted, there is still no knockdown argument that there is no possible world in which the heat of a gas is a fluid, but we are not thereby tempted to suspect that the heat of a gas might not after all be identical with molecular kinetic energy. When it comes to scientific identities, logical possibility is trumped by overwhelming implausibility.

The case at hand is similar. Much of the appeal of the inverted spectrum as an antifunctionalist weapon has lain in its intuitiveness: what looks to me to be THIS color (inwardly ostending red) could have looked to me to be THAT color (inwardly ostending green) without anyone being the wiser. This simple intuition has doubtless been aided and abetted by the wide currency of oversimplified models of color space, such as the color sphere and hue circle, in which the structure of color qualities is presented as smoothly symmetrical. But once we do the phenomenology of THIS and THAT, becoming aware of their intrinsic structure, and elaborating the functional structure that underlies them, the initial plausibility of interchange begins to fade, just as the plausibility of heat's being a fluid begins to fade once one understands how the ideas of the kinetic theory engage the empirical facts about heat. And when this paradigmatic example of qualitative interchange loses its grip on our imaginations, the idea of there being *abstractly specified* qualitative states being interchangeable in *abstractly specified* creatures with *abstractly specified* physical workings ought to lose its grip on our intuitions.

Merely schematic specification of the subject matter plagues both sides of the disputes about functionalism. On the one hand a defender of functionalism (Lewis 1980) gives us Martians with plumbing instead of neurons, and on the other, a critic of functionalism (Block 1980) presents us with the spectacle of the whole nation of China acting as a Turing machine. Amusing though these fantasies may be, they are as desperately lacking in the details of what is to be explained as they are lacking in constraints on the putative explanatory mechanisms. It is as if we were asked to judge the possibility of a physical account of living organisms based only on a thorough knowledge of Lucretius' *On the Nature of Things*. To judge rightly the adequacy of functionalism to capture the qualitative character of experience, we must carefully describe both sides of the equation. To do so, we need good ideas, the right distinctions, and lots of careful empirical work. That work must take place on several levels, regimenting the phenomenology, developing functional models that are capable of imaging that phenomenology, and investigating how those models might be realized by the available neural resources (cf. Clark 1993). The patient application of these methods can in principle capture any sayable fact about sensory qualities, and bring that fact within the ambit of scientific explanation.

Will there be a plurality of plausible functional models adequate to the total phenomenology, or will there be but one? Will the preferred future explanations of sensory qualities take the form only of correlations among the behavioral, phenomenal, and neural domains, or will they involve a proper reduction of phenomenology to neural mechanisms? We are simply too ignorant of the relevant facts to answer these questions now, and we ought not to pretend that clever conceptual analysis can offset this epistemic deficiency. We can responsibly judge these questions only on hand of a sufficiently rich broth of data and theory. Such a broth is not yet ready to be tasted, but the pot is already on the burner.

Notes

1. Furthermore, since the perceptions of both black and brown arise only as a consequence of simultaneous contrast, they depend essentially on the visual system. This poses a problem for a realist account of these colors. Cf. Hardin 1988.

2. In this sense, orange necessarily has both red and yellow as constituents. However, this will not be true for any plausible version of color realism that identifies orange with some constellation of extradermal physical properties. More generally, the unitary-binary structure of the colors as we experience them corresponds to no known physical structure lying outside of nervous systems that is causally involved in the perception of color. This makes it very difficult to subscribe to a color realism that is supposed to be about red, yellow, green, blue, black, and white—that is, the colors with which we are perceptually acquainted. Cf. Hardin 1988.

References

Berlin, B., and P. Kay. 1969. *Basic Color Terms.* Berkeley: University of California Press.

Block, N. 1980. Troubles with functionalism. In *Readings in Philosophy of Psychology*, vol. 1, ed. N. Block. Cambridge, MA: Harvard University Press.

Bornstein, M. H., W. Kessen, and S. Weiskopf. 1976. Color vision and hue categorization in Young Human Infants. *Journal of Experimental Psychology, 2,* 115–19.

Boynton, R. M., and C. X. Olson. 1987. Locating basic colors in the OSA space. *Color Research and Application, 12* (2), 94–105.

Clark, A. 1993. *Sensory Qualities.* Oxford: Clarendon Press.

Hardin, C. L. 1988. *Color for Philosophers: Unweaving the Rainbow.* Indianapolis, MA: Hackett.

Katra, B., and B. H. Wooten. n. d. Perceived lightness/darkness and warmth/coolness in chromatic experience. Unpublished MS, 38 pp.

Levine, J. 1983. Materialism and qualia: The explanatory gap. *Pacific Philosophical Quarterly, 64,* 354–61.

Levine, J. 1991. Cool red: A reply to Hardin. *Philosophical Psychology, 4* (1), 27–40.

Lewis, D. 1980. Mad pain and Martian pain. In *Readings in Philosophy of Psychology*, vol. 1, ed. N. Block. Cambridge, MA: Harvard University Press.

Matsuzawa, T. 1985. Colour naming and classification in a chimpanzee (*Pan troglodytes*). *Journal of Human Evolution, 14,* 283–91.

Quinn, P. C., J. L. Rosano, and B. R. Wooten. 1988. Evidence that brown is not an elemental color. *Perception and Psychophysics, 37* (3), 198–202.

Sandell, J. H., C. G. Gross, and M. H. Bornstein. 1979. Color categories in macaques. *Journal of Comparative and Physiological Psychology, 93,* 626–35.

Shoemaker, S. 1984. The inverted spectrum. In *Identity, Cause, and Mind: Philosophical Essays.* Cambridge: Cambridge University Press.

Sivik, L., and C. Taft. 1994. Color naming: A mapping in the NCS of common color terms. *Scandinavian Journal of Psychology, 35,* 144–64.

Sternheim, C. E., and R. M. Boynton. 1966. Uniqueness of perceived hues investigated with a continuous judgmental technique. *Journal of Experimental Psychology, 72,* 770–76.

Yoshioka, T., B. M. Dow, and R. G. Vautin. 1996. Neural mechanisms of color categorization in areas V1, V2, and V4 of macaque monkey cortex. *Behavioural Brain Research, 76,* 51–70.

Bibliography

Books

Philosophy

Recent philosophical books substantially concerned with color:

Broackes, J. *The Nature of Colour*. Routledge, forthcoming.

Clark, A. 1993. *Sensory Qualities*. Oxford: Oxford University Press.

Hacker, P. M. S. 1987. *Appearance and Reality*. Oxford: Blackwell.

Hardin, C. L. 1993. *Color for Philosophers: Unweaving the Rainbow* (expanded edition). Indianapolis: Hackett.

Harrison, B. 1973. *Form and Content*. Oxford: Blackwell.

Hilbert, D. R. 1987. *Color and Color Perception: A Study in Anthropocentric Realism*. Stanford: CSLI.

Jackson, F. 1977. *Perception: A Representative Theory*. Cambridge: Cambridge University Press.

Landesman, C. 1989. *Color and Consciousness: An Essay in Metaphysics*. Philadelphia: Temple University Press.

Maund, J. B. 1995. *Colours: Their Nature and Representation*. Cambridge: Cambridge University Press.

McGinn, C. 1983. *The Subjective View: Secondary Qualities and Indexical Thoughts*. Oxford: Oxford University Press.

Mundle, C. W. K. 1971. *Perception: Facts and Theories*. London: Oxford University Press.

Thompson, E. 1995. *Colour Vision*. New York: Routledge.

Westphal, J. 1991. *Colour: A Philosophical Introduction*. Oxford: Blackwell. (First published as *Colour: Some Philosophical Problems from Wittgenstein*.)

Wittgenstein, L. 1977. *Remarks on Colour*, ed. G. E. M. Anscombe, trans. L. L. McAlister and M. Schättle. Berkeley: University of California Press.

Goethe

Goethe's *Farbenlehre* has influenced a number of philosophers, notably Schelling, Schopenhauer, Hegel, and Wittgenstein:

Goethe, J. W. von. 1840/1970. *Theory of Colours*, trans. C. L. Eastlake. Cambridge, MA: MIT Press.

For a useful historical account see:

Sepper, D. L. 1988. *Goethe contra Newton: Polemics and the Project for a New Science of Color*. Cambridge: Cambridge University Press.

Color in Culture

The best survey of color in Western culture is:

Gage, J. 1993. *Color and Culture: Practice and Meaning from Antiquity to Abstraction*. Boston: Bulfinch Press.

And for fun:

Theroux, A. 1994. *The Primary Colors*. New York: Henry Holt.

Theroux, A. 1996. *The Secondary Colors*. New York: Henry Holt.

Papers

We have attempted to list every philosophical paper since 1950 in English whose main topic includes color. Aesthetics has been omitted, but selected historical material, book chapters, and book reviews have been included. We would be grateful to be told of errors or omissions.

Aldrich, V. C. 1952. Colors as universals. *Philosophical Review* 61, 377–81.

Allaire, E. B. 1959. *Tractatus* 6.3751. *Analysis* 19, 100–5.

Anscombe, G. E. M. 1974. The subjectivity of sensation. *Ajatus* 36, 3–18.

Arbini, R. 1963. Frederick Ferré on colour incompatibility. *Mind* 72, 586–90.

Armstrong, D. M. 1961. Problems about the secondary qualities. *Perception and the Physical World*, London: Routledge & Kegan Paul, chapter 14.

Armstrong, D. M. 1968a. The secondary qualities: an essay in the classification of theories. *Australasian Journal of Philosophy* 46, 225–41.

Armstrong, D. M. 1968b. The secondary qualities. *A Materialist Theory of the Mind*, London: Routledge, chapter 12.

Armstrong, D. M. 1969. Colour realism and the argument from microscopes. In *Contemporary Philosophy in Australia*, ed. R. Brown and C. D. Rollins. London: Allen & Unwin.

Armstrong, D. M. 1987. Smart and the secondary qualities. In *Metaphysics and Morality: Essays in Honour of J. J. C. Smart*, ed. P. Pettit, R. Sylvan, and J. Norman. Oxford: Blackwell. Reprinted as chapter 3 of this volume.

Armstrong, D. M. 1993. Reply to Campbell. In *Ontology, Causality and Mind: Essays in Honour of D. M. Armstrong*, ed. J. Bacon, K. Campbell, and L. Reinhardt. Cambridge: Cambridge University Press.

Arthadeva. 1961. Naive realism and the problem of color-seeing in dim light. *Philosophy and Phenomenological Research* 21, 467–78.

Austin, J. 1980. Wittgenstein's solutions to the color exclusion problem. *Philosophy and Phenomenological Research* 41, 142–9.

Averill, E. W. 1980. Why are colour terms primarily used as adjectives? *Philosophical Quarterly* 30, 19–33.

Averill, E. W. 1982. The primary-secondary quality distinction. *Philosophical Review* 91, 343–62.

Averill, E. W. 1985. Color and the anthropocentric problem. *Journal of Philosophy* 82, 281–304. Reprinted as chapter 2 of this volume.

Averill, E. W. 1991. Review of C. L. Hardin's *Color for Philosophers* and D. R. Hilbert's *Color and Color Perception*. *Philosophical Review* 100, 459–63.

Averill, E. W. 1992. The relational nature of color. *Philosophical Review* 101, 551–88.

Baldes, R. W. 1978. Democritus on the nature and perception of 'black' and 'white'. *Phronesis* 23, 87–100.

Beard, R. W. 1967. Analyticity, informativeness, and the incompatibility of colors. *Logique et Analyse* 10, 211–7.

Benardete, J. A. 1958. The analytic *a posteriori* and the foundations of metaphysics. *Journal of Philosophy* 55, 503–14.

Bennett, J. 1965. Substance, reality, and primary qualities. *American Philosophical Quarterly* 2, 1–17.

Bennett, J. 1971. Primary and secondary qualities. *Locke, Berkeley, Hume*, Oxford: Oxford University Press, chapter 4.

Berchielli, L. 1995. Representing color: discussions and problems. In *Bilder im Geiste: Zur kognitiven und erkenntnistheoretischen Funktion piktorialer Repräsentationen*, ed. K. Sachs-Hombach. Amsterdam: Rodopi.

Bigelow, J., J. Collins, and R. Pargetter. 1990. Colouring in the world. *Mind* 99, 279–88.

Block N. 1990. Inverted earth. In *Philosophical Perspectives* 4, ed. J. Tomberlin. Atascadero, CA: Ridgeview.

Boghossian, P. A., and J. D. Velleman. 1989. Colour as a secondary quality. *Mind* 98, 81–103. Reprinted as chapter 7 of this volume.

Boghossian, P. A., and J. D. Velleman. 1991. Physicalist theories of color. *Philosophical Review* 100, 67–106. Reprinted as chapter 8 of this volume.

Boyne, C. 1972. Vagueness and colour predicates. *Mind* 81, 576–7.

Bradley, M. C. 1963. Sensations, brain-processes and colours. *Australasian Journal of Philosophy* 41, 385–93.

Bradley, M. C. 1964. Critical notice of J. J. C. Smart's *Philosophy and Scientific Realism*. *Australasian Journal of Philosophy* 42, 262–83.

Brenner, W. 1982. Wittgenstein's color grammar. *Southern Journal of Philosophy* 20, 289–98.

Brenner, W. 1987. 'Brownish-Yellow' and 'Reddish-Green.' *Philosophical Investigations* 10, 200–11.

Broackes, J. 1992. The autonomy of colour. In *Reduction, Explanation and Realism*, ed. D. Charles and K. Lennon. Oxford: Oxford University Press. Reprinted as chapter 11 of this volume.

Broackes, J. 1993. Critical notice of J. Westphal's *Colour: A Philosophical Introduction*. *Philosophical Quarterly* 43, 233–8.

Buckner, D. K. 1986. Transparently false: reply to Hardin. *Analysis* 46, 86–7.

Byrne, A., and D. R. Hilbert. 1997. Colors and reflectances. In *Readings on Color, vol. 1: The Philosophy of Color*, ed. A. Byrne and D. R. Hilbert. Cambridge, MA: MIT Press. Chapter 14 of this volume.

Campbell, J. 1993. A simple view of colour. In *Reality, Representation, and Projection*, ed. J. Haldane and C. Wright. New York: Oxford University Press. Reprinted as chapter 10 of this volume.

Campbell, K. 1969. Colours. In *Contemporary Philosophy in Australia*, ed. R. Brown and C. D. Rollins. London: Allen & Unwin.

Campbell, K. 1979. The implications of Land's theory of colour vision. *Logic, Methodology and Philosophy of Science* 6, ed. L. Cohen. Amsterdam: North Holland.

Campbell, K. 1993. David Armstrong and realism about colour. In *Ontology, Causality and Mind: Essays in Honour of D. M. Armstrong*, ed. J. Bacon, K. Campbell, and L. Reinhardt. Cambridge: Cambridge University Press.

Casati, R. 1990. What is wrong in inverting spectra. *Teoria* 10, 183–6.

Clark, A. 1985a. Qualia and the psychophysiological explanation of color perception. *Synthese* 65, 377–405.

Clark, A. 1985b. Spectrum inversion and the color solid. *Southern Journal of Philosophy* 23, 431–43.

Clark, A. 1989. The particulate instantiation of homogeneous pink. *Synthese* 80, 277–304.

Clark, A. 1996. True theories, false colors. *Philosophy of Science* 63 (Proceedings), S143–50.

Clement, W. C. 1956. Quality orders. *Mind* 65, 184–99.

Cornman, J. 1969. Sellars, scientific realism, and sensa. *Review of Metaphysics* 23, 417–51.

Cornman, J. 1974. Can Eddington's 'two tables' be identical? *Australasian Journal of Philosophy* 52, 22–38.

Cornman, J. 1975. Naive realism. *Perception, Common Sense, and Science*, New Haven: Yale University Press, chapter 6.

Cottingham, J. 1989–90. Descartes on colour. *Proceedings of the Aristotelian Society* 90, 231–46.

Cummins, R. 1978. The missing shade of blue. *Philosophical Review* 87, 548–65.

Daniels, C. B. 1967. Colors and sensations, or how to define a pain ostensively. *American Philosophical Quarterly* 4, 231–7.

Dedrick, D. 1995. Objectivism and the evolutionary value of colour vision. *Dialogue* 34, 35–44.

Dedrick, D. 1996. Can color be reduced to anything? *Philosophy of Science* 63 (Proceedings), S134–42.

Dennett, D. C. 1981. Wondering where the yellow went. *Monist* 64, 102–8.

Deshpande, D. Y. 1982. An alleged case of factual a priori. *Indian Philosophical Quarterly* 9, 107–12.

Dolby, R. G. A. 1973. Philosophy and the incompatibility of colours. *Analysis* 34, 8–16.

Dummett, M. A. E. 1979. Common sense and physics. In *Perception and Identity: Essays Presented to A. J. Ayer with his Replies*, ed. G. F. MacDonald. Ithaca, NY: Cornell University Press.

Edwards, J. 1992. Secondary qualities and the a priori. *Mind* 101, 263–72.

Erickson, G. W. 1991. Wittgenstein's *Remarks on Colour*. *Dialogos* 57, 113–36.

Evans, G. 1980. Things without the mind—a commentary upon chapter two of Strawson's *Individuals*. In *Philosophical Subjects: Essays Presented to P. F. Strawson,* ed. Z. Van Straaten. Oxford: Oxford University Press.

Ferré, F. 1961. Colour incompatibility and language-games. *Mind* 70, 90–94.

Fales, E. 1982. Generic universals. *Australasian Journal of Philosophy* 60, 29–39.

Fogelin, R. J. 1984. Hume and the missing shade of blue. *Philosophy and Phenomenological Research* 45, 263–71.

Foti, V. 1990. The dimension of color. *International Studies in Philosophy* 22, 13–28.

Geach, P. T. 1957. Abstractionism and colour-concepts. *Mental Acts*, London: Routledge & Kegan Paul, section 10.

Gibbard, A. 1996. Visible properties of human interest only. In *Philosophical Issues* 7, ed. E. Villanueva. Atascadero, CA: Ridgeview.

Gilbert, P. 1987. Westphal and Wittgenstein on white. *Mind* 76, 399–403.

Gilbert, P. 1989. Reflections on white: a rejoinder to Westphal. *Mind* 98, 423–6.

Goldman, A. H. 1975. Criteriological arguments in perception. *Mind* 84, 102–5.

Goodman, N. 1957. Letter to the editor on W. C. Clement's 'Quality and order.' *Mind* 66, 78.

Grandy, R. E. 1989. A modern inquiry into the physical reality of colors. In *Mind, Value and Culture: Essays in Honour of E. M. Adams*, ed. D. Weissbord. Atascadero, CA: Ridgeview.

Guerlac, H. 1986. Can there be colors in the dark? Physical color theory before Newton. *Journal of the History of Ideas* 47, 3–20.

Hacker, P. M. S. 1976. Locke and the meaning of colour words. *Royal Institute of Philosophy Lectures* 9, ed. G. Vesey. New York: St. Martin's Press.

Hacker, P. M. S. 1986. Are secondary qualities relative? *Mind* 95, 180–97.

Hahm, D. E. 1978. Early Hellenistic theories of vision and the perception of color. In *Studies in Perception*, ed. P. K. Machamer and R. G. Turnbull. Columbus, OH: Ohio State University Press.

Hall, R. J. 1996. The evolution of color vision without colors. *Philosophy of Science* 63 (Proceedings), S125–33.

Hardin, C. L. 1983. Colors, normal observers, and standard conditions. *Journal of Philosophy* 80, 806–13.

Hardin, C. L. 1984a. A new look at color. *American Philosophical Quarterly* 21, 125–34.

Hardin, C. L. 1984b. Are 'scientific' objects coloured? *Mind* 93, 491–500.

Hardin, C. L. 1985a. A transparent case for subjectivism. *Analysis* 45, 117–9.

Hardin, C. L. 1985b. The resemblances of colors. *Philosophical Studies* 48, 35–47.

Hardin, C. L. 1985c. Frank talk about the colours of sense-data. *Australasian Journal of Philosophy* 63, 485–93.

Hardin, C. L. 1988. Phenomenal colors and sorites. *Noûs* 22, 213–34.

Hardin, C. L. 1989a. Idle colours and busy spectra. *Analysis* 49, 47–8.

Hardin, C. L. 1989b. Could white be green? *Mind* 98, 285–8.

Hardin, C. L. 1989c. Review of J. Westphal's *Colour: Some Philosophical Problems from Wittgenstein*. *Mind* 98, 146–9.

Hardin, C. L. 1989d. Review of D. R. Hilbert's *Color and Color Perception*. *Canadian Philosophical Reviews* 9, 47–9.

Hardin, C. L. 1990a. Why color? In *Perceiving, Measuring, and Using Color: 15–6 February 1990, Santa Clara, California*, ed. M. Brill. Bellingham, WA: SPIE.

Hardin, C. L. 1990b. Color and illusion. In *Mind and Cognition*, ed. W. G. Lycan. Oxford: Blackwell.

Hardin, C. L. 1991a. Color for philosophers: a précis. *Philosophical Psychology* 4, 21–6.

Hardin, C. L. 1991b. Reply to Levine. *Philosophical Psychology* 4, 41–50.

Hardin, C. L. 1991c. Reply to Teller. *Philosophical Psychology* 4, 61–4.

Hardin, C. L. 1992a. The virtues of illusion. *Philosophical Studies* 68, 371–82.

Hardin, C. L. 1992b. Physiology, phenomenology, and Spinoza's true colors. In *Emergence or Reduction? Essays on the Prospects of Nonreductive Physicalism*, ed. A. Beckermann, H. Flohr, and J. Kim. New York: Walter de Gruyter.

Hardin, C. L. 1993. Van Brakel and the not-so-naked emperor. *British Journal for the Philosophy of Science* 44, 137–50.

Hardin, C. L. 1997. Reinverting the spectrum. In *Readings on Color, vol. 1: The Philosophy of Color*, ed. A. Byrne and D. R. Hilbert. Cambridge, Massachusetts: MIT Press. Chapter 15 of this volume.

Harding, G. 1991. Color and the mind-body problem. *Review of Metaphysics* 45, 289–307.

Harman, G. 1996a. Explaining objective color in terms of subjective reactions. In *Philosophical Issues* 7, ed. E. Villanueva. Atascadero, CA: Ridgeview. Reprinted as chapter 13 of this volume.

Harman, G. 1996b. Qualia and color concepts. In *Philosophical Issues* 7, ed. E. Villanueva. Atascadero, CA: Ridgeview.

Harrison, B. 1967. On describing colours. *Inquiry* 10, 38–52.

Harrison, B. 1986. Identity, predication and color. *American Philosophical Quarterly* 23, 105–14.

Harvey, J. 1979. Systematic transposition of colours. *Australasian Journal of Philosophy* 57, 211–9.

Harvey, J. 1992. Challenging the obvious: the logic of colour concepts. *Philosophia* 21, 277–94.

Hatfield, G. 1992. Color perception and neural encoding: does metameric matching entail a loss of information? *Proceedings of the Philosophy of Science Association* 1, 492–504.

Hilbert, D. R. 1992. What is color vision? *Philosophical Studies* 68, 351–70.

Hilton, J. 1961. Red and green all over again. *Analysis* 22, 47–8.

Holman, E. L. 1979. Is the physical world colourless? *Australasian Journal of Philosophy* 57, 295–304.

Holman, E. L. 1981. Intension, identity, and the colourless physical world: a revision and further discussion. *Australasian Journal of Philosophy* 59, 203–5.

Illetterati, L. 1993. Hegel's exposition of Goethe's theory of colour. In *Hegel and Newtonianism*, ed. M. J. Petry. Dordrecht: Kluwer.

Jackson, F. 1973. Do material things have non-physical properties? *Personalist* 54, 105–10.

Jackson, F. 1996. The primary quality view of color. In *Philosophical Perspectives* 10, ed. J. Tomberlin. Cambridge, MA: Blackwell.

Jackson, F., and R. Pargetter. 1987. An objectivist's guide to subjectivism about colour. *Revue Internationale de Philosophie* 41, 127–41. Reprinted as chapter 6 of this volume.

Jacquette, D. 1990. Wittgenstein and the color incompatibility problem. *History of Philosophy Quarterly* 7, 353–65.

Jacquette, D. 1995. Color and Armstrong's color realism under the microscope. *Studies in History and Philosophy of Science* 26, 389–406.

Jarvis, J. 1961. Definition by internal relation. *Australasian Journal of Philosophy* 39, 125–42.

Johnson, D. M. 1984. Hume's missing shade of blue, interpreted as involving habitual spectra. *Hume Studies* 10, 109–24.

Johnston, M. 1992. How to speak of the colors. *Philosophical Studies* 68, 221–63. Reprinted as chapter 9 of this volume.

Johnston, M. 1996a. Is the external world invisible? In *Philosophical Issues* 7, ed. E. Villanueva. Atascadero, CA: Ridgeview.

Johnston, M. 1996b. A mind-body problem at the surface of objects. In *Philosophical Issues* 7, ed. E. Villanueva. Atascadero, CA: Ridgeview.

Johnston, M. 1997. Postscript: visual experience. In *Readings on Color, vol. 1: The Philosophy of Color*, ed. A. Byrne and D. R. Hilbert. Cambridge, MA: MIT Press. An appendix to chapter 9 of this volume.

Keating, L. 1993. Un-Locke-ing Boyle: Boyle on primary and secondary qualities. *History of Philosophy Quarterly* 10, 305–23.

Kenner, L. 1965. The triviality of the red-green problem. *Analysis* 25, 147–53.

Kraut, R. 1992. The objectivity of color and the color of objectivity. *Philosophical Studies* 68, 265–87.

Krishna, D. 1961/2. Colour incompatibility and language-games. *Indian Journal of Philosophy* 3, 55–60.

Landesman, C. 1993. Why nothing has color: color skepticism. In *Theory of Knowledge: Classical and Contemporary Readings*, ed. L. Pojman. Belmont, CA: Wadsworth.

Lauxtermann, P. F. H. 1987. Five decisive years: Schopenhauer's epistemology as reflected in his theory of colour. *Studies in History and Philosophy of Science* 18, 271–91.

Lauxtermann, P. F. H. 1990. Hegel and Schopenhauer as partisans of Goethe's theory of color. *Journal of the History of Ideas* 51, 599–624.

Leeds, S. 1975. Two senses of 'appears red.' *Philosophical Studies* 28, 199–205.

Levin, J. 1987. Physicalism and the subjectivity of secondary qualities. *Australasian Journal of Philosophy* 65, 400–11.

Levine, J. 1991. Cool red. *Philosophical Psychology* 4, 27–40.

Lewis, D. K. 1966. Percepts and color mosaics in visual experience. *Philosophical Review* 75, 357–68.

Lewis, D. K. 1987. Naming the colours. *Australasian Journal of Philosophy*, forthcoming.

Lycan, W. G. 1973. Inverted spectrum. *Ratio* 15, 315–9.

Macintyre, A. 1992. Colors, cultures, and practices. *Midwest Studies in Philosophy* 17, 1–23.

Mackie, J. L. 1976. Primary and secondary qualities. *Problems from Locke*, Oxford: Oxford University Press, chapter 1.

Matthen, M. 1988. Biological functions and perceptual content. *Journal of Philosophy* 85, 5–27.

Maund, J. B. 1981. Colour: a case for conceptual fission. *Australasian Journal of Philosophy* 59, 308–22.

Maund, J. B. 1991. The nature of color. *History of Philosophy Quarterly* 8, 253–63.

McCulloch, G. 1987. Subjectivity and colour vision. *Proceedings of the Aristotelian Society Suppl.* 61, 265–81.

McDowell, J. 1985. Values and secondary qualities. In *Morality and Objectivity: A Tribute to J. L. Mackie*, ed. T. Honderich. London: Routledge & Kegan Paul.

McGilvray, J. A. 1983. To color. *Synthese* 54, 37–70.

McGilvray, J. A. 1991. Review of C. L. Hardin's *Color for Philosophers*. *Philosophy of Science* 58, 329–31.

McGilvray, J. A. 1994. Constant colors in the head. *Synthese* 100, 197–239.

McGinn, C. 1996. Another look at color. *Journal of Philosophy* 93, 537–53.

McGinn, M. 1991a. On two recent accounts of colour. *Philosophical Quarterly* 41, 316–24.

McGinn, M. 1991b. Westphal on the physical basis of colour incompatibility. *Analysis* 51, 218–22.

McGinn, M. 1991c. Wittgenstein's *Remarks on Colour*. *Philosophy* 66, 435–53.

Melica, C. 1993. Hegel on shadows and the blue of the sky. In *Hegel and Newtonianism*, ed. M. J. Petry. Dordrecht, Netherlands: Kluwer.

Montgomery, R. 1990. Visual perception and the wages of indeterminacy. *Proceedings of the Philosophy of Science Association* 1, 365–78.

Morreall, J. 1982. Hume's missing shade of blue. *Philosophy and Phenomenological Research* 42, 407–15.

Mulligan, K. 1991. Colours, corners and complexity. In *Existence and Explanation: Essays Presented in Honor of Karel Lambert*, ed. W. Spohn, B. C. Van Fraassen, and B. Skyrms. Dordrecht: Kluwer.

Nathan, N. 1986. Simple colours. *Philosophy* 61, 345–53.

Nelkin, N. 1994. Phenomena and representation. *British Journal for the Philosophy of Science* 45, 527–47.

Nelson, J. O. 1961. y-Propositions. *Philosophical Studies* 12, 65–72.

Nelson, J. O. 1989. Hume's missing shade of blue re-viewed. *Hume Studies* 15, 353–63.

Noren, S. J. 1975a. Cornman on the colour of micro-entities. *Australasian Journal of Philosophy* 53, 65–7.

Noren, S. J. 1975b. The conflict between science and common sense and why it is inevitable. *Southern Journal of Philosophy* 13, 331–46.

O'Hair, S. G. 1969. Putnam on reds and greens. *Philosophical Review* 78, 504–6.

Pap, A. 1957. Once more: colors and the synthetic a priori. *Philosophical Review* 66, 94–9.

Peacocke, C. 1984. Colour concepts and colour experience. *Synthese* 58, 365–82. Reprinted as chapter 5 of this volume.

Peacocke, C. 1986. Reply to Michael Smith. *Synthese* 68, 577–80.

Pears, D. F. 1953. Incompatibilities of colours. In *Logic and Language (second series)*, ed. A Flew. Oxford: Blackwell.

Perkins, M. 1983. Vision. *Sensing the World*, Indianapolis: Hackett, chapter 6.

Pickering, F. R. 1975. Is light the proper object of vision? *Mind* 84, 119–21.

Pitcher, G. 1971. Colors: our perception of them and their ontological status. *A Theory of Perception*, Princeton: Princeton University Press, chapter 4.

Pluhar, E. B. 1986–7. The perceptual and physical worlds. *Philosophical Studies (Ireland)* 31, 228–40.

Putnam, H. 1956. Reds, greens, and logical analysis. *Philosophical Review* 65, 206–17.

Putnam, H. 1957. Red and green all over again: a rejoinder to Arthur Pap. *Philosophical Review* 66, 100–3.

Radford, C. 1963. The insolubility of the red-green problem. *Analysis* 23, 68–71.

Radford, C. 1965a. Reply to Mr. Kenner's 'The triviality of the red-green problem.' *Analysis* 25, 207–8.

Radford, C. 1965b. Incompatibilities of colours. *Philosophical Quarterly* 15, 207–19.

Remnant, P. 1961. Red and green all over again. *Analysis* 21, 93–5.

Rhees, R. 1963. The *Tractatus*: seeds of some misunderstandings. *Philosophical Review* 72, 213–20.

Ribe, N. M. 1985. Goethe's critique of Newton: a reconsideration. *Studies in History and Philosophy of Science* 16, 315–35.

Rosenberg, J. F. 1982. The place of color in the scheme of things: a roadmap to Sellar's Carus lectures. *Monist* 65, 315–35.

Rosenthal, D. 1990. The colors and shapes of visual experiences. Report No. 28, Research Group on Mind and Brain, Perspectives in Theoretical Psychology and the Philosophy of Mind (ZiF), University of Bielefeld, Germany.

Rozeboom, W. W. 1958. The logic of color words. *Philosophical Review* 67, 353–66.

Sahu, N. 1988. On 'this is red and this is blue': *Tractatus* 6.3751. *Journal of Indian Council of Philosophical Research* 6, 1–19.

Sanford, D. 1966. Red, green and absolute determinacy: a reply to C. Radford's 'Incompatibilities of colours.' *Philosophical Quarterly* 16, 356–58.

Saunders, B. A. C., and J. van Brakel. 1989. Review article: On cross cultural colour semantics: *Color for Philosophers* by C. L. Hardin. *International Journal of Moral and Social Studies* 4, 173–80.

Sellars, W. 1971. Science, sense impressions, and sensa. *Review of Metaphysics* 24, 391–447.

Sellars, W. 1981a. The lever of archimedes. *Monist* 64, 3–36.

Sellars, W. 1981b. Is consciousness physical? *Monist* 64, 66–90.

Sepper, D. L. 1989. Review of C. L. Hardin's *Color for Philosophers*. *Review of Metaphysics* 42, 834–37.

Shiner, R. A. 1977. Goldman on the non-contingency thesis. *Mind* 86, 587–90.

Shiner, R. A. 1979. Sense-experience, colours and tastes. *Mind* 88, 161–78.

Shoemaker, S. 1982. The inverted spectrum. *Journal of Philosophy* 79, 357–81.

Shoemaker, S. 1986. Review of C. McGinn's *The Subjective View*. *Journal of Philosophy* 83, 407–13.

Shoemaker, S. 1990. Qualities and qualia: what's in the mind? *Philosophy and Phenomenological Research* 50 (Suppl.), 109–31.

Shoemaker, S. 1991. Qualia and consciousness. *Mind* 100, 507–24.

Shoemaker, S. 1994a. Self-knowledge and 'inner sense.' Lecture III: the phenomenal character of experience. *Philosophy and Phenomenological Research* 54, 291–314.

Shoemaker, S. 1994b. Phenomenal character. *Noûs* 28, 21–38. Reprinted as chapter 12 of this volume.

Shoemaker, S. 1996. Colors, subjective reactions, and qualia. In *Philosophical Issues* 7, ed. E. Villanueva. Atascadero, CA: Ridgeview.

Sibley, F. N. 1968. Colours. *Proceedings of the Aristotelian Society* 68, 145–66.

Sievert, D. 1989. Another look at Wittgenstein on color exclusion. *Synthese* 78, 291–318.

Silverman, A. 1989. Color and color-perception in Aristotle's *De Anima*. *Ancient Philosophy* 9, 271–92.

Sloman, A. 1964. Colour incompatibilities and analyticity. *Analysis* 24, 104–19.

Smart, J. J. C. 1959. Incompatible colors. *Philosophical Studies* 10, 39–41.

Smart, J. J. C. 1961. Colours. *Philosophy* 36, 128–42.

Smart, J. J. C. 1963. The secondary qualities. *Philosophy and Scientific Realism*, London: Routledge, chapter 4.

Smart, J. J. C. 1971. Reports of immediate experiences. *Synthese* 22, 346–59.

Smart, J. J. C. 1975. On some criticisms of a physicalist theory of colors. In *Philosophical Aspects of the Mind–Body Problem*, ed. C. Cheng, Honolulu: University Press of Hawaii. Reprinted as chapter 1 of this volume.

Smart, J. J. C. 1987. Reply to Armstrong. In *Metaphysics and Morality: Essays in Honour of J. J. C. Smart*, ed. P. Pettit, R. Sylvan, and J. Norman. Oxford: Blackwell. Reprinted as chapter 4 of this volume.

Smart, J. J. C. 1995. 'Looks red' and dangerous talk. *Philosophy* 70, 545–54.

Smith, A. D. 1990. Of primary and secondary qualities. *Philosophical Review* 99, 221–54.

Smith, M. A. 1986. Peacocke on red and red'. *Synthese* 68, 559–76.

Smith, M. A. 1993. Colour, transparency, mind-independence. In *Reality, Representation, and Projection*, ed. J. Haldane and C. Wright. New York: Oxford University Press.

Smith, P. 1987. Subjectivity and colour vision. *Proceedings of the Aristotelian Society Suppl.* 61, 245–64.

Sorabji, R. 1972. Aristotle, mathematics, and colour. *Classical Quarterly* 22, 293–308.

Sosa, E. 1990. Perception and reality. In *Information, Semantics & Epistemology*, ed. E. Villanueva. Oxford: Blackwell.

Sosa, E. 1996. Is color psychological or biological? Or both? In *Philosophical Issues* 7, ed. E. Villanueva. Atascadero, CA: Ridgeview.

Srzednicki, D. J. 1962. Incompatibility statements. *Australasian Journal of Philosophy* 40, 178–86.

Steinle, F. 1993a. Newton's rejection of the modification theory of colour. In *Hegel and Newtonianism*, ed. M. J. Petry. Dordrecht, Netherlands: Kluwer.

Steinle, F. 1993b. Newton's colour-theory and perception. In *Hegel and Newtonianism*, ed. M. J. Petry. Dordrecht, Netherlands: Kluwer.

Strawson, G. 1989. Red and 'red.' *Synthese* 78, 193–232.

Stroud-Drinkwater, C. 1994. The naive theory of colour. *Philosophy and Phenomenological Research* 54, 345–54.

Swartz, R. J. 1967. Color concepts and dispositions. *Synthese* 17, 202–22.

Taylor, D. M. 1966. The incommunicability of content. *Mind* 75, 527–41.

Teller, D. Y. 1991. Simpler arguments might work better. *Philosophical Psychology* 4, 51–60.

Terrell, D. B. 1951. On a supposed synthetic entailment. *Philosophical Studies* 2, 57–63.

Thompson, E. 1992. Novel colours. *Philosophical Studies* 68, 321–49.

Thompson, E., A. Palacios, and F. J. Varela. 1992. Ways of coloring: comparative color vision as a case study for cognitive science. *Behavioral and Brain Sciences* 15, 1–74.

Thompson, E. 1995. Colour vision, evolution, and perceptual content. *Synthese* 104, 1–32.

Thornton, M. T. 1972. Ostensive terms and materialism. *Monist* 56, 193–214.

Tolliver, J. T. 1994. Interior colors. *Philosophical Topics* 22, 411–41.

Topper, D. 1990. Newton on the number of colours in the spectrum. *Studies in History and Philosophy of Science* 21, 269–79.

Tye, M. 1994. Qualia, content, and the inverted spectrum. *Noûs* 28, 159–83.

Tully, R. E. 1976. Reduction and secondary qualities. *Mind* 85, 351–70.

Valberg, E. 1980. A theory of secondary qualities. *Philosophy* 55, 437–53.

Van Brakel, J. 1993. The plasticity of categories: the case of colour. *British Journal for the Philosophy of Science* 44, 103–35.

Van Brakel, J. 1994. The *ignis fatuus* of semantic universalia: the case of colour. *British Journal for the Philosophy of Science* 45, 770–83.

Van Steenburgh, E. W. 1974. The problem of simple resemblance. *Philosophical Studies* 25, 337–46.

Vendler, Z. 1995. Goethe, Wittgenstein, and the essence of color. *Monist* 78, 391–410.

Vesey, G. N. A. 1968. Sensations of colour. In *Mill: A Collection of Critical Essays*, ed. J. B. Schneewind. New York: Doubleday.

Vision, G. 1982. Primary and secondary qualities: an essay in epistemology. *Erkenntnis* 17, 135–69.

Watkins, M. 1994. Dispositions, ostension, and austerity. *Philosophical Studies* 73, 55–86.

Wolfgang, W. 1990. Marty and Magnus on colours. In *Mind, Meaning and Metaphysics: The Philosophy and Theory of Language of Anton Marty*, ed. K. Mulligan. Dordrecht, Netherlands: Kluwer.

Westphal, J. 1982. Brown: remarks on colour. *Inquiry* 25, 417–33.

Westphal, J. 1984. The complexity of quality. *Philosophy* 59, 457–72.

Westphal, J. 1986. White. *Mind* 95, 310–28.

Westphal, J. 1989a. Black. *Mind* 98, 585–9.

Westphal, J. 1989b. Review of C. L. Hardin's *Color for Philosophers*. *Mind* 98, 145–6.

Westphal, J. 1990a. Universals and creativity. *Philosophy* 65, 255–60.

Westphal, J. 1990b. Review of C. Landesman's *Color and Consciousness*. *Times Literary Supplement*, 13 July, 758.

White, S. 1994. Color and notional content. *Philosophical Topics* 22, 471–503.

Wilson, M. D. 1987. Berkeley on the mind-dependence of colors. *Pacific Philosophical Quarterly* 68, 249–64.

Wilson, M. D. 1992. History of philosophy in philosophy today; and the case of the sensible qualities. *Philosophical Review* 101, 191–243.

Wilson, N. L. 1972. Color qualities and reference to them. *Canadian Journal of Philosophy* 2, 145–69.

Wolgast, E. H. 1962. A question about colors. *Philosophical Review* 71, 328–39.

Wright, C. 1988. Moral values, projection and secondary qualities. *Proceedings of the Aristotelian Society Suppl.* 62, 1–26.

Contributors

D. M. Armstrong
Department of Traditional and
Modern Philosophy
University of Sydney

Edward Wilson Averill
Department of Philosophy
Texas Tech University

Paul A. Boghossian
Department of Philosophy
New York University

Justin Broackes
Department of Philosophy
Brown University

Alex Byrne
Department of Linguistics and
Philosophy
Massachusetts Institute of Technology

John Campbell
New College
University of Oxford

C. L. Hardin
Department of Philosophy
Syracuse University

Gilbert Harman
Department of Philosophy
Princeton University

David R. Hilbert
Department of Philosophy
University of Illinois at Chicago

Frank Jackson
Philosophy Program
Research School of Social Sciences
Australian National University

Mark Johnston
Department of Philosophy
Princeton University

Robert Pargetter
Department of Philosophy
Monash University

Christopher Peacocke
Magdalen College
University of Oxford

Sydney Shoemaker
Sage School of Philosophy
Cornell University

J. J. C. Smart
Automated Reasoning Project
Centre for Information Science Research
Australian National University

J. David Velleman
Department of Philosophy
University of Michigan

Index

Adverbialism, 95, 101n3
Afterimages, xviii, 31n4, 85–86, 90, 91–92, 199–200, 222n26, 282n15, 289
Animal color vision, 19, 24, 294–295
Armstrong, D. M., xii, xxiii, xxvin29, 1, 3–4, 6, 31n5, 47–48, 53, 55, 67, 123–124, 173, 205, 236, 251
Averill, E. W., xii, xx, xxvn3, xxvin19, 45n13, 48–49

Belief and experience, xiii, 53, 153, 174–175, 188–189
Benham disc, 156–158
Bennett, J., 238
Berkeley, G., 36, 40, 71, 74, 96
Berlin, B., 294
Binary hues. *See* Unique hues
Blindsight, 282n15
Block, N., xxvn11, 250, 255, 268, 283n18, 300
Boghossian, P. A., xi, xii, xviii, xx, xxi, xxvin20, 141–142, 169n6, 231, 267, 282n15, 285n30
Bornstein, M. H., 294
Boynton, R. M., 291, 294
Boyle, R., 47
Bradley, M. C., 1, 2–3, 7–8, 38–39
Broackes, J., xii
Butterfield encoder, 156–157
Byrne, A., xii, xxiii

Campbell, J., xii, xxiv
Causation. *See* Explanation and causation (involving color)
Chevreul, M.-E., 198–199
Churchland, P.S., 192
Circularity (in account of color), xxi, 2–3, 86–90, 115, 175, 249, 252, 254–255
Clark, A., 300
Color blindness, 18, 216
Color circle. *See* Color space
Color harmony, 196, 220n13
Color illusions, 17–20, 21–22, 23–24, 29–30, 100, 156–160
Color language, xxvn11, 7–8, 68, 99–100, 107, 238–239, 250–251, 291ff
Color mixing, 197–201, 202, 221n17
Color space, 1, 37, 43–44, 129–130, 138, 247, 290ff
Concepts (of color), xxi, 42–43, 45n13, 51ff, 68, 83, 98, 137ff, 175–174, 253–255
Content (of visual experience), xii–xiii, 82, 84–94, 108ff, 172ff, 227–228, 232–237, 241–243, 263–264, 267ff. *See also* Intentionalism; Phenomenology (of visual experience)
and naturalistic theories of content, 68–69, 114–115, 133n6, 269–270, 285n25

Contingent identity, 5, 119, 133n5
Contrast, simultaneous, 28–29, 199–200, 202, 289, 295–296
Cornman, J., xxvin32

Davidson, D., 202, 206, 207, 211, 222n28
Democritus, xx
Dennett, D. C., 248
Descartes, R., xx, xxviin34, 139, 232
Determinate (colors), 11ff, 116–117, 122, 160, 266–267, 276–278, 280–281
Determinable (color categories). *See* Determinate (colors)
Discrimination (of color), 2, 7–8, 14–15, 38–39, 45n13, 48–49
Disjunctive properties, 3–5, 16–17, 20, 21, 39–42, 47–48, 75–76, 148–149, 266
Dispositionalism. *See* Dispositions
Dispositions, xii, xx–xxii, 58–60, 69–70, 83–101, 139ff, 172ff, 177, 181, 182, 185, 186, 191, 193–194, 202–205, 249–251, 263
Dretske, F., 270, 272

Eliminativism, xi, xx, 81, 107, 142, 174, 186, 263, 300n2. *See also* Projectivism, literal; Projectivism, figurative
Error theory. *See* Eliminativism
Evans, G., xxi
Evolution (of color vision), 185, 216, 247–248, 255
Explanation and causation (involving color), 6–9, 35–39, 41–42, 63, 68–69, 76–77, 138, 142, 148–149, 182–188, 191ff

Fodor, J. A., 206, 270

Galileo, G., xx, 35, 81, 95
Goethe, J. W., 199–200
Gold, I., 248
Goodman, N., xi
Grassmann, H. G., 197–198
Green'. *See* Red'
Grice, H. P., 206

Hacker, P. M. S., xxviin33
Hardin, C. L., xi, xv, xx, xxiv, 156–157, 205, 230, 279
Harding, G., 139
Harman, G., xii, xvii, xxiii, 169n7, 236
Harrison, B., 65n15
Headless woman, 6, 41, 42, 43
Hering, E., 291
Higher-order property, 108, 129, 130, 147–149, 173, 184, 192, 205

Hilbert, D. R., xii, xxiii, 139, 285n25, 285n32
Hume, D., xi, 37, 95, 113

Intentionalism, xiv–xix, 58–60, 91–93, 118–121,
    130–131, 172–174, 227, 236–237, 253, 255–256,
    267–272, 282n15. *See also* Content (of visual
    experience); Phenomenology (of visual
    experience)
  Boghossian and Velleman's definition of, 91
  Johnston's definition of, 172
Inverted spectrum, xiv–xvii, 1–3, 6–7, 38, 54–56,
    189, 228, 230, 232–234, 240, 242, 250–251, 255–
    258, 268–272, 290ff

Jackson, F., xi, xii, xvi, xx, xxiii, xxvin28, 31n4,
    132n3, 133n6, 148, 227
Johnston, M., xi, xii, xxi, xxiii, 248, 285n30

Kaplan, D., 61
Katra, B., 298
Kay, P. *See* Berlin, B.
Killer yellow, 203–206
Kripke, S., 13, 20–21, 160, 164

Land, E., xxi, 139
Landesman, C., xx
Leibniz, G., 289
Levine, J., 289–290, 299
Lewis, D. K., 1, 3, 4, 39, 41–42, 207, 251, 300
Light, color of, 195–201, 213–214, 265, 272
Locke, J., xiv–xv, xvi, xx–xxi, 2, 36, 67, 74, 77, 93,
    95, 144, 147, 183
Lower-order property. *See* Higher-order property
Lycan, W. G., 272

MacAdam, D. L., 264
McDowell, J., xxi, 177, 202, 211
McGinn, C., xxi, 191
Mackie, J., xx, 177
Martin, C. B., 1, 38–39
Matthen, M., xxiii
Matsuzawa, T., 294
Maund, J. B., xx
Metamerism, 12–13, 100, 195, 196, 198, 199, 200,
    201, 202, 265
Millikan, R. G., 40, 270
Mode of presentation, 51, 109ff, 244n5, 284n22
Moore, G. E., xi
Multiple relation theory (of visual experience),
    174–176
Munsell, A. H., 196

Nagel, T., 227, 249, 255, 259

Nassau, K., xxii
Newton, I., 95, 196–197
Normal conditions, xxi, 1ff, 11ff, 45n13, 48, 51,
    59–60, 63, 83–84, 100–101, 144, 155–158, 203–
    204, 215, 249,

Olson, C. X. *See* Boynton, R. M.
Opponent-process theory, 278, 291

Pain, 93–94, 98, 126–127, 130, 229–230, 238–239,
    251–252
Pargetter, R., xii, xvi, xxiii, xxvin28, 132n3, 133n6,
    148
Peacocke, C., xii, xviii, xix, xxiii, 90–94, 248, 249,
    282n15, 283n16
Phenol, 71–72, 238
Phenomenal properties, xvi–xvii, xix, 234ff, 256–
    258, 283n16
Phenomenology (of visual experience), xiii–xiv,
    43–44, 85–86, 93–94, 116, 130–131, 141–142,
    177, 186, 205–206, 227ff, 264, 267–272, 282n15,
    289ff. *See also* Content (of visual experience);
    Intentionalism
Physicalism, xii, xxii–xxiii, 1ff, 39–44, 53–56, 67–
    79, 82–83, 105ff, 147–153, 160, 162–163, 178,
    205–206, 263ff, 300n2
Primary quality. *See* Secondary quality
Primitivism, xxiv, xxviin33, 177ff, 263
Projectivism, figurative, xx, 233, 242, 243n4, 244n7.
    See also Eliminativism
  Shoemaker's definition of, 231–232
Projectivism, literal, xx, 94ff, 127, 131, 172, 242,
    243n4, 244n7. *See also* Eliminativism
  Shoemaker's definition of, 231
Putnam, H., 22, 118, 192, 196, 201, 218, 269

Qualia, xix, 38, 79n5, 96, 112, 114, 125–126, 127,
    131, 189, 216, 227–228, 231–236, 248, 258–259,
    290
Quine, W. V. O., 181, 259
Quinn, P. C., 296

Red′, xviii, xix, xx, 58, 90, 91, 93–94, 249–250,
    251, 252, 253, 281, 283n16
Reference fixing, 20, 106, 110, 117, 119, 132n3,
    160–162. *See also* Rigidified description
Reflectance, surface spectral, 82, 139–140, 195,
    196, 211ff, 264–267, 276
Relativized colors, xvi, 72–75, 144, 158–160
Representation (in visual experience). *See* Content
    (of visual experience)
Response-dispositional concepts, 143–147, 154–
    160

Revelation, xxiv, xxviin33, 138–143, 155, 158, 159, 160, 163, 164–168, 172ff, 177–179, 186
   Johnston's definition of, 138
Rigidified description, 39, 78, 144, 155, 159–160, 206 (see also Reference fixing)
Rood, O., 200
Rosenthal, D. M., xxvn11
Runge, P. O., 207–208
Russell, B., 138–139, 164

Second-order property. See Higher-order property
Secondary quality, xxi, xxiv, 33ff, 51, 67, 94, 143ff, 191, 205, 228, 230, 232, 239
Sellars, W., 35, 37, 64n3, 229
Sensational property. See Red′
Sense data, xviii, 172, 174, 216, 228, 231, 258, 283n16
Shepard, R. N., 247–248
Shoemaker, S., xii, xvi, xvii, xix, xxvin14, 53, 81, 172, 207, 248, 255, 256, 257, 268, 283n16, 299
Similarity (between colors), 43–44, 116–117, 122–125, 128–130, 138, 149–154, 163, 164, 185, 274–279, 285n32
Sivik, L., 294
Smart, J. J. C., xii, xxiii, 11, 12, 14–20, 23, 24–25, 28, 33ff, 53, 122–123
Smith, P., xxvin30
Sosa, E., 255, 257
Standard conditions. See Normal conditions
Standing colors, 45n6, 67, 69–70, 74, 77, 141–142, 156, 159, 169n11
Steady colors. See Standing colors
Stout, G. F., 37
Sternheim, C.E., 291
Strawson, G., 139
Strawson, P. F., 187, 206, 215
Subjective colors. See Color illusions
Supervenience, 40–41, 178, 181, 183, 192, 193, 207, 219n6, 289
Surface spectral reflectance. See Reflectance, surface spectral
Synesthesia, 171n33

Taft, C. See Sivik, L.
Thompson, E., xxvin30, 285n32
Tolliver, J., xxvn12
Transitory colors. See Standing colors
Transparency (of visual experience of color). See Revelation
Twin earth, 118, 269
Tye, M., 172, 272

Unique hues, xxvn1, 230, 272–274, 279ff, 291ff

Velleman, J. D. See Boghossian, P. A.

Wandell, B. A., xxii
Westphal, J., xxviin33, 205, 211, 213–214
Wittgenstein, L., 59, 62–63, 97–98, 126–127, 207–208, 217, 228–229
Wooten, B., 298

Yoshioka, T., 297